PRISONER 88

THE MAN IN STRIPES

PRISONER 88

THE MAN IN STRIPES

by

Roy D. Tanenbaum

as told to him by

Sigmund Sobolewski

Foreword by
Archbishop Oscar H. Lipscomb

University of Calgary Press

University of Calgary Press
2500 University Drive N.W.
Calgary, Alberta, Canada T2N 1N4

Canadian Cataloguing in Publication Data

Tanenbaum, Roy D., 1942–
    Prisoner 88: the man in stripes

    Includes bibliographical references.
    ISBN 1-895176-74-3

    1. Sobolewski, Sigmund.   2. Holocaust survivors—Canada—
Biography.   3. Auschwitz (Concentration camp)   4. Catholic
Church—Relations—Judaism   5. Judaism—Relations—Catholic
Church   I. Title.

DK4420.S62T36 1998   940.53'18'092   C98-910954-2

Printed and bound in Canada by Printcrafters Inc.
Cover designed by Robyn Herrington

∞ This book is printed on acid-free paper.

Contents

Dedicated in
Loving Memory of

Elizabeth Rose Herman
August 5, 1984 – February 17, 1995

For all the children

I survived until now that I could offer you me,

My pain and my joy, my hopes

And my fears, all on the altar of memory.

And still there is more.

Acknowledgments

In a time of cutbacks for the literary arts, I am grateful that this project was found worthy of the support and assistance of the Explorations Program of The Canada Council enabling the completion of research abroad. I also wish to thank my friends in the Canadian Council of Christians and Jews—Alberta Region for their warm-hearted support.

This book could not have been produced were it not for many long-standing friends who, recognizing the unique perspective this work seeks to provide, have willingly given of their time and expertise to provide much needed advice, assistance and encouragement: Arlene Kushner, Linda Kupecek, Dave Greber, Zelda Dean, Murray Zimmerman, Gillian Steward, Mary Krasinska, Caroline Russell-King, Gayl Veinotte, Windsor Viney, Nomi and Jack Kaston. My thanks, too, to Gordon Hoffman, Hal Joffe, Mark Shuler for their counsel; to Alexandra Cyngiser, Fred Wolf, Bert Baron, Dorit Truzman, Billy Cowen, Monica Schubert, and Ray Laycock for research assistance in elucidating specific details; to the students in Lorraine Miller's 1994 English 30H class who used the manuscript as a project; and to Maggie Siggins, Dahlia Beck, David Blitt, Syd Cyngiser, Baruch and Hannah Sirota, Sima Holt and Milt Bogoch for their suggestions.

I am deeply appreciative of the unwavering support and critical eye of my wife Loretta, and the insights of Miriam and Jeffrey Spitzer, Keren-Ami Armon, Tova Sperber and Shaina Tanenbaum and the rest of the immediate family. Special thanks are due to my daughter Tova, who has read and reread the drafts giving me many invaluable suggestions. She put her heart into this as much as I did, and it is certain that her assistance has made *Prisoner 88* a better project than it would otherwise have been.

Sigmund himself never failed in answering questions nor shirked in providing material even in those instances when we touched on subjects difficult and painful to relive. He opened to me his home, his library, his archives and his heart. I am also indebted to all the members of his family here in Canada and in Poland with whom I have met, in some instances several times (Ramona, Simon, Emilio, Vladimir, who helped me in more ways than one, Basia, Aunts Helena and Janina Sobolewski). They have become my friends. For their time and cooperation, I thank all those whom I have interviewed, either in person or on the telephone: surviving members of the fire brigade (Jurek, Dacko, Nowicki, and Mietek Tukaj); those appearing in the book (Jacques Mydlarski, Jack Downey, Leonard Zenith, Chaim Well, Gary Goldsand, Alexander and Barbara Krebs-Gehlen) and relatives of those appearing (Noa Heilman Schwartz). Simon Sherwood, especially, deserves to be singled out. He responded not only as a son but also professionally, reviewing the entire manuscript and offering innumerable suggestions for improving the dramatic movement.

Grateful acknowledgment is made to the archivists at Yad VaShem in Jerusalem and the National Holocaust Museum in Washington who were helpful in verifying details. David Schiff, president of the Tarnower Society in Israel, welcomed me into his home in Ramat Aviv and opened the doors of the society to facilitate my research. The connection was made through Gertrude Greenspan Greber of Toronto. Dr. Eugene J. Fisher of the Secretariat for Ecumenical and Interreligious Relations in Washington D.C. was extremely helpful, taking hours of his time on issues relating to the Catholic Church. I also wish to credit Tony Krzyanowski whose taped interviews with Sigmund led the way for my later research.

I wish to acknowledge, but have been unable to trace, the copyright owners of the photograph of Hössler on page 48 and the two drawings by Jerzy Potrzebowski (found on pages 175 and 179).

The editorial assistance I received from Shirley Onn at the University of Calgary Press has been enormous. She did not appear to mind when I called her on holidays at home, she did not appear to mind my taking long hours of her time thinking through an issue. Like her, so her staff, John King, Sharon Boyle, Cliff Kadatz, Robyn Harrington, and Eileen Eckert gave of themselves unstintingly in working out technical problems, giving their best advice, working diligently to assure a timely publication.

There are also certain people who choose to remain anonymous who have helped to see that this book became a reality. The reader will not know who they are, but when they see this, they will know my deep gratitude and appreciation.

Finally I again acknowledge Sigmund, in whose mind I have tried to live for the past few years.

Affidavit

This is my story. I attest to its authenticity. All reported experiences and interactions, as rendered by reporter, are accurate in overall content and mood, and faithfully represent my own memory of them.

Sigmund Sobolewski
September 3, 1998

Foreword

"Auschwitz is your reality, not mine." Those words of Simon, eldest of the sons of Sigmund Sobolewski, "the man in stripes" with the impossibly low number of *achtundachtzig* (88) among the numberless victims of Auschwitz, are a challenge and a reminder to every reader of this book. It was out of a growing conviction, the more painful as it became more evident, that the "reality of Auschwitz" was becoming less real that Sobolewski has produced this powerful and riveting account. The "reporter" has let him tell it, for the most part, in his own words. They speak with a passion for the truth, and an outrage at truth's betrayal, that surpass the niceties of language. They leave us hurting for a past that is part of our human story, and uncomfortable with some of the present as it still unfolds. That is what makes this book so important—it is about us, too.

Simply as a record of one man's ability to endure in the face of so monstrous an event of man's inhumanity to man, not only to endure but to survive, and more, should earn *Prisoner 88* a place among the classics. But it is more. The words not only open for us the frank and unflinching catharsis of the author, they invite, even demand, a participation in the process that extends to every race and nation, every political or religious persuasion. Any lesser response to the evil that is the Holocaust, and of which Auschwitz is only a part, is inadequate. It is important that we understand the implications of our response, or lack of it. Something basically right, human and decent is at risk here. Though worlds removed from the world of Auschwitz, we are not altogether unaffected by our reaction to the chilling reality of that place. As Sobolewski has noted: "The Nazis contrived to force us to make choices that would implicate us in our own spiritual death. This is a part of the evil of Auschwitz. Evil breeds evil, cruelty breeds cruelty. Bury it and you risk subsequent repetition. Expose it and you terrify" (Chapter Twelve). Exposure also has consequences for our own spiritual health.

Nor did exposure come early or easy to Sigmund Sobolewski. The manner and measure of his success in seeking and finding a life and family of his own in Canada convinces the reader of personal strengths, resources and balance that are part of the story of his survival when, in his own words,

"I became eighty-eight at age seventeen." By his own choice, in response to the appearance and advocacy of neo-Nazism by a West German leader on CBC-TV, to a local high school teacher for whom the Holocaust is less fact and more fiction, and to an "Alberta Aryan Fest" rife with racism and anti-Semitism, Sobolewski "became eighty-eight a second time at age forty-nine."

The consequence of his very public personal protest and activism on behalf of "Auschwitz awareness" is detailed fully, not always happily, for himself and his family. Its impact is, for that reason, all the more telling on the reader. "I am offensive to my own people.... But when I put that uniform on, it is like I have one foot planted back in Auschwitz. I am *Achtundachtzig*" (Chapter Eleven). This new role thrusts Sobolewski into national and international prominence. It returns him several times to Auschwitz itself and there he encounters further distortions of the truth he remembers so well. Efforts to sanitize or interpret the Holocaust as less than its actual horror amount to the worst form of denial. *Achtundachtzig* is a critic and a corrective, to national and international political authority, to religious authority, especially his own Roman Catholic faith, and to world opinion. The continuing necessity to such witness he explained to one of his sons: "There's old Russian proverb. 'Dwell on past, you'll lose an eye; forget past, you'll lose both eyes'" (Chapter Twelve).

Sobolewski finds particular outrage at the systematic official downscaling of Jewish suffering and Jewish death at Auschwitz. It is a theme that recurs again and again for the man in stripes as he remembers, sometimes to his own shame, and always to that of the reader, that such things should happen: specific incidents of degradation, torture and death. He was personal witness to mass arrivals of Jews by trainload. Inhuman selection for slave labour or worse resulted for some; speedy extermination followed for most. As a college student in 1952, well after the fact, I visited the concentration camp at Dachau. It left a memory as vivid as it is painful. The pain easily turned to anger for me many years later when Christian leaders in our community joined the local rabbi on a radio talk show to counter charges that the Holocaust was "manufactured" to justify the existence of Israel. I find it hard to imagine the effect of emergent neo-Nazism and worldwide reports of anti-Semitism on *Achtundachtzig* who lived their consequences and testifies to them eloquently. "To be a prisoner of Auschwitz was wretched and dehumanizing. To be a Jewish prisoner of Auschwitz was hopeless" (Chapter Twelve).

Memory is terribly, crucially important to the human enterprise. It is second only to truth itself. And where truth is to be found in the record of the contingent, free, fleeting interplay of human actions and relationships, memory mediates the truth. Individuals experience this first-hand. Collectively we acknowledge the role of memory as we capture, collect, analyze and judge the truth of history. Of course memory is not alone. There are records in the form of artifacts, writings and, thanks to technology, audio and visual resources that present the past to us as if we were there. But, generally, we were not. *Achtundachtzig* has drawn from all such sources to present the truth, at times so awful as to be all but incredible, of Auschwitz. But most telling of all is his first-person memory: "'I was there', I will tell them" (Chapter Sixteen). In the words of the reporter: "Sigmund is his own authority" (Chapter Eighteen).

The authority of the man in stripes cannot be denied as he tells his own story. In the course of that telling Sobolewski has drawn deeply from the living tradition of his own family, faith and nation, and from history, in a search for understanding of how Auschwitz could have happened. Who was to blame? Whether and how has guilt been expiated? His answers to such questions do not always carry the same authority as the truth of his personal experience. They must be judged on the strength, or weakness, of wider evidence and testimony. But here they are raised in ways that haunt us lest the Holocaust prove not to have been unique. "Auschwitz awareness" should not be a matter of choice.

The end message of *Prisoner 88* is, however, one of hope. It is personal and societal for an outcome that is admittedly fragile. The first arises from the immediate experience of *Achtundachtzig* and is offered with further witness to those who fear the price: "If you've got Auschwitz as part of your life, you know what most people think of as success is pure smoke and mirrors. With each day of my work, I'm happier and healthier." (Chapter Fifteen.) The second, Sigmund Sobolewski offers to his sons, but also to all who read his words: "Since Auschwitz, boys, can anyone ever say about some horrible event, 'I can't do anything about it'? I've finally learned from Auschwitz, you need more than survival. Before, if hungry, you bought snack. Inside no one could even say, 'I am hungry'. After Auschwitz it's necessary to stop hunger of others" (Chapter Twelve).

April 8, 1996
Oscar H. Lipscomb
Archbishop of Mobile

Chairman, NCCB Committee on Ecumenical
and Interreligious Affairs

Sigmund Sobolewski.
Photo courtesy of Ursula A. Krol, Digital Photo, Calgary.

Part 1
1992

Sigmund's moment came, quite typically, years into his life; and enough time has since passed to allow for analysis. If, in a reflective mood one dissects the human lot, one finds an almost elemental 'law of the moment': the average person spends half a lifetime building up to it, then in a flicker it is over, and he or she spends the rest of life in reaction. Most people experience only one such moment; a few might have two or three, not more. Those I have consulted concur: during that moment, the threads of life come together. Before and after, we are like someone knitting a multi-coloured sweater, trying somewhat unsuccessfully to keep the myriad balls of colour from unravelling all over the floor. Although the anatomy of moment is not given over to exact science, one thing is almost certain: when a person's moment comes, it will result in overwhelming consequences for the subject ... and, inevitably, for his family as well.

–the Reporter

One:
Enter the Subject

Fort Assiniboine, Alberta, 1992

 raised all three of my boys on the principle, 'Men don't cry.' Instead, Emilio had been telling me it is good to vent emotions. Naturally, I did not pay it much heed. Until the event with the dog....

Husky was more than just a dog. He was a cross-breed: half husky, half wolf, like something out of the wild. He could hear a mouse tunnelling under snow, catch the direction, pounce, and ferret him out. Yet he had a fastidious way about him, always scratched up ground on his own dirt. With paws larger than hands, legs rippling with muscles, a tail that arced up over his back, Husky hulked bigger than my present dog Samson—so broad, and what a friend! Whenever for one reason or another my wife was distant, Husky was closer to me than any woman. By some telepathic instinct, he just knew when to rub himself against my leg, when to curl up beside me, share his warmth, nuzzle the palm of my hand. Simon called him "a dog of a thousand faces."

Husky used to go out with me, jogging at my heels as I pedalled my bicycle. "Let's turn down this old logging path, eh Husky? Bet you can't outrace me

3

down this hill." His eyes would dance with pleasure as his tail flashed from side to side. "You're some pal," I would tell him. If for some reason I had to leave him, he would howl in loneliness.

Husky enjoyed grabbing shade outside near the back of the hotel. I was watching a beer truck, making a delivery, back into position. The dog kept sliding closer and closer. Before I realized what was happening, it was too late. The truck had got a wheel wrapped in the dog chain. I cried. For three days I cried, and not only for the dog. Why did I not react and stop the truck? I can hear the truck's roar, see the panic in his eyes. Why was I silent? Why? That dog still clamps into my life with the jaws of a pit bull. Except when I had decided to put my prison stripers back on, this was the first time I really allowed myself to cry. Thank God for Emilio with his "Men can cry, too." Thank God for my boys.

In the early days, such family bonds were quite numerous. But let Simon describe it. He is the oldest and the family storyteller:

> The day before Christmas, the Toronto house would be heated up almost to a glow, with piles of snow drifting outside. Around four o'clock, Papa would take us to Kensington Market. We'd forge our way from stall to stall, picking up whatever we could at the best prices: cheese; wine; fresh large loaves of egg bread, rye and pumpernickel. Then, on to the fish store. The fish man would roll up his sleeve, lean over nose to the water, plunge a net in past his elbow—the good ones were always on the bottom—and come up with the prize. "Nope, not that one." "Which one?" "That one." "This one?" more frustrated now. "No, that one." They must have had a magnifying glass over the tank because the fish was never as big on the table as it had been swimming. We'd be wide-eyed as the fish man smashed its head with a heavy wooden mallet. To think we selected the one to die.
>
> Late now, we'd whip off to Greenwood Race Track where we'd scoot around back for some fresh hay. By the time we got back, Mama would be preparing the meal according to a mix of Polish and Cuban customs, anxious for the ingredients. It'd be our job to spread the hay on the table, cover the hay with a quilt, and then cover the quilt with a fine linen table cloth. It was supposed to be the manger. When we set the glasses out, they'd wobble on the puffy spread. We'd set for one extra person, the Christmas Traveller, only it'd always be the five of us, no others.
>
> Whoever was a boy scout wore his uniform, and since Papa didn't have a uniform, he would dress in a burgundy dinner jacket. "It's the way we did when I was a kid," Papa would say. If Papa had been to church, he'd bring out the Host; if not, he'd bring out Jewish matzah. One year we even had a Host from Poland. Taking the Host, he'd face Mama. They'd break it in half and bless each other. Then with his half Papa would repeat with me, and then with each of my brothers.
>
> The first course was clear peppery borscht followed by the carp (we never ate meat on Christmas Eve). The Cuban part was lentils with onions, and salad. It wasn't a heavy meal, though there was lots of everything. Every year, it never varied: Papa would talk about his grandfather's Christmas dinner.

"Grandpa," he'd say, "would hold up an apple." While he talked, he'd do the same thing, slicing it away until it'd be just a core. Then he'd shell a walnut and slice off a sliver, stick it in the apple, and light. The candle always meant dinner was over and presents about to begin.

"Our Pride," I used to call the boys on our Christmas cards. In my position, children are more than just a natural result of marriage. Sometimes we would go fishing on the lake. I would let them take turns steering the boat, watch their smiling faces. We might catch a couple of frogs. At first, I would bait the younger boys' hooks. Soon they were doing it on their own. Soon, they did *everything* on their own. Sometimes I would just sink into my wicker porch chair and watch them playing 'cowboys' or 'war.' I could almost see them grow. I taught them how to swim. Starting beside the dock, I would get them to tread water, then dog-paddle, and soon I had them fish-tailing across the lake. The youngest, Vladimir, used to like to duck out to the YMCA with me. He would say, "You sure beat snot out of that weight bag, just killed the thing." I went to some of his volleyball games. Once the two of us took in a match between Poland and Canada. The teamwork is deceptively intricate. He explained the rules to me: "You can only volley the ball three times before batting it back over the net. Every player has to cover all positions, and no player can touch the ball twice. The trick is to position an impossible spike or catch the other team off guard."

"You surely know how to make it clear, Vladimir." I turned to catch his face glowing.

When does a father realize the family tapestry is beginning to fray at the edges? I've lost the very thing I hoped for, the dreams, the lungs that gave me breath when I could not breathe for myself. Thoughts rush in on me. The old genius Mark Twain once said something like this: "At fourteen I couldn't believe how ignorant my papa was. At twenty-one I was amazed at how much the old man had gone and learned in the interval."

I do not know the exact quote or even if I ever knew it; I read *Blueberry Finn* in Polish, that is about it. I recognize that it is not so unusual for fathers and their teenage sons to be at opposite ends of an emotional pole. You expect it; no problem. But my boys are already well beyond the great humorist's age of self-revelation: twenty-nine, twenty-seven and twenty-five. Yet, in the interval of their reaching maturity, they did not find that I learned much. I try to tell myself: it is simply that they have trouble admitting that deep down there are some things they really do admire me for. They find me exceptionally concerned about boosting the economy: "You spend all your money, all Mama's money. Why? Why'd a Polish Catholic sacrifice everything he's got for dead Jews?" They connect my work with good: "What's the good of parading around in striped pyjamas?" They note my accomplishments: "Hey, Papa was on TV with neo-Nazis and a burning cross."

I would like to make light of it, but I cannot carry it off. I wish my boys could see me as I see myself: a soul trying to do so much more than merely survive. When I tell them about my work, I see their eyes wander like prisoners who would like to escape. And I know that instead of seeking the blessing their heritage provides, deep down they reject it, as if sons could displace their father. They are certain their old man is a lingering tragedy, a victim of his own obsessions.

I have seen parents die for their children, and children die for their parents. More especially, I have seen the agony when they were prevented from making the sacrifice. Because I was taken, my father, sick with stomach cancer, was saved. And what do I hear from my sons? "You're not with it, Papa." My children look like me, but their actions come from elsewhere.

Recently, our middle guy, Emilio, drove up from Calgary just to talk it out with me. At first I was put off. But he is part of a group, one of those circles where you get together to tell other people about your problems with your parents. With the insight of self-awareness, Emilio has decided it is the best therapy for everyone else as well, his father included.

"It's time to forgive and forget," he tells me for the umpteenth time. It is 2 a.m. The customers have gone and we are cleaning up. I place the glasses on the shelf. To sweep, he up-ends the chairs—too carelessly, I think; Ramona says I behave like Husky with a bone, growling when anyone comes close.

"Emilio, I tried plenty to leave it. For many years that's all I did. Forgiving is much easier than forgetting, no matter how hard we try. Anyhow, he'd never let me."

"Who, Papa? Who is _he?_" Emilio turns from sweeping under the pay pool table to stare at me.

"_Achtundachtzig._"

"He talks to you?" Disgust is all over his face. How could he know what _Number 88_ means to me: _Number 88_ is my pole star. _Number 88_ is my foundation. From time to time my course might change, my footing might slip. At such times _Number 88_ is a lantern on the road. Emilio continues to stare at me. I note, though, that he closets _Achtundachtzig_ away in his mental cupboard to bring out and examine later, while going on to another topic. He has drifted under the wrought iron grillwork between the bar and pool table room. "Can you really forgive, Papa?"

"Certainly."

"O boy, you sure as hell don't show it," he huffs with the exasperation of youth. "You're _obsessed._ You pen ten letters to get one published. Then you call the whole damn world to tell them, 'Oh, I got a letter in the paper', and mail out copies."

"You know nothing of any of this, really."

He looks at his mother, who has just come into the tavern. "Sure it was horrible, Papa. There's been a helluva lot of research on this, though. In the big cities survivors even got therapy groups and all; I think they're open to Christians, too."

His mother nods her auburn head in agreement. "Listen to Emilio," she advises. They are teaming up against me. They look alike, too.

I try to divide the conversation. "Emilio," I say facing him, "You believe in this psycho stuff, not me. Forgiving isn't forgetting. You see this arm, Emilio, this tattoo, this 88 ... that's me. That was my *name*. They made of it nice little job, even called me by lousy number. In camp you lost command of every part of your life, even when to sit on can. One thing they couldn't control, though, was your mind. *That* was out of even their power. No one, not you or your brothers, or ten thousand shrinks, or for that matter anyone else," I glare at his mother, "is going to snatch that away from me. My past can't be erased or analyzed, and it's definitely not something to learn to get used to."

"That's funny—your whole life is Auschwitz, Auschwitz. And we're not even Jews."

"My point for doing what I do. If you need to see shrink, be my guest, but leave me out of it."

I feel like a child playing hide-and-seek; I'm 'it', and no one is looking. Once I picked up the translation of Rudolf Höss's autobiography. "You ought to read this," I told the boys. "It's Höss's memoirs. He tries to justify his role as camp commandant. Thinks we should praise his diligence. I saw him first in 1940, riding on his horse through Auschwitz like some English lord riding through his manor. His two oldest children, his son nine and daughter eight, followed in line behind. Then I got to know him when he returned to supervise, towards war's end, gassing of four hundred thousand Hungarian Jews."

Our youngest, Vladimir, read less than thirty pages. I do not know if the other two have even read that much. One evening after work—he's the only one of the three not to disdain manual labour—Vladimir went and sprawled on the floor. "Aren't you going to finish book I got you?" I asked.

"*The* book," Vladimir corrected.

"You know it never comes out right when I speak western language," I chafed. Mistakes upset me. I am very self-conscious about them. They detract from my message, and that is important to me. I try to read as much as I can to develop a better use of language.

"Yeah, it's the Polish influence. Polish lacks articles, uses different word order," Vladimir sing-songed like reciting a litany. "Don't worry about it. Sure, I'll get onto the book."

"Fine. Fine. When?" I pushed.

"Right away." He gave in so easily, I wondered if there was anything behind the words. The next three or four weeks, I let Höss's autobiography perch on the secondhand table pecking at my guts. Eventually, I put it away on a shelf to gather dust.

The firstborn toured Poland for several weeks. But he never went to the camp. Maybe Simon—we pronounce his name the Spanish way: See•mōne´— by virtue of his involvement in cinema, is interested in the camps from a historical point of view, certainly nothing more. He knew I wanted him to visit, but no. Once Simon answered my complaint, "Papa, your pain fills the air around me. Even the horrors you haven't told me, I feel. Everything I do pales in comparison. I can't even gossip about who's going with who, or talk about a new record, without it jingling in my head, 'My God, my father's a survivor.'"

Just when I was thinking it all might be sinking in, just when I was about to dare sharing a memory, he continued, "I've got to distance myself, to be independent. Know what, Papa? Auschwitz is your reality, not mine."

Simon's words cut a ragged tear in my past. My head buzzed. I could hear him saying, "You're like a character in an old-time cinema, jerking along as the screen flickers, mouth moving; but there's no one who can hear the sound." I felt a curtain fall between us. Jewish kids whose parents survived the camps devour every word, squeeze out every drop of information to better catch on to their parents.

The excuse my boy gives others for not going to Auschwitz is, "It was the time of crackdown against *Solidarność*. At every corner, military police were inspecting documents looking for Solidarity agitators. It was the coldest winter since 1944. And here I was all bundled up, knowing Papa was there in plain pyjamas. Going to visit that camp would've been too much for me."

Does he think I have learned so little over the years that I do not know visiting the camp would be difficult! "Boys," (I am always talking to them, even when they are not actually present), "Auschwitz might not be your life, but *Achtundachtzig* is your history."

I was there DAY ONE, 14 June 1940, part of the first Polish transport to Oświęcim, what the world would come to know, and not want to believe, as Auschwitz. *Achtundachtzig*, only two digits, prisoner Number Eighty-eight. All who lined up that first day were the same as number one!

And I was still there DAY ONE THOUSAND SIX HUNDRED EIGHT, 7 November 1944, four-and-a-half years later, when we fire brigade members were evacuated to Sachsenhausen Concentration Camp. Only a few weeks after our reincarceration, a Russian detachment, led by a Jewish Colonel, Grigori Davidowich Elishawetzki, entered Auschwitz. Around 3:00 p.m., 27 January 1945, they liberated the camp.

For those fifty-three months in the Auschwitz *Konzentrationslager,* I was "Number Eighty-eight." Even the dates themselves mean nothing. The sun rose and the sun set in weary rotation, but time did not pass. To paraphrase Einstein describing relativity: one day on the outside passes like a second with your lover; one day on the inside passes like a lifetime with the dentist. In Auschwitz, the only gauge of passing time was your dwindling endurance.

More than 405,000 numbers were issued at Auschwitz, leaving uncounted some one-and-a-half million Jews led directly to the gas. The first thirty numbers were German criminals brought in as officials. Of these, several survived the camp, though some were subsequently killed by former inmates in retaliation, others as a result of postwar trials. Numbers 31 to 758 made up the first transport. Maybe eighty survived. We had grabbed up the best jobs, and, more important for survival, we were not Jews.

"Look, boys, wherever you might be now, to understand numbers, think of your hand. Each finger is worth about 80,000. Of total 405,000 numbered, less than one fingernail's worth, about two thousand, were released, none of whom were Jewish. One nail clipping, two hundred, including some few Jews, escaped. About one third of total, finger and half, were transferred or evacuated before liberation; sixty percent of these died during evacuation, or in other camps, leaving maybe two knuckle's worth. Soviet Army liberated 7,650, less than knuckle. Altogether of those numbered, of whole hand, one pinky, about fifteen percent is all that survived. Most of those were latecomers, arriving in 1944–45."[1]

We do not need figures. The camp itself has remained undamaged except for the gas chambers, which the Germans dynamited right before liberation. The documents endure in the historical archives at the State Museum of Auschwitz-Birkenau in Poland. And those of us who lived through it have the numbers engraved all over our souls. As inmates, we lined up for canteen in order of our number. We non-Jewish prisoners could buy cigarettes, blades for shaving, powdered soup, a beet salad with '*Premiumschein*,' scrip converted from small amounts of money we were allowed to receive from home. When we lined up, sometimes hundreds of numbers intervened between one number called and the next.

I survived only to live with the nagging question, "What distinguishes me from them?"

Push
1945–1966

American war correspondent William L. Shirer wrote on Monday, May 7, 1945, "So it's finally over."[2]

—the Reporter.

Two: Jurek

Germany, 19 April 1945

lackout. We are lined up outside Sachsenhausen, to which we have been recently evacuated from Auschwitz. The hands on the clock show eleven. Distant flickers on the horizon are followed by a low rumble: the Katyushas pounding their targets. We, the last column to file out, waited our turn rummaging around the deserted camp looking for extra food. "The place is bare," I am telling Jurek in Polish. "Only found a couple of watches. In the shop where the Jews fix the loot from Auschwitz."

He gives a toothy grin. "Good for something, maybe."

"Who knows?" We depart. To one side I can see brick houses standing like soldiers, officers' quarters for the SS. Turning to the other side, visible in the glimmer of the half moon, I can see ordinary barracks—prefab row housing—and the experimental laboratories. Himmler had a passion for experimentation, and Sachsenhausen was his research centre. Human guinea pigs were used to test new medicines, to determine the absolute minimum iron rations necessary for survival, the minimum food. Prisoners had to run endlessly with different kinds of shoes on to test them through water, mud, and over rocks. I would try to look away when dogs were set upon anyone who lagged behind. And in Sachsenhausen, as in Auschwitz, experiments were conducted to make women infertile.

I shudder past the dimly outlined labs and now darkened greenhouses. Behind us we can hear the SS call, "*Feuerwehr, nach vorn! Austreten!* Fire brigade, step forward! Fall out!" We do not answer the call.

"We're going to get it now. We know too much."

"Just keep walking," I say, not even taking a parting glance at the gallows looming in the *Appelplatz* where we assembled for daily roll call. Over the past several days, the SS have been slipping away one by one, so now we are guarded by any available German they can issue a rifle to. Someone tugs at

Achtundachtzig's sleeve. That, too, is ignored. Three weeks after Easter, thousands of hunched figures forge through the darkness in front of us. Each clutches a loaf of bread and tin of bloodwurst. Those who cannot keep the pace just collapse by the side of the road. Not far behind, six or seven guards strung across the highway shoot the stragglers and kick them into the ditch. I force my feet along the death march, knowing Allied success will soon bring the Thousand-year *Reich* crashing to an abrupt end.

The word 'evacuation' plays in my mind. During our last months in Auschwitz, because of the constant Allied bombardments, we in the fire brigade were forever extinguishing fires in the surrounding factories. Now, while trudging along in the dark, I remember one evening in a rare lull when fellow brigade member Hulanicki (No. 443) and I shambled along Birkenweg Street, arm in arm in the European fashion, speaking hushed Polish. If you wanted to talk, the best place was always out in the open.

Hulanicki whispered softly, obliquely, "God, Zygmunt, another evacuation to Germany today."

"*Wiem o tym*, I know," I answered. From the watchtower, a guard followed our movements.

"The Russians are at the River San."

"I know." I was wary of the direction he was taking the conversation.

"They might attack Auschwitz. What'll happen then?"

"Don't know. Don't even want to think about it," I said, edging away a bit.

The normally cautious Hulanicki tightened the arm that was holding mine. "Zygmunt, the Nazis might evacuate us to Gliwice." Gliwice, we had learned from reports trickling back, was where prisoners were promised 'work' when they were really scheduled for liquidation. Gliwice meant death. "We've got to get out of here. These air raids may be the only chance we get."

"Don't know," I evaded. What if Hulanicki was a rat?

"We're cooked anyway. I heard that some former *Prominenten**3 are dying in quarries," he says.

"Hey, I'm as scared as you. But look what happened to the surveyors' commando after three escaped. We practically never fight a fire all together. If some of us escape, they'll kill the rest in punishment."

As we evacuate Sachsenhausen, this little conversation sticks in my mind. Even then I knew Hulanicki was right. But I was too wrapped up in my Polish girlfriend, Irka. Besides, an escape would have taken group consensus and we were convinced one of us twenty-four was collaborating with the SS. Some suggested Jurek, who, before coming to the fire brigade, had been close to the Head Foreman, Kapo No. 1. Was it paranoia? I never even went and discussed it with Tamborski, leader of Group One.

---

* A glossary is appended. Endnotes of an excursive nature are bolded to distinguish them from those that are solely bibliographical.

But now the situation has changed. For three days, we are goaded on day and night with only occasional half-hour stops. A light rain falls which we try to catch any way we can. The ditches to both sides of us overflow with the remains of the waves of prisoners who preceded us. Even while faced with the deathly consequences, unable to trudge on, ever more of our group join them on the roadside.[4]

None other than Auschwitz' head commandant himself, Höss, passes us, riding in his jeep. He recognizes our foreman, Tamborski. "*Ach,* my fire brigade," he shouts. "I'll meet you all in Schwerin."

"Not me," I think to myself.

As we walk, the green-shaded terrain becomes slightly more rolling; pine forests dot the countryside. Look, I note to myself, the guards are getting fewer and fewer, the confusion on the road greater. On the night of the third day, Hulanicki, Jurek and I gather. "It's time...."

Six of us, careful not to glance over our shoulders, just walk away.

When we leave the march, Hulanicki has second thoughts and remains behind. We quickly set out across country, then hide. "Jurek, this is it! What a fool that Hulanicki is."

Jurek is surveying the terrain. "Do you think we should we stay in the bush or march officially?"

"Let's march officially. It'll call even less attention to ourselves."

I am wearing civilian clothes issued in Sachsenhausen: a blue jacket for the fire brigade with Sachsenhausen No. 115318, and an arm band signifying my status as *Leiter Gruppe II* (leader, group two). On arrival in Sachsenhausen, we all forfeited our boots as punishment for failing to salute *Lagerführer* Höhn, who sprang in on us from the rear without our noticing him. But we were given regular shoes, and later we learned we had fared far better than the Gypsies that had replaced us at Auschwitz. They had been sent to the gas 'by mistake.' No one has given a thought to how we'll manage in the middle of a hostile country, wearing strange clothes, trying to act normal. We take a forest road, the rising sun creating a meandering path of light as it picks its way through the treetops at either side. "Got any wurst left?"

"Just a little bread."

"Me too." We troop along, a tiny band, singing in our hearts. Cool shadows invade from the edges.

"Shhh, you hear something?"

"Take it easy."

Too late. Barely four hours after leaving the main road, black-uniformed members of a German panzer unit, looking like a swarm of ravens with cigarettes dangling from their mouths, pounce at us from nowhere. "I can't believe it," I am saying. They dump us unceremoniously at a provincial prison in Neuruppin. Sixty to seventy dishevelled prisoners, Belgians, Dutch, Frenchmen and a few Russian, lie in the prison compound. And judging from the number of prisoners visible in the barred windows, the adjacent cells are already overcrowded. The German guards do not formally admit us, but shift about, avoiding eye contact. In Auschwitz this meant only one thing. My stomach churns.

"*Jezus-Marja,* they're going to shoot us," I whisper to Jurek. "It's written on their faces."

At such a time you have to take chances, and I am the one who, of the group, speaks the best German. After what they call lunch, I wander up to the SS. "Where's commander?"

"He'll be back at two o'clock," he says nonchalantly.

We are left in the courtyard of this four-storey-high old German prison. A balcony, reachable only from somewhere inside, runs along the second level on three sides. When the prison commander returns, I will myself straight to him, stand at attention, and salute. He is a sergeant of the dreaded SD, the German counterespionage service. Even in these last precarious days, he is still all spit and polish, ramrod straight. It is not an act of bravery on my part, just a last-ditch effort at self-preservation, more an instinct than anything else.

"Protective prisoner No. 115318 reporting, sir." He can see my group leader uniform and long hair.

"What do they want from me?" he says, half to himself. "Don't they know the prison here is full?"

Catching his words, I point to the prisoners lolling about the yard. "*Obersturmbannführer* Höss passed us on road. The lieutenant-colonel issued instructions.* We're supposed to take to Schwerin all this *Dreck.* I'll need for extra prisoners special permit."

He throws me a sidelong look. "Where were you born?" the strained commander asks doubtfully.

"West Poland, on border," I answer, taking one step forward.

Assuming I am a racial German, he asks, "Are you a *Volksdeutsche,* then?"

"No, sir. My mother is Czech, though." The Czechs did not resist the Nazi occupation.

"Sudeten Deutsch, huh?" His thumb goes up. "So you can be responsible?"

I sense that, just like that, the decision has been made. "Certainly, sir."

"You'll report in at Schwerin," he says flatly.

"Yes, sir." After he drafts the appropriate papers, affixing the stamp, I start rounding up the prisoners. It is then I notice I am being watched from the gangway above. I start swearing like the Kapos do, kicking one slow-moving prisoner, putting them in rows of five, counting. "Seventy-three, Herr Sergeant," I shout. Then one more pyjama-clad, bedraggled captive comes running over. I turn my head just enough to notice the commander is still leaning on the balcony rail, staring intently. Must show him I am the man

---

* A list of SS ranks is appended.

for the job. Must do something dramatic! With a string of curses, I hit the latecomer in the face. *Hit* him. I am wondering, why is this commander watching us? Has he got second thoughts?

Then I turn again to the commander, "Seventy-four."

His right arm jerks upwards and he shouts back, "Be careful you don't lose those devils."

Revealing no sign of relief, I reply, "Don't worry, Herr Sergeant." They line up in rows of five, the last row, four only. I place myself in the middle in my best military style. "Attention! Hats off!" Their hats slap the side of their legs with a loud clap. I bark like a sergeant major: "In straight order, march; in step, left, two, three, four." The gate opens, and we leave like a military company. I'm thinking, secretly the Germans are probably as relieved as I am. Now they do not have to be found with any battle-scarred Russian prisoners when the 'Ruskies' march in.

When we join with the main road, we see the bodies of German soldiers swinging from lampposts, each wearing a sign, "I am a traitor." They are the scapegoats of defeat; presumably, the voices of reason, calling, "Return to your homes; it is time for review." A parade of horse-drawn carts streams by, making ruts in the water-flat, sandy soil. The Russians, we hear, are just twelve kilometres away. We move through three or four villages on the outskirts of Neuruppin. In one, I stop by someone who seems to know what he is doing. A local farm lady, broad-faced with smooth light skin and darting eyes, is asking, "How is the situation?"

The road is teeming with grey-clad German troops, broad brimmed field caps, many unshaven, heading in both directions like steers at the beginning of a roundup, some running, some stumbling and lurching along. For they have turned and fled, shell-shocked, dirty and ragged, from recent battle. The end is already upon them. Some pass without a glance; others stare blankly.

"The situation is serious," the blue-clad village policeman replies in a deep dignified voice, "but not hopeless."

I stifle an inward laugh, and seeing my chance, ask in my best German, "Have you got bread?"

The officer studies my face. "You have money?"

"This pocket watch."

He goes in to check with his wife, brings out four loaves.

Back on the march, the turmoil is so uncharacteristic, there is no doubt that all that is around will soon be mowed down, as sheep mow the grass of the meadow. At such a time, who knows what can happen?

It is foggy, and a few kilometres north of Neuruppin we veer from the Schwerin highway, heading westwards because we know the Americans are west. We have no plan beyond that of escaping the soldiers on the road. Some of the prisoners we picked up in Neuruppin are trying to dig out beet roots in the mud of last night's rain. It is every man for himself. Our train of plodders still makes good time away from the thoroughfare. Each trudging captive, stretched across a kilometre, has already been through his personal fire and brimstone. Now he dares to think he might make it.

Achtundachtzig also walks away expecting to be free. But what is free? When Jews wish someone long life, they say, "*Bis hundertundzwanzig.*" In the group there is this Belgian Jew who is going around to everyone amending that to one hundred twenty-five, "*Bis hundertfünfundzwanzig.*" That is to say, the war years do not count; they are a horrible hallucination to be erased from human memory.

So, I am preoccupied with one compelling mission: how I will erase the two little blue digits, *achtundachtzig*, from my arm and, with their removal, erase the camp that has been tattooed into my life. Oh, that day when we were tattooed! We each filed by one of several tables. All around, more than the usual complement of Nazi officers stood ready. *Achtundachtzig* whispered with a wink to his technician, "Give me small, inconspicuous ones—in case I escape." He smirked his appreciation, and obliged with the smallest numbers of all my friends.

Now that liberation has come, I vow to Jurek, "I'm determined to get out of this befouled atmosphere, to nail shut its door forever, and to enter new life." And I really think I might.

"Halt! Halt! Who's responsible here?" an angry call hangs in the stilled air of the field. The procession of worn-out trekkers freezes. Again, I am the one who knows German. Taking another gamble, I face a furious corporal in the bluish uniform of the German Air Force, flying eagles on his collar. It turns out this same corporal had delivered the Jew that very morning to Neuruppin. "*Schweinehund*, you dirty pig, where are you going?" he yells while pointing a semi-automatic in my face.

My eyes are fixed to the weapon, my heart rattling all by itself like the assault rifle with its bipod flapping loosely below the barrel. He must notice my trembling. I can feel the sweat drenching my arms. I imagine us becoming fertilizer for the new crop. "We've got papers," I blurt out.

Still training the rifle on my head, its side magazine looms in front of me. One eye on me, one eye on the papers, he examines them for an eternity. "You're supposed to be on your way to Schwerin. What the hell are you doing this way?" The ragged column hangs back.

Jezus-Marja, this guy is going to shoot me any second. "These people are sick and hungry," I blurt out, "they can't walk, and it's getting dark. We were told they can put us up for night in village."

Still bristling, his hand on his gun, the *Luftwaffe* corporal turns to the group. "Look," he yells, "if you stretch out again, I'm going to shoot you all. Stick together." Then, throwing the papers back, he orders, "When you get to the village, you are to report directly to the council."

So now I know there *is* a village.

We dare not disobey. Once we are there, the local council wants nothing to do with us. They pack us on to the next village where we are joined with a work gang of Russian prisoners who glean the fields by hand, eating more of the winter vegetables than they basket. After three days of feasting, the guards have us on the evacuation trail again. Those prisoners we took with us still drag by the wayside, and being intent on my own preservation, I pay little attention. The Russian prisoners from the village, knowing they are fleeing from their own Russian Army, also shuffle along as slowly as possible. They have an excuse: they push carts laden with food and matériel, the Germans guards perched comfortably on top. So we are out in front, and it is already turning dark when we get to the main highway packed with hundreds of people. On the road there is a rumour that the first prisoners who made it to Schwerin were loaded onto a barge and sunk.

Again, the pounding of the Katyushas can be heard in the distance. Wasting no time for eating or resting, our little Auschwitz group picks up the pace and drifts away from the other prisoners—all living dead, *Muselmänner*, no longer maintaining the struggle for survival. Up and on the way before daylight, our tiny band fuses with many *Flüchtlingen*, civilian refugees. The road is clogged with cars, trucks, and wagons piled with family possessions and a few chickens, all headed to the northwest part of Germany and the Elbe, border of the Allied advance. Only those on foot progress at all; still, the going is fearfully slow. A German officer shows us a shortcut by an army camp.

Finally, there in front of us—the Havel bridge, a double arch-span affair painted a moulted green camouflage. Unlike the country spans of Poland, this bridge has room enough for two lanes of wide-load military traffic, testimony to a German technology capable of keeping up with the times. And on the far end, the same German countryside as on this, but with a difference marked by the taste of freedom burning in our mouths. The road approaches the bridge head-on. We are racing forwards. Then this German officer, legs stretched, waves his arms. "Only soldiers, no civilians. We're going to blow the bridge." When we argue, he has us arrested.

As soon as we are out of sight of the commanding officer, our guard loses interest, walking away without even so much as a glance. Ducking around the side to the river's edge, we see grey shadows quickly moving from positions beneath the bridge's roadbed. One drops from a rope not fifteen metres away, hits the ground running full speed in the other direction. "Come on, it's our only chance." From the marshy bank underneath, we slip behind the overwhelmed officer and scuttle over the swollen Havel River just as the bridge is blown up by the Germans.

A parade of stretchers passes through a sea of men. In no-man's-land now, the road turns past what seem to be hundreds of thousands of German soldiers camped on the sandy heath. Many soldiers walk around without tunics and in various stages of disarray. Officers pass unsaluted. As efficient as the Germans were in victory, they are inefficient in defeat. We rummage around through stacks of army supplies, hastily picking up what we want.

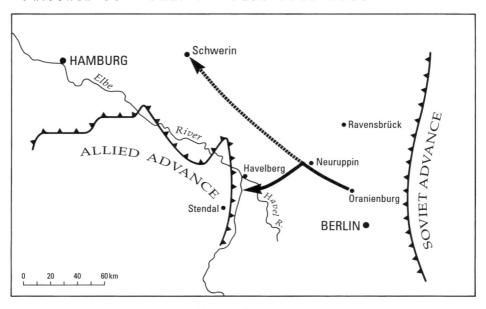

Route of escape.

No one ever asks us a thing. So this is what the end is like for supermen. A general apathy. Not too much different from the *Muselmänner* who, in the camp, spiritually gave up before actually physically dying. "They just want to be American and not Russian prisoners," Jurek observes. Those German soldiers with a flash in their eyes or who still hold themselves erect, we avoid.

At the Elbe, clamouring masses line the east bank. I finally jump into a military boat, only to be thrown out by two American soldiers. From their base across the river, they have a little side-business ferrying refugees for hire. After a mostly sleepless night, the same two souvenir-seeking GI's ferry me across in exchange for some German Lugers I managed to scavenge—just like bribing a guard in Auschwitz.

Jurek, meanwhile, has already made it over with a few others on a raft he cobbled together from driftwood. On the other side, I locate a ditched skiff, row back, and retrieve the remnant of our friends along with two wailing young German women. We have to beat off others wading through the ice-cold marsh trying to climb aboard. I am thinking, what a shameful thing. The whole time the women are crying, "Our sister, we have to get our sister." But what can we do? All around us, the crack of gunfire. No way to put back to shore, and no room to take in another, anyway.

Just keep your eyes on them, I say to myself, so they don't do anything foolish out in the main current or we'll all be washed away.

We are gathered, like medical students at their first operation, in a hastily abandoned stucco. Jurek is in charge. He is pouring scalding water to scrape the hair from the white hide of a little porker we caught bellying through the meadow behind the cottage. We found a bell in the kitchen with which to do the scraping. Jurek slits vertically down the belly, eviscerates the insides, carefully cuts away the liver so as not to break the gall bladder, and severs the lung from the rib cage. It all falls out in a heap.

I face the open window; farms stretch away as far as the eye can travel. We have come up from the river. It is 3 May, 1945, almost five years to the day after my first being arrested; we find ourselves in the American zone near Stendal. Outside is a lone red oak silhouetted against the sky. I fiddle with some windfall, absentmindedly juggling two little bereted acorns, the seeds of new life, from hand to hand.

"Where's it going to be from here?" I mutter, apparently loud enough for others to hear.

"Later. Let's eat," someone answers. Our tiny band consists of the reserved Jurek; Mietek Tukaj, a reliable honest fellow from Group One; Walenty Tukaj, the joker with a limp; a few guys from other commandos we met up with in Sachsenhausen; and me. We dispose of the pig's head in a garbage heap by the back shed, pausing only to superficially blot up the mess before the bloated pieces bubble in a huge black pot. What will the owners say when they get back? Are they just over there in the next village?

"Find some carrots and onions," Jurek yells.

"I could eat it raw," Mietek says, unable to take his eyes off the pot. He looks like he is going to fall in. We rest at ease for the first time in years, utterly exhausted and anything but elated.

Another looks at the pot, tears streaming down his cheeks.

"Some carrots and onions!" Jurek reminds us. Someone brings up some potatoes and onions from the cellar. He just stares at them and throws them in.

Jurek checks the meat again. "Won't be long now."

I am thinking of the women we saved, fled as soon as we hit the other side. Maybe they were so upset they could not bear to stand around. Maybe they were afraid to be alone with a group of grubby young foreigners. Someone yelled, "Come back, we're not going to rape you." But they were gone. I choked off my outrage at the implied insult.

Weary and wet, we lounge around the well-furnished living room. Everything has been left in place. We are filthy—but what do we care!

"Jurek," I yell, "did you see those Russians in German uniforms?" referring to the shortcut we took through the military encampment.

"Yeah, they had to be part of the Vlassov division," he shouts back from the kitchen. "Let us pass without even saying a word."

"No wonder," someone adds, "those deserters must have been scared out of their minds, what with Stalin's troops approaching. The Germans didn't even get them across before blowing up that bridge."

"Some gratitude," I say, laying with my back against a wall.

Voices from all sides call out together. "When we were arrested at the bridge, I thought it was all over," says a voice coming from a body stretched out on the couch.

"So'd I. I didn't think anything could scare me after Auschwitz," confesses Mietek.

"You're both a couple of grandmothers," a third voice says dryly. "I wasn't scared one minute." Strange laughter.

"Those Germans by the Havel River looked more scared than us," says the body filling the couch. "I'll bet some of them were SS. The Americans will take care of them if the Russians don't get them first."

"Those sisters looked rather pretty, though, don't you think, Sigmund?" The speaker, the one who was never afraid for a minute, kicks my foot for emphasis.

"Nah," Jurek calls in, "he only has eyes for Ir-ka." General hooting.

"May a duck kick you," I say, while vowing to find her.

The woman had a rooster, and she put it in a boot; oh, my dear cock, what are you doing inside that boot? Walenty starts the old Polish drinking tune, and we all join in. Then, softly, we sing the Polish national anthem. I look around at everyone, ragged and thin, arms around each other's shoulders; I am not the same person I was four-and-half years ago. The room goes quiet. It is as if we are all holding the melody against us to hang on to it better, as if it is slippery.

Mietek notes that today is Polish National Day, when in 1791 Hugo Kollantaj and his associates passed the ill-fated constitution freeing the serfs. So yesterday was St. Sigismunt Day. In our family St. Sigismunt Day was a festive event for my grandfather, my father and myself. Our custom was to celebrate the namesake's day instead of birthdays. There would be a party for all the relatives from Jarosław. My grandmother would bake a nut layer cake. I would get toys, *Tatuś* would get a gift such as a silver cigarette holder, and Grandpa would get a bottle of wine.

Now, it is only me. I know I am lucky; I spent years in Auschwitz without a trial. *That* is the reason I survived: once somebody went to interrogation you rarely saw him again. I look at the blood-splashed kitchen, listen to the boiling pot. I remember that for warming some soup, I once got five nights in the *Stehzelle*, a tiny ninety-by-ninety centimetre underground cell in the 'Bunker', a prison within a prison. Ohh, they made me kneel and crawl through a small opening, a dog entering its kennel, all the while kicking and pummelling me with sticks. The cell was then covered by a grating and a sealed door. I was lucky, though; only four of us were put in, not the usual five. We could not lie down. Could not stand up. Elbows and knees digging into each other's bent bodies, we could hardly breathe. There was one five-centimetre diameter pipe for ventilation near the ceiling. But the cell was not *completely* isolated. Through that breathing tube, we heard an interrogation going on in the Bunker's yard. It ended in an execution. A high-ranking officer was complaining about blood splashed all over. For the entire week, I was petrified they would realize there were cockroaches listening down below and kill us.

So here we sit, gorging ourselves on greasy pig in Germany. Germany the perpetrator! Germany occupied by the forces who refused to bomb the gas chambers! I must be out of my mind. Five years ago, I was confident *Tatuś* would get me out. A few days ago, I rose to the challenge. Today I am lost. The world is a crystal vase, a family heirloom, which, preserved for centuries, has slipped through the fingers of this generation. I find it laying at my feet. Now, the one who kept his head through the whole past few years, hears himself muttering aloud, "I'm not the one who dropped it! Not me!"

With a start, I look around self-consciously, hoping I was not overheard. While no one actually says anything, I can feel their sympathetic nods. Do not laugh, please do not laugh. As soon as possible, I crawl away from the cottage, leaving to anyone else, anyone but me, the task of cleaning up.

So is this it? I cannot grasp it. A few hours ago we were diving for safety into the bulrushes, kissing the mud on the Elbe's west bank, shells tearing up the ridge above our heads. We were among the last of the last. Like the Havel bridge. No sooner were we across when its bed rose up like a drawbridge, then plunged into the swirling river in massive fragments. A long series of chain-reaction explosions left a string of piers jutting up from their bedrock foundations with nothing above but a few swaying girders. The last act of a defeated army, a skill perfected by the retreating forces.

When I return to the cottage, everyone is asleep on the floor. The next day we are all sick.

After two days, we hear the grind of heavy trucks on the road. The U.S. troops are rounding up displaced persons. The Americans baffle us. They have been giving out supplies and cigarettes, and have a good record of who is here. Yet, we witnessed Russian troops crossing the river, meeting the Americans and hauling back refuge-seeking easterners who had risked their lives swimming naked across the Elbe. What do the Russians pay them, I wonder. What would they do with us? It does not take long to find out. The Americans ship us out in a canvas-covered lorry to a DP camp on the other side of Stendal. But when we hear they are going to pull back, ceding territory and people to the Red Army, we take no chances and head west once more. After Auschwitz, I will not be caught in the wrong camp again.

In Auschwitz, it was always, "When I get out, I'll kill the first German I see, kill him right away." The idea obsessed me for four-and-a-half years, sometimes making me shudder on the pallet at night, on the job, sometimes even in the brothel with Irka. This blind desire to throttle a German became a goal to live for. It was the reason for survival. Now the opportunity is here. Occupied Germany is in such chaos, and guilt makes many Germans so terrified of us we could fully requite ourselves and no one would interfere.

Jurek, Mietek, Walenty and I visit a German Air Force base next to the DP camp in Stendal, hunting for any SS we might report. Twenty American soldiers guard about five thousand Germans clustered all over the tarmac. They tell us, "Sure." Sticking our noses in everyone's face is actually quite dangerous. But nothing happens, nor do we recognize anyone. We do 'organize'—that is to say, steal—some socks and gym shorts from the officers' quarters for possible sale on the black market. Inside the barracks, we catch a soldier in a *Wehrmacht* uniform of the German army. We have him surrounded, and we all look at one another thinking the same thing. So does he; we can see he is scared.

"Disgusting," Jurek says.

"A pig," I say.

With Jurek, I follow the sun west. Ours is a strange friendship. Jurek is quiet, a chess-player type. I am well built and aggressive. We mostly move by night, rest by day. Sometimes we enter a farmhouse. Usually, a few religious pictures hang on the walls. I do not like to think about it. I was brought up on my father's dictum, "A Polish officer is a gentleman." I do not like to think about that, either.

"We need two bicycles and a couple of radios."

"We don't got nothing," they say, passing looks one to another. An older couple, they have wrinkled, leathery skin. He hulks, hiding something with his body. She is in the kitchen doorway.

"You pig," I swear like a Kapo, "five years we've been in *Konzentrationslager*, while you've wallowed here like nothing was happening. Who do you think you are? Okay, we'll search, then, your place." It is a bluff, of course. Usually we were too scared ourselves to go deep into the house.

The wife, hands shaking noticeably, glares at her husband as if to say, "I told you so."

"What about that radio?"

The man is beside me at once. "No, please," he pleads.

We choose not to listen. "We've no choice," Jurek says.

"You own this place?" I ask.

A red heat rises in his cheeks. "Here for twenty years. Take what you want, just leave us alone."

"No use reporting you then, huh?" I say.

"Maybe we could use some ham and bread," Jurek adds.

"We've only got a little," starts the wife.

I hold up a stick.

"Take what you want," cries the husband, motioning to the kitchen.

Jurek grabs some smoked bacon, with abrupt movements stashes it in a bag. I yell, "You're members of Nazi Party, that's why you won't help us. Soap, toothpaste, and a couple of sweaters." I am already rifling through the bedroom closet. "And blanket, shirt and pants," I add. It is all we can carry.

We donkey the stuff to some women we found, two young Poles, survivors of Ravensbrück. Have a party. Move on. So we rob cottagers to eat, and always flee westwards, westwards toward Hanover. We never kill anyone, simply do what we must to survive.

As a semblance of order sets in in the occupied zone, travel is restricted. When we meet a fellow from a camp with an interesting piece of paper, it sparks an idea. I write a *laissez passer* for each of us, which, in a DP camp, Jurek types and I sign, attaching a photo to each. With these 'documents' and our stolen bicycles, we make our way all around the western zones. We are checked maybe twenty times. The German villagers report us at a DP camp. But unless you are caught in the act ... nothing. American soldiers, retreating from their advance positions and passing land to the Russians, support us by giving us food in exchange for our bicycles. British military police do nothing.

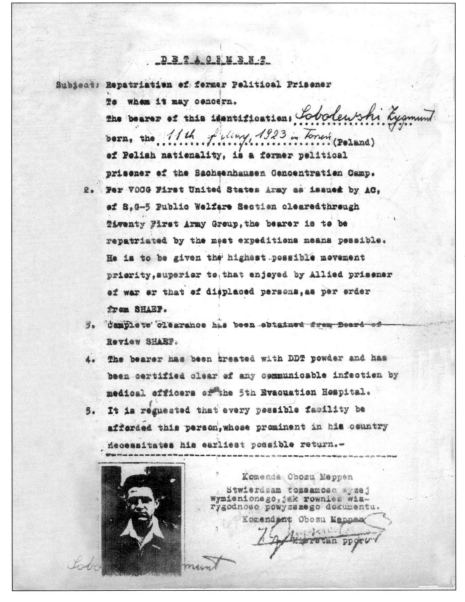

Detachment.

Three: *Tatuś*

Germany, May 1945

The numbers on my arm never do get erased. What good would it do? The brand that marked my body like an animal has seared itself indelibly on my soul. I feel it in everybody I meet, as if they can see, before I even open my mouth, this blue blemish deep down within me that burns whatever I will do or say. We are moving from camp to camp, never too long in one place. When I try to mix with others, it comes to mind something is different about me. Even the DPs say it. I hear, "Are you upset? Is something bothering you? Have I done something to offend you?" No answer. "Why did you leave so suddenly?" No answer. People edge away slowly, never taking their eyes off me.

At other times I give voice to my nightmares without ever knowing I am saying it. I confuse the flow of time. What appears before me, upon investigation is not always there: details ... expressions ... and always people marching, marching. I come to realize the brand in my flesh and my soul is permanent.

"Why have I survived and not the others?" This is not something *I* ask myself; *they* ask me. And I feel the unexpressed accusation. But I push it behind me. I will not allow Auschwitz to control my future.

Like shards under the archaeologist's brush, the broken vase again appears scattered at my feet. I push that away, too. Quickly! Surely after Auschwitz, no one would expect me to be like my ancestors. I can remember when, as a child, I first learned the story. Father had returned from being questioned at the local Nowy Targ police station during some civil disobedience. I saw he was very upset.

"Imagine being interrogated by the police! With my cross for valour and coat of arms!"

"*Tatuś*, what coat of arms?"

"I never told you?"

"No, *Tatuś*."

Afterwards, whenever my friend Leon Kapturkiewicz came over, I would prompt my father, "Tell him our story, *Tatuś*."

"Well," he would tell us, "in 1410, at Grunwald—you've studied that in school—the army of the Polish White Eagle poised for battle. Barely twenty-four hours later they'd engage the black-crossed Teutons. But this day, various minor noblemen were showing off. The bravado of apprehension as before all battles: 'What will tomorrow bring?' 'Will I see the sun set?' 'Will I stand whole and healthy and honourable?' Among them was a certain Pan Sobolew, who probably owned some land in the hamlet of Sobolew, maybe just a horse and a good name."

"Tell him about the ravens, *Tatuś.* "

"I'm getting to that. Either way, it happened that King Władysław noticed some shaggy-throated ravens light on a distant tree. Polish ravens can reach a wing span of a metre," Father would interject, as if ravens elsewhere are not as big. "Our ancestor Sobolew bragged, 'Not only will I shoot the bird, I'll shoot it right through the eye.'"

"Tell him about our coat of arms, *Tatuś.*"

"Yes, I'm trying to. He drew back his great bow. The arrow pierced the raven's eye. The king was so impressed, he then and there conferred upon

our ancient grandfather a coat of arms depicting a blind raven, a *ślepowron.* Grandfather was dubbed the 'raven killer' as a good omen for the day ahead."

I would revel in Leon's wide-eyed amazement. And, still only a youngster, something from all that talk permeated me as well. I knew my father's own name was Zygmunt Ślepowron Sobolewski. And Ślepowron became the sur-name for an early branch of our family tree.

"It *was* a good omen," *Tatuś* would add softly, "for the next day the Polish White Eagle entirely drove off the foreign raven."

Family coat of arms showing the ślepowron.

On the Nazi entrance into Po-land, Leon's brother was shot dead from an airplane. My friend eventually became a priest.

What will become of me? After four-and-a-half years in Auschwitz, why am I terrified now? *Tatuś* would not have been. After World War I, *Tatuś* was decorated for valour on the Italian front against Italy's bid to wrest Trentino and Trieste from Austria–Hungary, and on the Russian front against the Bolsheviks. As an officer, *Tatuś* devoted himself to the Polish White Eagle. But even more he was a man of principle. After Piłsudski's 1926 coup, he had reasoned, "I swore my loyalty to the President. Even if the former government looked like a lunatic asylum, I can't support a coup." Slowly, as time went on, I noticed he came to terms with what was. Then, in 1930, Pilsudski imprisoned opposition leader Wincenty Witos, a man who had been three times Prime Minister. Father abandoned all remaining chance for promotion in the Polish ranks by supporting the left wing opposition Partja Ludowa. He was blackballed from any position of worth in or out of the army, and it left us impoverished.

When the Nazis arrived, he formed a militia to keep order, becoming a town personality, part of the 'intelligentsia' targeted by the occupation forces. It was this act of assuming authority, more than anything else, that later landed me in Auschwitz. When the occupation force finally entered Nisko, my father met the commanding officer in full uniform, presented the militia, and in time-honoured ceremony turned over his sabre. I got rechristened *Achtundachtzig* because *Tatuś* stood by principle.

Initially, *Tatuś* being safely out of Auschwitz provided me the purpose to be in. My suffering mattered: I was a seventeen-year-old who counted; *Achtundachtzig* was saving his life. A father ought to preserve his son, I should think. In our case, it was the reverse. *Tatuś'* life had fallen into my charge. For what monumental reason fate had substituted the son for his father in the camp, I did not know.

Certainly, I thought of him often: *Tatuś* peddling through the village of Surochów, me on the crossbar of his bicycle, swerving around the sawmill where *Tatuś* had surreptitiously found work after being blacklisted. He kept the job, in spite of the ban against him, for four years. Then he found a position on the railroad near Piotrowice. He was always talking about a Polish senator who had been a buddy in officers' school. I figured he had something to do with getting the job. They knew the Germans were stockpiling gas, and *Tatuś* was hired to train the railroad personnel on how to face a gas attack.

Tatuś was non-exuberant, a quiet man, the opposite of me. And at home, we had not had much chance to spend time together. From the age of twelve, there was military cadet school. In this, I figured to follow in my father's footsteps, yet somehow during my adolescence a wall grew between the two of us. There was that row between my sister Barbara and me over the bicycle. Father smacked me with a stick. I clenched my fists. "How dare you strike me!" I wanted to shout. I was already quite tall, nearly as tall as my father. He simply looked at my fists and then at me. There was never an opportunity to tell him, "I'm sorry for that stupid fight with my sister, for my anger with you."

In the camp, sometimes the wall came tumbling down, and I felt us to be as close as if we were still together in the same house. His image loomed large. It was *Tatuś* and his friend Zelazny, also a retired army officer, who had taught us boys how to swim in the River Dunajec. They had thrown us in the water, yelling, "Move your arms and legs like a dog." Oh, how I had always loved that swirling river, especially in the summer, when the sun made its rapids glisten like a million daylight stars. I remembered the river bend

... remembered the blowing grasses along its banks, grasses you could get lost in ... remembered the eddy shaped by the twisting river, the canyon running up into the mountains behind, the quiet water where we swam. But I could not remember many accompanying words.

It was *Tatuś* who had taken me on long hikes on Mt. Turbacz. He was a soldier who did not believe in hunting. When we hiked the high trail, we had often barbecued a lamb on a homemade spit suspended between two vertical braces. I remembered the smell of the sizzling meat and onion and smoke of the fire in the clean air, the hiss of juices dripping onto the coals, us crouching close, minding the roast ... remembered the circling hawks overhead, *Tatuś* glancing up at them from beside the fire pit. But I could not remember any conversation about them.

It was *Tatuś* who had taught Barbara and me how to ski. I remembered waxing our skis with one of *Mamusia*'s old irons. We had trudged up the mountain for an hour or so, strapped our skis on with leather thongs, and carved our way down for a few minutes. *Tatuś* had been skiing since childhood. In his day, they had used only one pole, pegging it between the skis as a brake in downhill riding. An accident had forced him to lose time in first-year medical school, which, in turn, had led to his entering the army, the family career. We had learned to ski on the mountains of Nowy Targ, my childhood home, mountains so tall you had to stretch your neck back to see the sky. I remembered it all like it was happening, but no call of his voice rang my ear. He was an overwhelmingly warm, but mute, memory.

Barbara and I had always got excited when *Tatuś* unlocked the small, black, upholstered case and carefully began piecing his flute together. From the top of the hill on St. Anne Street, the dining room had looked out on Nowy Targ, and onto the Tatra mountains beyond. Mount Giewont with its huge Catholic cross visible from forty kilometres dominated the scene. The house had the steep-sloped broken roof typical of Tatra architecture, overhanging the length of the front to form a porch. A long, wooden, picket fence with 'hatted' posts surrounded our home. The notes of the flute floated out over our little Switzerland: the panoramic vistas, the valleys stretched between the hills, the thin waterfalls dropping right out from granite cliffs. And there I was, a kid, hushed, attentive to father playing heart-throbbing military songs on his instrument.

Only the knowledge of the role *Achtundachtzig* was playing in father's life gave me the strength to survive. In my reveries in camp, we would finally talk to each other, though sometimes he would be indicted in my mind for putting principle ahead of family. In the main camp, the Nazis built a museum that was to be a memorial to an extinct people; later there were concerts, played by emaciated prisoners. To me, this 'culture' underscored my feelings of absolute isolation. In my reveries I would inform *Tatuś* about amenities in the *Konzentrationslager*, maybe tell him, "They're talking about having concerts. Beethoven. I'll be one of the first to go. There's also a museum. I've had a glimpse of it. They've got many Jewish objects: Talmuds, prayer shawls, candle sticks; also national flags from all over Europe, a display for visiting SS celebrities." Then I would go on about a prisoner who works there. "He's from where we used to live in the Tatras, *Tatuś*. Maybe you know his family? And how are you doing at home? How are you feeling, *Tatuś*?"

I would imagine his words in return: "Oh, I'm fine, son. How are you bearing up? Be a good Polish soldier. Your father's proud of you. Your father's grateful." The reality, of course, was that we were in opposite worlds. But in some ways I would feel us to be closer than we had ever been. Or, maybe, that was the reality—I can no longer tell.

Both myth and reality came to a numb halt when, towards the end of 1942, a family friend showed up in camp. A letter from home had alerted the family's 'inside connection' to watch for him: "Atia's friend is coming to visit him." "Atia," as my baby brother Lucjan called me, was part of the code we had managed to develop to pass messages uncensored. These letters were life. I opened them like they were my mother herself come to visit. Until 1943 Polish prisoners were allowed two letters a month, Jewish prisoners none. What did it matter? By the time a Jew arrived in Auschwitz he had usually been shuffled around three or four times; chances were he had no family left.

Anyhow, it took six weeks to locate Marian Kornecki in the camp. By that time he was beyond help. Unable to keep up with his assigned work lugging stones to the river for flood control, he had been beaten. His eyes were swollen. His leg was festering and he could not walk. He just murmured, "I'm urinating blood." All that could be done for him was to get him admitted illegally to the hospital on the second floor of Block Twenty-eight; even that was no small matter.

Then, on one visit a few weeks following, his usual wooden slab was empty. "How's Marian?" *Achtundachtzig* asked an orderly. He merely pointed his finger towards heaven. Who knows if he died a 'natural' death or if he was given an injection? Many people were wiped from my memory, but not Marian, a man I hardly knew.

Before dying, Marian broke the news that father ... he had passed away the beginning of '42. "Zygmunt, I guess you know your father's dead."

"No! No! Don't tell me!"

Earlier, the news of my father's death might have devastated me. But by the time word came, *Achtundachtzig's* innards had become a fortified camp, so hardened it no longer mattered. This is something camp did. Under unnatural conditions, one quite normally has unnatural responses. Or perhaps my indifference was the product of an instinctual behaviour for survival. Either way, the knowledge of father's death left me undisturbed, as if his body was merely another corpse in a pile.

The only real emotion was an ongoing curiosity about what would happen to *Achtundachtzig* next. I observed that I had started to experience myself almost as though I was two people. I could see one me, Zygmunt, placidly settled in a cinema screening some motion picture in which another me with an eighty-eight on his arm acted the protagonist: *Achtundachtzig* is lined up in *Appel* waiting hours in the minus-twenty temperature for the roll-call's completion. *Achtundachtzig* is watching his comrade in front asking for a bottom scoop of soup. *Achtundachtzig* is waiting for a letter from his father.

One ghoul says to another, "I was killed in battle, how about you?" "I'm not a ghoul," answers the second, "I'm from Auschwitz." Like the story that made the rounds, this ability to step out of myself was the instinctual behaviour that saved me. I was the eye of the camera, wondering what might be next.

Now after the war, father's death first begins to hit me. Marion told me, "Until his death, he was writing letters to Governor-General Hans Frank, others, urging your release." A letter from my sister reaches me. She thinks he aggravated his sickness working in the underground. *Jezus-Marja*, was my being substituted for *Tatuś* in Auschwitz all for nothing? *Nothing?*

Four: Irka

Germany, May 1945

So now I am free, yet I still hear the songs we were made to chant: *"Im Lager Auschwitz war ich zwar,* I was indeed in Auschwitz camp."* Inside, I envisioned a banquet, children at my side—that is how I survived. Now, outside, it is the past that denies me peace—even when I desperately seek relief. This is freedom? Every face is a missing comrade risen from the dead like Lazarus. My mind leaps from one to another: This one saved my life when *Achtundachtzig* could barely drag his body out to roll call. That one amazed us with his sweet tenor singing in the night. "Aren't you Sikorski? No? I'm sorry." Now someone I recognize comes up. I stretch out my hand. It hangs in mid air. I close my eyes, look away, compel myself to picture Jurek or Mietek Tukaj, come back only to see the same face coming from another direction. Every plate of food the relief organizations pass out scares me. "What *Achtundachtzig* might've given for an onion, for a potato like this one, for a bowl of soup!" Every changing sky recalls another fright. Once there is this funeral procession, some German villagers following and weeping. I catch myself wondering, "What's the big deal?" Make no mistake, as much as you try, the images before your eyes will not align themselves to the simplest coherence in the real world.

Throughout the ordeal in Auschwitz, a boundless longing for that sleepy, friendly little provincial town in central Poland gripped me, sustained me when we lay three men to a pallet—Nisko, home! We had lived there only a short time, but home was family ... and home was freedom ... and home was a woman ... at least in the mind of a teenage boy yearning for life.

Our quarters in the fire hall faced the great oak tree by the main gate. From there, we could take in the skeleton-like slave labourers stumbling back from their work parties. They sang obligatory songs while carrying those who had died on the job. A most frequent was *"Willkommen Frohe Sängern."* The spirited melody about two wonderful dark blue eyes and a haircut that suited her well was repeated over and over. It pumped my heart with wild, unfulfilled fantasies. Which racked more, the physical cruelty or the torment of the mind, is hard to say. All I know is, I only thought of one thing. "Please, *Jezus-Marja*, where are the blue eyes now that I'm out?"

Sex. My mind remembers what I would rather forget. Prisons are notorious for sexual exploitation. I might have imagined that in the intensely male environment of an Auschwitz Block it would have been the norm. Not true. Or rather, it existed all right, but only in limited circles. Everyone's number had a triangle. Green for criminals. Red for 'political prisoners' like *Achtundachtzig*. Yellow for Jews. Known homosexuals wore a pink triangle, sometimes with the number 175 standing for the paragraph in the German code that outlawed homosexuality. Homosexuals not officially marked were quickly known anyway, and were afforded room to manoeuvre. Once, in the showers, a lad about seventeen years old was washing his genitals. The sacks hung like a small piece of shrivelled cloth. No outline of testicles showed at all. He confided, "I got caught in the act and castrated." He seemed mentally disturbed. And there was a guy whose voice suddenly changed and breasts began to enlarge. Was probably doing somebody favours, because he was made a Kapo in charge of the other prisoners in the Block.

Soon after arrival, I was billeted in Block Five, which, at the time, was assigned to the tradesmen and *Jugendtlichen*, prisoners below the age of eighteen. The Block hairdresser, remarkable for his long, slender, feminine fingers, bunked on the same pallet.

One night the barber reached across and started to rub *Achtundachtzig*'s leg. I could not see him, but I could hear his breathing. It was the only time I ever found myself in such a situation. A picture of father accompanying me on the train for my first day at cadet school popped into mind:

The undulating movement of the train. Our shoulders swaying from side to side. We faced each other in our own compartment. On yellow leather benches. With all my school gear, no one else had ventured in. Gazing out the curtained window. What was that? The wall of a tunnel? No. A freight train, unexpectedly blurring by in the other direction. Only the flashes of light between its cars flickering across *Tatuś'* face, distinguished it as a train. *Tatuś*, thinking, was staring on the wall behind me. Then, like he had reached a conclusion to an argument he was having with himself, he started to stammer in his mild, quiet way. Zygmunt, you're going to be at cadet school; all kinds of things happen; some things you'll need to know. He could barely be heard above the chirring of the train. I simply sat there not comprehending, terribly uncomfortable, not knowing what to say. Neither did he. He stopped and started three times: the stork doesn't really bring children ... you're a Catholic ... a Catholic shouldn't sin. What was he trying to say? Did I know? The son arrived at cadet school still thinking the stork brings children. Then our company captain once gave us a lecture: It's a sin to masturbate; masturbation is harmful to your health; it draws fluids from your brain; leaves you imbecilic; and when, one day, you get married, you won't be able to have children.

I pushed the barber's wandering fingers away. "Get out of here."

In the midst of the camp, this barber had an infinite capacity for happiness. The camp was good to him. The next day he approached me, smiling. "Why don't you come along to the *Blockälteste*'s tonight? You can have more bread."

"No thanks."

Right after lights out, another prisoner, a young guy—all the servants of the Kapos were handsome athletic young boys—wearing only his shirt, padded after the barber to the *Blockälteste*'s room.

"Jurek, there's somebody I've got to see," I say, not long after we reach the western occupation zone.

Relating immediately, he replies, "It won't be easy to find her."

"Fine, fine. If she's alive, I will."

It crosses my mind that back in March of 1942, when the first women inmates were brought to Auschwitz, women had not interested me yet: a thousand Germans and Poles from the Ravensbrück women's camp and, two days later, the same number of Jewish women from Slovakia entered the camp, and my main preoccupation was 'organizing' or scrounging more bread or soup. I could exchange cigarette stubs for food, perhaps smuggle some trinket from the *Tischlerei*, the joiners' shop where I worked. Eventually, I could not help but notice that women had come to occupy one third of the main camp, Blocks One to Ten. From the outside, these worn, two-storey reddish brick Blocks could have been apartment houses lining the street of any Polish town. On the inside, each Block contained approximately two thousand female prisoners. Some Kapos were soon shouting and gesticulating from the second floor of our two-storey barracks, over the concrete slab fence that divided men from women.

When the women's camp was transferred five months later down the road to the village of Birkenau, we in the fire brigade had to hose out their barracks. In the basement of Block Six, I thought I was hallucinating. Everything was wavy. Never had I seen anything like this floor, humming and jumping with a five-centimetre-thick carpet of fleas.

In our camp there was another group of women, the "*Kaninchen.*" Our fire brigade was housed near the gate through which they passed on their weekly excursions to gather daisies by the riverbank. We often eyed them in the colourful civilian clothes they were given to wear. They were all Jewish, some from Holland, Czechoslovakia and Hungary, most from Corfu or Salonika speaking Ladino, a wonderfully melodious cross between Old Spanish and Hebrew that nobody in camp could understand.

While still in the camp, before we escaped together and became real friends, I caught Jurek by the window, his baggy eyes fixed in space. "Jurek, tell Sobolewski." Among ourselves, we inmates always spoke Polish, and I did my best to reason with him. "Jurek, what are you going to do? Even if she doesn't die of her own accord, Dr. Clauberg will kill her one day anyhow; she's witnessed too much."

Block Fifteen opposite the main gate of Auschwitz. Room One, visible to the right, was where Fire Brigade II was housed. Courtesy of the State Museum of Auschwitz-Birkenau.

He remained rivetted to the window. "Zygmunt, do you see those warm, dark eyes? Her melancholy smile, her delicate turned-down lips? O *Jezus-Marja*, she's always with me."

I approached him from behind, whispering in his ear, "Those women are absolutely *verboten*, you know that." Contact with 'Clauberg's bunnies' was punishable by death.

But Jurek always had the variety of mind that is not waylaid by practicality. He fixed his face. "That's the trouble. If only they weren't Jewish, the rules might not be so rigid."

"Okay, okay. Jurek, you might be right. But you must stop this insanity."

He turned around then within my space. His eyes were gazing into the distance. He leaned into me. For a second it seemed he was about to hug and kiss me—he was that close. He came to a halt with his mouth practically next to mine, one arm on my shoulder, one extended, a satisfied, bowed smile filling his face. "See how she returns my gaze?"

"Look, Jurek," I said, backing away, "at least have an alibi in case they catch you. Go and get yourself assigned to check fire extinguishers over there."

I remember he did, quite often. Thanks to Jurek, we knew something about what was going on. Rosa, as part of the technical staff, lived downstairs; the women subjects lived upstairs. "It's top secret, got to do with something for Himmler," he told us. "The women are terrified Clauberg's implanting freaks in their wombs." Subsequently, Jurek told me, "You know why they get to wear those colourful dresses? To mock them. They're human guinea pigs, Clauberg's *Kaninchen.* He's injecting something that tears at them from within. No wonder Rosa's got doe eyes. We've got to get her out of there."[5]

Eventually, I was also aroused by the *Kaninchen.* But as the Block Ten women were strictly forbidden, nothing came of it. Years before, I had given a friend skiing lessons: held her between my skis and felt her breasts through gloves and jacket. Who knows whether she was even aware of the 'feel' through all those layers of clothing? I, of course, exulted in my 'conquest', but she never evidenced any outward notice. So I had never made love to a woman. Slowly, I became obsessed with the idea, "I might die without discovering the ecstasy of physically loving a woman!"

Jurek remembers; they all do, even when I occasionally meet an Auschwitzer in a DP camp. It seems so unbelievable now to even think about it; it is the only aspect of camp I willingly remember. In September of 1943, a brothel was established in the main camp. Four Germans and a few Poles, Ukrainians and Slavs, thirteen women in all, transfixed thousands of inmates. Mine was one of the Poles, room thirteen. Polish prisoners like myself were forbidden to visit the Germans, who were reserved for pure Aryans. Racial mixture was to be prevented at all costs.

Kapos and *Prominenten,* privileged prisoners like bakers, cooks and butchers—anyone with a shred of remaining energy—could spend three '*Premiumschein*' for twenty minutes. Nineteen years old and on my first visit, I had no idea what to do—except that I had 'organized' red shorts from a camp tailor so as not to arrive in prisoner's underwear. I just sat on the edge of the bed, staring. The women in the brothel wore civilian short-skirts, high-heeled shoes and makeup. Irka set her hair brushed up and gently curled forwards, a fresh rose riding the waves that fell in large soft curls to the collar. She had full, ruddy cheeks on a round Polish face, rose-red lipstick that accentuated sparkling white teeth, flashing eyes, and eyebrows reshaped with a pencil. Dark blouse, white collar, she held her hands behind her, making her body look like a stem. For me, she was indeed the one rose in the midst of Auschwitz' thorns. My inexperience surprised her. We talked a little. She smiled. She was not at all what I imagined, though I hardly even knew what it was I had expected. A friendship budded, then blossomed into deeper feelings. With petal hands, she took my head, put my mouth to her eyes, her cheek, her neck. My nervousness melted against her skin. Gradually we made love.

Well after getting the information that *Tatuś* had died, *Achtundachtzig* fell blindly in love. How strange that a woman I cared about and loved was taken by four or five men every day, and I barely gave it a thought. A human being wants to be unique, different from everybody else, more than a number. But Auschwitz dehumanized us all. I have observed dogs beaten by their masters come crawling, begging, wagging a tail, looking for a caress. Degraded by the Nazis, you took any shred—a smile, a look, a word—and made it yours to cherish, even if hundreds of others were also embraced.

Irka and I talked a lot, in Polish, of course. I would be sitting on the bed, she would be on a straight-backed chair. She would fix me straight in the eye.

Irka. This photograph was taken illegally in Auschwitz in 1943.

"You're such a good man, Zygmunt. Different, better than the others. You'll be my friend?"

I had no defence at all. "Yeah, I'm your friend."

"Even here?"

I glanced around at the peephole in the door, through which noncommissioned SS officers monitored the place like madams in civilian houses of prostitution—"No unnatural sex allowed."

"Yeah, even here," I conceded.

"You'll always be my friend, my special friend?"

"Good, good! Here and always."

She looked relieved. "You're so good, Zygmunt."

"Did you, uh, did you, ever have, before you were here that is, a boyfriend?"

"Yes, a boxer. I liked to feel his arms and shoulders." She maintained her eye contact. "That's over."

"It's over?"

"Yes. It's you and me." Her eyes crinkled again, drawing me in.

"You don't say the same thing to all the others?"

"No. For them I just do what I have to."

Before I encountered Irka, feelings that had once resonated like music within had been stifled. All but forgotten were the deeper human connections of participating in the successes and failures of others. Now out of this special friendship welled a flood of past emotions: closing my eyes, I could distinctly see the girl I had, as a shy twelve-year-old, taken to my first movie, *Mutiny on the Bounty*. I could sense once more my sister's pride when I returned from cadet school in uniform. I could re-experience my mother's anguished eyes as she was forced to choose between me, and my infant brother and sick father. How my anger had boiled when the soldiers forced her to tear herself apart like that! I relived her pain.

With the return of emotions, I fell deeper and deeper in love. As I could never get enough time with Irka, occasionally I dared visiting at night as well. I bribed supervisors and Kapos, stuffed my bed, and slithered out in the dark after the camp was quarantined and the brothel closed.

In many respects Auschwitz was more sinister at night than in daytime. After 9:30, the German ravens flew the camp. A *Blocksperre*, a Block confinement, would be ordered and the quiet *Konzentrationslager* was turned over to its regime of nocturnal predators, the prisoners' administration: 'green triangle' criminals. They could sentence you to death for no reason at all and the next morning you were gone. During the night, you often heard barking and screams.

When I got out there, everything was silent. Fleetingly I felt something in back of me and tried to pierce the darkness. Except someone bent on escape or self-destruction, all prisoners were safely asleep, grateful for any relief from their usual exhaustion. Dressed in black pyjamas, with a black balaclava over my head, I slid alongside walls, slinking from shadow to shadow. I was alert to avoid Kapo Jupp Windeck (No. 3221), a *Lagerpolizei*, police force prisoner, who cruised the brothel like a Bengal tiger. Some say Jupp had been castrated, like the guards of the old Persian harems.[6] If Jupp caught you after curfew, no questions would be asked. This time it was not my imagination— a sharp sound. I crouched in a darkened corner; heard my heart double-timing. The perimeter search light swept across the nearest building alive with the moving shadow cast by a tree, glittered over a glass pane, beamed down the gravel road, then was swallowed by the darkness behind me. My mind travelled all the different directions Jupp would be likely to take, forgetting not one cranny, trying to logic out his footsteps. Once you are out in the middle of the camp, retreat is as dangerous as pushing ahead. I held my breath lest the spray of vapour rising in the brisk black air give me away. Eventually I had to let my eye follow the inevitable trail upwards, thinking it was a smoke-signal damning my presence. Above, it seemed every star in the universe salted the night sky. My mind slipped away. What did God think of all this below? If He cared, He gave no sign.

Another wave of light brought me back. My body was a tight spring. I counted the minutes, then stole my way to the next shadow.

I had fashioned a passkey to the washroom underneath the brothel in Block Twenty-four. From there I swung open the bathroom window, slipped through, mounted the open panels and, catching the sill directly above, spidered my way up to where Irka was on vigil. It was the second floor transom I had to get through, being careful not to break the main windows with my knees. Warning for quiet, "*Cicho,*" Irka pulled me through.

I kissed her. "When was the guard through last?"

Her return kiss was passionate. I understood only partially the intensity of her lovemaking. She really risked her well-being to see me, yet when we were alone together, it was like nothing could touch us. They were intervals lived for themselves, unspoiled by the need to meet future responsibilities. Stretched out exposed on her cot, finding enjoyment in each other's naked-ness, we experienced a lifetime of Christmases and birthdays.

Once during the day, I had overstayed the time allotment. The orchestra had already started to play for the work kommandos returning at the end of the day. I let myself out from the bathroom window, and dangled for a minute in full view of the Auschwitz fence. Looking around, I saw no one, jumped, falling to the grass, knocking the wind out of my chest. "Made it," I thought. Within seconds, I saw from the ground a pair of boots. Then a belt. Then higher and higher until I was looking into the eyes of the biggest German Kapo in the camp. He had been standing in an alcove invisible from above. I whipped off my hat. "Um, sorry sir," I wheezed, "accidentally got stuck in the bathroom—had diarrhoea."

It might astonish the outsider that about that time, camp marshall SS Ser-geant-major Wilhelm Claussen, a good-looking tall blond sports fanatic, had organized the semblance of Sunday boxing. Once this Claussen spent hours with Irka after locking up all the others. "Talking," she claimed. I hated him. And as for boxing, in my exclusive cadet school in prewar Poland, boxing had been considered a vulgar, primitive sport, especially by our Latin teacher. We had practised the ritual and grace of fencing with a sabre, 'much more appropriate' for future Polish Army officers. Nazi ideology, however, stressed sport, and German boxer Max Schmelling was a Nazi hero even though he was beaten in 1938 by the black Joe Louis. And what choice has an unenlightened twenty-year-old, deeply in love, if the object of his desire adores boxers? Boxing it would be, and fast! The thought of Irka's strikingly high cheekbones, pearly teeth and ready smile outweighed any anxiety over even an opponent's dynamite-laden uppercut.

I discovered a Jewish prisoner named Max, a foreman in the attic of Block Twenty-three and a middleweight champion of Holland (1937). This former ring star supervised about ten prisoners. Their task was to hang the prison laundry out to dry on long lines of wire attached to the roof rafters of the Block. This Max could hoist a full basket of wet laundry like it was empty.

"You'll train twice a week here behind the wet clothing and underwear. I'll assign someone to be on the lookout for SS guards." Salamo Arouch, a Greek Jew who had been lightweight champ of the Balkans, was supposedly forced to fight in 220 bouts during his two years in Auschwitz–Birkenau. Each time he fought to the amusement of the Nazis who gambled on the outcome, he knew the loser faced instant death. Either he died, or he was responsible for the death of his opponent. Fighting to the death did not happen in our part of the camp. But it could have happened in Birkenau, so posting lookouts was no idle precaution. The Jew Max was particularly vulnerable. Just the same, he helped me. "Each class," he said, "will have three three-minute rounds of rope-skipping, two rounds of shadow boxing, two rounds of heavy-bag punching and two rounds of sparring."

"Good, good, and in return?" I asked.

"Bread, soup, one-half pound of margarine." Later, he sometimes added medicine. Occasionally, Max enlisted my influence as a *Prominent* prisoner to secure a 'better job' for some of his friends.

Max was good to his word, and the conditioning took about four months—all to impress Irka. Then, one evening in 1944, I became involved in a shouting match with a *Reichsdeutsche*, a German Kapo called Heinz, because he tripped a *Muselmann*. "Why'd you go and do that?" I exploded. In 1942, no one would have dared argue with a Kapo. But in the summer of 1944, with everyone, guard and inmate alike, knowing Soviet troops were but seven hundred kilometres away, and being a *Prominente*, I risked it. Why? Probably one of those dumb, helpless acts you do just to maintain a shred of humanity. I had forgotten that during the 'vicious years' of 1941 and 1942, Heinz was infamous for the short-handled sledgehammer he carried in his belt, discipline for a lazy prisoner's head. He had killed dozens.

At morning roll-call, Claussen, the sports fanatic who knew I had been itching for a chance in the ring, approached me. "*Achtundachtzig*, I have arranged for you to fight the former boxing *Meister* of Hamburg, 'Sledge-hammer' Heinz," he sneered.

Everywhere I look I see him, grinning, coming on me with flashing fists. "Jurek, I wanted to fight, yes, but not with a German. And certainly not with the 'Sledgehammer.' What did I get myself into?"

"You can do it if anybody can; keep practising."

"What if I should get sick and not be up to whatever strength I've got remaining?"

The days slipped by too quickly. One Sunday in June, in the intersection of Blocks:

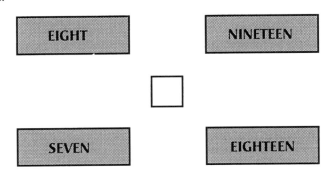

an elevated ring was built. Two three-round fights were announced. They made it seem like an ordinary card. The first fight was between two Polish prisoners. Ours was the second contest, a Pole against a *Reichsdeutsche*, which had never happened before. In their sun-drenched ringside seats, Nazi noncoms, 'smeltering' skin to smart dress uniform, were the society folk who came to see blood. Nine hundred prisoners squeezed in between the buildings behind them, cheering wildly when I forced myself to climb through the ropes. Claussen, in a white shirt and running shoes, refereed.

Heinz, who had done time for robbery, was a red-haired pig of a man. One blow with his huge paw could put a guy away for life. What am I doing on this steaming canvas with Kapo Heinz? I was saying to myself. And watch out for Claussen—he promises to be anything but a fair referee. My chest constricted, while my legs from thigh to calf felt as though they would melt into the mat. Heinz was taller and heavier than me (a Kapo, especially a German Kapo, never went hungry). The Sledgehammer's eyes glared with undisguised hatred above a huge grin. My first match ever had become both the testing of the four previous years, and also the measure of any future there might be for me. I had to keep reassuring myself: Aryan supremacy? No, the bell rings and each combatant is on his own.

It started at a fast pace. From the start I realized I was no match for him. He stalked me, chasing hard with his long right swing, a smile playing on his lips. His first swing ripped past my chin just scraping off a bit of skin, but I was surprised by the speed, and it spooked me. I could see he was out to cut me up bad. He took the next lunge, aiming for my neck. By sheer instinct I swerved, then danced professionally around the ring on my toes, sometimes as Max had taught, sometimes parrying as a fencer. The constant movement confused him, and my body was too fleet afoot.

"Come and say 'hello,'" I teased.

This boisterous Kapo snarled back, "I'll say, 'Bye, bye *Achtundachtzig*.' No Polish scum is going to mock me." He chased me all over the ring. Sweat poured off me; I took the heat as a personal affront from Nature. I knew one slip and he would go for the kill. The crowd knew it too, held its collective breath. Only an occasional shout of encouragement to Heinz from the German noncoms could be heard when he would graze my head. Just as he had me on the ropes in the corner, the bell clanged.

The prisoners' roar rang my ears as the handler rubbed me down. My parched lips gave off a salty taste of blood; in the next round, I could be eating blood on the mat. The faces of the crowd swam before me. "Where's Irka? Didn't Claussen let her out?" I tried to clear my head, "Focus on the job at hand."

In the following round, the Sledgehammer, twirling about the hot canvas, went right-hand crazy, trying several times to nail me with his powerful right, forgetting altogether to throw left-hand punches. I could hardly breathe. "Take this," he grunted with each intended blow.

Moving, shifting to the left, ducking, pulling away, carefully avoiding those spiked blows, I managed to skirt through the big hits, taunting: "Yeah, pretty good, *Meister*. You've got to do better, though."

"You'll be roasting on the floor," he growled. He looked to be true to his word. Heinz let loose with a walloping roundhouse. My head jerked back. Luckily, the heavy blow whistled just past my mouth. The wild swing pulled him forwards, and he lost his balance. The crowd started to laugh.

Between bells, I saw him throwing me killer looks, hardly able to sit still in his corner after that second embarrassment. I had the crazy idea that I'd again be lucky enough to avoid his sledgehammers; that he would trip over his own feet, knocking himself out on the floor. The handler's words broke into me from afar. "Get into him. Everyone's depending on you. And this is for a treasured title: Irka."

At the bell, the German Kapo bounced out enraged. Heinz's heavy punches gave way to crude anger and a sodden brain. His teeth jutted out in a snarl as if to say, "Now you're in for it." My attention fused onto this mad brute staggering out, stomping like a *klutz*. "Make a fool out of me, will you?" he snorted under his breath. A lacy vapour covered my eyes. The tripped *Muselmann* ... the shouting match ... an image of Heinz supervising the trench-digging detail, sledgehammer in his belt ... an image of Heinz hammering a prisoner's head in ... Claussen ordering the fight with a smirk—my mind was playing tricks on me. I looked him in the face, seeking vainly for any hint of an escape.

He was moving more slowly. Thoughts of Irka entered my brain. My former boyfriend, he was a boxer, she was saying. I came diving at him like an eagle, striking persistently with the left, crossing with the right to his heart. The blows struck home. He came back straining desperately to put me away, me watching those mad sledgehammer swings of his, him sweating like a stewed sow. The crowd was roaring. *Achtundachtzig* pressed the advantage, stepping into the overweight, chain-smoking drinker, mixing and landing. More twisting, pivoting, then drawing back his arm, *Achtundachtzig Slepowron*, raven killer, aimed for the eye. "That's what Poles do, you murdering son of a bitch."

While he was still smarting, another driving right went digging into his stomach. Heinz doubled over, his nose running red. "*Zabyi-go*," howled the excited crowd in Polish, "Kill him!"

In Germany, the Hitler Youth emphasized sport and strength. A programme of gymnastics had been formed to steel the Aryan physique. Each fighting Aryan was a knight in a holy encounter for the German destiny. I knew this at the time. We had heard much of it in cadet school. Apparently, no one among the SS had considered the unthinkable. It wasn't part of their Nazi consciousness, which saw the Aryan as the perfectly proportioned superior race whose energy was waiting to be released.

At that minute, Claussen in his impartial judgment stopped the bout. "You Polish prisoners are too unruly." It ended as a no-decision fight.

People pounded my back and shook hands, and I did get the two loaves of bread that were the prize. Irka, when she saw me, danced around without stopping, touching my arms and shoulders, kissing me. "Give me every detail," she demanded, even correcting me where she had heard something I left out.

Earlier, even a no-decision ending could have meant trouble, but by the summer of '44, the match earned us all respect. Afterwards, whenever our paths crossed, Heinz roared 'hello' like an old friend.

We had known it was coming, but you rarely face reality until it is forced upon you. After six months, Irka expected to be sent home; the promise of release had been part of the original agreement to get her to cooperate and join the brothel. She gazed out the window as I held her from behind. "Soon you'll be free." We were counting the days.

Staring out at the towers, she told me, "I'll memorize all the addresses, visit your family."

"Good, tell them I'll survive. Tell them I survive from their letters. Thank them for all they've sent."

"I'll love them as my own."

"But don't tell them too much."

"Don't worry."

"Here, memorize my aunt's address in case the family moves: Emma Ballas, NA Vozovce Nr. 44, Olomouc, Mähren Protectorate."

"Yes, I'll call on them all."

"You won't forget the address."

"No."

In what had become the bizarre experience of camp life, sometimes these reveries of ours so engrossed us it was hopeless trying to distinguish the authentic from the illusory.

When the hoped-for time came, Irka was instead transferred to the new *Schutzhaftlagereweiterung* section where she was made an assistant forewoman in construction. On the pretext of testing the water pressure in the hydrants, I met her there twice and we actually had sex. As the defeat of Germany drew near, Irka was evacuated suddenly without time for good-byes. I did not even find out where she was until she wrote a letter. Soon after, I was also shipped out. Each of us was sent our separate ways.

Even before liberation, Irka had written my Aunt Emma: "I'm a friend of Zygmunt's from the *Konzentrationslager*. I pray he survives. When you hear from him please tell him I'm alive in Bergen–Belsen outside Hanover." Details follow. In a postscript to me she writes, "I am so concerned about your well-being. You have my undying love." Her letter arrived before we left Sachsenhausen.

"She loves me," I tell my friend Jurek, and elated set out at the first opportunity.

Hanover, the railway centre of Germany. Soldiers from dozens of countries mob the station. Trains lurch in and out with a screech. Outside, the effects of bombing. The beech- and oak-lined Leine River divides the old town's narrow streets and gabled houses, or what is left of them, from the new. The fragmented roof of one centuries-old home intertwines with its top floor. Another survives, blackened by fire, still smelling like a blown-out candle. Yet another looms windowless to the elements, an eyeless skeleton, debris strewn on the brick walk, a flower bed still guarding its entrance path. We weave through the pock-marked streets on newly organized bicycles. Cleanup crews are sweating in the sun, sweeping and clearing, replacing broken glass, temporarily filling road holes for more permanent repaving later, quickly reinstalling the paraphernalia of middle-class domesticity. "German reconstruction," a man boasts.

"Is it?" I say, the indiscretion scudding out of my mouth like a bat through a bombed-out windowpane. "I could use some reconstruction myself."

Bergen–Belsen is posted with signs marked "Typhus." The concertina wire and SS have disappeared, but corpses are still being ferried about in wagons. Many hung on long enough to be liberated, but do not survive freedom. The allied soldiers have been trained to fight, not to govern or cater. Nor can they, with all their goodwill, do much for the typhus-ridden skeletons they have freed. Little medicine is available even to relieve acute agony. And since shortage makes for scrimping, they do not always employ even the bit they might possess.[7] God, I hope Irka hasn't been infected.

A shiver darts up my spine. Haven't I seen the German officers' quarters before? Whether at Belsen or Auschwitz, the character of the two-storey buildings connected by asphalt paths does not vary. I check the Block number, notice a tensing in the bottom of my throat. I focus my mind and force myself up the walk to the three-step stoop. A cherub-faced woman steps out in a print smock, a single rose in her hair. In a blink I am seeing Auschwitz all over again. Breaking into a tentative smile, she returns the stare, a vague question in her eyes. Uncomfortably, I watch her as she looks me up and down with warm curiosity. The rumpled pants, ill-fitting shirt and old cap, I requisitioned along the way; the fatigue comes with the territory. It is like old friends meeting after years of separation: "How did you survive the last days?" "How have you managed after liberation?" Then, "O *Jezus-Marja*, you're really safe."

Peeking into the dark austere interior of her barracks, I see faces peer out at me. News of my visit has obviously preceded my coming. I can grab sight of cramped, narrow beds, and an exposed hardwood floor. Its natural smell is decidedly female, or so it seems to me: mysterious. Or maybe it is merely an olfactory illusion. Whichever, to be alone, we meander down a path towards a pine wood, sharing our stories since we were last together. What barely a few days ago was a mass of emaciated bodies, has already grown serene, a tribute either to the regenerative powers of life, or the indifference of life.

I listen to this woman, her voice so familiar: "Remember the panic towards the end? We got sent to Belsen in a box car. Military transports held up our train for hours. We had nothing to eat. Many didn't arrive. What's the use of going back over it?"

"The complete opposite from me. We rode in comfortable coaches. For us, the worst was looking out at German people going about their business like Auschwitz was invisible."

"I still see it. In Auschwitz someone gave me a few thousand *złotys*. I went and bartered them for a little bread, or I might not have made it, either. The fifteenth of April, we were liberated."

"Only five days later I walked out of Sachsenhausen," I interject.

"We heard three large booms," she continues, "far away shouting. Word passed: '*Engländer, Engländer sind da*'. Then this grinding sound and the first British tank with its white star and Union Jack. It had a tattered Nazi flag stuck to it. At first the British were cheering themselves, celebrating, flashing victory signs. Then suddenly they got silent."

"When they saw you."

"Yes. One by one they began to throw food. Without moving, I watched others attack each other over the scraps, like it wasn't even happening to me." I take her hand. "I was so numb, I can't remember the slightest relief. I felt like scum in their eyes. Suddenly I felt nothing could ever wash away my shame. Not the shame of what the SS had forced me to do—oh no, not that, certainly not that. The shame of being part of the Nazi world, that all this had been *allowed* to happen, and us incapable of doing a thing."

Years after, I will remember her words like my own name. Now, I can barely concentrate on the conversation, such is Irka's power over me. The path has run out. But we have continued on. I move to comfort her. She is still the finest thing in the world. She responds in kind, the neck of her dress gaping open just enough to reveal a lack of undergarments as she leans forwards to greet the embrace.

"Zygmunt, there's a British officer; it was necessary; I'm glad I won't have to see him anymore."

What do I, barely twenty-one, know of complex morality? Inside the camp, this love was very positive: gratitude in the midst of agony. What could it matter that on the outside people wrote poetry, dreamt dreams, shared goals? In the abyss, our few seconds of love gave meaning to an existence otherwise lacking all purpose. But now I am confused. None of the hundreds bothered me. This one does. Maybe for her part she is still acting out of necessity, but it does not seem that way to me. I now see lying before me a boxing fan a couple years older than I, tricked into believing that if she consented they would release her after six months. Who knows what she now sees before her? I do not answer.

Now she is talking, fiercely on and on, like she has not spoken in a year. "Hössler, remember him?"

"You bet. Got me out of big trouble when I was caught jumping down from your window. Instead of shipping me the Mauthausen quarry, he ripped up the report with only a warning."

"For that I'll be forever thankful, only it doesn't change what he did to me."

"No, I guess it doesn't." As with many Poles, she had been taken in a street cordon.

She begins to break down, but catches herself. "When I got here?"

"Yeah?"

"He was assistant *kommandant*. The bastard had the gall to tell me he'd let me escape. Fat chance."

More than likely she is right. In an old game at Auschwitz, a guard would flip an inmate's cap, flip it by the fence, then order him to retrieve it. If he did, he was shot for attempting escape. If he did not, he was shot for disobedience. Great fun. True, once Dacko accidentally bumped into *SS Hauptsturmführer* Franz Hössler while fighting a fire and knocked him over. Dacko thought he was dead on the spot. Hössler simply got up, shook himself off and walked away. And once he shouted at a guard who was hampering us, 'By a fire there are no prisoners, only firemen.' But in the spring of 1942, I witnessed Hössler kick an old Jew to death, breast and ribs cracking. He was also known to have executed some prisoners after the 10 June 1942 escape from the *Königsgraben*. And from June 1944 to the evacuation of the camp, Hössler served Hitler's *Reich* as the *Lagerführer* of Auschwitz. Previously, he had been for a short time head of the women's camp at Birkenau, choosing Irka for the brothel.

"By the grace of *Jezus-Marja* I was there to see the British take him. I exploded, pelted him with rotten potatoes. 'You have betrayed me. You have betrayed me.' I had strength for that. He looked at me and said, 'I am very, very sorry.' He'll get his! They should string him up by his balls."

Hössler, former Auschwitz commander, in Bergen-Belsen in 1945.

"I don't think the British do that."[8]

"Guess what I heard," she asks.

"What?"

"During the evacuation, in January? when the open railroad cars were crossing a bridge? some prisoners pushed "Sledgehammer" Heinz in front of a train going the other way."

"Just like he did to others. To think he almost got me."

She gently smacks her finger between her lips, a gesture from the Auschwitz bordello. Her eyes go slightly dreamy. "Tired?"

"No."

"I've something important I want to talk about."

"Okay."

"You're not too tired?"

"No!"

"Zygmunt … I've got to see my family. Now that you're here, I'm anxious to return home. Let's up and get ourselves to Poland."

My mind can hear the high-spirited *mazurka* of earlier, better days; recall the youthful grandeur of fencing in cadet school; see the women gaily dressed at parties. But other thoughts crowd their way in:

A Polish language sprinkled with unknown locutions … subtle changes in street life—unbearable evidence that life has continued. There, too, mother, sister, brothers, other family and friends. Last time we were together, I'd just turned seventeen. Would they recognize that he who comes back is a fully grown man? Oh, I couldn't stomach the pity. The solicitude of my mother. Solicitude. *Mamusia*, haven't I proven I can look after myself! And then maybe even worse: a hint of disapproval. How did he survive? Hasn't it already happened to others? I could never stand that. Would they rather unrecognizable ash in the Silesian wind than the hands and lips of the living? Impossible to endure! And, all this time, why didn't my sister write? Basia, paralysed by anxiety attacks? Frequenting the church in our neighbourhood, constantly praying for me? What—only *Mamusia* knows how to write in German for the censor? Włodimierz never wrote either, not once. And my youngest brother Lucjan, born when I was fifteen. To him, I'm nothing more than a stick figure in a box called Auschwitz.

As Irka rambles on about returning to Poland, thoughts again balloon in my head:

They will be expecting their long-lost returnee to answer questions. How can I tell them, It's done, erased; I can't discuss it? Jewish children moving, moving continually past our Block. Children led by the hand. Children prancing out in front. Children, damn them all. Children. Another voice in my ear: Leave this bloody, hate-filled morgue; can you move ahead standing on a corpse? Try to visualize Nisko, my beloved village. Cold. Damp. That voice again: Find a better start, as far away as possible.

"Irka, Poland's not like it used to be, occupied by Russia." Unlike Auschwitz, Sachsenhausen had a library, primarily supplied with anti-Bolshevik literature I absorbed uncritically. "Read any newspapers lately?" She has not. "Who knows what the future will bring there? Irka, please, please understand ... the uncertainty ... how can I start up there under such circumstances?"

She does not say it, but the look on her face does: Because I'm a whore. You came to me and came to me, and now don't want me. Instead, she says, "I thought you understood me when no one else did. When everyone was using each other for their own purposes, I thought you and I——"

"It isn't against you, Irka. Too dangerous, the Communists might even keep Auschwitz."

And now I think of my father:

How I sometimes resented him. *Tatuś*, whose image sustained me until Irka entered my life. *Tatuś*, whose activities caused me to be taken prisoner. *Tatuś*, who did not even wait my return. Dead. Gone.

It comes clear. I can never return. All I am straining to remove from my life would come rolling back.

All this time Irka has been silent. She is talking on and on again, quickly, cheerily, a duck taking flight, skimming the surface of a dark mountain lake. Whatever her true feelings are, I can no longer tell.

"Irka, you know how I feel about you. This isn't about you. A Russian Poland I can't bear; and in many ways I'd be unbearable to those in Poland. Please understand, I have to make something new."

I am a stone pillar, just clamp tight whatever feelings I might have, like when *Tatuś* died. In Auschwitz, numbness was a skill you had to perfect.

Five: Ginsbourg

Brussels, Belgium, June 1945

urek and I are racing down towards the depot to catch the last train back to Antwerp. Suddenly, someone is calling me.

"What! George Ginsbourg! You made it! What a miracle you saw us!" We grab each other tightly, kissing. He has filled out considerably since last I saw him, but has the same toothy grin. George taught me English while in Auschwitz; but now, anxious to catch my train, we exchange stories in German.

"After leaving Irka, I went searching for the wife of a certain Dutch 'red triangle' we'd met in Sachsenhausen. He was so concerned about her, he'd asked everyone he knew to carry a message to her in Hilversum. No wonder he was concerned. Found her living with a guy."

"She was a delight!" says Jurek.

"When she heard her husband was still alive, in gratitude she went and had us arrested."

"I can't stand it," my old Auschwitz teacher says.

"It wasn't too terrible. You can understand, as camp survivors, we were something of celebrities. And there was no reason to hold us. When we learned some Polish troops were going to Antwerp for R&R, we convinced them to take us with them. And what about you?"

"We were evacuated from Auschwitz in an open train." There is a lull. "Half the prisoners died en route." George looks down, recalling the scene, then continues. "To keep warm on the wagon, the rest of us built a hut of the bodies." He cannot get his words out.

"Is there no end?" Jurek says.

Ginsbourg's deep eyes peer out from under his sun-bleached brows. "Three survived," he sighs. "Since liberation I've been translating for the Americans. Look, here's a picture." George hands me a photograph of himself in an American uniform, canteen on his belt, smiling between two American officers. He takes it again, inscribes it, "To my friend from Auschwitz," and hands it back to me. "Guess you'll be going back to Poland?" he asks me.

"Don't think so. What about you?"

"There's no place for me anymore in Danzig. I have an aunt in Palestine. Maybe I'll go there."

Jurek is motioning that we will miss the train. We part with regret. I put it out of my mind.

In Belgium we stay with an upholsterer. He had been an employee in a Jewish business. After the Nazis came in, when a Jew could not own a business, he was made partner. Then he had denounced his partner and become owner. I put that out of mind as well.

A short time later, Jurek and I illegally leapfrog from one car to another so as to board and disembark while avoiding the red sea of British military police checking papers. Escaping from the Paris station, we bump into a Polish uniform. Prewar Poland had excellent relations with France, and the French sent General Weygand to train the Polish Army. My father served as the Polish liaison to Weygand, a major position in the top echelons of the Polish army. In 1926, when Field Marshall Józef Pilsudski, the general who had successfully outmanoeuvred the Red Army when it attacked Poland after war, returned to power through a *coup d'état*. My father would not support him. If Pilsudski had lost, *Tatuś* would have most likely gone on to become a general like my uncle. As testimony to this French-Polish liaison, a Polish army barracks still stands in the heart of the Paris. This Polish soldier we meet buys us a bus ticket. Nazis escape through the very same routes. At Caserne Bessières, we find out about Hulanicki, who we thought was so foolish. When he decided to stay with the death march, he was simply liberated a few days afterwards in Mecklenburg.

Is this only another illusion? Why do I know this guy's moves before he makes them? My mind remembers horrible screams from the washroom of Block Ten where *Achtundachtzig* was then billeted. Paradowski (No. 323), a tall, phlegmatic youth about nineteen who gangled around like a giraffe, was being held under a frigid shower for two hours by *Blockälteste* Emil Bednarek (No. 1325) and his assistant Kala. "Wash your filthy arse and feet," they shouted while battering him continuously. He died the next day. His offence? Dirty feet during foot-review, *Fussparade*. At the news of Paradowski's death, Bednarek simply shrugged. "*Sowieso, Krematorium*, one way or another, one ends in the crematorium." Only the cruellest Kapos 'worked their way up' to the *Strafkompanie*, punishment gang, and Bednarek became one of them in 1944. The presence of Jurek and another Auschwitz inmate, Zończyk, who confirm my senses, is the only proof I have that I am not out of my mind. It is Bednarek's assistant, Kala, now a sergeant, strutting around the barracks barking orders. There is a counter intelligence-office on the site, and we go testify against this criminal to the Polish Secret Service.[9]

Soon after I left Irka, Ernest Bevin, British Foreign Secretary, issued a public statement that all members of the 'Free Polish Forces' not wishing to return to Russian occupied Poland would be welcomed to the U.K. and retrained. Bevin's statement leads us, on our first day in Paris, to enlist in the Polish navy. For back at the time of the raven invasion, our navy was caught outside the land of the White Eagle; so, fighting on the side of the Allies, it was based in England.

New culture. New language. New subtleties of exchange. Compared with Poland, with Auschwitz, England is a new planet: the double-decker bus that feels like you are going to fall over in Southampton's narrow streets; church bells change-ringing instead of the bong! bong! bong! of Poland; manicured grass. You meander aimlessly, buying trinkets, going to cinemas, finding nothing by which to steer a new course except a weird fascination in your own disorientation. Figuring out the money is impossible.

Eventually we make our way to Devonport. There we find our own Polish enclave at the Royal Naval Establishment barracks known as 'HMS Drake'.

Sigmund in Polish Navy in England, 8 December 1945.

When we were still back in France, I met a German sailor who taught me what I needed to know to prove navy experience. If not for me, Jurek would not have been accepted. But once in England and no longer dependent upon my German, our roles reverse. In the *Marynarka Wojenna*, everyone teases me at dinner. "Sobolewski, you've gotta be the biggest pig in the Polish navy." And those who have to march downwards from me complain I stagger like a drunken sailor—a leftover from camp meningitis.

"Jurek, I can't stand the ignorance. These guys who went through the Russian Gulag have no idea of the production-line gassing of millions. They think Siberian scarecrows equate with Auschwitz ashes."

"It's like what we went through never happened."

"But it did, didn't it? I think they try to avoid me. They say things like, 'Enough already', or 'Everybody suffered.'"

It is true that even this town is still marred by collapsed buildings: here a partial wall, there a chimney, bricks and rubble, a danger to inquisitive youngsters. In the Plymouth centre only the old Corn Exchange warehouse remains. And some of our fellow sailors were in submarine warfare. "You 'Kriegies,'" they say, calling me a POW from the German word, *Kriegsgefangen*, "had it made. While you sat, we seamen risked icy death convoying supply ships from Scapa Flow to Murmansk."

"Can't I ever get through any of your skulls that those arrested for 'political treason' were hardly treated like prisoners of war?"

"We liberated Bergen-Belsen, you know."

"But you don't know shit about Auschwitz. It was ten times bigger, ten times worse than Belsen."

Talk becomes like conversing two languages. They stuff up their ears to anything uncomfortable, and I am like two people: with a group, I become claustrophobic in the walls of their limited experience, and when by myself, I yearn again for the assurance of their clamor. I learn to talk about anything but Auschwitz. Jurek thinks that is the best policy. Every time I take a shower, I try to wash away my past.

Jurek, lean and handsome in his uniform, finds a girlfriend and occasionally takes me along to a dance. But he cannot fill the emptiness in my heart.

"Jurek, where's the girl with the dark blue eyes and the haircut that suits her so well?"

"Take it easy. The guy who swung boxing gloves for a woman in Auschwitz will find someone."

"Right. Except for the red light district, I can't get past round one."

"Maybe you should take up boxing again," he laughs.

When other guys are on duty, I am training. My trophy reads: "Plymouth Command/Royal Navy and Royal Marines/Boxing Championship/1947/ Heavyweight Winner."

The least frustration sucks at me, makes me irrational to succeed. I can get a 'no' twenty times at the door, and then try at the window twenty times more, right through the soft glass. Lately, I have become a hoarder, collecting wire, screws, anything which 'might have value.' Once, while I am foraging outside a row of Quonset huts, a shadow falls over me. I turn to encounter one of my officers.

"At ease, Sobolewski. I've noticed you seem to apply yourself. What do you do in your spare time?"

"Sir? I have programme: Study English. Learn welding. Take radio operator's course. Practise boxing. Look for women. Learn local customs."

"Sobolewski, I'm impressed with your work."

"Why, thank you, sir."

"I'd like to recommend you for an electrical course, to be an engineer. It will give you a start."

If he told me I was being shipped to Antarctica I would have believed him more easily. I am delighted. Ecstatic. But is it practical? "Well, I don't know. I don't know if I can. Thank you. I appreciate offer. I've got to think about it."

"Of course. But don't worry, there's a Further Education and Training grant for vets."

The same day, Jurek comes to me all excited. "I'm going to Canada. I've been speaking to an officer from the Polish Air Force on the volleyball court. Canada is taking some soldiers."

"You're leaving?"

"Yeah, you can sign on, too."

"Don't know. Just learned they're offering some education courses. Maybe I can finish high school."

"Oh."

"I don't think I should pass it up."

"Any idea what you'd do?"

"Two-year technical programme, electrical. My uncle was in construction; so was my grandfather."

"An FET is a big break, I guess."

"So's Canada. Jurek, take care of yourself, yes?"

Jurek is demobbed and leaves. There are too many separations in my life, too much agony. The school is not ready, nobody knows when it will start; and I learn the building trades unions do not at this time accept foreigners. I spot a notice on the base hoarding I frequent to practise my English, copying out any words I don't know and looking them up in an old dictionary. These exercises are no substitute for Ginsbourg's lessons, but I do my best. All through the last few months in Auschwitz, I would give him soup and bread in return for English lessons. Found him in July of 1944, part of one of the few Jewish work commandos housed in the main camp. When it started to get cold, I gave him a sweater for underneath his stripers. According to the announcement on the board, anyone who accepts demobilization can get an immediate salary on a merchant ship.

In the midst of making my decision, two letters arrive in rapid succession. "Włodimierz," my dear younger brother, "will have a growth removed from his belly." Then the second, "The growth, once disturbed, spread and settled in his brain." If I had known that afternoon with Irka that my brother would die of cancer at the age of twenty, I might have actually gone back. Now what good would it do?

Dejected, when a member of the seamen's union confirms entrance into the London union, I say to hell with this Polish army programme that is never going to start. In 1947, Great Britain honours its word and receives a new citizen. London, England. At first, I am in a stupor. The city is like a cold fish. The fog and rain penetrate inside as well as out. It seems I spend most of my life cocooned in bed, not literally, but still sleep-walking. I distrust. I cannot make decisions; for years they have all been made for me. The eyes see, the ears hear, yet all comes strained through a post-Auschwitz screen that distorts everything.

If you catch your reflection in a shop window, you see a body with your gestures and features. You cannot be certain if it is someone who just looks like you or if it is really you. Among the packed throngs of shoppers and textile vendors on Wentworth Street and Petticoat Lane, no one pays any mind to lost refugees, neither to me nor the others, unnamed others, as *Achtundachtzig* went unnamed. Then the haze lifts. By extreme exertion of will, I force my mind to swing into alignment with its new life. The now is now; I stab at submerging my feelings, attending every canteen dance at the Mecca ballrooms in London. There are four locations, all the same: clumps of men and clumps of women milling around in a semi-darkened hall, stamps on the back of each left hand like the numbers on my arm, the big band, maybe some decent women to dance with. Clinging. Hoping desperately. Faces passing in succession.

The Poles do not frequent the dance halls. Aside from a few Americans, I am alone among the British. Everybody, except me, seems to know somebody. And at evening's end, when others go off in pairs sitting over a glass of beer or embracing in the park, I feel sick with fear. "My body will wax old underneath my hand."

As arranged, I go down and join on with a merchant ship. Steaming where? Anywhere but Poland. Down, around, back and forth across the Atlantic. To the Ivory Coast, to the Gold Coast, to Nigeria. And even, by way of rail portages, down the Congo's thick jungle swamps like Henry M. Stanley, skimming by the overhanging branches where the river turns, now and again passing glistening-skinned ebony men and women in small colonies of thatched huts. Often they wave us in. They share smiles and a hot tea boiled over the fire. We break out some rice pudding and a few tins of meat.

Once, back staring into the purple-black sea on the late night watch, I am steering the ship and fall asleep at the helm. The third officer is dozing, too. It is a big ship, a 22,000 tonne tanker. I wake up to find it going in circles. Is it the same trip? We are transporting crude oil from Trinidad to England on the *TES Thaumastus*, a Shell oil tanker. A freak storm heaves the ship, catching me balanced on a peg painting the top mast. At one minute I am hanging far out in the air over the starboard on my back, the next minute far out over the port-side on my stomach. The tempest leaves us limping at half-speed, listing badly. We are forced to dry-dock in Galveston for six weeks.

After the long, agonizing trip, we bound ashore like the recently recovered from a confining illness. Barely past the port and warehouse district, some of our seamen get arrested just strolling down the street. They are fined their entire shore leave pay, have to remain battened down in their cabin the rest of the time. They are black. Then, on a bus, this little sign halfway down the aisle "for colored only" moves forwards as more blacks than whites get on and overflow the rear. Also, the contractor repairing our now lifeless ship sets up separate portable toilets for the black and white workers who swarm its sides and bilge. We have a mixed crew, and this is the first time outside of Auschwitz I have seen anything like this. To me, the honour of the craft has been sullied. Ports in Africa may be more primitive, but a feeling of fellow humanity always comes through. Galveston is brutal. The man from Auschwitz resolves never to settle in the United States. But action? The man from Auschwitz does nothing, and says nothing.

At first, nothing is more exciting than the merchant marine: the starlit nights away from city glare; Andromeda rescued by Perseus; Cassiopeia cast away in shame; the terrible archer, half beast, half man, Sagittarius. I love the idea that no nation-state can own or claim the high sea. The waves that wash the distant shore have been here before the Vikings, and will be here long after I am retired to a land-locked grave. We sail through, and a few minutes later there is no track or trace, not even a smell. In a world of porpoises breaking the skin of the ocean that I am beginning to learn and love, Auschwitz is but a piece of insignificant flotsam. But after a while, life at sea starts to repeat itself. The endless carping of the crew. The demands of the sea. The relentless routine. Even here, in the vast ocean, it closes in about me.

I try to put it out of my mind, and enjoy the women. Still, one port blends into another. Every port a different woman. That is to say, one evening's companion blends into another. We always have money though. On the *SS Takoradi*, making the route from Liverpool to Dakar, we deliver foodstuff, cotton cloth, and building materials to brown-skinned stevedores wheeling creaking carts in the misty heat. We watch as huge cranes supporting iron chains load flats of general cargo: skins, peanuts, and mahogany; and palm oil for Copenhagen. Whatever the port of arrival, my eyes grope in and around, like the finger of an Auschwitz beacon, for any women lolling about the bars and hotels past the wharf area. The worst is rotting on board for sometimes two or three days on anchor awaiting permission to disembark.

Travel broadens; but at the end of each tour, I return to the Red Ensign Club in Eastgate, London, with its cracked ceilings and paper-thin walls, where sailors stay only because the rates are reasonable. Chain the door at night, they advise. I go to bed by myself, keeping my shoes close. There are never enough blankets. Sometimes the sound of an ambulance wakes me, mouth parched, to find Nazis going through the dresser drawers, turning my meagre wardrobe out on the floor. I assure myself that I am okay, normal. At other times I hear a shot. Maybe a car backfires, I tell myself. Then a voice shrieks hysterically, mocking laughter. Noise from another room, I tell myself. I write to Jurek in Canada, "With you gone, there's no one who knows what we went through without long impossible explanations."

Life links me with Jews again. In the frequent empty hours, my body wanders streets with names like Aldgate East, Leman Street, Minories, Whitechapel Road, Old Montague Street, names bearing no connection to its previous existence. Scrunched among people whom it has but the vaguest affinity with, my jostled body often finds itself standing outside houses wondering what is going on inside. It works and sleeps and eats and hungers. Sometimes it wakes to the thought, "I'm all I've got."

Often after an exhausting day, I linger at the end of the long block to watch the children darting carelessly in the park. Sometimes after a shower, they splash wildly in brown puddles, redesigning their shorts and legs with chestnut polka dots. Always there is laughter. Mothers and fathers, each clustered in their separate little knots, hover around like guardian angels.

Frequently, they congratulate each other on a newly acquired house and garden that will soon lead them into a different neighbourhood. One brags, "My wife and my two tykes there, they're the people I care about most." Just then one kid smacks another, like he heard and wanted to test his father's sincerity. I, a silent monitor, listen with longing, unable to tear myself away from the scene. They are always gossiping about something like the Mothers' March or the children: "Jon, poor boy, is rather ill again." "My Sarah sat up by herself at five months."

A dwarfed juniper tree underneath a canopy of oaks and maples, parched and stunted, is barely managing to hold on to its gnarled existence. My ear can hear the juniper moan for its life, ignored by its fellows with their branches politely turned away towards the sky.

Six: Iris

London, 1949

The frail woman in the silk dress first catches my eye at the watering hole of the Hammersmith Palais, a dance hall frequented by soldiers. You go there to meet somebody congenial. She carries herself with the air of someone who grew up in a household of servants. Her figure first slenderly captures my attention, then her smile holds it.

"Would you like to dance?" In cadet school we learned the foxtrot, waltz and tango. In London I took tap dancing but never accomplished much.

"Indeed, it would be my pleasure." She combines an easy physical grace with a formal, deliberate use of words, which the Polish foreigner mistakes for good English. "You are a graceful dancer," she says. It is not long into the evening before a friendship blossoms.

Iris Snell comes from India, city of Bangalore, province of Mysore. In response to my questions, she recounts in a slow, studied choice of detail: "Ah, Sobolewski, imagine yourself tramping awesome wide-spreading valleys and plains, smelling the cool evening air of the Madras. You look out and there, there they are." Her delicate arm sweeps the dance floor in front of us. "There they are incredibly, our national symbol, the majestic elephant; and the deep chestnut sambar and the ibex in all its grace. There, too, languishes the horn-heavy buffalo comfortably settled beside a reed-filled hollow." Surveying the various dancers, standers and sitters, the eye in a flight of fancy identifies each animal as it is named.

"See yourself reclining in British shorts on the broad-gauge Madras and Southern Mahratta railway where my father is highly placed. Glass in hand, you drink in the exhilarating sweep of the panorama. You roll past the Kolar gold mines nestled in tangled folds of red hills and mountains, past thick-walled bush and grassy slopes between, past the dual Cauvery falls and its rocky canyon. The clatter of wheels beneath you, conductors provide the little extra attention that comes with my father's nod."

I can feel myself succumb to the bridges and streams she so carefully describes, and to her perfume.

"Sobolewski, it is all true, even the most famous British military hospital in India. In that very sanatorium, my mother once serves as nurse looking after many British boys. The rest is what? Life! Life, Sobolewski, you know: British bars, dancing, the bazaar, foods strange to the English palate, wonderful stories, people—all with most agreeable climate. Bangalore's silk and textile mills are renowned for the patterned interlacing of varied threads to produce fine intricate designs in fabric."

She reflects for a space, checks herself and then blushing remarks softly almost to apologize, "I am feeling extremely shy, actually."

I smile, pausing slightly in the dance to get a better look at her. Our eyes meet.

"Yes, you have a compassionate face, very trustworthy," she says.

I decide to let the compliment slide by, mainly because I do not know what else to do with it.

"My father is Indian, my mother English," she tells me. On her father's side, Iris descends from a wealthy, upper-crust family. From her mother's side she receives her religion, Roman Catholic. The scenes she weaves tingle the senses; but the odd, almost nineteenth-century manner with which this East Indian intertwines the English words, a language I struggle with, captivates me. It is easy to see she believes words should flow together like a pleasing silk design. I feel like the broken strand in the warp.

When we meet on that dance floor, Iris's husband of five or six years is billeted an ocean away in the United States on a six-week course. "I meet my husband," she informs matter-of-factly while dancing, "while he is posted in our province. He is a Commander in the British Navy, and Mysore hosts the most massive British cantonment in southern India. Our wedding——"

The band drowns out her thin voice. "What?"

She gets closer to me. "Our wedding is one of those typically British affairs. Lacking nothing, it combines a mixture of British and Indian foods. Men in white colonial uniforms, decked out with their coloured sashes and medals, gather in little knots toasting the bride and groom, sharing congenial stories. A multitude of women parade in every kind of elegance. 'Boys' slip in and out with bar trays."

Iris hesitates. "I hope it doesn't offend if I inquire how you are engaged since Auschwitz, or am I perhaps a trifle over-personal?"

"*Empire Seagreen*, small flat-bottom boat, formerly a landing craft Americans used on D-day. Impossible to steer on Channel, though good for navigating small inlets. Officially we import from Antwerp general cargo; actually," now I lean over close to her ear, "our main business is organizing, mostly nylon stockings." I use the camp word without pausing to find out if she understands it means smuggling.

There is no way I now want to bounce between the extremes of rock solid Auschwitz depravity and marshy morality. I do not want to change the world. I do not want to be bothered with thinking. I do not want to care even, except that for a pair of contraband nylon stockings you can get a woman to bed with you. Before Iris, I found a way to make women, one-night Bettys, move around my life like checkers on a board. I am unable to name three. Iris, however, is not of this type. My take-home pay equals about twenty pounds sterling a month as part of the crew, and about three times that much on the stuff brought in. So there is enough money to show Iris a good time; and I can see that, as the wife of an officer, she is accustomed to the tiny extras of rank.

We make the rounds of dances and are seen in the nightclubs of Picadilly Circus. While Iris never hides her marriage, for me there is no available alternative relationship, and little free time to develop one. Or maybe I enjoy the long odds. We stroll calm hours together in the park. But as we cross by the children's swings, I cannot help noticing she goes right on past. She does not stop and stare like I do.

"Marriage," she expounds, meticulously choosing her phrases like an artist might select her colours, "should be accompanied with a happy residue of feeling which, implanted deep within, carries one over the chasm of absence and temptation. Instead, I cannot tell you how lonely I am."

"I'm sorry."

I catch her biting her lip. "I hate each damnable day no end, diligently crossing them off on the calendar in anticipation of his return."

"We used to do that in Auschwitz."

"And then one day I perceive that even when he is home, it is like he is still on one of his interminable voyages." She pauses. I wait for her, and she soon goes on. "At first I do not even notice, because the daily words we exchange are the same. Then I perceive I am talking to stuffed ears. When I say something, he answers somewhere else, with empty flattery appropriate to all occasions. You cannot know the debasement I feel." She cocks her head. "My mother was quite intellectual, you know."

"How could I know?"

"Intellectual and sensitive. I imagine myself as having inherited something of that. Do you not think my husband should rather argue with me, take my thoughts to task and test them in fire, not simply pass them off as if they were empty fancies? His mother refers to me as 'Anglo-Indian', a foreigner forever. There is a child from his previous marriage whom they all dote upon."

She bites her lip again. "In my husband's little village, I feel everybody's eyes on me. Their attitude rubs off on him. He informs me that he will do what he pleases, and it gives him no mind what I do. Quite fair, actually, though disgraceful. As a result, I move to London."

Iris makes a point of relating this last bit of detail. I take it more as an invitation than a report.

Only eight hands are on our little boat, seven English. Whenever we berth, the English boys go home and I stay as watchman for extra pay. Iris meets me at the ship, stands in the spray of a wave breaking on the dock, draws me into moisture-laden arms and hair.

Iris is very attentive. She openly shares her budding feelings growing up as a child of a British nurse, marrying, coming to England, pretending to a life of mutuality, finding herself emotionally alone. I react to the nurse point, maybe because the other themes are too painful for me.

"You talk about hospitals. In Auschwitz, to avoid selections for gas chamber, sick would deliberately keep away from hospital. So at height of typhus epidemic, Nazis had to create special camp police force to keep workers in SS kitchen separate from rest of inmates who were wandering around sick."

Iris never seems to notice, as I do not at this time, that while relating event after event I share very little about my inner self. I survived because I had very few friends. One lesson of Auschwitz: never trust or confide in anyone, and speak only to one person at a time. Very few will not break under torture. So if you spoke only to one person, you could always claim, "He's jealous; he's against me because I stole his soap," or "because he's Ukrainian and I'm Polish." Nazis appreciate national differences. But if two witnesses were against you, the game was up: you would be quickly liquidated.

In such isolation, your only real companion was your own rage—that, and whatever fantasies you created to keep you going. To survive, you held within you a closed, steel box with a spring-trapped lid and iron jaws. I usually excuse my lack of sharing by saying my background is too difficult for people to handle. Deep down I am convinced it is me.

A letter arrives from Canada. "I've paid a local farmer a hundred dollars to sign for you to work on a tobacco farm. He's sending you a sponsorship," Jurek writes. As far as I am concerned, the further away from Europe, the better. And although I have never been there, Canada is one of my favourite countries. Why? It is an attitude that stems from my Auschwitz experience. Himmler warned in some of his speeches that anyone who took one mark, "one German mark!" would be shot.[10] Jews could be murdered indiscriminately, but always for the principle of the thing, never for personal gain, their goods belonged to the German *Reich*. Then, in October 1943, the prisoners' fire brigade to which I belonged had to extinguish a fire in the Kanada barracks. 'Kanada'—another one of the bitter jokes of Auschwitz—was prisoners' jargon for the place where all the baggage from the Jewish victims was sorted. I am pushed to deny to myself what I know. Those of us who stayed the night to protect against rekindling saw room after room of stockpiled goods: Rooms full of valises. Others with clothes, or human hair, or glasses, or piles of shoes one-storey high. Some with heaps of gold teeth, or silver fillings, or currency, or furs, or jewellery. There were tangled masses of crutches and artificial limbs; jumbles of dishes, pots, and brushes; mounds of prayer shawls, books, and phylacteries; mountains of children's clothing, even doll clothes. All marked for use in the *Reich*. During the fire, Dacko jumped on a truck in order to organize a bit. It was full of dead bodies.

The whole episode is vividly remembered because it was mostly women living and working in Kanada. Women who worked there sunbathed routinely on the only lawn in Birkenau, catching the odd interlude of rest and laughter within sight and sound of *Krematorium IV*. We were flirting with the women prisoners. Mietek had an affair with a Jewish Kapo from Slovakia that very night.

This association of Kanada with abundance and women disposes me favourably to Canada. The reading of four volumes on tobacco farming prepares me to meet Canadian immigration officials. I am accepted as an experienced farmer skilled in germination, fertilizing and transplanting, trimming, cultivating, disease control, harvesting and curing. But true to form, I did not confide in Iris.

On the last day, Iris and I sit in a White Eagle Restaurant by Hyde Park. She stretches her delicate arms as if after a person disappearing in a distant mist. "Why do you not discuss your plans with me a week earlier?"

"It just happened."

"I would have tried to arrange to accompany you."

"You're married."

"I love you."

"You're some strange woman."

That night is all tossing and turning. No good dwells in me. I want to do right; but, instead, I do wrong. Still, I must actually get some sleep, for the next morning the sun tattoos my cheek to announce time to go. I jump up early, pack my world in a stupor, and say goodbye to the steaming radiator. Iris takes me down to the railroad station.

Here I am again, in another cavernous train station of columns and arches. We briskly follow the crowd down into a dim tunnel. Vendors in various classes of dress sell magazines, combs and shoelaces, sweets and brollies. On the platform, it is mostly dark-suited business people at this hour in the morning.

"I know that you will do admirably well," she says, her voice much more peaceful than the night before. "Think of me, and I will be there for you."

I have no idea what any of this means, and at this time I do not give it much thought. We kiss between the steel sides of two hissing trains as a long low whistle is followed by a final call. "Good-bye, beautiful woman." I stroke her cheek, give the tips of my fingers a kiss.

"Be careful, Sigmund."

When boarding to Southhampton, were it not for a conductor, the reluctant traveller would have in his confusion wound up steaming down the track in the wrong direction.

Iris, then Irka, flit through my mind. Poland is far behind. Once in the port city, the Aquitania beckons me down into her lower cabins. Now reconverted to passenger, she was appropriated as a troop ship during the war. This will be her last voyage. The rumble of the old engines vibrates the boat. Shouts roll from ship to dock and from dock to ship, the gangplank grates into place, the fetid water between the ship and the city grows wider until it is all I see. Just mad waves of intense loneliness rolling over me, and the corrosive air of the brine stinging my cheeks. I am in mourning, though I am not even certain for whom—maybe for some version of myself left behind years before in Nisko.

The two hundred dollars I enter Canada with disappears in a week. Again, a quick series of jobs. In the few months after being led to port through the jagged Canadian coastline, I am bombarded with letters from the woman left so unceremoniously, the woman I have not succeeded in establishing a permanent relationship with, the umpteenth woman I had not succeeded with.

"Good news, I have plans to arrive in Canada."

"How can you come? It isn't easy to get a visa."

Then a wire arrives: "LEAVE HUSBAND STOP ARRIVE WEEK TUESDAY STOP."

While the tug nudges the grey liner gently into place, Iris spots me from afar, waving frantically from the rail. An hour for immigration and the dark woman with fine cameo-like features is in my arms.

"You finally made it. How are you doing?"

"Now I am fine. I have been awake since four in the morning, watching for the harbour to pop into view. It is so gratifying to see you."

"Yeah, same here."

Iris does not play the games other people sometimes do. "Tell me all about our home."

"I rented a place not far from here, on Barrington Street. Just a room and a kitchen, but it will do."

We walk. No car.

As a British citizen, my little charmer enters Canada without a visa though she is not allowed to work. Sometimes she finds me down on the Halifax piers, off to the side of the early morning bustle of fishermen staggering or wheeling their catch to the fish house. I am engaged as a labourer in the A. M. Smith fish factory for sixty-five cents an hour. We dry and pack cod and halibut, tonnes of silvery bullet-shaped prizes, for shipping to Trinidad, Tobago, and Jamaica. Soon I am made foreman, the youngest they have. I never do go to that farmer who expects me to raise tobacco. But I do mail Jurek his one hundred dollars. It is a matter of personal pride.

After she arrives, her husband is phoning and phoning, and writing her letters. After being a navy engineering commander, he became a Caterpillar salesman in England. He is in Iowa getting training; threatens to come to Halifax. Who knows if he loves her, or if his anguish is just the shock of being abandoned? As for me, what I have been searching for falls in my lap without planning. An unfamiliar sensation stirs inside and is recognized. "I think I might be happy," I write Jurek.

I move again. The Canadian National train surprises me: seats arranged like a bus, rather than in compartments as in Europe, and with thick upholstery. A few are flipped around in a party-of-four arrangement, but that is all. We take a basket of food with us, only to find a dining car with linen cloths and fine china. My mind rides a train slipping slowly up and down my life; calendar pages slip away into the past:

There go the chimneys disappearing in the distance; good riddance—I never want to see you again. This train, so much food, thanks to my passkey to the storeroom. Enough to share with the Nazis on board. So lucky. So lucky I'll never see another sunrise. Can't eat. Should force myself; who knows what will happen to us in Sachsenhausen—if we get there. Just like them to kill us now. Are these cushioned seats a trick? Is there even a purpose to force myself? Remember that other transport in 1941? A load of invalids to a sanatorium at Grafeneck. *Schreiber* compiling the lists refused to put me on. You're better off here, he said. Why? A ruse, all killed by gas. So why this special treatment now? A trap? Do we know too much? In the tension, two reported sick the day of departure. There's a plan to break out should the train stop unusually long at Gliwice. Gliwice, the latest place of no return, a Nazi euphemism for death. Past Gliwice? No. Yes! Relief. German countryside. How the spires of their churches stand out from so many kilometres away! By the look of the cows, it's been a plentiful harvest. Are the heavens as amazed as I am that these German folk continued about their affairs: the christenings, the funerals, the secret rendezvous, the office intrigue, the church singing, the little teas the women have, while only kilometres away thousands were gassed? Near Berlin the locomotive slows to a crawl. Devastation. Like someone unrolled a fiery carpet burning up everything in its path. Just like Krankemann's steamroller in the camp, running over a prisoner, leaving only a flat, bloody outline behind. Each night Allies drop delayed-action explosives. Every half hour or so, bombs explode in unexpected places. A solitude like that of three o'clock in the morning creeps through the daytime in the forsaken city. Although hardly deserted, its functionaries venture about only if necessary. One can see them scurry like cellar rats down a pathway in the street's middle formed by the rubble on both sides, which sometimes reaches as high as a two-storey building. Later, from nearby Sachsenhausen, we put out fires in and around the city. Gives us an opportunity to 'organize' to supplement our meagre rations.

When will these hallucinations finally leave me?

The rhythmic chapping and the churning of the chant on the track, forever chokes me with the changing situations in my life: I went to junior high by train, and to cadet school by train; went on leave by train; arrived in Auschwitz by train and left by train. Now Bill Knox is moving me to Ontario. Knox had been living next to us in Cape Breton, supervising the construction of a water tower. Iris got me a job with him, making more money than in the Canadian merchant navy, transporting limestone and iron ore from Newfoundland to Cape Breton. With Iris's help, I am working my way up in the world. After changing trains in Montreal and sitting up all night in coach, we arrive on a chilly winter morning in Toronto. I leave Iris in the station minding our luggage, grab a newspaper, and find accommodations the same day. Two taxis later, and everything we own is snugly placed in our new apartment.

After a month in the big city, a new Studebaker pulls up in front of our apartment. A man of medium height in suit and tie goes to the other side and helps a young lady out of the car. I am watching intently from the window. It is him, same lean abrupt movements and handsome smiling face, eyebrows sweeping far to the side, chipmunk teeth. Since arriving in Canada, we have been keeping in touch by mail, but we do not meet until I move to Toronto.

"Jurek, look how you're doing!"

The women and men separate. "Remember those days after the war? How about a trip around Canada like we did in Europe? We'll have a time of it. We could go to Niagara Falls."

"We'll ride around on bicycles, right? I don't know. Listen, Zygmunt, you're practically hitched."

"We can take the women."

"Maybe you can."

"What about you, Jurek?"

"Not the right one yet."

I am working at the Eastern Power Devices as a welder, a skill acquired in England. Soon I am lead-hand. Under my supervision, the department increases from three to twelve. And I keep a watchful eye, point out mistakes. "Look at this," I say, "if this work goes to galvanizing like that, it will come back after inspection and cost the company double."

Six months later Jurek shows me a ring. "If she takes it, fine—if not, to hell with her."

"Jurek, marriage is not a throw of the dice. If you're not sure, wait for something better."

"What do you say then?"

"I know? All I can say is this Ukrainian woman isn't as good looking as the other ones. Remember Rosa? Or the English girl you went to dances with? Or that one you brought with you to visit?"

"I think this one's Mrs. Permanent."

In 1951 I pick up a paper to see a small note. The final Jewish survivors have left the DP camps in Germany. When looking for a country, these poor Jews need another globe. It is just a fleeting thought. I wonder where Ginsbourg is. That thought also disappears from my mind.

After getting her working papers in order, Iris applies for a teller position in the Bank of Nova Scotia at Queen and Pape in Toronto. She is refused. She goes back again. "Sorry, we cannot take you."

"I am at a loss to know why."

"Why—aren't you Jewish?" Take an Irish Catholic mother and mix it with an East Indian father, and the Bank of Nova Scotia thinks the result is Jewish.

"No, I am baptized a Roman Catholic, raised a Roman Catholic, and all my days of the Roman Catholic faith." Then they hire her, much reassured.

We celebrate. Iris's kitchen is an adventure in new cuisine. It is her background, naturally. We celebrate her arrival, her job, every new event with a treat from the kitchen. The day she gets her job, the whole house smells of onion and curry sautéed in melted butter. She sings as she works, a curious

Iris and Sigmund, 1957.

lilting melody that draws me into the kitchen to savour my fortune. In India, her *ayah* would blend in a previously prepared mixture of flour, salt, sugar and ground ginger. Here, she does it herself. Removing the heavy pot from the heat, her slight brown fingers stir in some chicken broth and milk, then back to the heat, stirring constantly until everything comes to a slow boil. Diced cooked chicken and lemon juice are added. Then she serves the meal, its aroma preceding her. She washes her hands. I enjoy large helpings spooned over wild rice and sprinkled with mango chutney, served with roti. Some improvement over the old days cooking for myself.

"Iris, you make best chicken curry. Looks beautiful, smells beautiful, feels beautiful on tongue, and tastes beautiful, too. It's treat for every sense."

In 1954, within a week of Iris's divorce finally coming through, we celebrate our marriage, due to the divorce, without a priest's blessing. It is nothing like the would-be wedding I dreamed about in the camp:

A smorgasbord on long tables. Piled high. Pickled treats, mushrooms, spicy sausages and smoked meats, sauerkraut. Fish—pickled herring, herring in cream sauce, herring in wine sauce, ground pike with a pungent horse-radish, ground carp in sweet and sour jelly. Me hopping from table to table. In one hand I balance a glass of beer and a plate piled high with delicacies. With the other I shake hands. Aunt Halusia, isn't the bride beautiful! People come up one after another giving me no chance to eat. Others nibble from what's in my hand. I'm scraping an empty plate.

Instead, Iris and I go dancing to the echoes of the King Edward Hotel big band, order steak and sleep in the house of the lawyer who assisted Iris with the divorce. I never think about it; to me this is just the way things are done; once you have the divorce, you get married.

One Friday after picking up my cheque, a Yugoslavian fellow worker and I walk out together. He is in the rough white woollen turtleneck the English sailors wear. Running to swing his children waiting for him at the factory gate, he calls over his shoulder, "Hey, Sigmund, don't ya think it's time for you?"

There are no children, not in her first marriage, not in ours. Am I suddenly more sensitive? From this point on it seems fellow workers are always asking, "How's it you haven't got no children? How long ya gonna wait?"

My comforters. Now the question continuously haunts me, "Where are our children?" Like a man with a sin bearing on his conscience, I am possessed: maybe masturbation really does make you sterile.

We are enjoying ourselves, I tell myself. A basic comfort settles in, each day similar to the one before. Iris leads me upwards. "Do you not think it would be appropriate to don a jacket and tie before entering the bank to cash your cheque? Everybody comes in dressed so nice."

This time I purposely arrive at her downtown bank looking like a steel worker. "Look, many of the guys cash their cheques here. Are you embarrassed I'm not an office worker?"

Mentioning Auschwitz is like telling her a story about *One Thousand and One Nights;* and she corrects my English. In 1956, at a Dale Carnegie course, I meet a Ukrainian guy who sells mortgages. He recommends me to Brethour and Morris, and suddenly, I have another step up: selling real estate. It is a dog eat dog business, and I have been well trained in Auschwitz. I throw myself into the work. Soon I make a momentous decision, but like many such events in life, it comes with barely any conscious thought. Iris, who is more English than the English, has been suggesting, "Everyone has difficulty pronouncing our surname; nobody can spell it; we should endeavour to be more British." And then, our new office has a Sobolewski and a Sokolowski. Everybody confuses the two. So, when Jurek changes his name, I think, why not, it will improve business. I scan the phone book under 'S', and become Sigmund Sherwood. It just feels comfortable. It reminds me of Robin Hood, appropriate to replace the name of the man who shot out the eye of a raven with an arrow.

We often go out dancing, and there is a spate of great Polish weddings. Iris loves the dancing, both of us do. She looks up at me and tells me I am very smooth.

What a day! I've been trying to get my sister Basia to visit from Poland since my passage to Canada; the paperwork was convoluted. I am very excited when she arrives. We spend much time together.

"Sigmund, would you be good enough to please translate the conversation into English?"

"Iris, last time we saw each other was night I was taken sixteen years ago. It's too hard to keep up and translate at same time."

"It is impolite, do you not agree? Just like your friends who persist in conversing in Polish when there is a perfectly decent common language we all understand."

"Yeah, but do you have to bring out, in the middle of wedding reception, English newspaper to make your point?"

"Sigmund, I am delighted to have Barbara stay with us. All I request is to be included."

"Ah Iris, please, this is my sister. Only two or three weeks." It is a good job she does not understand Polish. Basia is saying she has a Polish woman for me.

After only three days, Basia finds it best to get other accommodations for the remainder of her visit.

Iris is still the most enchanting storyteller I know, so invigorating. We discuss a book by Burke critical of Indian child labour practices. "Sigmund, you must distinguish between truth and fiction."

Once, rummaging through the closet for some books, I find Iris's normal school certificate. Quite impressive. We get together downtown in the restaurant of Simpson–Sears, a usual meeting place. I work part-time in a nearby butcher shop to earn extra money. Sometimes I also join a manpower line downtown to wash cars. To me, the labourers lining up in hopes of being picked for work suggest the early morning work lines during the first few months in Auschwitz. Simpson–Sears is awash with well-dressed Saturday shoppers; this is downtown Toronto, after all. Iris goes to rinse her hands, then returns.

"How is it your school records show you finished, when you were two years old, Grade Six!" I ask.

"Pardon?" Her hands dart together in front in confusion.

"Well, when we got married, you claimed you were two years older than me. If school records are correct you're ten years older still. Also, date of birth on your travel document has been smudged."

Her lips purse in a coquettish smile, one you can only enjoy. She wore it when she first mused upon her marriage. It was the expression on her face the day she arrived in Canada. It was her look of satisfaction when something went right. She makes a joke out of my complaint. "If you will pardon the presumption, I am afraid there has been an error. In India, we register several years before school commences. I am well aware it is all too easy to confuse the registration date with the year of study."

Could it be? I know what I saw, yet maybe I made a mistake. She pretends it is unimportant, soon changing the subject with little ado. Since an element of doubt has crept in, I allow the issue to drop. She says we will not fight; we love each other. So we go to the cinema, make love that night, and the matter slips away. But there are no children.

I follow no guidelines. Nobody gives me priorities. I am a mass of tangled yarn. I absorb myself in my work: make great strides forwards, mostly selling low-priced housing. Everything is subordinated to getting ahead. Within a few months, I am the company's top salesman.

We go down to Florida to work on our relationship. There are some very reasonable touring packages designed to get you to Cuba. We take a side trip. Back home, I throw myself into work again. But I am puzzled: just when I should be happy, I feel tricked by life. Permitting no other explanation, I blame it on a lack of children. So without at first even recognizing it, a desperation for children creeps over me. Children give you what you thought you might not see: a tomorrow. After Auschwitz, one does not just 'have a child' like all other people in the world.

We are still living on 60 Ivy Avenue, Toronto's East End, rooms not much different from the one I rented in London, but filled with Iris in her long dresses. Some neighbours seem content to stay, but I detest the place. Give me a place with an upstairs and down, bright airy rooms, a little nook off the kitchen, a window looking onto children playing in the yard.

The train runs by the back, the fading echo of its whistle penetrating my sleep.

The trains come rolling in. I am always wearing stripes.

Awake, I think it cannot happen this time. It will not! But it does: *Achtundachtzig* is beaten in the *Lederfabrik*. Iris tries to comfort him. *Achtundachtzig* is thrown in the tiny *Stehzelle*. Iris attempts to rescue him. *Achtundachtzig* sees his fellow inmates float past his dinner table, dissolve one by one in a field of mist. Iris encircles him, runs wet fingers through his hair, cools his head. Like a reflection of daytime fears, *Achtundachtzig* wonders if he will survive, if he will ever have a family. Iris disappears.

At one point the thrashing around, as if to save myself from drowning in a sea of memory, becomes so bad I have to sleep on the sofa. "You are better to forget all this," Iris urges for the thousandth time.

Iris thinks it would be helpful if I went to church. After liberation, I pushed God from my life. Did not attend church for twelve years. As far as I was concerned, God had not only failed the world, the Church had failed God. Both were bankrupt, the second worse than the first. In Toronto, I briefly experiment with the Unitarian Church. And then nothing again. For me, Sunday has become the day the neighbours go to church. If I pray, it is a non-thinking reflex action, a residue from childhood: "If You'll be with me and give me children, then You'll be my God."

About three years after first coming across Iris's school certificate, it can, on rechecking, no longer be found. Suspicious, I confront her concerning her age and lack of fertility.

Through choked tears, she admits, "Several years ago one of my ovaries is being removed—a cyst."

"This time I believe you; I believe you to be telling half of truth."

She never hesitates. Her lips purse together into her special smile. "Sherwood, I rather protest. Should we not recognize that our love is worth more than momentary adversity?"

"It isn't that I don't love you. I just need, lest I die, children." I feel like a bum.

When we make a trial separation, Iris comes running. "Sigmund, I am pregnant."

Sometimes into my dreams floats an architecturally distinctive villa, surrounded by a paradise of flowers, greenery and an array of animals. Though I cover my eyes, the unwanted intrusion burned in my retina remains. I always recognize it at once. Only about three hundred metres from the camp, the striking grey stucco, two-storey house is the one that belonged to *SS Obersturmbannführer* Rudolf Höss, the Commandant. Dark wood frames the gables, the bay windows and a huge entrance way. Cement steps wrap around the right front and side. Inside a marble hall has the year of construction, '1938', designed into the floor. I don't remember having ever seen that before. The left corner of the villa is sliced away to form a fifth wall, diagonal to the other two, from which a balcony overlooks a camp gate below. A wire fence and gate run the perimeter of the estate.

In 1944, the fire brigade was called upon to excavate an underground bunker to shelter Höss and his family from the almost daily American bombing missions. Not a plain bunker, a labyrinth of cement and brick rooms, all fitted with air vents and electric wiring, even benches and tables. This was an illegal diversion of concrete from the war effort, so he used the fire brigade instead of registering a regular work crew. There were three entrances, one from the villa basement, one from either side of the garden. The bomb shelter was covered by a thick concrete ceiling disguised by a mound of dirt, bushes and trees.

While we were working there, *Achtundachtzig* saw the Hösses going about their everyday life. *Achtundachtzig* even spoke to Höss's wife. With the sun behind her, her face shone like a halo, the effect created by the light on the otherwise unnoticeable fuzz that covered her smooth skin. Everyone was afraid of her, though. She was always watching from behind the curtains. The gardeners warned us she sometimes denounced prisoners who were not working, but by 1944 she would also send us ersatz coffee.

Höss, himself, was a loving family man with five lovely children who had their own horses in the stables. The electrician told us Höss was brought up a devout Prussian Catholic, once determined to be an African missionary. He served in the German Army in Palestine during World War I. After the war, he joined the Nazi Party. Then in May 1923, he was incarcerated for murdering a school teacher accused of betraying the illegal Nazi party to French occupation forces. Six years later, upon release from prison where he had been confined as a 'political' deserving of special treatment, he joined the SS.

I thought to myself, maybe that expresses something about his obedience to authority. In any case, his religious training—my religion—did not prevent him from supervising the assembly-line murder. Once in 1941, I vividly remember Höss conducting a selection. During evening roll-call, he walked slowly along selecting one elderly man from each row of

Höss's bunker.

prisoners. Obviously, something else died at Auschwitz besides Nazi victims. Neither did his religious training prevent him from authorizing factory construction nearby for the exploitation of those prisoners temporarily set aside for forced labour. Nor did his religious training save him from a scandal in contraband, for which he was ultimately removed as Commandant. When Höss left, his possessions barely fitted into five railroad cars.

We Catholics in the camp could never understand why the Pope did not speak out. Nor could we understand why the Americans, in spite of their bombing targets all around us, never tried to stop the deportation trains. We could not understand why no attempt was made to stop boxcar after boxcar with Greek, Croatian, Albanian, Hungarian, Dutch, French, Italian, Transylvanian, Ruthenian, Belgian and Slovakian markings. Tracks are a military target, too; and all tracks led one way or another to Auschwitz.

Seven: Ramona

Havana, Cuba, April 1961

watch the American planes, painted with Cuban markings, dive-bombing the Columbia military airport. The Bay of Pigs operation, brief as it is, stirs in me long-suppressed memories of the Stuka attacks at the outbreak of the war, bitter feelings of a life cut short. Then, I was in Uncle's seventh floor apartment where I stayed briefly as a cadet student in Lwów. From his window, I followed the gull wing German dive-bombers as they aimed nose down at an old Polish fortress across the valley. Plane after plane came shrieking in, pulling out only at the last minute from almost ninety-degree angles. At the time, I thought it would be me distinguishing myself in the air in a few years, only in defence of Poland. The ravens would take note then!

Now, I am in a fourth floor walk-up near the University of Havana, combining business and politics, driving myself in my continuing effort to escape *Achtundachtzig*. I arrived 30 July 1960. As a former welding technician, I got a job recommended by the ministry of public works, purchasing welding machinery for the new government. Thanks to a lady friend, a doctor met on an earlier vacation, my Spanish was reasonably fluent. We were exercising our rights as Canadians, as much against the Americans, who were starting to boycott everything Cuban, as for our own business.

I also wouldn't be here if it weren't for my lawyer, Norman Endicott. He has been teaching me about socialism in ways not previously understood. His father was a missionary to China in the days before Chiang Kai-shek and his grandfather was Moderator of the United Church of Canada. After Auschwitz, most of us were anti-Communist. The Russian bear had never been a friend of the Polish White Eagle. And Stalin's Bialoy-Baltickoy Kanal connecting the White Sea with the Baltic Sea was said by Russian prisoners in Auschwitz to be paved with human skulls. Two million Russian lives sacrificed to its construction. Just one more reason why I had not wanted to go back to Poland. But Endicott introduced me to some socialist ideas I had never heard before.

It came slowly. It had to do with the doctor I had met, with the bombing that never took place in Auschwitz and with the little sign in the Galveston bus that kept moving forwards and then, after we passed the Negro district, irrationally moved back again. I felt myself changing quite against my own prejudices, centimetre by disillusioned centimetre. I would wake up in the morning as if in the middle of a heated debate, a question rolling off my tongue: what are the forces behind war, exploitation, minority-scapegoating and tyranny? Back would come answer: whatever they are, clearly no government yet developed has tamed them. Again, I would ask myself, have we met the social needs of the disadvantaged, unemployed, suffering and ill? Clearly not, and more is needed than just minor revisions. Those who advanced a programme of economic equality began to attract my ear. Did I believe they could do what no one else had? Not really. Well, yes, I suppose so. I tasted the feeling of being part of something bigger than myself; my little bit could be important. So, to aid the Cuban workers in helping themselves, I produced a book using material I had developed while teaching welding at the Western Technical–Commercial School in Toronto. Then I parleyed my job into head welder of a crew.

I am also down here to divorce Iris. Short of hiring a detective and catching your spouse *in flagrante delicto,* current Ontario divorce law is impossible. It was Nevada or Cuba. When a Cuban job came along first, I deeded everything over and left. There never was a child. She claims that when it comes to shared feelings, I am worse than her first husband.

My divorce comes through in May 1961. Surprisingly for something I engineered, I find my stomach churning inside. May. My father was ostracized from the Polish military in May 1926, beginning for me a childhood on the move. I slipped into the living grave in May 1940 when the Nazis crushed us in our cities, and, showing no respect for the old nor mercy for the young, turned out the young eaglet from his nest. In May 1942, my body was wasted by typhus and fever. The warm sun of May has long since become a time of failing eyes and depression. In May 1945, a shaking leaf frightened by its own sound, I walked away from Irka. With me, May has become a kaleidoscope of unrelenting events and feelings. I marched into the Land of Milk and Honey, an oppressive sack of hang-ups slung over my shoulder. I know this, but still cannot remove it. In spite of the fact I was born in May and my first day of freedom occurred in May, inevitably, as May progresses, my mind dwells on the dark areas of my past. In this month the worst nightmares terrorize my head until I grope in the sun as the blind grope in darkness. The angel of death vultures over my shoulders. I try to convince myself this feeling of doom is on the inside only, while in Auschwitz one was afflicted from within and without. Gradually, gradually, a survivor, if he focuses away, can get used to practically anything. Now this, a divorce. No matter how you cut it, good reason, bad reason, it is a failure, simple as that.

Again, I make the rounds of parties, dances, anything to cover up. I've been adding the cha-cha, merengue, *danzon,* rumba and conga to my repertoire.

Ramona accompanies her girlfriend to a dance in the hotel Havana Libre where we first meet.

"Enjoy my dancing?" she flirts, barely looking at me.

"Yes, yes! Exquisite, like Venus of ball."

"Who?"

"Most beautiful Roman goddess."

A laugh, lyric as the flight of a flute, acknowledges the exaggeration and weaves its thread around my heart. "*Por cierto,*" she scoffs, "Sure." Her cheeks flush with colour, though.

In Cuba, peasants call the Jews *Polacos,* probably because a good number of Cuban Jews emigrated from Poland. When we first meet, Ramona assumes that since I am a *Polaco,* I must be Jewish.

I pay a visit at her house, a three-storey villa with a baked white marble façade and a loggia of tall ionic columns. Wrought-iron gatework set in a glistening white cement bulwark surrounds the house; the same grillwork decorates the windows; real tile flooring leads to the door. I can hardly believe it, as she lacks the bearing of one brought up in wealth. She leads me through the many rooms and protected nooks out of breath. It turns out to be one of those unsoiled Havana mansions left with a housekeeper by an aristocratic family planning to return from Florida when Castro is ejected. Ramona bunks with a friend on the first floor, a few rolled-up clothes her wardrobe.

At her work place, an apartment in another well-to-do neighbourhood, I am relieved to find her working as a domestic. It piques my interest that this demure woman baby-sits a three-year-old girl in the home of wealthy Cuban doctors. She *likes* children. She is one of those peasants from the outlying provinces who came to the big city to find a job. I stem from noble stock; after Auschwitz, I, too, have become a wandering peasant. And I discern something else. After Auschwitz, I have been unable to relate to people whose only connection to the camps is a news story, protected innocents who see me as an object to be pitied, or who feel that, due to their ration card, they were like me. While her family was better off than some, since Ramona's father eventually owned a small patch of land, 'Daddy's Girl' suffered, especially during the Revolution. When I am with her, I feel relaxed, like I can tell her whatever I want, secure in the knowledge that she will understand.

Candida Ramona Tamayo-Corria (Ramona dislikes her first name) grew up on a farm in the humid heat of southeastern Cuba. From working as a foreman on a sugar plantation, her father had eked out enough to purchase the land on which he raised first other people's cows, then tobacco, then sugar cane. After her father died, the small farm was shared according to local custom among her brothers, who then assumed authority for her life. It impresses me to learn that when a relative notified her of a job opportunity in Havana, she leaped at the opportunity. This decision led her to me.

Fortune smiles. On leaving Toronto, the manager of our real estate office advised, "Sigmund, you'll be seeking another wife. Only a few things matter:

Is she a good, honest woman? Is she kind? Will she be a good mother? Essentials." On our second date we dine at a fancy restaurant where I show her the divorce papers. Her nose and forehead wrinkle up, she stares at the sheet, her lips move faintly. It takes her half an hour to read part of a page. I know.... Essentials though, that is what sticks in the mind.

We know each other barely ten days when I make one of those momentous decisions of life, which you always look back upon with wonder. Around eleven o'clock one morning I grab a taxi to the apartment where she works, one of those hoity-toity places with doilies everywhere. When she appears at the door, children in tow, her face is more than surprised.

"Take off your apron, we're going downtown," I tell her mysteriously.

"What on earth for!"

"You ask too many questions."

After she gets permission, we are off. In the speeding taxi, I propose.

How many couples have made acquaintance, attracting each other almost at once, recognizing a similarity of spirit that eventually leads to a long-lasting relationship? Several weeks following, we have already become one flesh; due to the divorce, again not in a church wedding, but surrounded all the same by her family, an exuberant bunch, down in her hometown of Bayamo.

Ramona's birth place is an area of political contrast: the Sierra Maestras provided Fidel Castro with a mountainous launching pad against Batista as well as the U.S. navy with a home for Guantánamo. Fidel, who comes from a wealthy background and who received Jesuit training as a youth, gathered about him Raúl Castro, his brother, and Ernesto 'Ché' Guevara, both known for their Communist leanings. An exalted, broadly humanitarian hope has spread through the land that his government will lead the masses out of the grinding poverty so prevalent throughout Cuba ... and in Ramona's family.

In the Sierra Maestras, Ramona carried food into the hills to those who would relay it to Castro's troops. "Far away, the Pico de Turquino, looking like a pyramid marked with furrows, called to me," she tells me staring into the distance. "I went there. But with Batista's *casquitos* roaming during the day, and Castro's *barbudos* controlling the night, I never got a chance to climb it. Isn't that something?"

She can go on about nature if she wants; I just wish I could be like everybody else, simply carry on life as usual. In Toronto, I absorbed myself, lost myself really, in business. Now, in Cuba, I absorb myself in a cause. Stories represent Batista's Cuba as the picture of capitalism at its worst, a huge bordello for Americans with sixteen flights a day between Miami and Havana. And tales of Batista's police remind me of the SS: killing indiscriminately, shamelessly accusing poor illiterate peasants of being Communists. Have I not experienced well enough the threat of both Fascism and Communism, each side denouncing the other? For me, Cuban reform is not an issue of Communism nor even of ideology; it is an issue of ethics. Is the United Fruit Company immune from criticism? Maybe the Americans mock

Castro's long speeches; I find them interesting. You learn if you listen. I sympathize with the underdog.

Castro's talk of a new society is validated for me when Ché Guevera, himself, meets me to get help with a Russian welding machine. Here then, at long last, on this small island, emerges a Cause to which energy can be productively directed for the good of all. The push to escape *Achtundachtzig* takes the form of an unseen grip that, from time to time, seizes me. I leap without looking.

In my mind, Cuba and Ramona are wrapped up together. Both provide something to believe in. For me, it is a special sign Ramona is a virgin, important in a country like Cuba, where a groom can return his bride to her father the next morning if she turns out unchaste. Even Castro, a lawyer educated in the Sorbonne, influences my decision for Ramona. "Peasants," he says, "are as important for our society as the middle class." In fact our marriage affects my work in an unexpected way.

One day, when working for the department of public works, I am taken blindfolded down to a secret area in Pinar del Rio, Cuba's westernmost province. It is rough going and I stumble on the steep slippery slope worn down by whose feet way out here. Finally, when the blindfold is removed, we stand in front of what looks like a massive network of half-caves and tunnels cut into the elevated coral reefs that streak the northern cliffs. If the one we are in is an example, each cave is fortified with heavy coastal artillery. For strategic purposes, the units are mounted on tracks camouflaged by palm and pine trees and a yellowish scraggly undergrowth, all growing right up from the coral. From under shadow of the armour-plated Russian guns, I look out across the sea towards the Florida coast beyond the horizon. I am surprised at how well they are prepared to confront ships on the high sea. Just the steel hydraulic carriage on which the cannons mount is almost as tall as I am. And the barrel assembly alone must weigh fifty tonnes. Do not ask me how they so quickly chiselled those caves and hoisted such massive artillery into place, all in secret. It is Ché Guevera's choreography, tribute to his conceptual and administrative skill.

The welds on the rails on which they trolley the weighty artillery in and out are cracking, and no one knows why. Under the bare field lights, the solution clarifies itself immediately. But I pretend to be working out an obscure problem so as not to disgrace the army engineers who stand around silently tearing off my skin with their eyes. They are using welding electrodes designed for ordinary steel when they should be using electrodes for cast steel. Meanwhile, while being led blindfolded, I had overheard them whispering, "Who's this?" "He's a Canadian." "A Canadian! Why's he being brought here?" "He's married to a *campesina*." "Ohhh, one of our peasants, okay!"

Ramona has been absorbed for days. Then it comes out, softly, tentatively. "Simo, they got you in Auschwitz, didn't they?"

We are making our way to a friend's apartment. Pools of water shimmer on the sunlit asphalt of the city streets, which melts underfoot. The slim tattered boles of the royal palm poke high in the air, while from inner courtyards the broad glossy leaves of smooth-barked breadfruit trees cast the odd shady relief. Few people venture about.

"You don't want to know."

"I do, tell it."

"It'll disgust you."

"I lived through the Revolution."

Reluctantly, I open up for once. "They got you physically, yes. But real attack was spiritual. As hot as it is now, picture cold. Only you didn't have coat, just thin pyjamas, like dress you're wearing, through which wind cut sharply. You stood in frigid roll call for hours outside Block Five. It was winter of 1940. On road in front of you, some prisoners were laying down with their heads in snow; they were dead or soon would be. Another, not far from you, was laying down, but supporting his head on one elbow. Yesterday you lost one of your wooden shoes working. You've been walking with one shoe and one bare foot in snow. Guys who were breathing death rattle already had their shoes taken. This guy who was still propping his head up had good shoes. He had been in same cell with you in Tarnów prison. If you waited for this one to die, maybe in two hours, his shoes would be gone, too. Did you take anyway his shoes even though he could still muster enough strength to hold up his head? Your freezing feet told you that if you didn't, you'd have gangrene and soon be finished. For women, it was even worse."

"What about women?"

I whistle air through my lips. "Same thing, only worse, much worse. You arrived in women's camp, saw before your eyes skeletons walking around half naked, hallucinating, with swollen legs and dysentery with blood coming from their rectums. You knew that it would soon happen to you. Because you were young and pretty, some SS man, maybe Franz Hössler, came up to you. 'You look smart', he told you. 'I'll give you chance to survive. On word of SS, if you join brothel, you'll be well fed, cared for, never be kicked or beaten. You'll see no more than three men per day, and after six months you'll be free."

She removes her hat and wipes her damp forehead with the back of her hand.

"Soon you couldn't stand yourself," I say. "Soon you were Nazi looking down on piece of immoral dung, agreeing with their imposed judgment of you. Let's say you became servant of Kapo like somebody I know, and Kapo saved your life and looked after you. You were straight, but now and again your Kapo wanted extra services. Or you were Catholic priest, sick and hungry like everyone else. Guy came to you for confession. You said, 'Yes, but give me first piece of bread."

She is crying. I decide the best policy is still obliteration. I resolve never again to get caught in a flicker of weakness, telling stories. Away! Away! Let the new world begin!

Rounding the corner, we almost collide with a squad of soldiers. "Do you have your identity papers?" Oh, how our visions do crumple! It becomes apparent all too soon faith in Castro cuts two ways. True, I think Cuba is unfairly ostracized by American policy; all Latin American countries support him. Yet the words 'glorious', 'hallowed', 'valour', 'sacrifice', 'in vain', especially disturb me. Germany exposed nothing glorious either in victory or in defeat, and to me Cuban jingoism remains just as empty. Life has cheated me, repeatedly altering my fate. A chasm between me and everything else again sets me adrift.

"Sigmund," Ramona tells me, "on the bus to hairdresser classes, I got sick and went to the doctor."

She is laughing and does not have to finish the sentence. "Wee-oh." I just lift her up and swing her around and around. Now I am shouting, "Send a telegram to everybody." I take a bottle to the clinic for the nurses, and that night we go out and celebrate with our friends.

Ramona is self-conscious. She is worried that everyone must be counting the months, she got pregnant so quickly. And it is a hard pregnancy: vomiting, swollen legs. It makes me think of the *Muselmänner* with their elephant-like swollen feet; how the Kapos would make them run as a big joke. It is no help to Ramona that her husband has been putting in long hours ranging from province to province, raising a dust on sandy roads in a government jeep. But Ramona will share with her friends how I took her to the doctor who recommended visiting her family. "He went and took me down south; and it helped, that is for sure."

Ramona's slim stomach soon balloons. The heavier her belly, the more elated I become. Somebody is going to look like me, carry on the life that at one point had hung by such a slender thread. Ramona puts my hand to the movements, my ear to what I think is a heartbeat. God, a heartbeat! When it reaches eleven months after the wedding she is cleared in the eyes of all her relatives and friends.

Summoned to the clinic at work, I leap from my torch, scorching the wall. The foreman of our department, José Eskanazi, accompanies me for support.[11] Arriving out of breath, the husband has no role. We are sent to *La Red*, a nightclub facing the hospital, which, ominously, is one of those places so dark you have to be led to your seats down in the pit. A thin luminescence emanates from some fluorescent strips on the wall. Even when your eyes accustom themselves to the half-light, it remains hard to glimpse anything beyond the next table through the screen of smoke. To the right, four *trabajadores* discuss the singers on the stage. On the other side, slightly behind the labourers, two well-dressed *caballeros* celebrate the new times. They speak very softly. But we are perfectly positioned to catch a snatches of the conversation: "Once the sugar refineries are nationalized, Cuba will be sitting pretty."

I am more interested right now in what José has to say. We were married about the same time, and his wife just gave birth to a boy a week ago. "Both mother and child are doing wonderfully," José tells me. "My boy has a voice like mine, and good taste, too—always nursing."

Every so often I check across the road. "No, not yet." Her sisters have gathered, a coffee klatsch possessed of proven sisterly balm to allay pain. Back to *La Red* with José again.

A matronly woman in a frilly apron serves the tables. She moves about easily, quickly, remembering all the orders in her head. I am wanting to ask her what her pregnancies had been like. She picks me out first. "Your wife would be in the clinic, isn't it so?"

"Yeah, she's——"

"I can always tell. Don't worry."

"You have no idea what this means——"

"Everything's always okay."

What can possibly be taking so long? On seeing my approach, the nurse on duty shakes her head. "Go back to *La Red*, we'll tell you."

"José, did it take so long with your wife? No? Oh, my God."

How long did yours take, I want to ask the waitress. But first I check across the street.

"It's only twenty minutes since you last asked," the weary desk nurse tells me.

In the cabaret, they are singing '*Vamos a la playa*,' '*Cuando Calienta el Sol*,' and '*Sabrosona*.' Late in the evening, José has to leave. I am swimming in the music, diving like a loon, my feet no longer able to find the notes falling over and around me, my lips mouthing gibberish. Soon I can no longer distinguish one song from the next. Soon I am numb worrying about Ramona, thinking about what is going to happen after the baby is born and I have to leave.

When the bar is closed, and with still nothing happening across the street, I carefully tack my way home. At least I try to, for Nena, Ramona's sister, is helping me, alcohol breath in her hair. Like a bear out of hibernation, I lumber over the stairs on all fours. She leaves me there.

Nena returns in the morning to proclaim I have a son. "*Un varón*."

"*Un varón!*"

"*Sí*."

Simon's birth temporarily wipes away the despair that has been building. I immediately visit Ramona. She is without the slightest complication. When the nurse exhibits our son, he looks like a little dark-skinned monkey. It is the proudest day of my life to be an ape.

"How many dead have I seen, and now you are here," I tell him in Polish. "A duty fulfilled. A future. New growth for those who have gone."

We planned to name the baby Sigmund like me, my father and grandfather. But since Ramona pronounces my name "See•mō," leaving out the final consonant of each syllable, the hospital staff heard "See•mōne" So in Spanish they wrote 'Simon.' So our firstborn was anointed with a name meaning, according to the name book, "[the Lord] has heard."

"You'll one day appreciate how much of an answer to a thousand prayers you are," I tell him. "All the years in the camp, all the years I lived with Iris, all those years, I thought I would never have children. My cadet commander's words about masturbation kept ringing in my ears. I remembered my bout with typhus. I was plagued: this is the end of the line. And now my grave is opened ... and I suppose it can't hurt us, my little one, the name book says the Lord has heard.

"As soon as we're back together, we'll play. You'll see, my little one, we'll play under the sun and the clouds. They'll bear witness to the rest of the universe of our joy, that this is what life is all about."

It is a hectic time: preparing to bring the baby home, simultaneously arranging to leave Cuba. We have been counselled that if I am away longer than two years I can forfeit my Canadian citizenship. So in the midst of everything, I have had to push like crazy to get a new welding machine up and operating. At the last minute it is done. Ramona and Simon are only one day back from the clinic before I must leave. She is moving about drag-footedly, sitting like a butterfly; he sleeps. Nena is there to help.

The time comes for goodbyes. I go over details. "Now don't forget, I've registered, at Canadian embassy, our baby; and you, at food store for foreigners."

"Will we ever see each other again?" Abandonment of Cuban women by their American husbands happens enough that it has become a recognized problem.

"Yeah, yeah! I promise you."

"*Simo, te quiero.*"

"I love you, too."

I am two years less three days in Cuba. The first day in Toronto I send a pram by mail. Within three weeks comes the reply: "Simon loves to go for a stroll; he sleeps before we are barely out the door."

For once, I rest without the recurrent nightmares.

We foolishly expect our family to be in Canada within a month. Month follows month; in a curious replay of history, the months drag on. In 1920, after the Treaty of Versailles awarded the city of Teschen (Český Těšín) to the Czechs, Poland broke diplomatic relations. My parents had just been married, and *Tatuś* could not get *Mamusia* to Poland for more than two years. The separation produced an out-of-wedlock daughter we kids never met. *Tatuś* paid child support for many years.

Ramona, as a native Cuban, is soon cut off from the food store for foreign families. And I find out on a visit that with all my work and running, they were never able to get the welding machine going after my leaving. My work succeeds, bears fruit. But somehow, like Ramona's Canadian immigration, it always seems stillborn. She is writing me, "Sigmund, I feel so alone without you; Simon, he needs his father." I picture her in my empty arms, try to reassure her, as a husband should; but I am no more assured than she. After all that has transpired, what is happening with my son? They tell me, "It's all due to the Cuban missile crisis." True or not, Ramona is refused admission until a year after; and, even then, permission is granted only "because of Simon's Canadian citizenship."

My lawyer, Endicott, warns me, "Understand, it is possible there can be a last-minute glitch which will send them back. The immigration officer can still refuse entrance."

Two hours have passed since the plane landed. "A plane from Cuba takes a long time," he tells me. "There are a lot of people to process. If there is a problem, they'll tell us."

"Endicott, I am so glad you came with me."

Ramona, half the belly since last I saw her, parts the swinging doors, a fat lump of flesh in her arms.

"You're really here."

Soon Simon is learning to walk. He was born with a clubbed right foot, probably genetic. Two of my wife's brothers also have this. Every time he sleeps he wears a special brace. How we watch his every step! "Is he toeing properly?" "Only a few more months of this brace."

In rapid succession there are more children. Emilio Ernesto is named after my mother's brother Emil and Ernesto Ché Guevera. Like his brother, Emilio inherits a club foot. Unlike his brother's, his is surgically corrected at birth.

There is a miscarriage when Ramona slips down the stairs (also a boy). Then my mother finally gets her visa to visit—our first reunion since 1940. "Zigmush, Zigmush," she's calling, waving.

"*Mamusia!*" I have been at the Montreal harbour immigration for what seems like hours and she sees me first. "How are you? Were you seasick? How good to see you. I never realized how short you are."

"It's you who's changed. But I recognized you all the same. A mother never forgets."

"How is everyone at home? What is with Lucjan's stomach problems?"

"After what happened to my brother Włodimierz, I'm worried about cancer."

I take her to a restaurant in the revolving tower, then drive right home to Toronto, alternating conversation with long awkward, but happy, silences. The visit is a good one though she cannot appreciate, especially after the miscarriage, why we do not all settle in Poland. "How you liked to spend so much time in our courtyard in Nisko; something kept you for hours." She does not know I was quite fond of the Jewish landlord's daughter Rifka, though she was slightly older than I. Her pitch black hair, sometimes cascading down her milky white neck, sometimes pinned up in some fashionable way, captivated me. Her body had what it takes to attract, a nuance girls my own age either did not have or were not quite as adept at exploiting. I would watch her from the balcony like a foreign undercover agent as she rested against the leaning beech tree in the courtyard. I think she knew I was there. But no secret rendezvous occurred, except in my overactive imagination. In reality, she was nothing more than a sigh. *Mamusia* goes on, "Your Aunt Halusia asks about you all the time; your poor mother never knows what to say." "Remember how you used to fetch water at Grandpa's, how grateful he was?" "Remember how much you used to like me to cook plum cake?" She returns home, mission unaccomplished.

Then, there is the arrival of our third son. Picking a name, the precise name, is no simple business; words count. You can influence a whole life with

Our Pride. Vladimir, Emilio, Simon.

a name. But above all, a name requires mutual consent: "Ramona, ever since *Mamusia* came to visit, I've been thinking about the family back home. This one will be my hope, completion of what shouldn't have ended." She more than agrees. Our youngest is named Vladimir in memory of my brother Włodimierz.

Ramona keeps herself well groomed. Her eyebrows, made up in Toronto style, arch over wide, pronounced cheek bones. When we first met, I was most struck by her warmth. I love the way her smile fills her face when she grins, reflecting in her eyes. She is a strong woman, a good woman, a good mother. I enjoy watching her catch their fingers with her toes. Do they laugh!

Each time a child is born we have a big party, invite all the old fire brigade members who are in North America. Jurek and Tukaj are both there. Ramona cooks Polish food: red borscht, sauerkraut, pork chops, beet root salad, Black Forest and poppy seed layer cakes. "Good as it is, can't beat the pig we cooked at Stendal," Tukaj is saying. At the christening party, I say, "I'm so glad godfather will look after my son if anything should happen." Ramona, just out of the hospital, is telling everybody about the birth they missed in Cuba. "Isn't that something? It was the first and only time he got drunk." Between us, we have even begun to laugh about the year we were apart.

The inconceivable has transpired: the former prisoner has become a family.

Like Arachne of old, we weave, some with great skill, some with less, a garment that, in the end, we ourselves wear. Sometimes I wonder if, in striving to remove *Achtundachtzig* from my life, I haven't actually unravelled something of myself, something which, once lost, will not be regained. I have nagging doubts. Deep down I sense I am different than everybody else, a leper unsuitable for society. When I walk about I feel like shouting, 'Unclean, unclean!' Again, I throw myself into my work. Survive. Survive. Escape. Escape. I glory in my growing success on the job. I glory in my family. Why am I still asking myself, "Is this all there is?" I thought all I needed was children.

Do all young boys go through a stage where they refuse to eat? Ramona sings for him; he bashes the potatoes with his spoon, often in rhythm. I think he'll be a musician. She makes faces; he laughs but still refuses to eat. She cooks his favourite foods; he says, "The spaghetti is white worms." She counts: "Only three more bites"; he takes but he does not swallow. She solicits his family spirit: "Eat this one for Papa"; he gives back what was not swallowed.

I am happy my son has food to eat, but I deem it my duty as a father not to allow him from the table until he finishes eating: "Some liquid and piece of bread, that's what we lived on." I think I must sound like any typical father: "When I was your age I would clean my father's shoes; I'd never question him."

He grows sullen, a pattern for life. What could he know, of course, about nine to thirteen hundred calories per day? (It takes two thousand just to maintain the body at rest.) My food disappears with a few quick swallows. He sits for an hour, Buddha-style.

"Look, when you come to table, you should concentrate on job at hand and have a go at it," I try to explain, never very successfully. "I learned, from experience in Auschwitz, that lesson. In Canada, people want to eat and watch, at same time, TV. You want to have social party? That, you do after you eat." I know it seems incongruous, but I have to say it anyway. A pure clash of wills.

You do not go and yell at your children to be a bully. I will read it somewhere and it fits: I get so upset over threats to their well-being, Simon's failure to eat not excluded, because an injury of theirs puts me in jeopardy. This I cannot even try to explain, barely realizing it myself. In spite of myself, though, I have to secretly admire the fortitude of a child who takes on an adult to win. As the boys grow older, I resolve to take advantage of these mealtimes as a place for learning and constructive criticism.

I have been working night and day back selling real estate, and I am proud of what I have accomplished. But somehow I don't feel successful. What does that mean? The long-term satisfaction of the soul is eluding me; at fleeting glimpses of self-doubt I recognize it—otherwise, I revel in my accomplishments and plough on obliviously. In summer, we vacation on the Georgian Bay, what locals call Blind Bay near Parry Sound. In winter, we ski near Orillia with its opera house and Stephen Leacock museum. Each in its season is warmly anticipated for its rare leisure time with my family.

Carting the gang from city to countryside, packing and unpacking, means jobs to be done: scrubbing rust off the stove, airing out blankets, straightening wall hangings, planting seeds, reconnecting with last year's self. But try to get Simon to help: police the area, pick up stones, anything. The summer of 1966, just when the last one is born, I ask Simon to clean up around the yard. His little face gets red, jaw juts out. When he gets a little older, he will let slip that I want him to behave like children in Poland in 1935. Exasperated, I lose my temper. Then I hate myself for it, feel broken like a spoon tilted in a glass of water. Instead of doing what I know I should, I find myself unwittingly doing what I hate. What is this deep pain that wars against my own mind, imprisoning me anew? I race outside to try and escape the unseen power that grips my life. With her usual sensitivity, Ramona soothes, *"Por cierto*, the Papa really loves you; it is not like it seems; he gets angry because he loves you, my love."

When we return from the cottage, Professor Malatynski awaits me in downtown Toronto. He wants to persuade me to go back to Poland. We serve together on the Polish Political Ex-prisoners' Association in Canada, Inc., my sole organization related to Auschwitz. While the members share common experiences, we rarely talk about them. We simply enjoy the sound of Polish splashing around our tongue and flooding our ears. Sometimes somebody who was there will mention the boxing match. One guy tells me, "Once in the end, when an SS officer got mad, we just said, 'Come, take on Sigmund.'"[12] I cannot help a small smile. "Yeah, Heinz never asked for a rematch."

For the most part, though, we get together to forget, to drink, to fight over who should be our officers, and to argue about how we will collect German reparations. In this the Jews have it easier for once. The German Federal Restitution Law and the Federal Indemnification Law legally confirm the Jews as victims. But Poles have to prove they had been incarcerated for opposing the Nazi party, not for activity against the German occupying forces. This is a distinction next to impossible to document. Therefore, the clumsy name of our group: Polish *Political* Ex-prisoners' Association.

After Germany bounced my request to the UN High Commissioner of Refugees in Geneva, I did receive $1,878 from the UN; $1,878 compensation for my incarceration and years in Auschwitz—about $1.11 for every day spent in the camp. From Germany most of us, like myself, have received only polite letters. Nobody cares about the money. You cannot compensate for a day in Auschwitz. What we need for our own peace is that Germany officially recognize our unjust suffering. That would mean something. Instead I get this bloody UN cheque. It takes me a long time to decide to cash it. At first, I thought about sending it back. Then I realize it was sent from Zurich, covered by German accounts in Swiss banks taken over by the UN. Now if only Germany would own up to its responsibility, it would provide some validation that what no one wants to listen to was real, that we are not hallucinating, that our feelings are not unique to us alone.

When in 1965 the ex-prisoners' association decides public representation should be made in Europe, General Secretary Syput and Chairman Kašzuba appoint me. It is a spur-of-the-moment decision. Ramona's way is to speak in English when she is angry. When she is calm, she speaks in Spanish. Mostly we converse in Spanish. Ramona is concerned, not angry. "Why you?" she asks.

"They know that I am outspoken. Also, delegate must pay his own way. I'll use my UN cheque."

"Simo, what about your work?"

"I'll ask permission, I know they'll give it."

"You will have a chance to see your family."

"If authorities let me; I hope so."

"What is going to happen to you, Simo? Will we be separated long? When will you be back?

"In two weeks."

"They won't arrest you?"

"Nah, it's dedication of international monument at Birkenau. They can't arrest me. Dedication will be broadcast all over world."

"I'll pack for you."

"You're some fine woman."

But for me, after twenty-two years of exile and avoidance, the next few months resemble the months before my fight with the 'Sledgehammer.' I feel it in my chest.

Part II
1967

On 13 July 1948, the British government had issued a telegram to all Commonwealth countries proposing to discontinue trials of Nazi war criminals in British occupied Germany and to "dispose of the past as soon as possible." To this message, Canada had responded: "The Canadian Government has no comment to make."

It would only be in 1985 with the establishment of the Deschênes Commission of Inquiry on War Criminals that the Canadian government would commence any organized investigation of its own.

—*the Reporter*[1]

Eight: Zygmunt

Toronto, Ontario, 10 January 1967

It began with an ordinary news report; on the face of it, nothing spectacularly dramatic, a small item in the *Toronto Daily Star.* "West German neo-Nazi leader Adolf von Thadden is definitely coming to Toronto and will appear on CBC-TV's 'Sunday' program January 29, the CBC announced today."

But von Thadden, leader of the *NPD* in Germany, is no ordinary subject. He invokes the same themes Hitler so successfully exploited, but instead of attacking Jews directly, he castigates the State of Israel. He denounces postwar foreign domination of Germany, demanding an end to the "fallacy that Germany is to blame" which "extorts thousands of millions" from Germans. "Certainly there were situations like Auschwitz which were regrettable; very badly managed. Have we got to live with it forever?" he asks. In the 1966–67 elections, he is enjoying unexpected success, shattering West Germany's mythology that Nazism died with Hitler and arousing world alarm.[2]

What I tried to erase from my arm and my life comes back with force. This is the man the CBC—funded by the government of Canada, my haven— invites to speak to all of Canada! Are the horrors forgotten so quickly? In the midst of my preparations for Poland, I am conscious of an uncontrolled rage rising within me. Usually I fall asleep immediately; tonight I thrash and turn. The news account buzzes my head. Burning anger. Impotence. Failure. *My* failure over twenty-two years. Can I realize my own image of myself, that paragon of virtue we all take ourselves for? "Please, *Jezus*, favour me with compassion; I'm greatly distressed." I find myself alone, wandering beside Lake Ontario:

Mist encloses the boardwalk like a womb. Spine shivers. Is it the cool air that penetrates the light blazer? or the dark silhouettes that blow in and out of the white in front of me, slither around me? *Not* a favourable time to happen upon a stranger. He speaks first: Excuse me. What?—I can barely hear you. Could you tell me where Sobolewski lives? Me? is it me he's looking for? my name has been Sherwood for years; don't know of anyone else, though. Sigmund Sobolewski?—Yeah, yeah, I reply. He whistles like he is surprised himself, switches to Polish: What luck, finally! Then still testing, You—he drags out the *you* like an old man recalling the distant past—are Zygmunt? To hear my Polish name pronounced with a Nisko accent! How does he know me? What claim could this nocturnal apparition have over me? Check around. Except for us no one is about. Try and gain his favour. With a cigarette. The stranger waves it off. But who are you? I say, and he says, sidestepping the question, I've been looking for you for a long time. This one's words seem to hang in the night air. You with anyone? he asks. Oh *Jezus-Marja*, what should I answer him? Tell him or not tell him? Tell him. No, I'm alone. He seems relieved. Got time? His *words* are a question, but his *voice* is practically a demand. Watch his eyes—his eyes search my face as if they can see something hidden to others. This moonless night. All *I* can see is a shivering body cloaked in striped pyjamas like we used to wear in Auschwitz. Why didn't I notice it before? Why does it seem normal? Couldn't sleep anyway, I hear myself tell him. And he says, Then let me introduce myself, no one else knows; I'm not very proud of where I've been. His words begin to tumble out agitated, one after another: I'm here, that's about all I can say; they killed, I was silent; one man saved my life, I couldn't save his; one man, my friend, was left lolling outside with fever; why didn't I get him any medical attention? why? I wouldn't be around if others hadn't got me to the infirmary. And then his breath grows heavy, like, like what? like a train toiling up a hill, and he worms along more painfully: When I cleaned soup kettles, had to push away other prisoners; and, and ... and once ... when I was made *Stubendienst* in my Block ... I beat this guy ... bad ... I was prejudiced against him because he was ... *a pink triangle* ... they told me he'd molested children ... didn't like him, either ... one of these transplanted German *Volksdeutsche* who presumably lived in Poland all his life, yet never learned Polish; you get me? ... flayed him up something awful; didn't kill him, mind you, but it frightened me. On cresting the top, his rhythm spurts forth again, frenzied, reckless, like trying to escape from under an avalanche. Afterwards I started to reflect: I was so glad to have been made assistant Kapo, so proud, one of the youngest, and now this, am I really a criminal? is that why I'm in Auschwitz? will this moral slide continue? I was so scared; once you begin to sink, SS never let you wriggle out; they like to cover you with blood, until there is no turning back; so when women came and Blocks got switched, I managed to give up my position; but that pink triangle never leaves me, never leaves me.

I am left speechless. His words, making me for the first time wish I could make the faces that jump in front of me mine as he has done for his, dredge up long-suppressed memories of my own past:

Am I to blame? It was another era. Nothing was the same; and I was a kid, a prisoner. Long ago I have put it out of my head. Now I see no matter how much you will it away, it is always lying in wait, eager to undermine and to discredit; to make any attempt at new life seem like self-deception. If I know I'm a decent person, why should I be feeling guilty? And why this urge to flee home, locking and bolting the door behind me? Careful. Divide yourself from your camp. If the worst happens, at least the family is free. Take him away from the stucco on Pine Avenue, past the beaches and tennis courts to the park. Boughs creak and sway, winter air bitter from fallen vegetation, roots of maples bulk out of the ground making walking in the dark like climbing a series of little hills, branch on my cheek. Double-bodied, I feel myself pulled as if by an invisible string on a child's toy; no, I walk of my own, a sheep to slaughter. The stripes stumble after like a matched brother. City noises fade. In perfect tandem now, tuned to an unheard march, we walk together. Path twists narrowly, meanders through tangled scrub, straightens at a clearing, I feel the mowed park grass underfoot. A mystical affinity like that of two sports rivals settles between us. He stands about my size. I am poised, ready. We close in on each other as do youngsters making acquaintance, and we are well matched, surprising for someone as thin as he is; two moving shadows wrestling in front of a stone bench. Silvery flecks of dust catch light. There's more than what you've so far revealed; tell Sobolewski, I pant. Frightening concerns, a hollow voice replies first from below and then from above. What? I ask, and he wheezes and says, You saw today's newspapers? how is it possible! Von Thadden, to spread his racist hatred on CBC; sponsored with taxpayer dollars! And I say, To enhance his reputation in his own country. And he says, Yes, we must up and fight this. The challenger assumes my agreement as if our minds are as similar as our physical bearing. A chill wind rustles my thin blue blazer. I want to say, Not me! ask somebody else. But this time it remains choked inside; neither do I give in, though. I've got doubts; I'd be scared, and feel ... a bit unworthy, I tell him. The visitor, his intent clear as cards laid out on a table; too clear— the consequences of *not* acting loom like a mass of arrows flying in my direction. The visitor. Can't let him win this. Too long I've journeyed from land to land making my way: marriage, longed-for children, security, especially the last; in this Sherwood has been successful, all right. The visitor, aiming his words, pierces my barricade. Yeah, yeah! I understand; what responsibility do victims have? we have right to be left alone. My God, it's as if he *can* read my mind. Still, what choice do we have? he asks. He can say that generally; surely there's a wrong; but he wants to point the finger at me. The tussle continues. Zygmunt, you follow? very few who've experienced the truth of Auschwitz are alive. He uses the classic veto formula of the old Polish parliament, quaint but decisive: *Nie pozwalam*, what is left of us cannot again abide such dividing between Aryan Christian and non-Aryan Jew, making no sound like *Muselmänner* enduring living nothingness. He breaks off, a tinge of regret in his voice, Thank you, Zygmunt, everyone needs someone who understands him.

I bolt upright. In a moment of introspection, I realize emptiness steals the spirit before it is recognized as missing. In any case that is the way it has been with me. Maybe it was just my inability to admit failure. Told myself I was happy, and I almost believed it. Then I am thrashing and rolling around again:

Concede nothing. We must be at it a considerable time, for I feel my chest is heaving when first I speak again: Auschwitz? Unfortunately, my double breathes, also panting heavily. Neither of us has prevailed against the other. Block Fifteen, fire brigade, I say, pushing myself up and brushing the dust of crushed leaves from my jacket. Block Three, he mouths, still panting. Block Three? Did he say Block Three? We originally were housed in Block Three before the rest of the buildings were ready for occupancy, but he presumably was taken in later. I light a menthol to examine his features undetected. Looks distantly familiar: a Polish face, except for its emaciated pallor, like a younger version of myself; eyes set deep into a round head, forehead a heart with his shaven hairline; pointed inverted-V eyebrows; bowed mouth stretched resolute, a man with a mission. Shivering more than ever, I extinguish the match, rubbing it into the soil with my foot. What is it about his face? It's time for me to leave, he murmurs. Wait, don't go ... you haven't told me your name. And he says, I've got something for *your* name, though; until now you've been masquerading through life; from now on, your name shall no longer be Sherwood, but *Achtundachtzig*. What—in the *Konzentrationslager* we used only our names; *they* used the numbers. A rising draft rustles the aspens. Like that of a rain. Above, a kaleidoscope of darks and dawning lights plays tag in the shifting branches. Below, the nameless contender, gone.

Morning finds a new, freer man in my bed. I went to sleep tormented, full of anguish, and wake up considerably lighter. If, in spite of myself, it is all going to come out anyway, I might as well decide to live with it. My mind runs wild. I am so unworthy; what have I accomplished besides surviving? Children? Money? None of it has mended my torn soul. Could I not change? That a great abyss has been crossed, is instinctively understood. For the first time since cadet school I am whole. Viewed from the perspective of past, present and future, the same moment always looks different. So who can account for why stripes appear and suddenly past and future come together, a road on a map? An angel's view.

For the first time ever, I am ready to admit what I have always known: anyone who has been in Auschwitz remains in Auschwitz. You can wrestle with your spectre—like all such pivotal moments, it comes in a blink and in a blink it passes—but afterwards, you limp. My physical manifestation is represented by this knotty cane, my cross to bear, an unenvied legacy from Auschwitz. So now each day refreshes with an old reality: "Hello, you vile insolent leg, you that wrenches my hip so."

Some might say, "That is a less than productive way to start the morning." Yet it does wonders for me. There is a blessing, a fresh role, a meaning. "Ramona, I've got to show that son-of-a-bitch, von Thadden." My blood surges with electric energy. "That raven will find no place here."

A decision of the Will has knitted the disparate strands of my life together again. I go to Henessey Tailors. "Light fabric, vertical stripes, grey, buttons to the neck," I tell them, trembling.

I wait till I am alone in the house. The stripers lay spread out on my bed, the number staring me in the face. Until now, I have been ashamed for having survived, ashamed that I climbed over the barbed wire where others laid down their lives, as if it is a sin to live. And I was concerned lest people think me a collaborator. In self-defence, I let this dull cold fog twist around my brain and anaesthetize it. Now it is those twenty-two years of nothingness I am ashamed of.

The number on the bed continues to stare up at me. I go downstairs, have a coffee, come back, roll the stripers up, spread them out again, turn away, come back again. I see my knuckles are pearly, I am clutching my throbbing thigh so hard.

When I put them on, this raw lump chokes my throat; tears spill out uncontrollably. Before, I would have stared in disbelief if somebody had told me that I would so much as shed a teardrop. It is as if during all those years a swollen pool of polluted ooze has collected inside. Now, by my own decision, the sandbank collapses under its force, sending my body into sobbing spasms that cleanse my soul. Then I am back in the camp, like in a trance, shuddering at my own memories:

When you arrive here, the Nazis take everything away. Everything! Your identity papers, your ring, your watch, your cross on a chain, your clothes, your hair. Silence. Who is prepared for the complete loss? See the others. Is that what I look like? Stark silence. Then the first hesitant attempts to reestablish human contact. One of the young guys looks at me and says, Sigmund, is that you? No, no, that's an ostrich egg on legs; I'm underneath the table. Someone else says, I'm a ghost. I'm an alien from outer space, says another. Idiotic laughter. The older guys still haven't said a word. We in the first transports get our civilian clothes back for a few months; on every piece we've got to sew white bands with that number of ours. When our official prison pictures get taken in November, we still haven't been issued stripers. I appreciate how much suffering my strong heavy boots save me only when I see that later prisoners enjoy no such fortune. Shoes first, then pants, shirt, fold your bundle neatly, quick! Your last links with the past, never seen again. Naked and shaved, regardless the weather, you enter a new world where even

Prisoner No. 88, Auschwitz, October 1940.
Courtesy of the State Museum of Auschwitz-Birkenau.

your name is stripped away. Why do they do this? I ask at first. Then I realize a naked person cannot confront clothed guards, cannot explain how everything is merely one big mistake. He cannot carry on human conversation at all. Our entire worldly possessions become a thin striped shirt and pants often too small or too large, underwear changed once in several weeks, wooden sabots or shoes, a beaten tin spoon, bowl and cup. Hang on to that bowl with your life. Your bowl is your soup.

When Ramona comes home, she finds me with my stripers on. She catches a glimpse; then, so as not to disturb me, quickly turns and tiptoes out; but not before I catch the look of satisfaction on her face.

The protest in the Coliseum against von Thadden's appearance becomes the first time I publicly stand up. It is surprising to me that but a few days ago I would never have dreamed of participating in a demonstration, let alone a Holocaust rally; it was the last thing I wanted to remember. But then the polite Canadian government minister responsible for the CBC said she "would not interfere with the CBC interview plans." And what did they show? A man who loves his children and dog? What Nazi did not? Since making my decision, I have become conscious of a growing exhilaration, an unexpected lilt in my heart. I feel like I have found a part of myself that has been wandering in the wilderness for twenty-two years. And with six thousand present—representing various religious, veterans' and women's groups—I feel sure Canadians are going to rethink the whole subject of hatred against specific groups.

Holding my sign, I stand erect, a witness as politicians recount the horrors. As we march in the bitter cold to the International Peace Memorial, I stand erect, a witness. As Cantor Bela Herskovitz begins chanting the memorial prayer for the dead, I stand erect, a witness. Then I hear his voice echoing in the empty synagogues of Poland. Without warning, I lose my grip on the placard and crumple sobbing into the arms of two men beside me.

Dishing out soup. The Blockälteste is serving. Next to him, with the stick, stands the Stubendienst. The camp-smart prisoners line up with their bowls toward the end, hoping they will get the heavier soup from the bottom. Prisoners would joke, "Someday you'll be at a dinner party and ask the hostess to ladle the soup from the bottom."
Pen and ink by Mieczysław Kościelniak.

At the CNE Coliseum. Toronto Star/D. Glynn.

"Here's an official assignment to help get your foot in the door of European newspapers," Martin Goodman, city editor of the *Toronto Daily Star*, tells me.

I am going up to Auschwitz. The stripes appeared and I am already flying into my future life backwards. I shaved my head as it was then, used my UN compensation on a ticket with stopovers in five European cities. In each airport I conduct a silent vigil, carrying signs with a message for fair reparations. It is my first introduction to grass-roots action, and the response is tremendous. I learn that, even without my having to show the letter from the *Star*, the media appears. "Why did you shave your head?" "What are you trying to accomplish?" "This will be your first time back after all these years?"

"Yes."

"How do you feel about it?"

"I don't know. Ask me afterwards."

In Vienna a surprise awaits: in addition to the media, neo-Nazis. *That* makes headlines. The politics of confrontation turn out to be the easy part, though. All the media coverage wrests no recognition from the German government. And what awaits proves even more difficult. Next stop....

Poland. It seems to me I am walking with less of a limp. The language around me sings in my ear. From the bus, my eyes shake hands with each farmer turning his soil, earth turning green. Before anything, I visit *Tatuś'* grave in Racławice. My first physical confirmation of his death is seeing his name chiselled in granite. For the first time in years, I hear his voice, the shy, strained sound of his staccato words stumbling over themselves as he struggled to tell me about women. I have come home.

"Your father's a man of principle," I remember *Mamusia* telling me bitterly. Mentally reviewing how he confronted powerful political forces that would inevitably change his life and the life of his family, I re-experience his courage. What stands out is not his courage on the battlefield, which he had, but his courage of conviction, his quiet courage. Seeing ZYGMUNT SOBOLEWSKI on that stone puts into perspective, for the first time in my life, the man he was: a true raven-killer. At the same time it strikes me, Jews can't do this; there aren't even graves for them to visit.

I kneel on the mound that represents his ashes and cry out, "Don't be dead. I am sorry I fought with you, sorry I didn't apologize, sorry I never said 'good-bye.' How I underrated you, I see that now. I thought you were blind to your own family. Sorry I resented your nerve. I can finally appreciate what you went through. Could I ever live up to your example? Please be with me now." The silence overwhelms me. "*Tatuś*, in Auschwitz I kept your trust with honour."

I am fifty years old. One day I will be facing my own adult sons; will I have to wait for them as long as *Tatuś* did for me?

Someone gives me a copy of father's will written during his last few days: "I ask Zygmunt, as the eldest, to take care of the family." I will have to live with the fact his last words went totally unfulfilled. And I will keep the copy hidden, like poisonous gas, in a place where I am unlikely to accidentally stumble onto it and breathe it in.

Nothing is like it was, of course. The family is no longer: *Tatuś* and Włodimierz are both gone. Basia is married. My youngest brother Lucjan, the one who was a baby when I was taken, the one who never really knew my father, is a mystery to me—he does not like Jews; thinks he knows everything best. *Mamusia* is living in a different place. Shortly after my arrest, the family was given three days to move. But one thing has remained constant: *Mamusia* wistfully pleading with her son, her prodigal son, so rudely plucked from her bosom. "How is it that after going through the whole of Auschwitz, you turned away like that?" The figure, seemingly grown smaller through the years, has lost none of the sharpness of her mind: "What was it about the courtyard in Nisko...?"

"That kept me hanging around there for hours?"

She looks pleased. "You surely loved that courtyard. And how you loved your Aunt! Zygmunt," she asks nonchalantly, "did you know your Aunt Halusia asks about you all the time?"

"You have trouble knowing how to answer, right?"

She looks away. "It's lonely without you, Zygmunt." Now she looks back. "Do you remember how you used to fetch water at Grandpa's?"

"How grateful he was?"

"Wasn't he! Remember how much you used to like me to cook plum cake?" I stand up. "O Zygmunt," she pleads, gazing up with those soft eyes of hers. "Zygmunt, your mother is an old woman; wouldn't it be nice if you brought the family home?" Long-repressed images surge up in me:

Yes, after all these years, the survivor still has a *home* here in Poland, an open door, a mama, a sister and baby brother, uncles, aunts, cousins and friends. What does somebody like my Jewish friend Ginsbourg have? His neighbours and fellow countrymen—his best friends, even—occupy the space he once called his own, hang his pictures, use his silverware. From Kielce, out of twenty-five thousand Jews, what? Two hundred survived. After the war, after everything was public record in Poland, a pogrom! An organized massacre against the remnant! Forty-two murdered, some forty-five seriously wounded. My brother Lucjan said, Didn't the communist authorities appeal to the local bishop to calm the mob? And I said, But the clergy delayed twenty-four hours before responding. Lucjan said, Cardinal Hlond, the primate of Poland, called the event *regrettable*; the cardinal clearly explained: it had occurred not for racial, but for religious and political reasons.[3] I practically yelled, Regrettable? before the war, this same cardinal recited some facts: it's a fact that Jews fight against the Catholic Church.... it's a fact that the Jews are embezzlers and usurers and that they engage in white-slave traffic.[4] There were other 'lesser' postwar pogroms in Kraków, Chelm, Nowy Targ and Rzeszów. Of the small number of Jewish survivors, my compatriots murdered hundreds. How can I return to that? O yes, my family is safe; I have maybe fifty relatives still alive. The Jewish survivor? My arrest had some shred of reason. His? Is any additional fault other than being Jewish necessary? My children will reassure themselves their father was taken for a reason that can be avoided. Jewish children will harbour the knowledge it could happen to them whatever they do.

This same Lucjan had wanted to go to polytechnical college, but when the Russians discovered I was in England, he was given the run around. With what I thought of communism at the time, they wonder why I never returned.

"No matter what you do, I still love you," *Mamusia* says with a sad, well-placed sigh. "After all, you're my son."

"*Mamusia*, let's not spoil the visit," Basia placates.

Mamusia has the last word. "Remember your Auschwitz friend Julek Zończyk? I saw his picture in the paper. He has a big factory in Łódź, bigger than most in Canada. Even though he lives in New York, he visits Poland all the time."

As the day to return to the camp draws closer, I feel like a person about to jump in a pool blindfolded, not knowing if any water is in it. Is this my family rushing to a crushed and bloody body on the pool bottom? Before, I arrived against my will. Now, I am actually contemplating jumping into the hellhole of the world voluntarily. While mentally the decision has been made, psychologically the die is not yet cast. I imagine myself in the centre of the camp, an indifferent procession of shadows dancing before me. Am I among them? What if I am *not* among them?

I resist. I take a tramp through the streets and alleys of Nisko, recognizing and not recognizing. Figures leap at me from nowhere. I glimpse our Jewish neighbour with the glossy hair. We used to play volleyball in the courtyard. "You're alive!" I shout in joy. The figure passes by, dumb.

I see *Tatuś* whose grave I so recently left. He stops. He is beside his marker, standing like an aristocrat. He looks around like he senses my presence, and recognizing me, mouths the words, "Be a good soldier, Zygmunt." He points to the road. The road is a rail track and it leads back to the camp.

The rhythmic chuffing and the churning of the chant of the train too swiftly generates a chamber of grim chills in my brain. For a while I'm back in 1940, creeping along slowly, early in the morning:

How long does this trip from Tarnów prison last? Seems hours already. Going west. To Germany? Stretches of indigo, pink and red poppies in the grassy meadows of the pleasant Polish countryside. Eyes hurt. Overwhelming. Haven't seen such colours in a month. Better try to get some sleep. *Jezus-Marja*, who knows what's to become of us? More fields. Babushkas in constant motion: walking a bicycle beside a cow on the road; following two cows in the field with a branch in hand; bent low to make a furrow, plant or weed. A dusty road. A horse-drawn wagon transports its family to the local market. Land still farmed as it's been since the days when Poland was the breadbasket of Europe. A Polish peasant-farmer might be poor, but in surveying his few hectares, he would assert: this land was my father's, and his father's, and his father's before him. So with the German occupation, what? For us a farm represents more than just another occupation; rather, it's an inviolable commitment. The train churns on. Nazi guards are so cocky. They laugh. You Poles are a sorry lot; a few weeks, and your country is finished, *Kaputt*. More laughter. And shouting: *Deutschland über Alles!* Germany over all! And singing the Nazi anthem: the *Horst Wessel Lied*. They swagger around. Simply scrunch down wherever they push you. What chance do we have against their well-oiled blitzkrieg?

My body tenses all over again as if I were living these events for the first time. Well, we *did* show them. In the sober second look of a postwar perspective, did our armies not persist longer and mount a better fight than those of any other western country in Europe? Yes. And in spite of the most brutal subjugation of all the occupied countries, did the Germans not learn that our spine was stiffer than all others'?

The conductor comes by, briefly waking me from my brooding. We in the first transport were taken to Auschwitz in an ordinary passenger train, sitting on ordinary seats like these. Again my mind rambles:

Rumbling. Slowing. Scraping on the tracks. Jewish detainees arriving in sealed box cars. See them coming down the branch track. See them coming day after day. Long and slow. Several times a day. Sliding into Birkenau. Car after car of packed humanity, excrement and dread. By what right did I arrive in Auschwitz like a human being ... an experience enjoyed by so very few others? Those Jews. There they are again. Men, women, children, old people. The hundreds of thousands shuttled from every corner of Europe, for days without food, without water, with barely a bucket for the most elemental needs. Blue frozen corpses in winter, bodies rotting and bloated in the hot and dry central European summer. One train of twenty-five cattle cars containing 3,000 arrives in the hot summer of 1944, every 'passenger' dead.[5] *Jezus-Marja*, how could anybody ever believe?

Now, this new Polish train returns me to the land of the smokestacks, again rushing me by fields where my Polish Babushkas toil. Passengers, mostly ex-prisoners travelling at government expense to the dedication ceremonies, move along the aisle outside the compartment. I recognize the guy that kicked me out from unloading railroad cars in the *HWL* after I was discovered with peas in my pocket. He tries to be friendly. I do not want to have anything to do with him.

Someone else starts up a conversation. "Sigmund, do you know that Irka survived the war?"

"Yes, I met her in Bergen-Belsen after. Do you know where she lives?"

"No, but I heard she married a colonel." Then he laughs. "Read one of your love letters in camp."

"How did you get ahold of it?"

"Somebody must have pinched it. Every prisoner in the camp kitchen read it. It was hilarious."

Our sliding door, its latch broken, bangs open and closed with each change in grade. There are no empty seats, some passengers sit on the floor. The door flies open with one last bang as the coal-burner comes to a halt, disgorging its passengers by a rail yard much larger than a small town usually requires.

My eyes see beyond the external. The gates of Auschwitz are set off by a flaming red sun on a wavy green sky. I pass a tour guide surrounded by a large crowd, for today the Polish government will dedicate a monument "to the memory of the four million who died here." The guide is pompously funereal, speaking Polish, grey dress, about thirty, long on Communism and short on facts.

As her group moves to the next site, I go up to correct some details. "You crawled, not walked, into the *Stehzelle*; all while they beat you. Though it looks like it's big enough for only one, five were put in."

"I've had extensive training," she retorts, "and the way I said it was the way it was." I leave her as I am about to vomit.

As I pass the expansion camp, old feelings overwhelm me:

Irka. There, that building, there you work since being transferred from the brothel. In the *Schutzhaftlagereweiterung,* a manager for the construction of twenty new blocks. Hössler arranged it. Doesn't take too long to walk over. Worth it. Hit the ground! Figures stumble about in the dim smoky light, then crumple, arms over head, buried by a shower of bricks and plaster. I run forwards. One left, a Jew, ghostly white from dust and broken plaster. Gasping. Beyond help. A stray American bomb has blown away the entire end of the Block. Basement ceiling hanging only by a few iron reinforcement bars. I call. No answer. Forty Jewish tailors, lost in a flash, their stripers soaking up their own blood like blotting paper. Burning odour pervades the scene. Wait! Ah, a thin voice crying, Help! He will surely die. I start to crawl my way under the precariously swinging basement ceiling. The wood crackles. I see the fire brigade has arrived. Jedrek Czurawski is in the front.[6] Zygmunt, where are you going, you crazy? he calls. Somebody is crying, *Hilfe! Hilfe!* I shout back. *Zostaw tego zasranego Żyda niech zdechnie,* Jedrek yells, Leave the fucking Jew to croak, he says. And he's right. Why risk my life for one of these Jewish cowards? What makes me care about these *Saujuden, Hurengesindel, Mistvieh, Elendshaufen, Drecksau?* this Jewish shit. What? An image of a Polish Jewish soldier pulling *Tatuś* from the line of fire when he was wounded in 1917? Nah, it's merely what a fireman is supposed to do, no more, no less. Scooping with bare hands, crawling in the still smouldering dark hole, I follow the groans of *Hilfe.* Lift into my arms a blood-caked Hungarian Jew, bone sticking out where leg should be. Grasps onto me, not letting go. Does he think once I know he is a Jew, I will abandon him? *Mein Retter ist da,* Varga Szarkady calls out gratefully when *Achtundachtzig* visits him later in Block Twenty-seven, My rescuer. He is a tailor. Full of life. Always smiling. One leg is broken in two places; the other, mangled. The wounded are unusually well treated: single beds, white linen, flowers, milk, double food rations. What is this? The *Lagerführer* actually came to visit with a

Typical fence posts made by the prisoners in the cement works.
Courtesy of the State Museum of Auschwitz-Birkenau.

photographer, Varga says, smiling like he was just given a honourary citation.
Soon after, I visit again. All the white linen is gone; the ward empty.

Here I am, *Achtundachtzig.* I left this place determined never to return. Yet
the more it is erased, the more it draws like a magnet. I owe it to all the people
who have never left this place, to tread where they stepped, to teach my boys
back home—I live for those kids; they can be seven thousand kilometres away,
to me they are like in my back pocket. "I'd like you boys to one day be able
to say your father was here, and to talk about it with your children." I tell
myself some day they will come with me, find myself addressing them as
adults, that is to say, with the hopes and aspirations of a father. "Boys, walk
around. This calm was once teeming with people. Imagine here snow, here
mud, all under heavy, low hanging clouds. Corpses everywhere. There was
no grass then, though there was same thick forest. This building I helped
build. This door I made, and there I slept, on that board, and there, and there.
Crawl here. They beat you when you entered. There, you see? That's how we
dried fire hoses. These cement poles looking like friendly beckoning fingers,
they held through their glass rings electrified fencing. From these watchtowers every ninety metres or so machine guns pointed down at you." The air
is thick with the scarecrows of men behind every tree and door, speechless
until the visitors have gone through. Once, I am certain I hear a Nazi guard
break into laughter as a Kapo kicks his Jewish victim into oblivion.

Józef Cyrankiewicz, Polish premier and former prisoner, unveils the monument. The date, April 16, exactly 557 years after the defeat of the Teutonic

Order of German Knights at Grunwald in 1410. My mind again wanders to our little guys at home. I am telling them, "That foundation surrounding this unkempt mess of cement and grasses outlines where once *Krematorium IV* complex stood. Where each of these flowers grow, naked people once stood under dummy showers. These twisted rails are remains of tracks over which bodies were rolled from gas chamber to crematorium. Do you see that man fishing? That's where ashes were dumped. Listen, do you hear wind murmur from ground? Look, look well, there where flames lick sky. Can you see babies, children and sick? Jews, Gypsies, Poles? Can you? Can you? Boys, pray tell your children what you've seen here. We owe that to all who've perished." I notice I have just unconsciously crossed myself.

Ready to leave, I hear a guide telling her group, "You can purchase souvenirs here by the cafeteria."

Nine: *Mamusia* and *Tatuś*

Toronto, Ontario, July 1967

The last twenty-two years, I was pushed to forget. Now, thanks to von Thadden, 1967 marks the first time my life is reconnected on the same wheel, a gigantic wheel of time around which I am once again free to move unafraid of the past, around which I must move. I love to know the background, the reasons for things that happen. The 'why' to *Achtundachtzig* harks back to well before Hitler's invasion; those with a long view might even say centuries. I will teach my boys repeatedly, "Current affairs aren't result of present alone." What has happened to the Jews is precisely what happened seven hundred years ago to my native Poland, and that, in turn, is what brought the Jews. But even with this long view, I have put the cart before the horse. I tell them, as my teachers taught me.

Already two centuries earlier, in the days of King Bolesław 'Chrobry', Poland became an extensive European empire, boasting even the overlordship of western Russia. Then, in 1241, a ruthless wave of drooping-mustached invaders surged from central Asia. They swashed away every man and animal, catching the women and children in their grasp. The stand of Prince Henry the Pious proved valiant but futile, not even a finger in the dike. One looked out and thought one had seen a hill. Then one realized the hill was heaving like an ocean swell composed of masses of horsemen. And that was the last one would know. Wave after wave, the Polish people disappeared inundated, and none was left to shed a tear.

Then the tide reversed. Poland was not occupied by the Tatars, but she was left ruined and void, as if all the oceans of the Earth had washed over her. After the last of the Tatars rode off, no middle class, no commerce, no business, no craft remained. More than four hundred villages were wiped away, sixteen cities gutted and destroyed, a hundred thousand dead. Scarcely a handful of crushed serfs with their impoverished aristocracy appeared here and there in isolated tiny tide-pools of life among great stretches of coniferous forests and barren but fertile land begging for care.

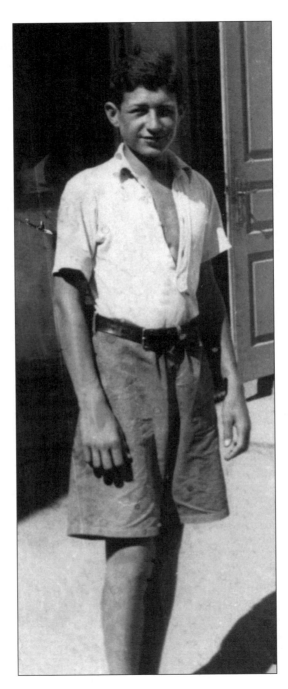

Sigmund. Nisko. August 1939.

Even though I have known this all my life, it is amazing that I only see the parallel since my evening struggle. As with the Tatars, in the fall of 1939 the *Wehrmacht* burst into Poland with the force of water through a broken dam. It was as if all the sky's windows had opened. Then, slowly, the flooding stopped. But this time, the mud and debris carried in the wake remained:

School starts. My Rawicz campus in German-held territory, I report to the eastern cadet school in Lwów. But invading ravens blitz their way through Poland. Before I can even unpack, an unfamiliar banshee-like whine. The first time I see dead bodies, smell cordite. Twelve classmates. These were my friends; we were like seeds of a pomegranate. If I hadn't been in the other room. Why did they do this? why? No time for ceremony or sentiment; though I am barely sixteen, orders come for me to report to the field. Sustained shelling greets our arrival. Worming my way on the soft ground in the dark. What am I doing here with no training? The next day, 13 September, we move forwards to a big winery several stories high. Sobolewski, up there; you'll help the forward observation officer. Where are they sticking me, for God's sake? Tighten my stomach and creep up. Windows on every landing blown out. What fire shells have been raining down on this field? On the top floor, I am barely capable of peeking out on the surrounding vineyards, many of them in long shelled-out glass greenhouses. Visible for kilometres. The officer I'm to help explains we'll be directing the fire of a heavy artillery battery in a culvert behind and below. Cadet, look front! I see three trails of dust kicked up by Pzkw tanks closing in from the west. Main body will follow, he tells me. What's he saying! We instruct the gunners by telephone. Bursts of the battery take me by surprise. The panzers are too far away to zero in on us yet, but they have advanced in range of our big guns, which nonetheless have trouble closing in on the moving targets. The Germans are dangerously close now. Can hear the whine and clank of the motors. Fortunately, the morning sun glares over our shoulders and into their eyes. A twist of the field glasses catches the flicker of light off the grinding treads; I can see their short-barrelled cannons rising and falling with the tanks' movements over the terrain. Soon they'll be pointing directly at us. Exposed ducks. My stomach moves to my throat. What am I doing in a tower in the middle of a field? I look around for ways to escape. You have to last; don't think about it; make yourself tight inside. My first battle test. I'm not ready for this. I can hear a pulsating dull rumbling, the distant echo of successive explosions on both flanks. *Jezus*, are we winning or losing? don't dwell on it, the troops are either holding or not holding; concentrate on what's in front of you. My officer speaks slowly, coolly, like we were out bird-watching on a lazy summer day. *Unbelievable*—how does he keep so calm? I repeat his words over the telephone, try to imitate his self-control. Only my mouth and eyes work, the rest is frozen to my spine. Smaller fountains of dust spatter up the area of their advance, our shells pocking the sand in ever-closer patterns. My feet can feel the vibrations with each thump of the mortars. Now dancing all around them. Now forcing the tanks to veer. Now, exposing the two-tone formée cross on their flanks winking at me through the red dust. Bent forwards on his elbows, glasses to his head, my officer maintains his even drone of numbers—if anything, even more subdued. We have their range and the last raven gets clipped. In the eye. I cheer. My officer looks me over. I watch our troops advance below, taking the crew.

Down below. Grapes in my mouth. Who's this tall red-haired German? I should escort him to the POW cage? He's shamefaced. Being assigned to me, a cadet, has to be beneath his German dignity. Or else, he's taking a broader view, ashamed that here in eastern Poland our nonmechanized forces under Sosnkowski have succeeded in checking the German blitz. On my return, regulars from elsewhere in Poland arrive to replace us cadets. Several soldiers lie dead. My God, look at that one caked with white powder like an Egyptian mummy; I thought people died with their eyes closed.

We're back in school only a few days; that is, those who remain are back. Where are our officers? it's a morgue here. Outside, the same stillness. Only yesterday, what seemed like thousands of Polish police slid along the streets. Where've they all gone? A shout pierces the silence: The Russians have invaded! change into civilian clothes, quick! It's 17 September 1939. The Germans back off to the west and the Russians lumber in from the east. I watch from an uncle's apartment. Look what a motley group these Russians are, Uncle is saying, especially compared to our boys. Yeah, some even carry their rifles slung on ropes. Their songs, too, strange, bouncing back and forth like newsreels of the U.S. marines, nothing like the way our troops sing with one voice. On 28 September, Nazi Germany and the Soviet Union sign the partition. Is it possible? Within a month of the first invasion, my country has disappeared; the family is left on the German side, the eldest son on the Russian. My only goal: to get home quickly.

It wasn't easy getting that Russian travel permit. Wonder if he really believed I was cycling to Przemyśl? Damn strutting Germans, turn me back at the Jarosław crossing. They can't separate a kid from his parents, war or no war; is this river a wall? I peddle north along the San, find two Ukrainians to help me cross. On reaching our side, I go to pay. Bounding from their Trojan horse and catching me unawares, the two of them thump me from the raft, make off with all that I have, including the bicycle, and escape back across the river while I'm still sprawled in the reeds. So long, sucker, they call.

I walk to Nisko mad. Mad. On a pearly steed, I, Zygmunt the Freedom Lover, vanquish the enemy. It started in school when, even as a lad, I used to fuel my patriotism by the example of our Polish heroes, imagining myself acting out our history. With the few nobles remaining after the Tatar invasion, I would survey our once-blossoming lands. Then I would call: "This land will hum again. Dig the foundations, build for expansion. Time will come when we'll be more than we ever were under Bolesław Chrobry."

With a cold eye, I, Zygmunt the Clever, outdo Casimir the Great, uniting Poland's scattered towns, bringing law, prosperity and culture to my country.

Partition of Poland 1939.

In the mid-1300's I set the first legal covenant in Europe. I reform the currency, establish universities, confirm and then extend the charter of rights and protection of previous monarchs. To advance the level of economic and cultural life and to populate the provinces, especially in the east, I throw open our gates. The storm-tossed masses of the Germanic principalities, its peasants, burghers, craftsmen, merchants and financiers, all come pouring in. This time, it is like a blessed river in a flood plain. Poland becomes a nation with an extended arm, an immigrant nation, bringing out the smitten from the dungeons of the world. With them come the Jews.

Jews. Since my visit to Poland, the floodgates of memory have been pulled wide open, overwhelming me with details I had for so long tried to suppress. In October of 1939, soon after getting back, I remember watching from our balcony as Jews were unloaded at the railroad station down the block:[7]

Nine hundred Jews plod past our house. My first sight of people with two crisscrossing yellow triangles stitched to their clothing. Several horse-drawn carts follow. Loaded with suitcases in various shades of brown and some medical equipment. I don't believe I'm seeing this. Under Nazi guard, the sad-eyed newcomers purchase supplies. Then word spreads around town: food, bedding, money, dishes, coats, all get confiscated. That's war, I guess. Our merchants for the time being get the money, the Germans get the goods, and the newly arrived Jews get dumped in an empty field surrounded by barbed wire. During the night it rains. Soon another transport arrives, then another and another, each more pitiful than the one before. No outcry emerges; does anybody even thinks about it?[8]

Now I wonder, why had I seen no yellow stars earlier in the occupation? Many Jews lived in Nisko when we were growing up. In the building where we rented, lived two Jewish families: the Habers and the Feits. Our landlord's family, the Feits, lived behind the storefront downstairs. It was their daughter I used to watch in the courtyard. The father operated a bicycle shop on the main street, very small, old-fashioned wooden shutters, three or four bicycles in front tied up with a chain while he did repair work in the back. His wife ran an equally small haberdashery in the front of our building. People do not realize how many poor Jews there were in Poland. Although religious, the Feits wore modern dress except on the Sabbath, when sometimes I was asked to put up the house lights for them.

After the sudden invasion and before the border had been sealed, more than a quarter million Jews lucky enough to live in boundary towns had escaped from the German to the Russian side. In the general anarchy that followed, many former Jewish homes were looted. Since the Polish soldiers and police had run away to save their necks after the invasion, *Tatuś* formed an interim militia to prevent the stealing. He trained about fifteen volunteers, and wore his Polish captain's uniform.

By the time I managed to get back across the border, all the local Jews had fled to Mother Russia. My parents told me they escaped before the occupation forces issued the edict for yellow stars.

Soon after arriving back home, I sneaked downstairs to see what was in the Feit's abandoned store:

Tatuś! you'd pull a revolver on me? He's yelling: The son of a Polish officer thinks to steal! His efforts, all in vain: what Polish looters have not stolen, the Germans haul away in trucks, convert the synagogue into a warehouse. After the Germans vacuum up everything? *Tatuś* is of a different attitude. Bicycle parts in the attic. He barters them: This is a loan we'll repay after the war. Fine, reasonable; but the Zarzecze area, where the foreign Jews are, why do I keep thinking about that? Don't go there, *Mamusia* admonishes more than once. Ah, so she doesn't want to know if I go. Those foreigners draw me as salt draws liquid. Don't get too close, just ski out and steal a look. It's not what I expect; *Jezus,* these black-uniformed SS with their death-head insignia give me the willies, as do the flat empty fields behind the barbed wire, and and how is it that nothing has been done to prepare for the Jewish arrival?[9] Other days, safely in my apartment. Peer from behind a curtain, watch the sleighs come to town. Always the same, too: in back, two or three well-fed SS men sprawl out drinking; up front, a Jewish coachman shivers, bootless feet wrapped in a blanket. I catch the coachman's eyes, have to turn away.[10]

I helplessly watched the Germans, while it was my ancestor who helped chase the Teutonic knights out of Poland. That was when, in 1410, Zygmunt Ślepowron Sobolewski was knighted by King Władysław, and we vanquished the German ravens. How proud I was as a child to learn that the White Eagle soon flew from the Baltic Sea on the north almost to the Black Sea on the south, from Prussia in the west past Moscow to the Urals in the east. Poland comprised parts of what later would be Lithuania, Latvia, Estonia, Byelorussia, Russia, the Ukraine, Germany, Hungary, Bohemia, and Transylvania, and soon expanded southwards to swallow Moldavia, becoming an uneasy neighbour with the non-Christian Ottoman Empire. Poland was the première mercantilistic, intellectual and scientific centre of Europe. The paramount fairs were here, the leading universities were here, and that a Copernicus made his debut in Poland was no accident of history.[11]

Lately I am making connections I never made before. "Boys, do you wonder, like I do, why Polish Jews had German sounding names? Why they spoke Yiddish, language like old Rhine Valley German?"

This part they never taught me; it has opened my eyes to what could have been and set the tone for my present work. In the Rhineland from Mainz to Speyer to Worms, the lasting mark of the Crusaders was a trail of 'infidel' Jewish blood. When Polish princes encouraged immigration, they simultaneously enacted laws to incorporate Jews expelled from neighbouring Teutonic dukedoms. His contemporaries dubbed Casimir the Great "the king of the serfs and the Jews."[12] I am always anticipating to myself my children's future interest. "This is how, boys, the Jews entered by invitation and assisted in reviving our business and production. Most Polish families with 'ski' names dating back before nineteenth century, descend from gentry. So when your grandfather was lieutenant in Austrian army, his name was Germanized to 'von Sobolewski.' Maybe some ancestor Sobolewski was minor potentate who invited Jews to people Poland's wilderness. Anyhow, through centuries we've shared much, even to coincidence that both Polish and Yiddish languages look like their writers are too poor to buy any vowels."

Into what had become this seething hotbed of culture and growth, entered also the beliefs of the Reformation: "Let us eliminate priestly celibacy like the Lutherans." "What we need is a state church like Henry VIII instituted in England, a church with Polish, not Roman, rites, and with clergy dependent upon Polish leaders." Then, in 1565, the Jesuit foot soldiers of the Counter Reformation appeared.

King István Báthory continued the policy of enlightenment towards all people, granting charters to various individuals and groups. With the approval of Báthory, there developed the *Va'ad Arba'ah Ha'aratzos*, the Council of the Four Lands. Through the Council, the Jewish community was recognized

The Sobolewski home. Poniatowski Street 30,
Jarosław, custom built by Sigmund's grandfather in 1903.
A plaque on the wall still bears the name "Zygmunt Sobolewski."

as an autonomous and distinct society within the Polish national framework. Jews received the right to maintain their own schools and courts and to govern by their own legislation, a right not contingent on territory. More significantly, Jews were taxed not as individuals, but as a body politic; and the *Va'ad's* administration was authorized to determine the community's own method of tax distribution.[13]

Several times the *Va'ad Arba'ah Ha'aratzos* convened at the Jarosław fall fair, and it would have been amidst the stalls that the Sobolewskis would have come into contact with Jews. Poland flourished and its peoples flourished, trading skins and grain for cotton, silk and spices from the Far East and West. It was the golden age of Poland. With respect to Jews, no other country has such a history.

And I keep learning more; for me it is like peeling away layer after layer of an onion. History is the story of society, not individuals; but often an individual is a window to the whole, sometimes even representing an entire generation or period. The following is a complete epoch. This Saul was the forebear of many with whom our family shared a fate. I remember the story in practically the same words I heard it.

In the mid-fifteen hundreds, a Jesuit influenced the Prince Nicholas Radziwiłł to revert to Catholicism after his father had apostatized. As an act of repentance, the young Radziwiłł travelled to Palestine, recorded in his *Journeys to Jerusalem* in both Polish and Latin. Returning from his pilgrimage, Radziwiłł solicited Rabbi Samuel Judah Katzenellenbogen for charity, which he received. Reaching home, the prince sought out the rabbi's son Saul, who had been attracted to Poland by its *yeshivos*.

Somewhat later, King István Báthory suddenly died. The prominent magnates assembled to elect a successor on Tuesday, 18 August 1587 when, by law, a decision had to be concluded. They deadlocked. "These will never rule," each faction said of the others. That the date not pass without electing a king, thus contravening their own legislation, they offered Prince Radziwiłł the position of temporary monarch. According to Hebrew tradition,[14] he declined, stating, "There is one in discernment and virtue considerably preferred to myself. If the Diet would proclaim him unanimously, I will reveal the name."

"Agreed." All the magnates acclaimed the celebrated Saul *Rex pro tempore*, king for the interval, cheering: "Long live our Lord, the King."

Centuries later a debate arose. Some said, "He governed all night." And some said, "A few days." All agree, however, that the distinguished Saul issued many salutary laws for the welfare of Poland.

Rather than choose from among themselves, the nobles finally elected Zygmunt III Vasa, son of John, King of Sweden, permanent king.[15] As for Saul, he became known in history as Saul *Wahl*, marking his having been *chosen* King of Poland by the unanimous vote of the landed gentry.[16]

These are stories I never tire of. "You understand, boys? Sobolewskis and Wahls, just two individual examples of Polish families. Yet we're representative of many others, and we interact again and again."[17]

On my trip to Poland, my sister gave me our family history, gathered by Uncle Karol on odd sheets of paper from various sources. I work on it like a professor pouring over an ancient text. Sobolewskis were an active part of Polish history: army officers and priests. In our family chronicle, I can trace the entire outline of Poland's decline beginning with the 1587 election of Sweden's Zygmunt III to the throne.

Border fighting with Sweden, Russia and Turkey quickly drained the economy. I dislike thinking about it even. Decade after slow decade, the proud Polish gentry, relying on the principle of 'republican liberty', proved unprepared to commit the means necessary to support the national cause. If Sobolewskis were among those unwilling to grant the king rights to recruit troops without each time having to make debilitating concessions to the nobility, I do not know. "The kings, after all, must not become dictators."

Then, too, the monarch who in Sweden had been Lutheran, pledged, "In Poland I will be Catholic." Zygmunt Vasa adopted Catholicism with narrow-minded zeal, thus stirring an element of religious dogmatism and tyranny into a stew previously noted for its tolerance. Little by little, clerics were successful in churning the pot. In consequence, the Jews steadily wandered away from the cities of the west, migrating particularly to Galicia and the

Ukraine. If the priestly Sobolewskis participated in the searing blood defamations enkindled against the Jews, I do not know. I would like to think that maybe their sentiments agreed with Zygmunt Augustus, who, some forty years before, had fumed indignantly, "I do not wish to be regarded as a fool who believes blood may flow from a pierced Host."

As for the blood libel, I first heard it from my priest in Nowy Targ, so I figured it had to be true. No one ever told me the pagan Romans used to accuse the early Christians of slaughtering Roman children to use in what we ourselves call the "flesh and blood of Jesus." The accusation against the Jews represents a classic example, not for the first time in history, of one group placing its own situation onto another.

Maybe everybody thought antisemitism a necessary expedient to nation-building. Most people meander like sheep, following the spirit of the times. It is clear to me that, against Orthodox Russia and Protestant Germany, what I regard as this new anti-Jewish policy supposedly unifying Poland did not save our country.

According to our family chronicle, the end, when it came, erupted from east of the Bug River. Three groups simmered in the kettle: The Cossacks, steeping on vast Ukrainian estates to the east, were Greek Orthodox and barely tolerated Uniates.[18] The absent Polish Roman Catholics owned the land, subjugating the peasants and taxing them mercilessly. The Jews became intermediaries between the city and village economies and between the nobles and the peasants, the object of Church scorn. A Polish proverb illustrates the tension: "What the peasant earns, the noble spends and the Jew profits by."

The volatile cauldron boiled over in 1648, the end of Poland's golden age. Led by the Cossack Bogdan Chmielnicki, a country gentleman whose possessions had been confiscated by a Polish official, the Ukrainians surged forth with Tatar allies in armed rebellion. "*Voruzhye! Vperyod!*" A seething, rampaging flow, they scalded hundreds of thousands of Poles and Jews, raping women, killing children. For us, we were one of the thousands of Polish families blistered in the hot froth of unleashed rage.

For the Jews it was like a flame kindled upon them, the worst mass slaying until Auschwitz. After two years, the Jewish population of Poland had in some sectors lost nine-tenths of its whole. More than seven hundred Jewish communities were wiped out. It is almost as difficult to comprehend as what came in our own century. So brutal was the explosion that an eyewitness reported, "They said: if we wait until the Ukrainians invade, we will all perish or be forced into baptism.... It is preferable that we fall captive to the Tatars.... This they did ... some three thousand people."[19] Still today, you frequently find Jews with a yellow cast or eyes slightly slanted, reflection of some distant Asian connection.

Then came my scorching:

It's 18 May 1940, 4:30 in the morning. Barely after my seventeenth birthday. A *komisarz*, actually a major in the Polish army, leads a Nazi officer and two helmeted soldiers into our apartment.[20] Pulling books from the wall, dumping drawers, seizing years of little stuff meaningful only to us. Stop, please stop, my mother is shouting in German. The baby wailing. Me hiding under the blankets in my room. Someone slaps my bed and demands, Who's here? And I hear *Mamusia* blurt out, Just our young son. A subterfuge to no avail. Get up and get dressed! the German officer yells, ripping the blankets away, my body left huddled under nothing. They turn towards my fifteen-year-old sister, Basia. And who's this? She's eleven years old, I say. The black-shirted SS, like the holy Teutonic Knights, the select of Germany. Actually come for my father; when *Tatuś* appears to be dying, they seize his son instead. Maybe they figure my arrest, as much as his, neutralizes any influence he, as head of the disbanded militia, might wield against the occupation. Or maybe I'm simply the fulfilment of some German quota.[21] Whatever, they allow me no opportunity for farewells. Not to my sick father vomiting blood. Not to my brothers and sister huddled under blankets. Not to my aged, watery-eyed grandmother. Not to the garden where I played hide-and-seek with my chalk-skinned neighbour. Not to the San River over which I had returned home. No big deal. When everything's cleared up, won't I soon be back?

Mamusia gets arrested with me. I'm asking, What happened, where are they taking us? And she looks at me and whispers, Zygmunt, you didn't have any leaflets, did you? No, I whisper back. The next morning, still in Nisko. Temporarily incarcerated in a large gymnasium. I'm sawmill worker, I tell them in German. *Mamusia*, you think all they want to do is register us? look, those guys over there are lawyers; I see some teachers; and the priest! that beer-stomached guy, the one by the wall, he's the hotel owner, and there's Dr. Pizło. None of this makes sense, she says. Her wits about her, Mother has latched herself to one carefully chosen German. No one can beat my mother. Hers, a well-delivered appeal in fluent impeccable German: a baby at home … a sick man … no way one can care for the other … no way to care for either of them … work for German post office.... Her long neck erect, her head back. She does not stir from her goal. Speaks so calmly that his surprise parades across his face. You're a young man; perhaps you've got a young sister or brother, perhaps a baby of your own; whatever offence caused my arrest, can we convict a sick man and baby who have no blame? Just a short distance from the door where they stand, I can barely hear her; if I didn't know better, I'd think them socializing in a coffee house. I'm a Czech citizen, she says, family name Kreutzer; my sister lives in Sudetenland.... Smart, use the Czech treaty with Hitler. At four o'clock in the afternoon, he relents and looking in the opposite direction says, Out, quickly! Didn't she pick him as susceptible to her cause? With my son. *Nein!* Not that susceptible. *Mamusia*, leaving me to go to the others. Takes my hands in hers, looking into my eyes. They say you're off to Tarnów; I'll get our cousins to visit you; see to it you're released in no time.

Good job *Mamusia* can go back. She'll be my advocate. So far the Germans have treated us decently. I tell every German guard, It's mistake. Their only response, a shrug. As they load us up, don't I catch a glimpse of my little brother Włodimierz with a backpack? Probably brought sandwiches or clothes from *Mamusia*. She probably felt it unsafe to send my sister. Probably *Mamusia* told him how crucial his job is, and the Nazis stopped him from fulfilling it. The normally jolly face is crumpled into tears. I'm sitting on the last seat towards the rear, next to the soldier battening down the canvas back. Włodimierz, even though you can't hear me, I'll be off this lorry and see you soon.

Haven't slept since the arrest. Tarnów. *Jezus*, we're being herded into the depths of some prison. The rhythmic noise of marching feet is punctuated only by the Nazis' shouts, *Los! Los! Ihr verdammten Hunde!* and, every once in a while, by the slam of heavy iron doors as they prod us forwards. Hurry, you damned dogs! Without any food, twenty-six of us get shoved into a cellar dungeon designed for four. Place reeks the musty smell of dank, undrained concrete floors. Freezing. We more or less snuggle into each other. No privacy. Can't believe that nobody knows why he was arrested. A junior judge from Nisko, Kazimierz Andrysik, protests, The Nazis are in an untenable position, there have to be charges against us. The hotel owner, who believes it was because some Germans got in a fight in his hotel, says in a low voice, I know the name of one of them; he'll explain it. Klocek, another lawyer from Nisko, chimes in, Oh yes, this is just an ugly joke—isn't it? I feel sorry for him. He tells me his son jumped out of the first floor window and escaped. Some of the older guys are telling stories. Say nothing, their stories are much better than anything you could tell. What? something from school? you call that a story? And what about you guys? enough about families and food and the unaffordable time missing from the job. Soon the smell is us. Rivulets run between our legs when the men can no longer hold themselves in. Then the stench. I'm slapping at bugs. How long can I stand this? I'm so hungry, the growling stomach cramps, the thirst—worst of all the thirst. Light from a crack in the upper wall. Sun has come up and down and up again. Are they going to starve us to death? Let them just come for us. Then I can explain; they will realize I do not belong here. They are in no hurry. I'm so thirsty.

Is that scuffling outside the cell? Forty-eight hours—about time. Forty of us from various locations are jerked into another, somewhat larger, cell. A small single window. Vents downwards from the ceiling out. Higher than I can reach. Outside, the sun lingers longer each day; inside, barely enough light filters through to reveal parts of faces in the dark. Though it's May, we shiver night and day due to the damp. Impossible to lie down. The dry bread and gruel are nauseating. *Jezus*, when will I get used to the smell? No linen. After two weeks, killing lice is our only distraction. One guy has a fester on his leg. Leave it alone, will you! Guys are starting to complain; then real conversation peters out. People break the silence just to hear the sound of their own voices, assuring themselves they are alive. Again we are moved. Twelve to fourteen of us, mostly thirty- to forty-year-olds, are shoved into a smaller, third floor cell. You can't move around, but at least you can stretch.

A hole in one corner. Two bunks on each side that we take turns using. Why do I usually get the concrete? just because I'm the youngest? I'm never taken on a walk, never interrogated; they call some people but never Sobolewski, maybe because I registered as a sawmill worker, my new job. Although it is strictly forbidden, we tap on the pipes to those above and below in Morse. So we know a little about what's going on, a mixed blessing. Even though the Germans rev up their trucks to muffle the sound, we can hear executions in the yard below, confirmed by our taps. A man who has been sobbing a lot on the opposite side of the cell mourns, Now we're in for it. A semiconversation breathes on the floor in front of me: What's it like? What? To be shot? I heard they line you up against a wall. Do you think you feel the bullets? Yes, but hopefully not for long. A priest is in our cell. Rests knees to chin in the corner, the best spot. Keeps complaining he was only arrested because the parishioners sang 'God who always saved Poland' at Sunday mass. Right. I attended church that day—when everybody started singing, he bolted away in fright. I'm glad we're allowed to receive parcels. The priest, supplied with almost daily packages from his church, does not share. *Mamusia* was right, *Tatuś*'s cousins do bring bread and pork skin, once even launder my underwear. When will they let us write home? Meanwhile try not to think of anything, especially the gunshots outside. Thinking will get you into trouble. A seventeen-year-old knows enough to wait till things are cleared up. A seventeen-year-old is unafraid. If *Tatuś* cannot come, *Mamusia* will. Just wait.

Something has been happening to me. I am richer, fuller. Even others seem to notice. Since my visit to Auschwitz, I have been getting asked to speak on Polish history. At first I find it scary speaking to so many people. But it takes over me. I limp up to the front of the room and into my past.

Ladies and gentlemen: Especially for those who have never been in eastern Europe, I will cite my own family experiences to illustrate today's topic.... About forty of us were in group day I got my wedding invitation and was thrown in Tarnów prison with group of Poles and Jews. No further Nazi arrests of Poles took place in Nisko. I feel, naturally, close link towards one particular ancestor on our family tree. Turks captured, in 1672, Cavalry officer, distant-something grandfather Stanisław Sobolewski. They imprisoned him for twelve years until family could arrange for ransoming our *Zakladnik*. Why did it take so long? I don't know. Our family had, evidently, some resources, so maybe it took time to locate him. On his return, he stated, "I'm not sorry I was a prisoner in chains. But I am sorry I couldn't fight for my country [in the heroic rescue of Vienna]."

Circle of time spiralled Sobolewskis to prominent positions. Jan Sobolewski fought as officer in Potocki's cavalry. In 1685, King Jan appointed him supervisor of Podolia and Volhynia.[22] Along with King Jan's associates from Sobolewski family, two of Saul Wahl's descendants by marriage, Rabbi Aaron Gordon of Wilna and Rabbi Simha Doctor of Lwów, served as the king's personal physicians. And, while Wojciech Sobolewski was viscount, Jewish settlement in Drohobycz was enabled.

Partition of Poland, eighteenth century.

Following Cossack rebellion, ever-jealous nobles made *liberum veto* unavoidable principle of Polish law. Based on radical democratic notion, "Every Polish nobleman is equal to another," one deputy rising in *sejm* to exclaim, *"Nie pozwalam* (I object)," defeated any bill. As result, with all of Poland's emphasis on freedom and equality, our country never developed workable form of central authority to sustain that freedom. Each magnate felt *he* was Poland.[23]

Despite brief periods of triumph, wheel of Polish glory ended.[24] Countries of Europe turned on Poland like famished wolves who assail injured pack mate, tearing it limb from limb.

After 1795, neither Russian nor German occupation was calm, but Germany took steps to make its control permanent. Prussians changed all place names from Polish to German, and transferred populations, bringing German nationals, *Volksdeutsche,* into occupied Polish territory.[25]

Our family continued, as most Poles did, to intersect with Jews. Fighting with true Polish patriotism, Sobolewskis, right along with many Jews, joined in 'November Uprising' against Russia (1830–31), keeping foreign wolves at bay for two years.[26] *"Jeszcze Polska nie zginęła póki my żyjemy,* Poland is not lost

Germany by 1938.

while Poles still live," states anthem that preserved hope of White Eagle flying again. Sobolewskis, like their Zionist counterparts, came to recognize that, if its society remained loyal, nation could overcome temporary loss.[27]

Following World War I, Poland, its severed parts resurrected as one, resurfaced on map of Europe soon to look ominously like lamb caught alongside jaws of German wolf.

History's wheel churns inside my head as one vision now generates another. I got this photo on my visit to the *Konzentrationslager*. To my sons it is merely a photo. They will stare at it and observe nothing. Even when Simon, whose eventual field is cinema, studies the picture I will spot in his eyes a lack of full comprehension.

"You see, Simon, this photo." My hands tremble as I speak.

"Is it a railroad station?"

"Yes, German troops are surrounding these Polish prisoners. You think it can ever be over for me?"

Staring for some time into the depths of the picture can make it come alive. "Night between thirteenth and fourteenth of June 1940 we in Tarnów prison awoke to great commotion. Soon rumour spread that they were deporting us to Germany. Practically everyone's opinion had it we were going

119

as chain-gang workers in agriculture. Someone declared, 'I've got a premonition of something more sinister.' But for most part, we told each other, 'Everything'll be okay.' That we were leaving prison, you can understand, even relieved some tension. Proverbial die had already been cast; but, unknowing, we chatted among ourselves like at any gathering.

"Soon they moved us to this building with wooden benches arranged in a semicircle like an amphitheatre, Tarnów's communal bath. Older guys settled in to try and sleep. We younger ones were too wound up. Broken pipe was steaming, so this plumber was called. One student attached himself to mechanic. Envy ran through group when he left pretending to be plumber's apprentice."

"That was smart."

"I think so, too," Ramona joins in from the kitchen.

"Today, you can say that. Then, I thought by marching out he had more than likely put himself into bigger trouble. Besides, no opportunity to follow his example presented itself."

"Too bad you didn't think of it," Ramona says.

"I was still clinging to hope that everything will soon be sorted out."

Simon examines the picture. "How would you ever know how to interpret, if it wasn't for me, this photograph, Simon? Bunch of people at some dim railway station? Group of sombre, sallow-cheeked, unshaven men waiting for doors of this old type passenger train to open on foggy morning? Suits and wide-brim prewar business hats, cassocks, workers caps, knitted stocking cap, two uniforms and steel helmets in foreground. You're interested in military history."

"This isn't merely a snapshot. This is an historical document," he says.

"Right, in many ways it's all I've got."

"How'd it come to be?"

"Well, while still dark, they marched us through streets of Tarnów. SS guards shouted '*Dali-Dali*, hurry, hurry' as they pushed us through the deserted streets. Short while later they loaded us onto train. This is only photo that survived war. The Museum made copies."

Before me, while we are still discussing, my eyes play tricks on me. We peer at what has become for me a sacred scene. One by one the inhabitants of the picture, first prisoners, then grinning Nazis, slide, silent as the grave, from the world contained by its frame. Soon, as if in a trance, I am all who is left, holding an empty photo. I stare at myself from another corner of the room. All the others have disappeared. Human beings with promise all done in. I replace the photograph in its protective yellow cover, tender its history to the box from which it came, to be preserved with the shadows. With a sigh, I continue the story.

"Noon, train stopped at Kraków station. They ordered us to keep windows closed, so air quickly grew stale. Guards stood ready at both ends of our car. I got up to use, at front end of car, washroom. Nazi guard came with me. Hadn't eaten since previous evening and I was starving. The reason is, eating or drinking means more trips to washroom, more trips mean more confusion, and, for guards, more work. So it's not that they planned to be heartless, and everything followed from that. Rather, as normal routine, it was simply more efficient to give nothing. Except for their mania with Jews, you can explain core of Nazi heartlessness as German efficiency.

"Anyway, we saw outside, under red swastika-emblazoned flags, German troops swarming along busy platforms empty of tourists. Carts laden with duffle bags butted their way through masses of soldiers who parted and then came back together. Then we heard German station master squawking: 'Attention, Attention, we have a news bulletin. *Paris ist genommen. Paris kapituliert.* Paris has fallen to the German forces?' Exultant shouts and shooting as German troops went wild. Martial music was blasting from public address system. Our steam engine started up again, puffing out of station, gradually picking up speed, sliding smoothly past stucco houses and little gardens. You might get idea we stopped merely for this announcement of German triumph. At the time, I put it out of my mind and slumped down on my wooden bench. German guards laughed."

In my public speeches, I begin gradually to introduce other elements. Jerzy Sobolewski, the son of the same family that brought me bread and pork skin in the Tarnów prison, is now living in Montreal. When his daughter is married to a Jewish medical student, I speak of Jewish suffering during World War II while toasting the bride. It does not go over very well. But do we not have to learn history's lessons? If a place with Poland's early tolerance could turn upside down, could it not happen anywhere? The older my sons get, the more I will try to teach them. "From Chmielnicki on, we were well on track, boys, towards Auschwitz."

Ladies and gentlemen: ... I've been wondering, isn't there something to fact that brief period of Ottoman rule in Podolia and Volhynia gave rest to Jewish community? There's dark side to Polish history. Demise of Polish entity also brought, against Jews, new and frequent pogroms, resulting, for first time in centuries, in reversal of Jewish demographic march: westwards rather than eastwards.

Between 1846 and 49, Austrian *agents provocateurs* excited, in Galicia, local peasants against their landlords and estate managers (mostly Jews). Again our fates interconnected. One of my grandfathers, owning land in Dziedzice, was bound and placed on wooden rack. Then he was sawed in half by local mob. According to my aunt's account, someone shouted, "Cut him slowly, he's a good *Pan*."

When Pilsudski signed pact with Germany, Catholic-Jewish relations further deteriorated. Burghers and peasants blamed, for all Poland's problems, supposed world Jewish conspiracy. Bloody pogroms took place in Grodno, Lwów and other towns, blood accusations in Lublin and Vilna. Immediately preceding World War II, all Polish political factions other than Socialists and Communists, including ruling Sanacja Party, were dedicated to antisemitic policies. Guilds and universities alike instituted tight Jewish quotas. Free Poland pursued, with French Colonial Office, idea of exiling Jews to Madagascar. At the same time, one third of Polish Jewry was forced to rely upon support from U.S. charities.

"When ravens swooped in on that fateful Friday 1 September 1939, I'm sorry to have to admit, boys, I was simply product of my times. Nazi Final Solution only completed what we'd already begun quite well on our own. It was two weeks before Rosh HaShanah. Jews were reading in their synagogues passage from Isaiah, 'Nations shall walk by Thy light.'"

A month after our arrest, we were standing in front of our first *Lagerführer*, SS *Hauptsturmführer* Karl Fritzsch.[28]

Mounted on a wooden chair, Fritzsch shouts: I want you to know you haven't arrived at a sanatorium but at a German concentration camp; if you don't like it, you can go right now to the high tension wire and commit suicide; Jews got no right to live longer than two weeks; priests can't live any longer than one month; all the rest of you should be finished off in three months. Man next to me shoots me a frightened pleading look like a cornered rabbit. I just shrug. These old guys take things too seriously. Just take things as they come. Open space? Daily sun? A whole lot better than the century-old Tarnów prison. SS guards and thirty *Szwabs* dressed in blue jackets and blue berets supervise us. Blue jackets and berets? At first I thought they were seamen. Turn out to be German convicts. From seven a.m. to seven p.m. we're doing *Sport*. This reception is rough, remarks an obese fellow who's having trouble keeping up. As for me, I'm neither beaten nor kicked. Like army recruits, we march while singing in German, *Dark brown are the hazel nuts, dark brown are our shirts*. To the Nazi blackshirts and brownshirts, a tribute. Spread your arms, bend your bodies, do push-ups, run around in a big parking lot. Like my evening and early morning exercises in cadet school. Wasn't my hope then to become a long-distance runner like Nurmi, the Finnish marathon winner in the 1937 Berlin Olympics? Now who knows? It can't hurt. How quickly the Sport loses any resemblance to the Rules of the Marquis de Queensberry! Those who cannot run, the old men and the sick, are shouted at in a German they cannot understand, then beaten with sticks. Or they must race around as *Strafe* while the rest of us lie on the ground watching the punishment. This whole workout would be a joke if it weren't for them. By the third day, the first dead prisoner. Stricken by a heart attack while sprinting back and forth in the hot humid weather. A pall hangs over us. After that, ever more deaths daily. We've got to stand in pairs facing each other, a tall prisoner with a short one, a fat man with a skinny man. Then, on the order *Rollen*, we've got to put our arms around each other and roll on the gravel parking lot in clouds of dust. Alternatively, we must squirm on our elbows and toes, all at a brisk pace. No letup. Tears our clothing to shreds. I'm such an optimist; still cling to the hope *Mamusia* and *Tatuś* will push the right button and everything will turn out all right. But these little games are wearing me down. This evening when we finish eating our bread and tea, a new game. All the

Jews arrested in that first transport are pushed to the front of the hall. Sing your Hebrew psalms, they're told. A guard shouts at Father Stanisław Węgrzynowski, No. 90, You, lead the choir. My Nisko parish priest. Almost two hundred centimetres tall in his ankle-length black cassock. One, two, three. Awkward, hesitant, mournful music. The SS burst with glee! A reluctant witness, I refuse to look. God, I'm sorry for my priest. I go to him later; Father Węgrzynowski looks me straight in the eye. How could the Pope be doing so little for the Catholic priest of Auschwitz? he asks.

His voice comes to my mind so clearly; it is as if he speaks now in my ear. It turned out to be his last words with me. Węgrzynowski got transferred to Dachau where he perished.

Part III
Pull
1968–1992

The year 1967 was a momentous one for Jews and Christians. During the weeks that led up to the Six Day War, Israel the country and its people, were threatened with annihilation. The secular press understood clearly the spectre of a second Holocaust. The Christian world was silent.

About those few weeks, Emil Fackenheim wrote: "The Jew after Auschwitz exists with the knowledge of abandonment; the Christian cannot bear to face his responsibility of this abandonment. He knows that, as a Christian, he should voluntarily have gone to Auschwitz, where his own Master would have been dragged, voluntarily or involuntarily. Hence the Christian failure to face Auschwitz. Hence, too, Christian silence in May 1967. It failed to recognize the danger of a second Holocaust because it has yet to recognize the fact of the first."[1]

—the Reporter

Ten: Achtundachtzig

Toronto, Ontario, 1968

 limp into my future. Involuntarily, I became eighty-eight at age seventeen. By my own decision, I became eighty-eight a second time at age forty-nine. By the strength of my resolve, I will be number eighty-eight for the rest of my life. Having had my education snatched away from me, being eighty-eight is the one area for which I have been truly prepared, prepared like none other. With the flood of memories, I begin attending political meetings wearing the prison stripers, my number sewn on the left breast. Every time the stripers go on, I cry. At first, before each new protest rally, I swallow a Valium. But do what I must, since that nocturnal struggle, I will not be got the better of. Ever.

Because of my return to my Auschwitz past, I meet Sabina Citron No. A-15134 at a demonstration.

"Sigmund, I'd like to introduce you to Andrew Mittelman."

"Auschwitz?"

"Yes, No. 30193, deported to Auschwitz on arrangements of Father Józef Tiso."

I let pass the reference to the president of the New Slovak Republic, a satellite state of Hitler.[2] "It's amazing Jew with such low number survived," I exclaim.

"After four months, only eighty-eight people remained from our original transport of 972," he tells me. "I think I'm the only survivor."

"His proficiency in German saved his life," Sabina interjects.

"I became a *Schreiber* in the IG Farben chemical plant keeping production records at Monowice. Seventy percent of IG Farben's workforce perished, but being a clerk I survived."[3]

Citron, Mittelman and I form the Ad Hoc Auschwitz Memorial Committee, with me serving as chairman. I am impressed with the quiet and organized way Mittelman goes about making arrangements for demonstrations, creating lists of invitees, seeing to details.

Auschwitz Remembrance, now I welcome it. When we first arrived in Auschwitz, we were 'quarantined' in the Polish Tobacco Monopoly building:

We sleep on concrete floors. No washrooms, 728 prisoners in 'protective custody.' Two oil drums, open at one end, stand watch on the landings of the staircase. At dawn, the Jews have to wrestle the barrels down two flights of stairs, sloshing urine and faeces onto the floor and themselves. Then, without washing, they must join the rest of us doing sports. Immediately, the SS guards fall upon them shouting, You *verfluchte Juden*, you cursed Jews, this will be the last month of your lives. Some promises the Nazis keep. Shortage of water. Wash in potato salad buckets outside. Wash! on the double. No matter the weather, we run out without shirts, scrub up in the same bucket as the guy before, then show the *Stubendienst* you're wet. Don't I come here from cadet school where life was also communal and regimented? Strange how that discipline helps me now. For survival's sake, I gotta keep clean, exercise.

Work details commence. A relief from daily sport? No. Sport ends, but the Nazi oppression escalates. And no reprieve arrives. *Schweine*, clean the stucco from these buildings, on the double, you pigs. My first assignment. I scale the lattice-work scaffolding as high as possible cornering into an abutment because the Kapos can't observe the top very well. Will the blustering toughs venture where they might slip and fall? Too risky. From under me, the dull cloud of white plaster chips rises and fills my nostrils. Work *Kommando* assignments not fixed. So I try a few days as a road sweeper where I can scrape up cigarette butts to trade for an extra mouthful of soup. Green triangle one-armed German Kapo strikes up a conversation: How do you come to speak such good German? I tell him the truth, My mother and father both speak; my family respected German culture. And he says, So, what were you doing before being arrested, then? I was translator; for German engineering company. Really—why don't you join our work detail? we unload cement bags from railroad cars in the industrial yard, love to have you. He's got a warm permanently turned-up mouth, and leaves a friendly impression. Well, I think I might. Good, he says amiably. O yes, very friendly!

First day, he yells at a dying guy: What! you stinking animal, you're laying down instead of working! On similar occasions he is known to look around with eyes that betray a background of murder and robbery, calling to a prisoner: Hey, you there! take him and pull his overcoat, jacket and shirt off, and lay him in the snow; that'll shock him, and wake him up to work; move it! This Johann Siegruth (Kapo No. 26) uses his one arm more effectively than most men use two. Right in front of me, he pulps a prisoner's head against the iron bumper of a flatcar. Maybe he was interested in me because I'm young. Find any excuse not to go back. Report to the infirmary with a skin rash. Male nurse aims a spoon of sulphuric ointment in my palm and a kick on the ass. If I catch you goofing off again. Thank God they put me peeling potatoes for the day, at this time an activity reserved for the old and infirm. For once, it's good to be one of the elderly![4]

I begin to have these dreams: Fresh dark rye, aroma filling the kitchen; *Mamusia* made it. She brings potatoes, borscht with sour cream, hot yeast meat *pierogi*, sweet and sour stuffed cabbage, chilled Ukrainian stewed eggplant, *mazurek* for dessert. I've got this stomach ache, can't eat a thing. And food has become the subject of conversation: My wife used to make poppy-seed cake every birthday, says one. Mine would make veal with mushrooms, says another, warm and dripping in sauce. The hunger gnawing in our stomachs disappears as we tell each other what delicacies we'll eat when we get out. One will be a cook in a fancy French restaurant, permitted to taste whatever he wishes. Another will live on a farm, produce appearing from the soil all year long. For some, work won't be necessary when a grateful Polish nation showers food upon the former inmates. Even so, when I mention my would-be wedding dream, everyone can hardly suppress their laughter.

Arthur Balke, German prisoner who was in charge of the Tischlerei.
He saved Sigmund's life.

Pfahlhängen.
Watercolour by Władisław Siwek, 1946.

Of all people to get married, the seventeen-year-old, Sigmund. The discussion gets merrier and merrier. I never get a chance to explain.

It has been getting colder each day; to survive you clearly need a job under a roof.

Once during 'story time' I made the mistake of telling my sons, "Even when we were forced labourers, some jobs were better than others. Main thing was to do anything to avoid assignment outside. Exposed, outside labourers were more vulnerable to mistreatment and loss of food. Any low number who survived had to have made his way into one or another of Auschwitz' 'better jobs', always indoors.

"Carpentry, my first long-term job in *Tischlerei*, was 'good'. If you worked in Fire Brigade, as I did later, you had door to whole of Auschwitz, useful for 'organizing' for barter or sale. You made point of getting guards used to you marching in and out with fire extinguishers, modified with double bottoms."

"Did you have good jobs and all?" naïve Emilio asked, looking up with those deep brown eyes of his. Ramona reminds me how he used to sit in one of those overstuffed easy chairs, a little nothing curled up in a big cocoon. In the growing-up years of our three boys, he was the most anxious to please.

To explain the irrational in rational terms is impossible; any comparison to normal life would be absurd. "Yes, but not the way you might think. I went immediately after indoor job; managed to get assigned to *H.W.L.*, main food storage warehouse for SS troops, unloading boxcars packed with sugar, dry peas, macaroni, rice, every kind of canned food."

"What's good about that?" Emilio wants to know.

"There was chance to liberate some sugar. We split, 'accidentally', bag against hard edge. Three days later, they discovered in my pocket some dry peas. Sentence was one hour of *Pfahlhängen*. They hoisted me from wrists handcuffed in back, legs dangling about thirty centimetres off ground."

"You will scare him," Ramona says.

"He should know this. Four of us got punished this way: one Jew and three Poles. I was trying not to move because of shooting shoulder pain. Someone came in, each step tearing at my shoulders as he jounced attic floor. 'Hello, Roman', *SS Blockführer* called to the newcomer. Herbert Roman (Kapo No. 25) answered, 'Hi! How goes it today? Well, what do we have here?' Kapo Roman took over like he was in charge. He tied, to foot of Jew, rope, and swung him back and forth. Cold sweat covered Jew's face. After tiring of this amusement, he jumped and hung himself around Jew's neck. I could hear his tendons rip and his shoulder joints break. There was piercing scream. Jew did not survive." Roman, Kapo of the painting department, had no reason to be there except his simple pleasure at watching people suffer. Hated Poles practically as much as Jews. Later he volunteered to murder Russian PoW's. His favourite tactic was to kick the prisoners in the kidneys to make their urine red. The Nazis had an unerring knack for choosing Kapos who relished their work.[5]

"When they finally took me down, my back was breaking and my arms were like rags. Couldn't wipe the dribble from my mouth, had no control of my bladder. Lights were coming at me from walls and ceiling. I could feel bone in my shoulders for hours. I was surprised at how glad I was not to have been Jewish. Before Auschwitz, Emilio, I considered myself normal and honest boy; after this I began to wonder. One by one, any illusions to which I tried to cling were destroyed. Why don't I let myself forget, Emilio? *Achtundachtzig* pulls me."

Out of necessity, your education in survival started immediately upon entering the camp:

You learn: never call attention to yourself. Never be *aufgefallen*, never stand out in any way, be totally inconspicuous until you just blur into everything else. But even that, you learn, does not go far enough. It's more than just a physical thing. A person can be sensed without being seen. So you must curl up inside, diminish your presence to zero. Forced to run wherever you go. But you must develop a prison shuffle of the brain. Once that happens, the guards will no longer harass you. You'll get a better assignment, maybe pulling a cart, cleaning latrines, peeling potatoes, other such favours. What of a large nose or hunched back, or one who walks with a limp? He'll be marked like the fox on an English hunt. Prisoners with glasses? Considered

Pick and shovel gang. Watercolour by Władisław Siwek, 1950

members of the *intelligentsia*, singled out for particular abuse. Play the role of being dumb well, and your chances of survival increase.

Every day I told myself I will live. This, and the ability to be invisible, were the reasons for my survival. Worrying about hunger or pain soon drained your hope away:

How many there are who see no chance for freedom, who constantly fret, I'll never make it. And with that attitude, they don't. One about my age, Karol Siciński. Knew each other in cadet school. A lifetime ago. Karol, never reveal you were in a Polish military academy, they'll kill us immediately. Karol is caked in bruises. Falls a lot during exercises. Also, he worries constantly, I don't think I'll make it. With reason: he's got no survival smarts. Misty morning, 5:30. Why, why does he replace a broken lens with a fallen leaf? Only succeeds in attracting attention of the guards. I once witnessed an SS guard slowly and gently remove the glasses from a prisoner's face. Please be very careful with these glasses, guard said. Then a fist bashed the man's head in, flat. You're free to put your glasses back on, he sugared to the crumpled pile on the ground. To survive on your own is next to impossible. Someone else also has to be helping. First and foremost yourself, then others. You do unto another in hopes you both live long enough that one day he will likewise do unto you. I've just become *Scheissmeister* in my Block. A very prestigious job! Could save your life, a fellow inmate says with jealousy. Hope he's right. Scouring the latrine, even though often full from dysentery, is inside, and when we wash the wooden food barrels, there'll be an extra few swallows of soup, yes? Poor Julek Zończyk (No. 821) often shows up at the back window. Pick and shovel today, he whispers, continually looking over his shoulder and pretending not to be addressing a window. Got a morsel for a starving man? God, he looks like chaff that, beaten from the kernel, blows in the wind. Yeah, yeah, don't worry; somehow we'll find some soup scrapings. Just a futile act? Maybe, maybe not; these little gestures keep you human.

We ... I, that is, don't think about God much. But one thing, even under these conditions—no, *especially* under these conditions, you've got to be a *Mensch*. I knew German from before, but this camp jargon has a different meaning for the word. It's the way the Jews use it: You have to be a decent person. Monks are in the camp, still wearing their grey habits. Be careful what you say, Zygmunt, some will report you to the SS. I've met the much-maligned Jehovah Witnesses. They don't report you. Working in the *Tischlerei*, I bunk with tradesmen from other commandos. Actually most aren't tradesmen. The more savvy lawyers and teachers pretend to a trade. Appears more useful in the Nazi hierarchy of what gets one a better job. One such a person is a round-faced, well-nourished priest who sells confessions. I know it's bad religion; I'd rather be without it, but then again, it fits the place. Haven't the older guys warned me? He likes young boys. Your smooth skin will drive him nuts, they joke. It's clear that all groups have their share of saints and rogues. What counts? Being a *Mensch*. Yes, and there are other lessons. The Kapo of the *Lederfabrik*, the leather factory with its attached joiners shop, is exceptionally cruel. If Walter finds you stealing, he beats you with a pipe; and the more he beats you, the more excited he gets. Inside my shirt, an engraved cigar box. Could get me an extra ration. Oh oh, Walter starting a body search. Ah, he inspects someone downline. Step into the line already searched even though those guys are not my height. Misses me. Completely. An unscheduled visit to Irka. SS? Quick, ditch into the bathroom. Irka grabs a mop and sloshes soapy water outside the door. Another time, I again hide in the bathroom, with a Russian on a similar jaunt. The SS examine the stalls one by one. Oh, a Russian! They drag him out holding his hands together, kicking his head in, come back, check the remaining stalls. No one. I slithered over the partition into one already searched. The Russian never betrays me, which changes my mind about Russians. Indecisiveness can mean death.

"Death, as graceful product of old age," I tell Ramona, "did not exist in camp. In Auschwitz, death was always premature, symptom of delicacy, degeneracy and decay. Senseless. Failure Kapos mocked." People who were never there can pontificate about 'noble martyrs.' But I saw it again and again:

A nauseating splattering of flesh and fluid. Weaker a prisoner is, harder he gets beaten to finish him off. Bodies of the dead are quickly stripped naked by others who need shoes or trousers. A new guy asks, What happens around here? You go and *organize*, I reply, summarizing what the uninitiated newcomer will require months to fully understand. You want something? find something else you can trade for it. As for the dead guy? The *Blockälteste* senior prisoner spits onto the chest of the naked body to wet the copy pencil; writes the dead prisoner's number in large fifteen-centimetre-high figures. Must have the right one. These now-stripped bodies lie on the ground in pairs—in winter, blue-white from sub-zero cold. Side by side, we, the living and the dead, are counted, hours on end, during *Appells*. The guards set down the rules: During roll call, you're forbidden to enter your building or use the washroom. That can be deadly. Especially in winter. Doing the big job in your pants can be the first step towards becoming a *Muselmann*. July 6, three weeks after we arrive, a punitive nineteen-hour roll call following a successful breakout. From seven p.m. till two p.m. the next day. Attention! Squat! Attention! Squat! The orders that teach us prisoners a proper appreciation for authority. Following a second escape on October 28, there's a bitter cold roll call from noon to nine. Two hundred die. Don't look. What does it matter? Is there any other place to look? The son of raven killers, impotent.

Shared struggle makes for camaraderie, not friendship—a dangerous luxury. A friend. Yes, I do have a friend here. Stefan from Kalisz. Succumbs to meningitis; probably contract my own affliction through him. Stefan's death upsets me so much I write his mother: Know he was one good Pole; he died martyr's death. *Jezus-Marja*, what did I go and do? They'll kill me, no question. They're going to call me into the *Politische Abteilung*. How can I retrieve that letter? Why didn't anybody take him to the hospital? The *Stubendienst* should have done something. No. Am I a fool? Such a waste, so young, so patriotic.

From this point on, I realize I'm trapped.

Maybe the censors miss it. Or maybe some prisoner shuffling papers in the office manages to do away with it, saving my life. Two weeks later meningitis strikes, and nothing is ever heard about my attempt at *belles lettres*. On exit from the Block Twenty isolation ward in March 1941, the last of my individuality slithers away into darkness. I'm issued stripers for the first time. A baggy elephant in zebra skin. Thin zebra skin. Zebra No. 88. Everything I came with is now gone. But I'm lucky, very lucky. In the hospital they let me do a little switching, even get pants with elastic; many have to do their work trying to hold them up. As for me, I'm falling down a lot, but from lack of balance due to my recent illness. Owe my survival to the fact head Kapo Balke takes me back. Never says *yes* or *no*. Just takes me back. Who knows why? Maybe because I'm valuable to him as a translator.

New dreams begin: I'm on the second floor of a building. Have to leave. Something looks like stairs, but it's not. I can't get down. Then I'm standing in a field. A sphere, yellow, blue and green wafts in the sky. Then another one comes and it turns into a globe. I'm staring at the whole world. It turns into nature scenes. Birds dart out of it. There is a baby two years old. I'm hugging and kissing it. All the birds die. Everything disappears. But I'm not finished kissing the baby. I'm calling "Atia! Atia!" the name my baby brother was calling me the night they took me.

On 27 January 1970, my labours with Citron and Mittelman come to their climax. Frost glistens from the branches, painting pictures onto windows; in the distance, muffler-clad skaters pirouette on an outdoor rink. Frozen to the marrow in my stripers, I track through Toronto's grimy snow; a crunching sound confirming my hesitant steps. I am thinking, this is the first time I've worked with Jews; I've never even been inside a synagogue. Mayor Dennison has proclaimed it Auschwitz Memorial Day. Soon I see people funnelling into the YMHA on the corner of Spadina and Bloor to observe the twenty-fifth anniversary of the liberation of Auschwitz. Lots of them.

Six Jewish children light candles for the six million. There are slides of atrocities. I have tears in my eyes when Sabina speaks. Now it is my turn. I pause, then step forward:

> Before being arrested, I had visited, in Jarosław, my two aunts, on errand to get for my family food. My mother had given me sheet in which to wrap up sugar. I remember it was freezing, and I was wondering if I would make it. On road, group of Jews, age sixteen to sixty, were working under guard. It was getting dark. They were doing highway duty, clearing with their bare hands snow, or with their hats or their coats, while their guards lounged around in warm clothing making sport. As non-Jewish witness to suffering of Polish Jews, I speak not for me but for them: for Jews I knew in Jarosław and Nowy Targ, for all Jews of Poland. Train after train they came, seventy-six trainloads just between 5 May 1942 and 21 May 1943. Few survived.

While I am talking, a Toronto councilman by the name of Rottenberg breaks down and cries. I wonder why it took me so long to come to this. The success is due to Mittelman's organizational skills.

The next day, all the posters are in the garbage.

Jurek joined us. Tukaj came up from Chicago. Sikorski from New York. I had invited them all. And they came! Jurek was in charge of the music. While I showed slides of the camp, he played records of Paderewski's Symphony in B minor, a musical depiction of the tragic history of Poland. Tukaj was a spectator.[6] Sikorski helped direct people to the seats.

Everybody stays with Ramona and me in our house in Missisauga, a split-level bungalow. It is the first time I have seen Ed Sikorski No. 439 since Devonport. While in the fire brigade, we had not known he was an officer in the Polish navy. Sikorski tells us, "So after the navy, I became an electrical engineer. Since then I just try to live my life, mind my own business."

It is my friend and mentor Jurek, unaware of course of his impact upon me, who gives me my first clue of what is to come. Jurek knows the workings of Auschwitz better than I do. His first job had him mixed up in the highest levels of the prisoners' administration. He had been *Kalfaktor*, personal servant to the *Lagerälteste* Bruno Brodniewicz (Head Kapo No. 1). Although Bruno was himself a prisoner, when addressing him we had to do 'hats off' like in front of an SS guard. When Bruno took a shower, the room was vacated while hundreds of prisoners waited naked outside. All he had to say was, "Fifteen strokes with an *Oxenschwanz* (an ox's penis with a steel rod inside)," and it got done. Bruno collaborated with the *Politische Abteilung*, routinely reporting any suspected resisters to the Nazi security authorities.[7]

After Bruno is put away for having had sex with an SS woman, Jurek joins the fire brigade. We hardly have one word, except on the subject of his girlfriend Rosa and the Clauberg bunnies. We work different shifts, which decreases our contact. But, primarily, we share so little because we never know who is an informer. We become friends only in the last days, after we walk away from Sachsenhausen.

"Sigmund," Jurek says, "need I remind you how the two of us learned to walk holding hands in the sick bay; how, through my connections, the two of us escaped *SS Unterscharführer* Joseph Klehr."

I have no recollection of either. I do remember Klehr, a practically illiterate guard, who would dress up in a doctor's coat, stethoscope around his neck, and, on his own accord, select prisoners unworthy of continued existence. They would then be led to the washrooms in Block Twenty where he would inject them with phenol directly into the heart muscle.[8]

"This is crazy," Jurek says in Polish. "What are you doing?! Zygmunt, is it for this I helped you get to Canada? Are you some kind of baptized Jew?" My other friends are nodding assent.

"What?! Maybe our only possible response is to react ethically," I suggest. Now Ramona nods. Camp life obviously affects people differently.

"Very commendable. What are you going to say? That those who outlived the others were the ones who were ready to adopt any means, upright or otherwise, to preserve themselves? That the finest of us remain in the camp? Is it ethical to stir up ashes that should be left to rest in peace? For what purpose?"

"Jurek, not only to recover. To rise above what we were before."

Later Ramona tells me, "You surely have changed."

Buoyed up by the success of efforts at the twenty-fifth anniversary demonstration, I have a desire to spread it. When I hear that Simon Wiesenthal, the famous Viennese Nazi hunter, is coming to Toronto, I have Henessey Tailors customize another striped jacket for Jurek. It is all in vain.

Most of my fellow officers in the Polish Ex-prisoners' Association also have what to say. They do not let up either: "Zygmunt, why are you parading around?" "Zygmunt, are you still one of us? Those Jews are clever. They can change you without your realizing it." "Zygmunt, can't you get it through your head you're playing into the hands of the Jews keeping this Holocaust thing alive!"

"Are we then against the Jews? Aren't we trying to create a new world, a world of truth, a world where life isn't in vain?"

Less than two years after that first demonstration, Mittelman dies. To the end, he was dedicated to making the memory of Auschwitz a warning for the world. I set up a correspondence with his widow, make an effort to carry on his work. The press fixes on my stripers, so my efforts achieve notice. Holocaust consciousness is a new theory, and I know my work is having an effect.

While I am working alone one evening, a straw-blond fellow strides into my real estate office shouting, "Why are you spouting all these lies! Spreading anti-German propaganda!" He approaches quickly like he is about to throw a punch.

"Don't even think of it." It is *Achtundachtzig* who answers his stare. The intruder backs down.

I take down his licence plate number and call the Toronto police. "Oh, we know about him. He's a good law-abiding citizen. Yes, we know he belongs to a neo-Nazi group."

That I am making new associations helps to overcome my disappointment with my old friends. There are those I meet at demonstrations. Then there are the socialists plying me with new ways of thinking. Our home has become a magnet for discussion and socializing. Ramona and I are living on the same street as Stephen Lewis, soon to be Ontario New Democratic Party leader and later Canada's UN ambassador. Every Sunday evening, people in shirtsleeves dance in the kitchen. Stephen Lewis is at the house. So is Cheddi Jagan, left-leaning Prime Minister of Guyana deposed by the British, probably with CIA complicity. Simon's godfather, Oscar Pfeifer, an Austrian who fought in the Spanish Civil War, is also there. He teaches Simon his swimming strokes, and some of his paintings decorate our house.

"The U.S. will force Diefenbaker to break relations with Cuba, just like they forced him to buy their rejected Bomarc missiles," a member of the Iron Workers' Union is saying.

"Why do we let them have their way?" asks the publisher of a labour paper.

"You don't *let* them," Cheddi says. "They push their way in; support whomever will kowtow."

"We had that during Batista," Ramona says.

I sit taking the whole thing in. We are making some good friends, I think. Later that night, though, people are slowly driving by, flashing lights on our house. Who is watching us?

One new friend, Max Buechler, is the son of a colonel in the German Army. He is president of a real estate company, and I have become his general manager, supervising fourteen branches, interviewing new people, training salesmen. After I start my own real estate office, Buechler also helps me. Maybe it is his form of reparations. Just the same, I think his support says a lot for both of us. He appreciates that I never raid even one of his realtors. As a way to attract salespeople, I advertise for realtors who know languages. My real estate office becomes a multi-cultural hothouse. We have over fifteen languages represented, Urdu, Pakistani, all the various western and eastern European languages.

Sigmund Sherwood Ltd. opens three offices in Toronto, one in Orillia; over sixty agents are employed. Our agency consistently outsells others in west Toronto. Those who work for me say I am a hard driver. Sometimes a client has trouble making up his mind. I say, "Look, how many times do I have to keep coming back to you? What do you mean you can't make up your mind? Are you a man or a...?" Real estate is very competitive, like the survival of the fittest. And I learned that in Auschwitz.

Saturday nights Ramona and I usually dress up and go out with the Buechlers, often to the O'Keefe Centre in downtown Toronto. We are jacket-and-tie socialists.

Now that I am taking control of my life, no longer do I live like two individuals who do not know each other. A tremendous pressure has been lifted off my chest. I feel healthy. I feel grand. But externally my relationships with my old friends are slowly coming undone, at first unnoticeably, then more conspicuously, like a piece of thread pulled from a Polish wall hanging. I tell myself, this must be a normal experience among those who examine their place in the world.

At least Ramona has no objection. *"Haga lo que quieres,* do as you like," she says. Her acceptance provides strength for the real involvement I know is yet to come. Simon is reaching the age when he, too, will begin to make a judgment. I am confident all three boys will join me when they are older.

"Don't question so much, just do." So I tell the boys. "It was well-educated people, doctors and lawyers, who most often became *Muselmänner*, committing suicide after only two or three weeks in camp. They figured out right away there was no hope for them. Ordinary workers or peasants, those who didn't realize seriousness of situation, survived best. They simply grappled on."

With the opening of memory's floodgates ever in front of my eyes stalk the once-functioning people turned into hungry animals, *Muselmänner*, walking zombies who completely lacked the will to live. *Muselmänner* were dying skeletons of men or women mumbling incoherently, disoriented, paralysed with hunger, half-crazed from beatings, with swollen eyes and swollen legs, dirty and smelling of dysentery. You recognized them by the way they shuffled:

Halt! Halt! I hear several times a night. Guards shout: Are you crazy? Beat it! or Why are you doing this? or I'm going to shoot! Each time, an inevitable rifle shot cracks the air. The guy next to me whispers, Another poor creature caught trying to cheat the Nazis by walking into the fence. One morning the *Konzentrationslager* is ablaze with news: A Polish priest went and volunteered his life for another marked for death. Who is it? Prisoner from his Block tells me in the washroom, It's Father Kolbe, he's come to the *Muselmann* stage. So Kolbe, well-known Franciscan missionary with two PhD's and publisher of an antisemitic journal *Rycerz Niepokalanej* widely distributed through the Church, here in camp just a couple of weeks, is already acknowledging, I'll never survive.

I argue it out with myself:

To this prisoner in Kolbe's own Block, his noble act was his way of committing suicide, I tell myself. Then I answer, Surely no one could be expected to have understood then the symbol Kolbe would become today, that the Roman Catholic Church would recognize in him the finest that was wartime Poland, 'the patron saint of Auschwitz'; are you in a position to say the camp explanation has more truth than the Vatican's? The first me: No, who can penetrate the heart? but a saint? granted, a saint doesn't have to be perfect; but wouldn't editing a journal containing antisemitic articles disqualify him? And I reply, Jews aren't the measure of Catholic sainthood, you know. The first me again: All the same, doesn't it eat you up inside to hear Church leaders consider sainthood for one who helped create the atmosphere that enabled the Holocaust on Polish soil? The second me: Didn't Pope Paul VI describe Kolbe as probably the brightest and most glittering figure to emerge from the inhuman degradation and unthinkable cruelty of the Nazi epoch? The first me: Paul VI? as former right-hand man to Pius XII, he was himself accused of being implicated in the Church's zeal to secure refuge for war criminals.[9] The second me: Judge each man by his own record. My *coup de grâce*: Okay, grant even that Kolbe, in replacing a Pole, Francisek Gajowniczek, was the hero the Vatican claims; isn't it still to our everlasting shame that the Vatican has no moral stance of its own to exult, and even after the fact, no theological response? though the *reasons* may not be, history's *facts* are clear: despite information concerning the systematic killing of European Jewry, there was silence from Pope Pius XII, the Vatican's former emissary to Berlin; only after long delay, in his 1942 Christmas message, the Holy See obliquely referred to the hundreds of thousands of people who, through no fault of their own and solely because of their nation or their race, have been condemned to death or progressive extinction;[10] he knew!—and never even mentioned the Jews by name;[11] then, weary silence again.

On 27 April 1941, three months *before* Kolbe's event, Marion Batko, a Polish Greek-Catholic school teacher, made an equal stir when he substituted himself for a fellow prisoner. But Professor Batko, who edited no antisemitic journal, has hardly received recognition from the Church. And the Auschwitz Museum, which made a shrine for Kolbe, hardly mentions Batko.

"Look, boys, question is: Don't we as Catholics have to do something more?"

The thought of both Batko and Kolbe perishing from starvation in the cellars of Block Eleven, later marked as the "Block of Death," pulls my mind. Certainly, they were not alone. In these early months, the whole camp was starving. Behind the *Tischlerei* or joiners' shop, where I worked, was a *Schweinestall* in which food was prepared for pigs. We devised all sorts of strategies to get at it:

What do you think of this *Luftka?* Guard is running his fingers over the contours of the naked female torso we have carved. You have, back home, son? Not old enough for this, he says, smiling at the thought. I've struck the right note. A fellow inmate catches in: Well, maybe then the wife, he suggests grinning. Yeah, right! the guard says. Okay to talk to a Nazi guard, but keep your eye out. Don't want to be caught if Kapo Balke comes in. Kapo has to worry about his position whereas the Nazi does not. Have to time it neither too long nor too short. Does he have to examine the wood like we're engaging in high finance or something? I say, It's awfully nice little job, no? And it is, too; one of our master craftsmen carved this one. Delicate, like a Chinese medical doll. Everybody's watching, got to make this good. For cigarette holder like this, you should get fair sum. Not nearly as much as you think. Who does he think he's kidding? Can't I see he's calculating the market? Careful, though, don't jump the gun. Well, it ought to be worth anyway few potatoes, *erledigt?* Okay, agreed; come out by the back door in about ten minutes. The *Luftka* disappears in his pocket. The other guys crawl back to their work, the rhythm of which seems just a touch faster. Tomorrow maybe a cigarette box or some such trinket. In the middle of the shop squats a round stove looking like a steel drum. Used for heating carpenter's glue in a double boiler hissing steam. When the Kapo turns his back, one of the guys boils his potato in the bottom. If caught, it means *selektion* for assignment to the *Strafkompanie*. In the penal company you work at the most arduous labours, always outdoors, always double time. When you inevitably stumble, you are beaten and trampled, then carried home for your last roll call. Even if you've got to soften glue, don't linger one warm second more than necessary. Later, during the bitter winter of '41, Ignacy Sikora (No. 5814) appears. Oafish *Muselmann* can hardly walk—or talk, except about food. He's assigned to our workbench, making hutches for the angora rabbits raised here. Look, we'll cut the lengths; you join them; if you don't look productive you'll be out of here. It's more an act of defiance than kindness to him. Amazing how quickly he mends merely by being sheltered from blue air of outside work.[12]

The boys think of a concentration camp as a relatively small place. Not so. Auschwitz–Birkenau, population in 1944 exceeding 135,000 inmates, encompassed the same area as an average town of 50,000.

The camp lay adjacent the town of Oświęcim, our Polish name for Auschwitz. A camp that size, however, constitutes a city unto itself. The *Konzentrationslager* contained its own Political Department, run by the Gestapo. This *Politische Abteilung* was in charge of reception, registration, interrogation, internal security, legal, records and the crematoria complexes including the gas chambers. Auschwitz had its own Administration, run by the SS. Its own Division of Labour, Bureau of Public Works, Housing, Kitchen, Sanitation, Supply and Services Departments, Waterworks. Its own hospital. Its own penal institutions—a prison within a prison. The all-important Transport Department. Even its own Agricultural Department. And its own Fire Department formed, 27 December 1941, with twelve men and eventually expanded to three trucks and three teams of nine.

A chief Nazi authority in the camp was *SS Hauptsturmführer* Hans Aumeier, *Lagerführer* from end of 1941 to August 1943.[13] These memories, chiselled into my mind, are changing my life:

Aumeier's two-storey mansion. Heavy oak double-door opens to a wide carpeted stairway. To the left, the drawing room, home to many parties.

SS Hauptsturmführer Aumeier.
Pen and ink by Fire Brigade member Edward Sokol.

Through the open sliding panels to the right, Adolph Hitler, who they say Cardinal Faulhaber credits as possessing greater diplomatic finesse and social grace than a trueborn king. When Hitler committed suicide, I believe the cardinal sent a message to all churches ordering a funeral mass.[14] And alongside this picture of *Victory Himself?* Swords and several plaques of merit from different concentration camps: Esterwegen, Lichtenburg and Buchenwald. We're here to repair doors that are sticking. You sand them down here; I'll measure and cut as I take them off upstairs, Bartośek, my journeyman, tells me. Guard lounges around smoking, first with me, then upstairs. Now what's this? A cigar box? From concentration camp Flossenbürg? I pick up the next door for sanding, tell Bartośek: Of all the hobbies, this Aumeier collects souvenirs from concentration camps. Doesn't even let me finish my sentence! Bartośek turns and, pointing at me without putting down his plane, cautions, Hope nobody saw you nosing around, Zygmunt. So this is the extent of small talk here. This Aumeier is only about a hundred fifty centimetres tall, wizened and hunched, with a Roman nose like a raven. Looks clownish in his SS officer's cap. He's in charge of the *Bunker*. When, on Saturdays, he flaps drunk through the camp prison with his metallic high-pitched croak, a painful murmur rises from the inmates. Preying at random, he selects prisoners for execution, usually by marking a big cross on his list, leaving no doubt to everyone, including the potential victim. Aumeier can't stand Poles, especially members of the intelligentsia. *Abstauben* he calls it, dusting off. Like some exterminator removing vermin.[15]

We who came into camp with an innocent belief in our own worth were soon disabused of such notions. Besides the Gestapo and SS, the Nazis established a parallel prisoners' administration:

In other camps, red triangles get put in charge; here the choice falls to the green triangles. By design. Höss' assistant, Palitzsch, handpicked the first contingent of such prisoner-administrators from the Sachsenhausen concentration camp. We've arranged it so your *Kameraden*, your own fellow prisoners, will supervise you, so there should be no complaints; they'll maintain order, distribute food, and administer the rules. The menagerie of thieves and murderers glower at us politicals with sadistic glee. By the red triangle we wear, we're first labelled as *politicals*. To distinguish us from the green triangle habitual criminals, no? Then they tell us the greens are our superiors. What's the implication of such an arrangement? To be governed by people who have no respect for property or person? What could I know? But we find out, soon enough. Don't we, for the most part intellectuals of one sort or another, picture ourselves as part of society? They picture themselves as at war with society. The regime of general corruption that these *fellows* of ours create is harder to endure than if coming from the Nazi guards. How the Nazis revel in such contradictions. Or is it just that criminals are less tiresome than us *intelligentsia*? Criminals, at least, can be counted upon for a little mayhem. One such German prisoner-administrator, an obese barber with crossed narrow eyes, is brute force, *perfect* for Auschwitz authority. Amazing that in a few short weeks Ernest Krankemann, No. 3210, has become notorious. For his one-punch elbow hit. Usually produces a cracked skull when a prisoner is placed to attention about fifteen centimetres from the corner of a brick wall. Auschwitz' version of cosmetic surgery. And I have to witness him perform for the benefit of some SS *Blockführers!* Will I ever forget the second day after Krankemann's arrival? This big heavy man goes strolling happy as a pirate on a ship. Whenever he comes across a yellow triangle, he nonchalantly clubs the Jew down. Like this is normal behaviour on any street corner. I scurry out of harm's way lest he think me a Jew. Endlessly creative, he hoses water down the throats of his victims. Or, for variation, through their rectums. The gravel yard beside the Bunker that for nine months now I am billeted next door to in Block Ten. Even though the windows are boarded, we catch an eyeful through the cracks. Krankemann harnessing his victim to a post with a five-metre line. Runs the prisoner in circles like a horse, until he falls, is pushed on, drops again, going to his knees, and is eventually kicked into the ground itself and thrown into the garbage box in the corner. Spring of 1941. To prepare for 20,000 expected new inmates, prisoners have to fill in small pond in the middle of camp. Served the Polish artillery as a place to wash horses when after Versailles they appropriated the base from the Austrians. Krankemann devises a Ben Hur chariot, below which, instead of wheels, is an old three-metre-diameter steel cylinder, filled with concrete. About fifty Jews harnessed with wires and ropes in front, another fifty priests, monks and other dangerous Poles behind. Can't help but see Krankemann riding the top beam like a Roman soldier, cracking a bullwhip six metres long. The emaciated Jews in front treadmill their legs, the heavy *Walze* barely slugs along while Krankemann shouts, On the double! cracking his *Peitsche* on their heads. They fall over one another. Krankemann metes out appropriate punishment. Before the war it took six teams of horses on either side to move the roller. Who am I sympathizing with? Jews?

After a few days, the priests escaped this duty; as I found out in the years that have gone by, due to the protests of Archbishop Adam Sapieha. What might the Church have accomplished if it had attempted to exercise a bit of clout for the Jews! After the Holocaust, some people ask, 'Where was God?' But I have an even more traumatic question, 'Where was Christianity?'

The mind that ran the camp claimed in its memoirs that it could not be responsible if those put in authority exceeded their mandate:

What's this? The Nazis use the green triangles, join in, actually. If a Kapo holds back food to elicit bribes, the SS collect part of the take. They even enlist us prisoners to clean their shoes, *organize* and smuggle for them. What goes on in the guards' minds? Is it difficult to convince themselves that we skeletal smelly dregs are inhuman? And the treatment? Having to run, then stop, then run again so the whole group crashes into one another. Great game. People stumble, fall, get trampled and killed. They've been doing it since Day One. Is it some diabolical design, though? Being a guard is boring; I can appreciate the desire to perk things up. And the stuffed airless boxcars lacking sanitary facilities, food or drink; the unnecessary frenzy of arrival with its orgy of German shouts incomprehensible to most newcomers, followed by kicks and punches; the division of families; the forced public nudity; the haircutting and shaving of women's pubic hair, mostly by male barbers; the insufficient number of latrines; the failure sometimes to provide newcomers with spoons; the ill-fitting garments. All part of the dehumanization of Auschwitz. Could it be to condition those who carry out the policies? Like the doctors making selections. Auschwitz is physical and spiritual murder, of those killed, of those who kill, and of all of us forced to witness. Inmates do have ways of getting even, though! *Lagerälteste* Leon Wietschorek (Kapo No. 30), deputy to Head-Kapo Bruno, is both cruel and stupid, a vicious combination. Didn't I recently see him beat a guy, hear his bones crack? Then a fellow prisoner tells me, Wietschorek went and pushed an iron concrete-reinforcement-rod down a Jew's throat. During the typhus epidemic, Wietschorek takes sick. An inmate confides, We took lice from a sick body and put them in his sweater; at the hospital, one of our Polish orderlies injected him with air; bye-bye. Yes! Sheer luck, that's what survival is; I hear the latest word: Between the Gestapo and the SS, or among the many levels of official and prisoner administration, papers for the first transport are lost, and Nazis don't want to admit it. So main office isn't constantly shuffling *Achtundachtzig*, or calling him for interrogation or for periodic weeding-out.

When groups of *Ślązaks* started to arrive, they had to undress on the street, dropping clothing, possessions and bread before going to the showers and having their heads sheared like spring sheep:

When the SS turn their backs, some veterans dash towards the piles. Grabbing pieces of bread, they bolt it down on the run back. Whole operation must last less than thirty seconds before guard turns around. Hunger compels me to risk it. Only crumbs. On the return, there's a prisoner still wolfing a piece. Give me half. No. I tear some from his hands and disappear. Guard does not notice. But the *Blockälteste*, looking through the window of his cubicle, does. Walking legs apart, a little bent, like a guy with haemorrhoids, he stalks me, combing Block Three section by section. Where to hide in an empty barracks? Try desperately to blend into the shadows. *Heraus! Heraus!* he yells, Out! My mind recalls *Mamusia* searching for me when once as a child I had misbehaved and hidden. Her light was poking in around the cans behind the house, causing everything it touched to sparkle. I heard her exasperated calls. Eventually she gave up. Two days later, her anger had given over to concern. This *Blockälteste* Max Küserow (Kapo No. 17) is much more determined. That's his breathing; he's systematically probing the dark air between us. Trapped. You Polish scum, he shouts, it is *verboten* to steal from a fellow prisoner. I face front, eyes downcast, conscious of the sweat eating at the back of my shirt, fearing from his reputation what is to come. To my office, on the double. The room is small but immaculate. A single window looks onto the street where we were running. He bears himself up with pride, standing like a general behind his desk. Green triangle upside down, '▲,' an ex-soldier discharged for some infraction. Finally leaning back in his chair (I still stand like a stick), folding his hands across the back of his neck, he asks, What is the problem? And without giving a chance for reply, he launches his own response: The problem is, you're not allowed to steal. *The eye is the mirror of the soul;* his betray no soul at all—only icy steel, ice and the arbitrary power of one man over another. My eyes drift to a smudge on his lapel, contenting themselves with this obvious imperfection. After a pause, they look up to catch a twisted smile playing in the corner of his mouth. A tiger. A tiger who, having tasted human blood, longs for it again. He lights a cigarette, butts it out, then orders: *Drop trou* and bend over the chair. Suddenly, with the authority of *der Führer* himself, the dispassionate Kapo's face flushes. He draws himself to full height, compels me to count in German seventeen strokes applied to my naked buttocks. A caning is supposedly milder than a birching or a whipping, which produce an open wound that can turn gangrenous if not treated. But even the first stroke at full strength is fire ... the rest, an inferno. Don't give him the satisfaction of crying out: think of other things! Anything to keep your mind off the pain. Insulted, his blows get fiercer. I'll burn you, you insolent bastard! ... Twelve. My mind reviews my life. How my father beamed the day I decided to follow family tradition and go to cadet school to become an officer. Oh, *Tatuś,* if you saw me under this cane. Thirteen. I recall *Mamusia* drilling me with my German, telling me how it would help my future. Fourteen. Why—these Nazis first starve us, then this German criminal has a mind to teach Poles not to steal. Fifteen. I ought to grab him and throttle him. Sixteen. The stirred-up dust twinkles in the sunlight streaming through the window. Seventeen. I have to bow my head to the panting *Blockälteste* and express my appreciation, *Danke schön.*

My bottom healed over time. The damage to my spirit never did.

The Buechlers, my real-estate mentor we go out with on Saturday nights, are to take us to Venezuela. Ramona and I are talking about it every day. Max loves to travel, has his own plane. In fact as a young manager for a large transport firm in Karlsruhe, Germany, he came to Canada on the first leg of a trip around the world, liked it and stayed. Still travels all the time.

For Ramona, it will be almost like going home. "I want to see the country villages in the mountains, the interior tropical forests and the coastal pearl fisheries."

"Ramona, this trip is tribute to our friendship with Buechlers." And Ramona's enthusiasm rubs off on me. I do my homework. It is the history I am interested in.

A few days before we are to leave, our boys take sick. Reluctantly we have to bow out.

Main gate at Auschwitz.
Courtesy of the State Museum of Auschwitz-Birkenau.

His plane crashes into a mountain. "Ramona, why'd he have to go and crash?"

Our boys being little, it is hard to explain to them that 'camp' was not some kind of summer holiday. The Nazis pretended that, too: "ARBEIT MACHT FREI" was the cynical slogan emblazoned in wrought iron over the camp entrance, "WORK BRINGS FREEDOM." In the camp, though, I often over-heard the Nazis vaunt among themselves another expression, "*Vernichtung durch Arbeit,* Extermination through work." That was introduced at the outset by the skinny, arrogant SS Hauptsturmführer Karl Fritzsch, *Lagerführer* through the end of 1941, who announced to us through a Ger-man–Polish translator: "The only exit from Auschwitz is *durch dem Schornstein,* through the *Krematorium* chimney."

No crematorium yet existed; the dead were buried in the municipal cemetery, so we could not comprehend his warning. "What a weird expression," I remember saying to the prisoner next to me.

Eleven: Simon

Orillia, Ontario, 1974

In the winter the boys and I go skiing. When you ascend a mountain, peaks and clouds, lakes and valleys, spread before you. Every day is different, every hour is different: sometimes you can almost stretch out and touch the neighbouring peak; sometimes a cloud veils it in mystery. We soar down the slopes together, wind in our faces, laughing. A graceful blending of body and nature, our legs absorb the changing contours of the terrain, powder flies up from our feet, our tracks become part of the scene. We are four figures of different height flying in the free. We set out early and turn in only when our fingers stiffen or our stomachs growl. "I have something hot and good ready for you," Ramona greets us.

From the beginning, Ramona and I played Spanish nursery rhymes on the phonograph during meals. They have learned to recite the poems, and all three are learning to speak both Spanish and English fluently. We decided to make each dinner a learning experience.

"Simon, how's your homework?" I ask, one dinner at the ski chalet.

"Papa, come on, this is vacation."

"I'm not nagging. Really. I'm interested in what you do. Education cuts, cleaner than anything else, Gordian knot. Don't you know Caesar's rule for life, '*Veni. Vidi. Vici.*'"

"What?"

"I came, I saw, I conquered. It's only pattern for life."

I have learned to enjoy physical work; I find it relaxing after selling houses for weeks on end. And at the cottage in Parry Sound we need an embankment, even though the neighbours tell us it is unnecessary. I decide not to take any chances. So, since we reach the cottage by boat, allowing no way to bring in equipment, we have to do it ourselves. There we are, pick and crowbars, breaking through the Canadian shield, organizing soil wherever we can find it, running it in wheelbarrows to our dike.

I can hear Simon muttering under his breath, "Some wonderful vacation! Pick and shovel."

"Yeah! We're goddamn forced labourers. Like the Jews in Auschwitz. And our own dad is Kapo," chimes in his brother Emilio, pushing a wheelbarrow.

"Shameless! Just build wall. If you lazy bums worked in Auschwitz like you do here, you'd be dead."

I later overhear the oldest tell his brother, "As soon as I can, I'm off to Lost Lake or Bald Eagle Point." He is grumbling, "Stuck nowhere, all by ourselves, working like slaves! I didn't want to come in the first place. All my friends back home are probably playing ball in the park, enjoying themselves."

"You run off in woods, and you're in for it," I call. Can anyone explain? How I look forward to some time with my boys! I schedule them in on my calendar. The days with the warmest glow are the quiet days: Ramona teaching them how to skip rocks, or me just watching them play together in the yard. They have these little characters: Colonel Custer, Johnny West, Jamie West. I love the way they set up their game. An outcropping of rocks marks the site of a homestead. A bunch of sticks becomes a ranch house. Then one guy will jaunt over to visit his range neighbour. A whole scenario develops. Emilio relishes the game, I can see; and maybe it is Simon's first step towards film-making. Whenever I observe them enjoying each other like this, I have a sudden desire to join in. Yet, often when we finally capture a minute with each other, they invariably trigger my pent-up emotion. At such a time, the longed-for opportunity ends in a disaster: my family wall-hanging fraying, the boys crying, and me not knowing what went wrong. These family events never have the dream ending I imagine.

Their lack of understanding drives me to try to bring together my passion and my life. I try to interpret to the boys what I have seen. "You think because what I tell you isn't in your school books, no such thing existed? Well, it was real. I don't want to give you bad dreams, but you can never tell when life as you know it will end." If people were to ask at that second what I want most from life, they would still receive the plain truth: "My boys should live normal life without agony I went through."

In spite of the brace Simon used to have to wear, if my eyes do not deceive me, he still walks with a barely perceptible limp. I also walk with a slight limp, an inheritance from life.

Simon turns into a voracious reader, like his Papa, so much so that he is forced to fight off the bullies defending his right to read. It is the start of his becoming counterculture, beyond the herd. Once, when fourteen-year-old Simon and I share a quiet time, a gentle patter of rain taps a background to the memories that pace through my head:

Rain! One evening in November 1941. Our Block. Recently equipped with three-tier bunks. Bits of hay linger, for until now we slept on straw on the floor. There must be some splits in the ceiling as tiny drops of rain sporadically dance through, darkening the wood floor. Despite the coal-fired stove, we are freezing in the dampness. I look up to see SS Hauptscharführer Gerhard Arno Max Palitzsch, camp executioner, blow in immaculately dressed, breeches tucked perfectly into his shining wet boots. Not even the swaying of his pantaloons can conceal his intoxication. A *Blocksperre*. Eight hundred prisoners stand to attention in ten rows, heads uncovered, the shortest in front, the tallest in the back with me. *For nothing*, for wiggling, an enraged Palitzsch begins beating a prisoner just two metres away from me. "*Schwein! Da ist der Mist!* Pig, there's the shit." My head goes wild: You can't, for no reason at all, do that, someone says. Is it me shouting those words? A swelling in my throat. Hot and red my face. I'm pushing the brute down, holding his clean-shaven boyish face to the ground. Look how his conceited eyes blaze as if to say, How dare you! So attractive this Hauptscharführer, Palitzsch. Barely old enough to be out of school; yet he, wife and kids sport on the grass outside camp. Smell his cheap cologne. Notice the veins in his neck. Feel his sweat. *Jezus-Marja*, what have I done? The air is so heavy. Yech! The nearby swamp fills my mouth. The rain greases my hands. Oh, feel his neck twist in my fingers. Just let those Nazis come and try to pull him free! How his legs kick and flail! Help me, someone. Why do all 799 prisoners stand like stuck pigs, eyes forward? Shame! Be brave! Not one stir a peg? My God, that's the emergency siren; I'll be blown away beyond recognition. Who whispers, Poor Devil? Should I grovel for mercy? Let go? Never! So your specialty is shooting two prisoners dead with one bullet: men, women and children. Other SS let Kapos do dirty work, content to look on. You, you pig, you volunteer for job. *Jezus-Marja*, let me squeeze with every ounce of strength I can still muster. My hands, they're shaking. Should I flee? Escape like a rat leaves a ship? No mooring lines to follow, no plan of action. See the electrified fence, the dark objects silhouetted in the moving lights, the sentries poised beyond. Too late! Why's everything in slow motion? See my hands float before me. Watch his long thin lips turn a purple-blue under my fingers. How his eyes protrude from his high well-groomed forehead! I am the descendant of raven killers. Ha-ha! Those limbs and eyes and death. Are those my limbs and eyes splattered about the assembly? My death? God! Oh oh, shouting: The trouble is over there. See the guards one by one bob into place. Assault rifles at the ready. From under their helmets narrow slitted eyes roam the crowd. No chance of escape. That's Kapo Krankemann from Block Eleven loping forward. When they no longer have a control over my family, will they go after *Tatuś* again? I'm lost. Krankemann's boot wafts towards me. Hold my breath! But do not loose my grip!

In Auschwitz, you learned to see without seeing, never speaking, never reacting. You had thick walls; your face revealed nothing. It was an achievement of self-mastery, or a measure of the depravity to which you can sink, to be forced to watch a person beaten or flogged until his sinews shined through the slices, and to show no trace of compassion, or outrage, or even the slightest notice. I learned this early. Blasphemous silence. You stood totally helpless and simply concentrated on not answering the call of nature that grew ever more insistent. The Nazis knew that standing by like a eunuch, with no ability to intercede, could overwhelm the inmate's spirit. You were no longer yourself. You could not alert them. Could not comfort them. Could not even hold them by the hand. For you were nothing, a wisp in the air, an accidental leftover. Once you saw an old man hit and did not respond, once you saw a fatty razzed by being made to run around in a circle like a horse, once you stood at attention while a man was kicked to death, you were implicated. By the time you had realized that it was the first stroke you should have objected to, you were so hungry and weak yourself, so mentally exhausted and morally broken, that the possibility of response was no longer realistic. You were then a prisoner, a soulless, empty prisoner. If not then, then a few months later, or days ... and your body, too, would be splayed out on the ground.

In the split seconds before the Kapo arrived, I looked out in stark fear: Palitzsch's arms and legs still thrash the form at his feet. Kapo Krankemann joins in. I'm still holding my breath. All eight hundred of us never move! It takes the full strength of my imagination to overcome the desire to act. Another light blinks out inside *Achtundachtzig.*

Fourteen-year-old Simon's words call me back to the present. I have difficulty hearing him, a legacy from camp meningitis. Should sit to the left so I can hear on the right. He is drumming his fingers, and the question blurts out in starts and stops. "Are we guilty ... Papa ... for crimes ... we didn't do?"

"For almost two thousand years, Church failed to live by its own message: love your neighbour as yourself. Instead, it preached against Jews for centuries, helping to set scene that made Auschwitz possible.[16] Then, when things got out of hand, Pope failed even to condemn murder. Only those directly involved are *guilty*. But are we *responsible* for commission and omission that even now continues? That's decision we make: to take Auschwitz to heart or to treat it as irritant to be rejected out of hand. Just decide we are not responsible and whole issue evaporates."

"Why doesn't the Church fess up?"

"This is not easy for me to discuss with you, Simon. I figure Church feels need to maintain it was blameless. Church says it *had to* stand by and helplessly support, in occupied Europe, Nazi civil authority; that doing more than saving individual souls would have been harmful to Jews."[17]

"Papa, isn't that a good point?"

"Judge for yourself. Hard to imagine how things could've been worse for Jews, or for Christian message. I ask, doesn't Church need what we call act of contrition?"

"I suppose other religions were better?"

"No better. Mind you, in 1947 Evangelical Lutheran Church, urged by Pastor Niemüller, did publish public 'declaration of guilt', then only church to do so; but still without mentioning Jews. Maybe, as some have said, Christianity emphasized obedience too much, and responsibility not enough. And it continues, Simon. Vatican has recognized since Auschwitz all kinds of countries, even Communist enemies of Church, all but State of Israel. Aren't Jews supposed to wander eternally as their punishment?"[18]

"What's with Vatican II then?"

"Pope John XXIII preached, in Second Vatican Council, tolerance.[19] It was big step forward. He also grappled with Church antisemitism by removing some offending parts of prayers. But in my opinion, later Popes don't follow it up nearly enough. And there wasn't express attention given to Holocaust or Israel. Don't we have to wonder, Simon, what it is about Christianity that causes Church to be so active in defending Nazis, though so hesitant in condemning them?"[20]

My survival in the camp, of course, was mainly due to the fact I am Roman Catholic and not Jewish. I think the boys have trouble appreciating the full implications of this. They are not to blame. They grew up in a world where their greatest crisis was failing to make the hockey team. And they are not stupid. Like reaching out to touch a mountain peak, they can see clearly enough my work's effect on Ramona and the family. The cause, though, remains for them shrouded in mist.

When it was pointed out to me that wherever I have been, favourable circumstances have resulted, I had to stop and think. In Auschwitz, I rose to *Scheissmeister*, then *Stubendienst*, then *Gruppeleiter*. In England, for my service in the navy, I earned a scholarship. In Canada, during my first years, I became a foreman in the fish factory, then rose to welding foreman making high tension towers. In Cuba, I headed a welding crew. Back in Toronto, I ascend to real estate manager, then owner of my own company. *Something* has been with me. *Something* gives me a Midas touch. *Something* leads me to find approval in the eyes of others. Is it God, or is it something more mundane?

They say sheep nibble themselves lost. Like a lost sheep, success brings me, nibble by nibble, to spend like there is no tomorrow. Ramona has had three trips to Cuba. I have seen to that. We take a family vacation in the Bahamas, driving from Toronto to Miami, finding every gas station rest room God ever invented. We also stop with the boys at all the tourist sites along the way, revelling in their excitement, enjoying our own. Emilio says, "I loved flying kites off the back of the *SS Monarch Sun*. With the boat moving and all, we didn't even have to run. And then dropping off in Disney World on the way back. Since everything on the trip was sort of new to everyone, we all shared. No one had one up on the other. Only, it must have cost you one helluva pretty penny."

Then there is a six-hundred-foot shoreline vista in the Bahamas. The deep blue Bahama sea has drawn me back along with a lady realtor I am training. A local realtor shows us properties on the island of Eleuthera. "These are something to die for; you can sell them in Canada," he advises. The next day I discover a beach-front property inherited by a servant who now lives in Spain. When my friend goes to Spain and makes a deal with him, I rejoice in my good fortune.

As a direct result of a too-carefree attitude, I soon have financial problems. But whether sirloin steak or thin soup, as far as material matters are concerned, you have no choice but to accept what life dishes out. After Auschwitz, financial failure is not the worst tragedy.

Other problems are more tragic by far. It is the start of the most wrenching event of my marriage. To put it up front, Ramona has her way of handling every issue, I mine: she closes the store; I go shopping elsewhere. Fact: in the brief time of training my new partner, weird and wonderful things start to happen. Fact: I do not measure up as I should. I have an extended affair.

I am forced to tell Ramona because I am seriously considering leaving. "It's something that's been bothering me for long time. I don't want to hurt you, but there's another woman."

"What?"

"It isn't you. I just don't know what I want, what life is supposed to be like. I thought, I thought when liberation came, when I got out, everything would sort itself out. There'd be woman, like you; I'd have family; everything would be smooth, nothing would touch us; we'd live for the hour, not bothered by outside concerns. But life didn't turn out way I thought it would."

"Why?" she grimaces.

"I don't know what I was looking for even. Nothing, perhaps. Excitement. I don't know. Then I met my real estate partner."

"Your *partner!* No wonder you are never in the house."

"That's not it. I was working, long before I met her, long hours—working to have good home with bright rooms and backyard boys can play in, working to send you to Cuba when you want, working."

"Think that is what I wanted? Being alone all of the time, raising the children by myself? I no ask you to work all the evenings and the weekends; that is you. Know something, Simo? Sometimes during the night I sit facing the door; the clock chime and I worry someone attack you. There is not much doing, but waiting for you to come home, I sit and make up something cheerful to tell you. I think he has to go to one of his meetings. But instead, you are out with this woman."

"This is new."

"No wonder you pick on me; you no realize it, but lately nothing I do can please you."

"Please, Ramona, you are making it so hard."

"Is she prettier than me?" she asks softly.

"Please, Ramona."

"Is she? Is she prettier than me? I have to know."

I scramble to get an answer. "She makes me want to be with her."

"So you want to leave your wife and your children?"

"No! Yes. I don't know. Give me time to think." I leave, for a day, two days, come back, then go again. There is a lot of crying and shouting. Each time I leave, I think of Ramona, and then I feel guilty.

"Simo, your place is here. I have thought it out. I no come from Cuba to divorce you."

"I'm confused. Leave me alone for while, I don't know what's happening."

"You can no keep popping back and forth." I see her hands curl up into fists.

"I have to think."

"Okay, you think of the boys; they realize what is going on."

Ramona does not go with another man; and when the time comes, she takes me back, accepting my fingers in her hair until they are lost in the forest. That is Ramona. But it is the Fall of Sigmund Sherwood. Within a year of the Buechler's plane crash, I gather the family, pack our goods, and go with what we have in the car.

The corn and lettuce crops of Ontario soon give way to the long expansive flat monotonous lonely treeless ribbon of yellow waving prairie grasses empty of beast or human punctuated with occasional stretches of dry moonscape badlands and tiny little repetitious towns each with its own set of grain elevators along a single railroad siding which finally ends in Calgary, the city of the Stampede, at the base of the majestic Canadian Rockies. We arrive in peace, take a plot of land, spread our tent.

We come to Calgary at the end of the summer, yet we are all amazed to see the mountains on the western horizon still capped in white. I have timed our arrival so the boys can enter school with the least disruption. As for me, I am in limbo again. Until I get my realtor's licence, I do some welding. About this time, I also come to realize that even in Auschwitz there was Something; there must have been. Not that I was more deserving than anyone else. But the fact I survived does show God's grace. And I survived without succumbing to Nazi methods. "Come to mass with me," Ramona says.

"Okay."

The shards cannot remain at my feet forever.

It is 1978, and Calgary is experiencing an economic boom. Soon I am a member of the Calgary Realtor million-dollar-sales club. We buy a small house, then another, somewhat bigger. "Simo," Ramona says, "dealing in private homes is no way to live if you want a family life. You research the market all day, attend open houses, take clients out every evening, Saturdays and Sundays."

It is true. I am at the beck and call of my pager. Cannot even go to Mydlarski, my tailor, without jumping, amid fabric cuttings everywhere, to use the phone. If only he could, as a Jewish survivor, sew the threads of my life's relationships together.

"I'll look at commercial real estate, something with normal business hours." The choice includes selling rural hotels. Still having trouble making friendships, I do not get to know the people in my office very well. But I do an energetic business. It is boom time. Soon I am number three in the city. In my first year with Canada Trust, I earn a holiday trip to Costa Rica as top salesman; in the next year, Hawaii. After only two years in Calgary, after Ramona's fourth trip to Cuba when she found out her sister had died without her knowing, I can go and say, "Ramona, I've managed to pay off all our debt at Toronto banks, and even to put away few dollars. Hotel is available in Fort Macleod that seems sweet deal. How would you like to open family business? I'll run hotel and tavern, if you can take care of, please, restaurant. In our country, I knew lots of such rural inns; and I've become more familiar with hotel business through selling real estate. This looks like good one; could lead to many trips."

"Simo, what do I know about a hotel?"

Before buying the Fort Macleod hotel, we take the summer and go back to the Georgian Bay, the only return after Calgary. A new neighbour bundles along, swaying sideways, the typical movement of a person during a lengthy climb. My first assignment in the *Tischlerei* runs through my mind:

Tall and skinny. Oh, what was his name? Number 101. Think! Same kind of walk. Mephistophelian smile on his slightly twisted face. Józef. Yeah, Józef Chramiec. He is a journeyman carpenter, not bad either, not like one of those just looking for a better job. I am his apprentice. Has many callers who whisper. My type of guy, Chramiec. Specializes in crafting skis for the SS men, especially the officers. *Lagerkommandant* Höss wants skis for his wife and all five children. It's fitting! Höss's nose, narrow at the top, broadening widely at the bottom, looks like a ski jump. Later, we make doors. Heavy doors. About five centimetres thick. As assistant, my job is to file around the spy hole. Chramiec explains, The hole, small on the outside, flares out on the inside so they can monitor without prisoners checking them in return.

The best time to talk with my boys is on vacation. We are sunbathing on the dock. "Simon, we used to install doors in Bunker with wrought iron hinges. Also went and installed them in *Krematorium I*, later called 'old crematorium.' 'Old' because, in contrast to those that got built in Birkenau, one in main camp only had three-hundred-person capacity. Over to right of ovens, was large mortuary where they stored bodies before cremation. We were called back three or four times over next many months. Had to reinstall doors to gas chamber. 'It's the water,' Chramiec told me, 'those who die by gas lose bowel control, so they need to hose the floor after each gassing; that, in turn, swells the doors.' [21] How we in *Tischlerei* looked forward to Kapo Balke assigning us to crematorium complex! Twelve Poles and Polish Jews working there supped over half cauldron of soup. Whole cauldron usually served what, fifty prisoners? No way they could put away all of it. So when guard went for cigarette, there we'd sit on bloated, stinking bodies, men, women and children, their limbs shifting underneath us until we'd adjust our position. Finally resting normal, like that is way everybody sits, we stuffed ourselves with leftovers."

"Gross! Like, how could you do it?"

"To get extra soup was more important than corpses. 'Balke,' we'd say, 'please send us again.'" [22] I can see he is disgusted with me. "Simon, I only hope you never face such choices. Look, we saw every day bodies being loaded for burning: one body hands at sides, a second laying in opposite direction with its legs on first one's head. It became so commonplace, you understand, I got used to it. This was small second-rate crematorium with only four or five ovens. And it's still there. *Krematorium I, 'Das kleine Krematorium,'* with

Gas chamber of old crematorium.
Photo courtesy of Bob Krieger, Vancouver.

connecting gas chamber was being used by Germans as air-raid shelter in 1944 and was spared destruction from retreating SS."

"Wait, were they just inmates who had given out from hard labour getting cremated," Simon asks through a mouthful of apple, "or newcomers?"

"Yeah, during first winter as many as hundred per day were dropping off 'naturally' from rough treatment, lack of food and medical attention. In fall of 1941, when installing doors, gassings began in small crematorium. Then, trainloads of Jews started coming from Silesia. I saw it all."

Then and there I decide that each of my boys will visit Auschwitz.

When we get back from our summer at the cottage, it is time to pack up: emptying closets, wrapping glassware, filling boxes, a few sticks of people waiting for the van in a bare house. I cannot help but think of the night I was taken, the Nazis rifling through my *Tatuś*'s desk, ripping open all the drawers; I have done a lot of moving in my life. And then the dislocation at the other end: Ramona's vase from Cuba is broken; my shaver disappears for weeks; the boys mope around without friends. I hate it all.

When we move to Fort Macleod, the old perennial problems with Simon crop up; he refuses to do his share in the hotel. This is a family enterprise. For some reason I cannot figure out, the closer he gets to the age I was in Auschwitz, the more irresponsible he appears to get. Simon is in his first year at Lethbridge College, a short distance from Fort Macleod where he lives with us at the hotel. By the time a young man reaches college, some sense of discipline should have sunk in. Otherwise, strict measures have surely to be taken to avoid future problems. I do the necessary and throw him out; put him up in another hotel. In complete silence, at 2 a.m., I drive him and his suitcases the forty-five minutes to Lethbridge.

He storms and rages, his brown eyes flashing. "You've never been there for me. You just want me to be an example for the others, to force me to go and do things I don't want to do, ever."

I tell Ramona later, "Okay, he doesn't want to share with everyone else in hotel responsibilities. He's on his own." Her face boils anger. And Simon does not visit us for three full months.

Naturally, the Papa pays for the hotel at first, so Simon is living on his own at Papa's expense while going to school. Many teens might wonder, "What's the punishment?" I want him to recognize that to get along in this world people depend on each other. What did I survive for, if not for that?

Eventually, he gets his own job. But instead of feeling a need for family, he learns to count only on himself. It is not what I meant to happen. Am I destined to die bereft of my son?

On the fortieth anniversary of the 1943 Warsaw Ghetto uprising, again asked to represent the Polish Political Ex-prisoners' Association, I am back for a second visit wearing my stripers. Ceremonies take place in the little green park at the corner of Zamenhof and Anielewicz streets. My sister Basia, the Canadian ambassador and I parade a large Canadian flag. Dominating the plaza is an eleven-metre bronze memorial to the Ghetto's Jews who held out for forty-two days and nights, longer than all Poland before the raven onslaught. Two menorahs, symbolic of Judaism and the State of Israel, flank the Warsaw Ghetto memorial. The slab of Swedish granite on which they sit is the same one Hitler ordered for a Berlin victory monument he never got to build. And all around the park, postwar apartments mark the spot below which lie the bones and ashes of tens of thousands of Jews who perished in the Ghetto.

The commemorative ceremonies; renewed fellowship with relatives and friends; an obligatory visit to Auschwitz-Birkenau; the opportunity to reacquaint myself with the Polish countryside, checking out the village inns for our new business back home; and searching Warsaw for Irka—all squeeze me dry.

I meet a former prisoner. "Do you know what happened to Auschwitz's Ben Hur?" he asks.

"Krankemann? No, what?"

"In the power struggle between the camp *Kommandant* and the head of security, Krankemann sided with the latter. So when Höss won, he ordered a search. In Krankemann's quarters, they found gold dental crowns and six thousand *Deutschmarke* in the leg of a heavy oak table. Krankemann was sent with a transport of invalids to concentration camp Grafeneck. Some say six prisoners held his head in the door of a boxcar. Others say the prisoners hanged him. Either way, he arrived at Grafeneck dead." [23]

The return flight frightens me. In Frankfurt, changing from LOT Airlines, I kill time wandering the many duty-free shops buying some good whisky, cigarettes and PARFUM No. 5 CHANEL PARIS for Ramona. I never go away without bringing Ramona something. Lufthansa extends a hospitable flight home. To give my pulled left leg stretching room, I get my usual seat on the right side of the second aisle.

"Is the gentleman comfortable, sir?" asks a courteous young blonde in polite German.

"Fine, fine, *danke schön*."

"Can I help the gentleman with a pillow?"

"Yeah, thank you."

"Would the gentleman like a drink before dinner?" After meal service, the young lady circuits again. "Would the gentleman like coffee or tea? Anything else to make the gentleman comfortable?"

She smiles like a dear friend. My mind wonders what her father was doing during the war when the German language I was treated to was anything but polite. "Thank you, everything's fine."

An American movie flashes onto the screen. After a quick glance, whatever it is about does not catch my interest. I prop myself with the miniaturized version of a pillow airlines like to distribute. Then I flip on the private light, rummage pen and paper from my carry-on, and begin another article, this one about my latest visit to Poland. Onto my internal silver screen are projected reruns of my recent experience:

The apartment of my two old aunts in Jarosław just like I remembered it, its indoor washroom behind a curtain, its richly tiled fire wall by the old round heating stove. The communal well around the corner where, on summer visits during my youth, I watched the servants fetch water in two buckets suspended from a wooden shoulder harness. The picture of my mustached grandfather, straight and tall, who had designed the Jarosław home with its unusual copper-roofed turret. The synagogue in Warsaw with its arched doors and windows, carved wooden pillars and crowns, and great domed ceiling arcing over the holy ark. My oh-so-futile search for Irka. An argument with the Auschwitz Museum director.

One period's vision meshes with another's. The plane's pressurized cabin transmutes into a gas chamber packed with people. Far in the distance, I hear a father calming his whining young son. Others cough. A high-pitched beep announces the placement of the Zyklon B canisters. A rush of gas is heard.

Instead of screams, the beep is followed by a hollow voice over the speaker system: "Please fasten your seat belts and return your seat backs and table trays to the upright position." I wake with but two lines on my paper, barely in time to shove my things away. Across the seats to my right, I catch the sweeping countryside tilting against the looming Rockies as the plane banks on its descent into Calgary.

What I return to is more frightening. Eckville, a town of 890 people in rural Alberta, makes page two of the *New York Times* thanks to a high school teacher. There are Holocaust deniers all over the world; Keegstra is one of ours. Welcome home! Happy Birthday! It is 26 May 1983.

Thinking of Simon, a young man in the same shoes as James Keegstra's students, helps me clarify my own response. I slip into my stripers, and using the organizational techniques I learned from Mittelman, call a press interview with the *Lethbridge Herald:* "Just having got back from Auschwitz, I publicly offer Keegstra free trip to camp."

Simon says, "Papa's response to Keegstra gives me my first true understanding of my father."

A newsman conveys the offer. As I would find out, the affable Keegstra just shrugged and never answered. Keegstra has been teaching there were no extermination chambers: Hitler knew Jews were far safer in concentration camps than outside where undisciplined soldiers might attack them. No survivor witnessed his relative inside of a gas chamber. All he actually saw was someone being led off somewhere. Even what looks like verification for the existence of gas chambers could have been fabricated after the war when the camps in Poland lay inaccessible behind the Iron Curtain. "That is why I declined the offer to visit the European concentration camps," he tells Stanley Barrett.[24] He has fashioned his mental constructs so no personal confession, no eyewitness testimony, no on-the-ground facts, no accumulation of evidence no matter how voluminous, can ever prove otherwise.

It is not just the drivel. I keep thinking, what if Simon had a teacher like that? The district school board dismissed Keegstra for failing to comply with the board's directive: "Follow the Alberta Social Studies curriculum and cease teaching the Jewish Conspiracy ideology as if it were a fact." Keegstra, popular Mayor of Eckville, with the support of the Alberta Teachers' Association, lodged an appeal with the courts. I decide that Simon and his brothers will have reason to be proud of their father.

"Keegstra threatens our community," I say. "Those who were never there, who tell you history on basis of ideology, know better than liberators, better than confessed Nazis, better than we surviving victims. *Achtundachtzig* is answered by all those who know better than I."

"Well, what was the Holocaust? I mean, the Holocaust is a name of a movie." This, out of the mouth of Stephen Stiles, a member of our provincial Legislative Assembly.

Newspapers quote a university-educated Eckville businessman: "Keegstra is a good man, a sincere man, who has been greatly maligned by the media. Keegstra is not antisemitic, but only anti-Zionist. He doesn't deny that Jews were killed in the Holocaust, but only questions the numbers—perhaps seven hundred thousand or so, rather than six million." Like Keegstra himself, he believes "Keegstra's undoing only came about because of his Christian orientation."

A report quotes a devout member of the Christian Reformed Church. "Keegstra turned out more Christian students than did the majority of actual Christian Bible schools. Everything that Keegstra says about the Jews is absolutely correct."

The same report tells us a local farmer and devout Christian, a member of the United Church, philosophized, "It is absolutely essential if democracy is to survive that there are alternatives to the public education system. There is no record that Hitler ordered Jews to be destroyed. Keegstra is simply an extraordinarily competent teacher, and he threatens other members of his profession."

"We have no other choice than to defend Keegstra; he has to be presumed innocent until proven guilty," reasons the Alberta Teachers' Association. It is as if Keegstra denied teaching his belief in a Jewish conspiracy and the nonexistence of the Holocaust, instead of bragging about it.

Edwin Olsen, the principal, has defended Keegstra throughout, and finds him an "inspiration" to students previously uninterested in their studies. Olsen is said to have remarked that, since he himself is not Jewish, Keegstra's antisemitic thrust is not his concern. "Keegstra is a God-fearing person who had no intention of indoctrinating the students. I'd be happy to see him reinstated."

Now I feel like the attack is against me as a parent and a Canadian. I initiate an active program of writing letters to every newspaper and journal in the province.

The judge decides Keegstra "refused to comply with the lawful and reasonable direction of his employer."

Keegstra blames Madame Justice Elizabeth MacFayden's judgment on "the Zionists," alleging the decision proves a Jewish conspiracy does exist. "She had no choice. It was either me or her."

Meanwhile, Keegstra is elected national Social Credit Party vice-president, only to find himself suspended by an unusually wary leader. Ninety-four of the 116 senior high school students have petitioned in favour of their teacher. They like the man, and agree with what he has taught them.

How is it possible so many people cannot distinguish between personality on the one hand, and racist views on the other! They think if a man is evil, he must be a monster; so conversely, if Keegstra is a nice guy, then his ideas must have some merit, too. Such a perspective minimizes the Keegstra threat. James Keegstra represents a living practical instance of a supposedly theoretical impossibility, one I saw many times in the *Konzentrationslager*: the fusion of Nazi thought and Christian theology.

Keegstra is the son of Dutch immigrant farmers, both members of the Social Credit Party.[25] In his youth, Keegstra studied the works of C. H. Douglas, the party's founder. Simon is interested enough to ask questions. I explain, "C. H. Douglas blamed failure of his theories on Jewish conspiracy, and once wrote Adolf Hitler accusing 'the Jewish financial system of sowing discord between countries.'"

Keegstra, a sincere and otherwise virtuous person, searched the Christian Bible as a teenager to 'discover' Jews are essentially anti-Christian. He found they believe it sinful to sell a farm or to give a gift to a Christian. Any evidence to the contrary is an individual aberration. Through his subsequent study, he also discovered that Zionists both command the apparatus of capitalism and inspire the rise of Communism. It is they who caused the Second World War and fabricated the Holocaust.

Keegstra depicts himself as "a bit of a Calvinist." By this he indicates his belief that, since the spiritual and mundane cannot be separated, he feels obliged to get involved publicly as a Christian. "It would be impossible for me to teach outside the parameters of the Christian faith. I wonder if the entire mess is anything more than a massive Jewish attack on my Christian principles." He says:

> I say that whites are where they are and have a better standard of living, have a better, and have more freedom and all these things and therefore are in that sense blessed—they have been blessed by God because they, in their culture and that, they do follow Christian principles and institutions and this kind of thing. Now, I'm saying that the blessings which we have … is simply because of … the Christian factor. I'm not saying that we are superior. I'm saying that we are receiving blessings which I'm beginning to think now that we don't deserve, because—but you see how I would explain it; rather than on a race basis, I'm saying no, it's religious basis.[26]

In this, Keegstra actually returns to Nazism's earliest philosophical roots. Christian white-supremacy is what prevailed a century before Nazism adopted and spread biological racism.

Out come my stripers again, this time for visits to Alberta schools. Two mothers, Marg Andrew and Susan Maddox, have been standing alone in a small community. It was Andrew who had originally sent class notes documenting Keegstra's antisemitism to the school board superintendent. And it was Maddox who had lodged the first formal letter of complaint. Slowly, others now begin to follow suit. Of note: the Alberta Teachers' Association, which had been so zealous in contesting Keegstra's dismissal, has finally begun hearings into whether he should forfeit his teaching certificate.

When the ATA eventually orders his suspension, the indomitable Keegstra launches another appeal. Then with a ninety percent turnout, Keegstra loses his position of mayor, 278 to 123. "The Zionist Conspiracy," he claims, has again engineered his defeat. And belatedly, the Province of Alberta has brought an action against Keegstra under the Canadian Criminal Code for promoting hatred against an identifiable group. Now "Bud" Zip, a Conservative member of the provincial legislature, follows Stiles by announcing that six million is a trumped-up figure. Both 'apologize', so retain their positions.

"You were in Auschwitz; were there crematoria in the camp?" The speaker looks familiar: pocked face, reddish complexion, blonde, about fifty-five years old, slim. It is Keegstra's criminal trial, and I, together with members of the Jewish Defense League and two Dutchmen, am demonstrating at the Red Deer courthouse. She places me first. Now her heavy German accent jogs my memory. It is my teller from the bank in Toronto where I had had financial difficulties. She has travelled from back east to support Keegstra.

"Yes, of course," I answer, unaware of her design.

Her line of debate gives the impression of careful planning; it has to, for here she does not embody the authority of the bank. The massive columns of the courthouse dwarf us, just two individual citizens. "What did they use for fuel?"

What an effective question to cast doubt on your testimony! Most witnesses would have been too far away to note. I answer, "Sometimes coal, sometimes coke." A few people have gathered around.

"How would you know?"

"I saw them. I was in them."

I can feel her surprise. "You were in a crematorium? Well, isn't that fortunate?" she says. Then she turns on me, giving me half a smile. "Tell us, what was it used for?"

It is hard to discern what point she is hoping to make. "Burning corpses from gas chambers."

"You witnessed that?" she triumphs, her voice radiating the assurance of one convinced.

The sign in my hands suddenly grows intensely heavy. For her, the only proof would be if you yourself were gassed, but then you are unlikely to testify very well. My thoughts burn like drops of hot wax. For this, I endured four-and-half years in Auschwitz! The words just tumble out, tripping over themselves as if tiptoeing on hot sand, braking by the side of the woman, now bereaved. "Yeah, I wasn't member of *Sonderkommando* working in gas chamber, but I am witness: With my own eyes I watched from all over Europe trains roll in. Each day when I went to joiners' shop, they were there, marching from station, this wave of colour, hundreds of Jews in its tow, while only few people were added to prisoners working in camp. Then I saw in small crematorium their gassed bodies. I remember a pregnant body, young, her stretched belly taut. And when I came back at night, another river of Jews spilling out from trains, no firm ground under their feet, no stopping for rest. You picked wrong person to try and demonstrate your theories on. I witnessed with my own eyes gas chambers, even installed and reinstalled doors." I shove the words down her throat, feel the blood coursing my temples like a drum roll. The words are coming without my head intervening. I cannot stop, cannot stop, cannot stop. "Saw corpses—newcomers, not emaciated prisoners— waiting for burning. Saw crematoria, saw burning. Saw, when checking fire extinguishers in the later years, warehouses of goods: eyeglasses and shoes and hats and mountains of children's clothes. As part of fire brigade, when *Sonderkommando* revolted, I was present at gas chamber–crematorium putting out fire; saw whole thing. I saw and smelled, repeated day after endless day, after each train came in, smoke belching from chimneys. When smokestacks were cracking from nonstop burning, wide iron straps were mounted onto chimneys to prevent them from falling apart. Piles of gassed bodies waited disposal." Bystanders applaud my retort. It rolls through my ears. I pause, then finish off exhausted: "I'm not Jewish;

161

got no axe to grind. Unfortunately for your theory, I was there."

I try to explain it all to my son, Simon. In affidavits at the Nuremberg war crime trials, Höss vaunted his efficiency. He claimed that under his supervision there were two-and-a-half million deaths by gassing and burning, and another half million by starvation and disease.[27] The Soviet government, which investigated the camp after the Red Army liberated it in January 1945, put the figure murdered during Auschwitz' years of operation as four million. These being mostly Jews, the total figure the Nazis murdered would soar above the six million usually quoted. However, Höss later gave lesser numbers.[28] Many think he exaggerated in his first figures. Having been there, I think he understated his second figures. Whatever the exact number, Auschwitz was the biggest and most infamous murder factory in history. No one really knows the total figures: six million plus or minus.

Strangers say my firstborn, tall and slim, looks like me—arched eyebrows, full-bridged nose, strong. In fact, some people say that, except for the ears, we both resemble Star Trek's Mr. Spock. After a few detours, Simon will finish Montreal's Concordia University with honours in film making.

"Simon, you're interested in cinematography and imagery; if you want to understand what six million means, look out your window. Here they come, men, women and children; five abreast every five seconds; all day, all night; seven days per week; month after month of marching day and night; twenty-four hours per day, 365 days per year; almost two years of steady marching past your window, to be exact, twenty-two months, three-and-half weeks— 694.44 days. Boys, scholars can debate up or down actual numbers. Event is what was, and is, important."

We distribute leaflets outside of the court until the judge enjoins against our action for fear "it might prejudice the jury." After I leave the courthouse steps, I hear another Torontonian shows up. Ernst Zundel, worldwide purveyor of anti-Holocaust literature, parades in front of the court with a sign proclaiming "Freedom of Speech."[29] He faces his own legal problems in Ontario and West Germany. My co-worker on the twenty-fifth anniversary celebration of Auschwitz's liberation, Sabina Citron, launched a prosecution against the hate-monger. When I find out Zundel was there repaying Keegstra for testifying for him during his own earlier trial, I regret missing the opportunity to confront him.

For Alberta and its government, the Keegstra affair and the hatred it brings to the surface is a time for soul-searching. Keegstra believes his difficulties result from the strength of the "Zionist Conspiracy."

Nie pozwalam; as a Polish Catholic survivor, I cannot allow such a gross misstatement to pass. His ability to teach his warmed-over theories for fourteen years in the public school system; the failure of anyone to find his philosophy objectionable enough to protest; the belated response of government and churches when complaints finally arose; and the presence of countless Keegstra supporters within and out of government—all illustrate to me the strength of antisemitism even after Auschwitz.

Jurek, after all these years, still brands my stripers "a publicity stunt." I am offensive to my own people. True, the idea spawned from some Austrian protest I had read about. But when I put that uniform on, it is like I have one foot planted back in Auschwitz. I am *Achtundachtzig*. The mountain peaks come close again. I am those who have perished. The stripers are my form of the Jewish *kaddish* for my cadet school friends who perished, for our family friend I could not help, for the Jarosław student beaten to death because he did the big job in his pants due to dysentery. I remember the women with children in tow. I remember one father carrying his son and a broken piece of crutch. I remember husbands calling for wives, sisters for brothers. I remember those looking back for the truck with their suitcases, books or samovars, bags of care and betrayals, pettiness and concern, forever dragging ant-like past our Block. An endless rosary of Jews filing towards nothingness.

Twelve: Vladimir

Fort Macleod, Alberta, 1984

pon taking over the American Hotel, we decided to appeal to a Native clientele. In the tavern, which stretches over the whole of the first floor, we displayed a gallery of Aboriginal art, installed a big TV screen and pool tables, and laid new carpets. Even years after liberation, walking on a carpet is still something special to me. Outside, a huge spear-carrying, befeathered Indian standing beside his faithful horse, both silhouetted by a full moon, festoons the façade of the red brick hotel. We sponsored the Peigan band's hockey team, and helped support the Blood tribe's educational system.

Being inexperienced, at the slightest sign of a brawl, I called in the RCMP. They responded right away. After several calls, they explained to me they are not a bouncer service. The bouncers I hired caused more problems than they solved. Subsequently, the RCMP did post officers outside the tavern.

Fort Macleod was the initial RCMP post in Canada, until this time considered the model for the others. New recruits who frequently get their first posting here were not prepared for the American Hotel. The RCMP presence, which I initially sought, soon became a problem. In the course of one year, by personal count, the Mounties entered the hotel 259 times 'checking on' patrons. I interpreted that as harassment of our clientele; the RCMP accused me of pampering Natives.

"What's wrong with pampering once in while customers?" I asked, and then continued, "By law, you can't drive with open liquor. Is it open if locked in trunk? Yes? Come on. I mean, that's abusing Natives." And this is where Ramona tells me I made my biggest mistake. "What's happened to six hundred some-odd cases confiscated from private cars?"

"We keep it for evidence."

"Show me where."

Too late to catch back the words, I watched them slap a fine on me.

In a bus stuffed with drumming Indians, we 'rode the warpath' to Edmonton where I spoke for Native rights.[30]

"I earned it," fourteen-year-old, dimple-chinned Vladimir insisted, jutting out his chin like General Motors had installed him as their newest president. You could have balanced a Chinese figurine on it.

"Five hundred dollars," I yelled, "under your pillow? Where your mother finds it?"

"Guess so."

"How?"

"None of your business. Don't worry about it."

I could feel the blood pound behind my eyes. Ramona was saying to me, "I was so mistaken, I thought Fort Macleod was a great town with such nice kids, I let Vladimir do what he wants."

After a long interrogation, Vladimir finally said, "A man, he gave me a small package to deliver to Lethbridge."

"What's his name?"

"How should I know?" Vladimir mumbled, looking like a puppy who just messed the carpet.

As a father, situations like this always find me unsure of myself. I have spoken with other parents in this position, and they concur. "You don't know his name, but he went and handed you five hundred dollars? Cash?" I screamed, waving the bills at him.

"Sigmund, easy," interjected Ramona.

"Ramona," I shouted whirling around, "we don't need referee." Then turning back, "Vladimir, a guy you don't even know gave you five hundred dollars?"

"Yeah, that's right."

"Doesn't that seem funny?" Ramona still hovered over and I knew I had shouted at the wrong person.

"No."

We both groaned. I could not detect even a flicker of doubt or remorse. "What! And you had no idea what was in package? You think you can guess?"

"No."

"Give back, today, this money." I was wagging the bills at him again.

"I won't."

"You'll catch it if you don't," I said, now shaking my fist in his face.

"Can't."

"Why in *Jezus*' name not?"

"Because."

A withering look on my part.

"Because he's gone," Vladimir whispered.

"And you got no idea where he went, or what was in that bag?" I was aware it was not simply a matter of teenage pride; fairly likely he saw nothing wrong. Much rumbles in a father's mind, "How did I fail?" being prominent.

Ramona told me later that night, "Do not worry. Vladimir will not do it again."

I was the one to initiate the next step. I gathered the family, then arranged an appointment with Leonard Zenith, my Calgary lawyer, who I knew volunteered with teens in his synagogue. I never told Vladimir why we were going.

"When we moved to Fort Macleod," I told Zenith in front of everybody, "we were both busy with opening hotel. Vladimir started to stay at 'friends' houses, come in late, all kinds of things. We never allowed this before." It was true. Once when Simon was around sixteen, he had phoned to say he was sleeping over at a friend's house. We spoke to the parents; agreed. Then nervous, we had both looked at each other and jumped in the car. Simon was already bathing, but we took him home anyway. Then when this happened, we were caught up in the middle of the Keegstra affair.

Zenith laid down the legal implications.

A year and much trouble later, Vladimir quits high school with only three months left, floats God knows where. We dig around for clues: missing clothes, stolen money. "Sigmund," Ramona says, "Vladimir is in trouble. Maybe one of those druggies, something too horrible to imagine."

All the 'maybes' of modern living flash before me. I suspect he is 'doing his thing'. But, I confess, I am not sleeping well. It matters little *why* your son is out there, that is when things can happen. What self-defence can a teenager marshal? I see him hitchhiking, a car stopping to pick him up. My mind prevents me from conjuring up what happens next. Although I keep my fears from Ramona, I worry plenty. And with every passing day it gets worse. How much power one person holds over another! How many names of his friends do I know? Not many. Those I manage to contact know nothing.

The school phones to find out why Vladimir has been sick.

"I'd love to know," I tell them.

Ramona and I check his hang-outs. We are in this together now. Mutual recriminations have given way to a common fear that draws us back to each other. No one we talk to has a lead. "Here's our number. Contact us immediately if you hear anything at all."

People are speculating. Every foolish remark fuels Ramona's mind: Vladimir is laying dead somewhere. Someone has kidnapped him (if that is true, they will be calling soon, so every time the phone rings we jump; it does not have to ring twice). He is drugged (that part seems plausible). The baby-faced boy has been turned into some male sex-slave; God knows what. I am certain that, like me, half the things she imagines she dares not utter. We hang on every newscast, check the hospitals, scour the papers, everything but call the RCMP. Is he wandering around somewhere sick, a sleepwalker suffering amnesia amid hundreds of thousands, any one of whom threatens to do him harm? Lost in the bush, leg broken, a prey to some animal? Swept away by a raging icy torrent of water? A natural disaster almost sounds preferable to the harrowing possibilities that riddle the imagination.

Weeks pass. He did almost drown—in the swamp trying to skirt around the bay to reach the cottage. It is only when he calls for money that I put it together. Vladimir always loved the hiking with his brothers, the games of war they used to play (we never allowed toy guns in the house, so they used sticks), the canoeing. Unlike the other two, he even enjoyed helping build a boat house one summer. Why I never figured out where he had stolen off to, is impossible for me to say. The likelihood of his hitchhiking so far just never penetrated. Ramona wires him a package like I should have been sent in Auschwitz.

I have to face the fact that we are a family out of control. None of the boys hesitate to throw my old affair up to me a thousand times: "No wonder we can't study." "No wonder we're emotionally scarred." "No wonder we have difficulty committing to anyone."

Suddenly I have this picture of myself repeating my father's life. "Boys, boys, go on! My father also had, with woman who ran Nisko tobacco store, ongoing affair. Did her books. I remember my mother crying. It wasn't nice— matter of fact, I remember I sided with my mother, too. Still, *Tatuś* came to his senses; they went on with their lives, and I with mine. You can do same."

In spite of my exhortations, Simon now tells somebody, "I was only a kid, fourteen, but, as the oldest, I felt the burden of keeping the children together fell on my shoulders. I felt depressed for my parents. Then their yelling two floors below flew at me through the ducts. It was like I was crawling through my own shit. I was going to kill myself, was wondering how to do it. Then suddenly I said to myself, 'No, fuck 'em. I'm not my mother's son; I'm not my father's son. I can be who I want to be.' From that point on, I found myself withdrawing from the life of my parents. It made for some distasteful times, but it was not intensely painful."

Ramona, too, is still saying to me, "Can I ever trust you again?"

"Ramona, it's too long to be chained to past," I say. If I could have one wish, it would be that some things could go away over time. It is not that easy. I made a mistake. I regret it. I made atonement. But once you lose your wife's trust, how do you win it back?

Wrapped up in daily concerns, we rarely realize how much our family mean to us, how much we sacrifice to our daily involvements. It is plain as a neon sign in the bush that, despite all the good intentions, this experiment with a hotel has failed miserably. The tension leads me to sell the hotel to buy another in Nanton where the pace will be slower and work easier, where we will enjoy more family time. Is it not always that way? We lock the barn door after the cows are wandering all over the countryside. Even so, learning from experience beats not learning at all. "Boys, that's another reason why Auschwitz pulls me. There's old Russian proverb, 'Dwell on past, you'll lose eye; forget past, you'll lose both eyes.'"

The Nanton hotel is partially burned, so we get a good deal. Our lawyer is vacationing, and since much sweat has yet to be put in, by agreement with the vendor, we move in before closing.

As soon as we finish extensive repairs, almost like she is awaiting the minute, the previous owner's estranged wife shows up from Texas claiming half is hers. It is not such a good deal after all. Nanton, known for the purity of its spring water, becomes our second economic bust. This time we are forced to sell the cottage and the Bahama home as well. I do not even get my money out of the property I had once hoped to subdivide and exploit. The Bahamian government passed a law that only Bahamian-born citizens could own seafront property which limited the market and brought down the value. It is the final fall of Sigmund Sherwood.

"Ramona, with economic downturn in oil patch, I'll never be able to get back into real estate," I say after the Nanton fiasco. Like other survivors, I am chameleonlike in accommodating myself to new circumstances. With misgivings right from the start, I choose the best of what is available at the time. We pack our goods, travel with Ramona, Emilio, Vladimir, and Husky—Simon has already left the nest—and come tired and hungry to Fort Assiniboine.

"Simo, we are very far north, very far from Calgary, not even on a main highway."

"Yes, but this hotel was grossing $300,000 per year before the oil slide. We can do it again." We find little on the street besides our new hotel and a couple of houses up the way; in the facing bush, nothing—except, well, snakes and bear. Nonetheless, it is of a friendly sort, in a homely kind of a way, a rectangular box of a building perched in a clearing surrounded by pine and spruce and twisted bush. To every approaching soul, its big signs say:

SPORTSMAN'S INN

HOTEL CAFE

BIKERS WELCOME   BREAKFAST ALL DAY $3.99, 6:00 a.m.–8:00 p.m.

HEPY HOUR 3 TO 6, DANCE MUSIC THIS FRIDAY

A sandwich board, a phone booth, an *Edmonton Journal* vending machine and two potted plants all huddle around the building like children lined up to enter the warm halls of their school. A shed and a fallen phone pole, squeezed between the hotel and the parking lot, keep the column in some semblance of order. On the other side of the parking lot is the trailer we now call home.

Ramona, looking at our trailer, sighs. "We can store extra things in the basement of the hotel!" True to form, the dog of a thousand faces stakes out a warm spot on the sofa before it is even brought into the house.

"Home," supposedly the most melodious of words. Here, life goes on at the desired slower, more relaxed pace—"reviving the dead," as the Polish Jews sometimes say, would be a more apt description.

"Emilio and Vladimir are beginning to make friends," Ramona reports.

"For me, I feel like tiger in cage." I can feel myself slipping into pre-1967 resentments. "Ramona, according to today's *Edmonton Journal*, Alberta Farmers for Peace are forming technical brigade to help in war-torn Nicaragua."

"Simo, I hope you are not starting to get ideas."

"It's like Cuban revolution."

"What do you mean?"

"Sandinista government's emphasis is on land reform, 'idle land to working hands', and Americans find that too socialist." The whole situation reminds me of post-seventeenth-century Poland: Christians first persecuted the Jews, denying them land and occupations, then pointed at their poor state as a demonstration of divine disfavour. Similarly, the U.S. first destabilizes the country, then criticizes the Sandinista government as one unable to cope.

After some checking, I reach a farmer named Klassen who, they tell me, is going on the Nicaraguan mission, and hear his raspy nasal voice. "Hello. Sigmund? Oh sure, I remember, you're the one who's gone and taken over the hotel in Fort Assiniboine. Yup, Irving Bablitz is organizing the trip. We're a bunch of Alberta farmers planning to set up a machine shop, establish a small factory in farm tools and train farmers to repair agricultural equipment. You teach welding, eh? Wonderful. Don't know if it's still possible to join in. You speak Spanish? Yup? Excellent. Most of our guys don't. Lemme give you his number. Our group's out to prove individuals can work out of a Christian feeling for the people, without political constraints. We'll make a real time of it. Well, good luck. Lemme know what Bablitz says." Four days later we are en route to Nicaragua.

The captain's voice comes on. "We will be making our descent into Managua International Airport in a few minutes." When we touch ground, someone jumps up to liberate a box from the overhead bin. It starts a chain reaction. The flight attendant has to come on again. "Please remain seated with your seat belts fastened until we have come to a complete stop beside the terminal building." More hullabaloo in the airport leaves me, loaded with duty-free cigarettes to use as gifts, separated from the Farmers for Peace. The confusion in the airport reception area left behind, my Spanish and technical welding skills combine to commend me to the Sandinistas. Immediately, the Ministerio de la Construcciones of Managua engages me to upgrade Nicaraguan welders in basic techniques.

It is one step forward, two steps back. Again I function as if I can drown *Achtundachtzig* in a swirl of distant, unrelated activity. While in Nicaragua, I am an advisor for the construction of a bridge over the Rio Coco. It is a wondrous river glade in the rugged central highlands near Telpaneca, close to the border with Honduras. We work under the constant threat of U.S.-backed Contra attack from across the river. To remind us, an army squad bivouacs nearby, and our construction trucks bear protective steel sheathing around the cab. But I am feeling better. There is renewed purpose to life.

My fellow crew-members could never dream what associations buzz my mind as we interlace the steel beams. Laying the concrete bridge bed over our fabricated steel support structure, I soon find out, is much like laying the roof of Höss's bunker. And the construction of two nearby irrigation canals reminds me of the Jewish slaves who built the *Königsgraben* in Birkenau in 1943: men digging their shovels into clay, the clump of the thrusts reverberating back on their thin shoulders, others throwing and tamping crushed stone, all sweating. One backhoe could easily complete, in less than an hour, what it takes a crew of twenty many days to accomplish. Only here in Nicaragua, the workmen eat properly, and we sweat for the benefit of the peasant population with their small bean and coffee farms.

The morning of the day the bridge is to open, we drive up to the work site eating the dust of preceding vehicles. No matter. My Nicaraguan companion and I congratulate ourselves. I am saying, "Fine little job we did, eh?"

"Yeah, be painting the exposed steel, and tomorrow be moving on. They tell me it's another bridge."

"Okay with me." The road curves and the columns of dust veer away to the left. In front of us we look over the edge of a steep drop into the now-familiar gorge stretching down to the river. Then we too curve around shrubs that have already become landmarks, descend through the bush and rise over a smaller shoulder to the water, swift, clean, and surprisingly deep. As we turn, we see those who preceded us have clumped on the bridge in small knots. "Wonder why they're not going to their crews?" I remark.

My companion parks the *camión* and bounds through the mud and gravel, me at his heals. Reaching the scene, we find Edgardo, our night guard, face down in a pool of blood. He has fallen forwards, arms underneath, his rifle at his feet where it must have dropped. A metre more and his body would have rolled down the gorge. The bridge's newly laid concrete lies blasted full of holes, the surging river visible below, its steel girders ripped in ragged patterns exposing shiny raw edges. People shake their heads, faces twisted. "Patching will be impossible," the foreman is saying. "Support structure's shot to hell. We've got to tear out everything." Then looking up, he says with terse remorse, "Form a burial crew."

The military presence proved to be a paper tiger in deterring the Contras from swooping over the Honduran border. It is not the first life claimed. I gaze out across the river to the glade in the distance, shaking my head. "These people will never be left to live in peace," I say to no one in particular.

You often hear people say, "This can't happen." Nonsense! If you can think it up, it can happen. Shortly after, I witness a brand new rural hospital completely razed in a Contra mortar attack. When they demolish a rural school, leaving its children bits and pieces here and there in the mud, I remember the Jewish children wasted for what great cause? I am back with *Achtundachtzig* gazing at the children in the 'family camp' from Theresienstadt, all destined for destruction.

It is the fortieth anniversary of liberation, January 27. Even casting my lot with the Sandinistas, I do not lose an opportunity to talk about Auschwitz. The *Barricada* reporter, given the Sandinista problems with the Reagan government, rephrases my words to political statements. "These neo-Fascists you say are spreading the lie that the concentration camps are a Communist invention, are they in the United States as well?" Just as *Achtundachtzig* helped Cuba, he now supports Nicaraguan workers with a how-to manual on welding, the newspaper's readers are informed.

The month ended, I wing home knowing that what my flying crusade has contributed, though potentially useful, was just a drop in the bucket. I entertain myself with the thought that my drop counts. When the Jews streamed into the gas chambers of Auschwitz each one was an individual drop with individual potential, each one was loved and respected by someone. "Since Auschwitz, boys," I'm talking to them in my mind again, "can anyone ever say about some horrible event, 'I can't do anything about it'? I've finally learned from Auschwitz, you need more than survival. Before, if hungry, you bought snack. Inside, no one could even say, 'I am hungry.' After Auschwitz it's necessary to stop hunger of others. You crawl between two extremes: Either you turn against society in bitterness, or you learn that life only has meaning if you attempt to sustain it for others. You try and put yourself at one side or other, but usually you waffle back and forth."

When I get back, the others are complaining about their local politicians; me, I am refocussed. I recognize that, as in Cuba, 'necessity' brought excesses. But for me, the difference between the Cuban episode and the Nicaraguan is immense: the first, before von Thadden, left me empty; the second, after my pivotal moment with the stranger, gave me renewed purpose. If both Sandinista and Contra remind me of the camp, if family changes and my experience with the Natives all dredge up old memories, the realization hits me that I should concentrate my work at the roots. The dog recognizes its owner, the house cat its basket; but I failed to recognize the lesson of my own growth. It is a delusion to think I can move away from Auschwitz. Life keeps pulling me back. Eventually I begin to call it "Auschwitz awareness."

In Auschwitz, there were also political distinctions. I saw German Communists and Social Democrats arrested for their political opposition to the Nazi regime. There were also BVers, hardened criminals, who, after release from jail, the Gestapo rearrested for having no jobs. Jehovah Witnesses were taken because they refused to bear arms. But the Nazis grabbed Gypsies and Jews simply because they were who they were. *No* Jews survived from 1940. None from '41. None even from the first six months of '42. Only a few after that. To be a prisoner of Auschwitz was wretched and dehumanizing. To be a Jewish prisoner of Auschwitz was hopeless.

The Jews of Auschwitz were highly visible with the Star of David stitched to their clothing; the two intersecting yellow and red triangles sent a beacon reminding the SS guards and the criminal Kapos, "Some Jews still live." They were first to start work and last to get food, allotted the biggest shovels, the deepest wheelbarrows. If the kitchen failed to send enough soup, it was the Jews who went back to work hungry in the afternoon. Upon returning from his lunch, an SS guard asked no questions when he noticed four Jews laying dead on the ground. He simply called to the Kapo, "Don't forget to write this one's number on his breast so there'll be no mistake as to his identity." There was no punishment of Kapos, nor any inquiry of any kind, for killing a prisoner.

In 1940, Himmler, the chief of the SS, had redesigned the old Polish cavalry camp at Auschwitz as a punishment camp. On 1 March 1941, Himmler arrived for his first visit to the camp. That September, Zyklon B gas was employed on some Russian prisoners, first in the Bunker's basement, then early in 1942 in the morgue adjacent to the crematorium. One morning in the middle of July 1942:

What are we doing on the parade grounds instead of going to work? SS are excited, expectation in the air. Around 11:00 a.m., Himmler arrives. The *SS Reichsführer* himself. Ah, so that's the reason for the inlaid cigar box we crafted in the *Tischlerei*. Gothic crest dedication on the outside, another on the inside. Höss came personally to inspect our work. Twice. Really wanted to please Himmler. Strip of about forty Nazi dignitaries in the *Reichsführer's* wake. Crossing on foot under arch ARBEIT MACHT FREI, not the grand entrance in his Mercedes as in 1941. The convoy pauses? Can't see. Oh yes, Himmler is pointing at the wrought iron street sign: a Jew, a priest and an SS man with a rifle on his hip marching one after another, underneath in the Gothic alphabet, *Dali Dali Strasse*, mispronounced Polish that means Rush-rush Street. Laughter. Quite a joke, the bastards. Prisoners must move in and out of camp, at evening lugging their dead, running, always on the run. Real funny. *Reichsführer* struts forward again. *Mützen ab!* Nineteen thousand right arms tear off their zebra striped berets in rhythmic unison and with a loud clap slap them hard against the outside seam of their trousers, then absolute silence. He is receiving the cigar box. After the ceremonies, prisoners' whispers pass from one to another: You know Himmler never reviewed the SS honour guard assembled inside? but he did check out progress at the IG Farbenwerke at Monowice; watched the Jews knee-deep in the ice-cold Sola River, bending picking lugging stones for road construction; then in Birkenau, he inspected two cottages made over for gas. From Day One Jews got much worse than us Poles, though the policy of arrest appeared identical. Now all-Jewish transports are arriving. What?—transport from Holland with 1,135 and Himmler participated! the bastard vomited?[31]

In 1867, the six times great grandson of Rabbi Saul Wahl, Dr. Paul Felix Mendelssohn-Bartholdy, a Christian, founded AGFA. In 1929, AGFA joined the IG Farben Chemical Corporation which became, in a terrible irony, one of the companies consuming Jewish slave labour like so many spare parts, though its synthetic oil plant never produced a bit of synthetic rubber.

As a result of his tour, Himmler authorized construction of four gas chamber–crematoria complexes with ventilators, electric lifts for bodies and batteries of ovens; he also ordered a ring of factories around the camp. Thus began, with the presentation of our cigar box, a new era at Auschwitz.

In response to Himmler's visit, the *Konzentrationslager* was gradually en-larged to hold two hundred thousand prisoners and to kill thousands more

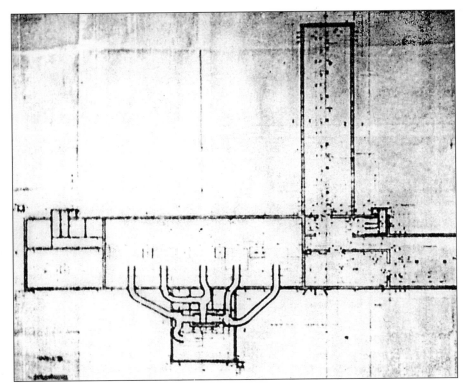

Plans for gas chamber and crematorium, dated 23 January 1942.
Courtesy of the State Museum of Auschwitz-Birkenau.

in the huge new gas chamber and crematory complexes. Meanwhile, in
Birkenau the mass-gassing began immediately, mostly on Polish Jews in
the two brightly whitewashed cottages surrounded by flowers, known
simply as the 'white house' and the 'red house.' The gas was routinely
brought in a Red Cross ambulance. Back and forth the van with the big
cross rumbled, calming the silent lines of people. Birkenau: Dante's
inferno with goose steps.[32]

From a multitude of documents, we know that bids poured in for the
authorized construction from throughout Germany and Silesia. These
included, in addition to IG Farbenindustrie, such notable German con-
cerns as Berghütte, Deutsche Ausrüstungswerke, Deutsche Erd- und
Steinwerke, Energieversorgung Oberschlesien AG, Friedrich Krupp AG,
Hermann Göring-Werke, Oberschlesische Hydrierwerke AG,
Rheinmetall-Borsig, Siemens-Schuckert, Weichsel-Union-Metallwerke.
Then Hoch- und Tiefbau AG of Katowice built the crematoria. J.A. Topf
und Söhne of Erfurt supplied the ovens and related equipment. DEGESCH
(Deutsche Gessellschaft zur Schädlingsbekämpfung) produced the
Zyklon B gas, and TESTA (Tesch and Stabenow) distributed it. The firms

Forced march. Until the 'Ramp' at Birkenau was completed, Jews were unloaded at the freight station in Auschwitz. Then they were forced to walk about four kilometres to the gas chambers. No sign of any kind marks the freight station. Watercolour by Jerzy Potrzebowski, 1965.

of Aleks Zink of Roth and Färberei Furst AG bought the hair. The Deutsche Bank realized more than a billion dollars in profits from the operations at Auschwitz. Local civilian staff was employed by the hundreds along with outside engineers and thousands of prisoners. Jewish forced labourers dug the foundations and dragged the materials, building factories for other slaves to work in.[33] The economy was booming, the surrounding populace was grateful. Himmler called the steps, as his dream reeled into place, a mega-community enterprise built right on top of the Soła swamp:

Cruellest Kapos are gravitating to Birkenau [Auschwitz-II] where the Jews now are. While conditions in Birkenau are worsening each day, in the *Stammlager* [Auschwitz main camp] they're improving. Beating and killing are less, roll calls shorter, care packages from home arriving with more frequency. Just having better bunks can mean life. Come home to our Block and not only sleep better but more easily. God, compared with Birkenau, we live in a resort hotel. First a museum is opened, even—a collection of Jewish artifacts that would, to future generations of grateful onlookers, testify to the Nazi contribution to world racial purity—and then later propaganda films, usually a news clip, and concerts and Sunday boxing and other athletics. Everyone's got his own method of coping, too. To stave off depression some think of escape, thoughts you dare not share with another due to the camp spy system. Some pray, especially before a *Selekcja*. See them make the sign of the cross that someone else was selected and not them. A link between religious faith and human responsibility? Are you kidding? Wish I could do as the Jews do, though: afflicted worse than anyone else in camp, they explain that God has hidden His face from them; yet, no sooner having said that, they pray all the same. Have to admit that those who have a higher purpose, whether religion or communism, seem to cope better than others. To preserve the equilibrium, some also develop a morbid humour, both as self-defence and as an act of defiance: How does Christianity differ from Nazism? I don't know; how? In Christianity, one man died for everyone; in Nazism, everyone has to die because of one man. Often the humour is at the expense of the *Muselmänner*. But if you are caught laughing, trouble. Why are you laughing at me? a Kapo would ask. Then he beats you. At lights out, no talking allowed, but sometimes in the safety of the dark, singing breaks out: Dizzie Gillespie's "Caravan," maybe something from the Polish hit parade, other songs. Rises from somewhere deep down in the shadows like from a well or a cistern and then hangs in the air like a cobra swaying to the charmer's pipe. Stefan Sikorski, No. 414, is the pipe whose sweet lilting notes never seem to disappear from your ear, and gradually we all join in, hungrily and almost spellbound, giving the words meaning they never had before.[34] Later, when the guards decide we do not sing the Nazi songs with enough fervour, all the barracks must sing for half-an-hour before sleep like at a children's summer camp. If you draw, you might sketch some pictures and get them smuggled out. Though strictly forbidden, it happens. In fact, someone sketches me.

With the gradual lessening of harassment, my brain broke out of the prison shuffle it had, in self-defence, adopted. When I noticed, because of luck, opening in the fire brigade, I assumed a new strategy:

Otto Küssel (Kapo No. 2), in charge of job assignments. Position just opened in fire brigade, think you can get me in? How do you know there's a vacancy? Saw George Thomas locked between the two fences, white fire brigade uniform full of blood; he was called to *Erkennungsdienst*. Don't have to say anything else, Thomas got the order for photographs, and, knowing no one ever returns, escaped. Baaad luck. SS Hauptscharführer Palitzsch— the guy I had so dearly wanted to throttle—happened to be peddling up the road. Recaptured him. Oh, authorization could be worth $5,000 American, you know. I've got nothing to give. Küssel staring, taking in my low number. Here's a *Zettel*. New white linen drill fatigues like the *Wehrmacht*, not striped pyjamas like other prisoners, (F) on our breasts, one red vertical stripe on each trouser leg, red stripe on the jacket following the spine from top to bottom. New knee-high polished boots! Fighting fires, we wear ordinary SS helmets painted white with a leather neck-covering resembling the French Foreign Legion. Warning: after Thomas is executed, Engelschall,

SS Hauptscharführer Georg Engelschall, a Catholic, chief of electricians and fire brigade of Auschwitz.

our SS fire brigade commander, assembles us, scowls, two circular spots on his forehead over his left eye. You're all cleared with security, I've seen to that; we'll have no more calls to the registry; but have no *Dummheiten* in your minds—in case of any escape, those remaining will suffer reprisal. How could we escape in these clothes, anyhow? Our serial numbers stencilled onto the jacket's left breast, and a second number onto the trousers' right leg. Never forget that warning; but will this man, contrary to everyone else here, keep his word, always getting us out of trouble? Yes. Soon we get permission to wear long hair, the sign of *Prominenten*. Usually only super Kapos get to grow their hair! New job makes me part of the *Prominenten*, entitled, due to the work, to better treatment, food, lodging and access to the brothel. And a *Prominente* is no longer forced to risk stealing; you've got others stealing the same food for you. Difference between a *Prominente* like myself and an average prisoner, and between an average prisoner and a Jew? Same difference between being caught in a hurricane or a volcanic eruption; life as a *Prominente* is better, but only by comparison.

In remembering Auschwitz, you hesitate to be entirely honest. To do so is often to dishonour the memory of the dead. How can you explain some *Prominent* prisoners had three or more personal slaves, and as many mistresses? How I pity the Jewish slaves who were often the sexual playthings of the guards! Words both memorialize and dishonour. The Nazis contrived to force us to make choices that would implicate us in our own spiritual death. This is part of the evil of Auschwitz. Evil breeds evil; cruelty breeds cruelty. Bury it, and you risk subsequent repetition. Expose it, and you terrify.

After the war, the Polish government decorated the man who assigned me to the fire brigade, green triangle No. 2, Otto Küssel, for his compassion towards the Poles. Nonetheless, he became a recluse, suffering for the guilt of having selected who to put in various positions. He never hit a man, never mistreated anyone. So there is guilt, even if you never physically attack another. In this world, there is a train waiting for everyone.[35] The Catholic Church correctly, I think, recognizes a special morality for *in extremis* situations. Under extreme circumstances virtue lies in survival, not in deliberately choosing to let oneself die.

Following Himmler's visit, they were still burying the gassed victims in long trenches. Shovelling quick lime to accelerate their decomposition proved futile, and water wells in the area became contaminated. By mid-1942 the ground above the mass graves was heaving and large puddles of stinking, reddish slimy fluid oozed to the surface. Unlike other prisoners who saw only their Block and workplace, being in the fire brigade we saw everything. When we had to go over there, the stench got sharper as you came nearer, creeping between the folds of your clothes. The third *Sonderkommando*, that special detail of about three hundred Jewish prisoners assigned to the extermination process, was forced to dig out the 107,000 corpses. They burned them in open pyres. When I went over to Birkenau and smelled its sweet pungency, squeezed my smarting eyes, rubbed the ash between my fingers, all for the first time, I could not imagine what it was. Soon I knew. Soon we all knew. Even indoors, checking fire extinguishers in Birkenau warehouses, it was in your mouth and in the soup they give you. It was worst in the morning, when the wet mist pushed the smoke down like lava rolling across Birkenau.[36]

Of the boys, Vladimir stands out as the most interested in my mission. We are working together in the rafters of a train trestle near Calgary, when we spot some mule deer on the floor of the valley. I tell him, "We never saw in Auschwitz any animals, except German police dogs and bloodhounds."

"No groundhogs? Not even birds?" he asks, braced by the wind against the girders we are welding.

"Once in great while," I answer, "bird flew by to tweak your attention to outside; in Birkenau, not even that! How could there be? Smoke from chimneys purified air. Blood fertilized soil. All it could give forth in return was accusation."

"Accusation?" Vladimir asks.

"Many of us prisoners felt hopelessly guilty. The bloodied soil cried out to the inner soul."

After the four gas chamber–crematoria complexes were constructed and Jews were herded in by the thousands to get baked, an orchestra of inmates played Wagner—SS overtures to die by! With the grace of a conductor's baton, Dr. Josef Mengele severed who would live from who would die. Who lived? Only a few able-bodied Jewish men and women. Mothers who dared to stay with their crying children automatically and unknowingly condemned themselves to death. If a Jew made the *Selektion*, his life expectancy as a forced labourer, mostly in factories of exploitation outside camp, was at best six months. The lucky one endured subsequent *Selektions*, usually naked in the shower. Then one day, casually as selecting a carp in the vendor's tank, he would get classified *Arbeitsunfähig*, unfit for further work. End was the same gas chamber he supposedly escaped.

To meet the evolving needs of the camp, the *Sonderkommando* developed into a detail of about four hundred Jews drafted to work in the gas-chamber complexes. The opened door revealed a pile of bodies who had struggled

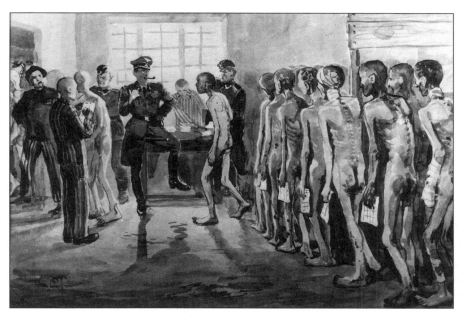

Selektion. Watercolour by Jerzy Potrzebowski, 1950.

against each other, clawing their way to the top where the gas was last to reach. Their job was to disentangle the naked corpses, sometimes with a crowbar, extract the gold teeth and then cut off the women's hair with three clips, shearing them like sheep. The hair was destined for production of rope and hair-felt used in boots, upholstery and to insulate against moisture buildup in submarines. Then, the *Sonderkommandos* had to stoke the crematoria with the bodies. Every few months the Nazis executed the current group and replaced it with another squad of Jews.

Only a few of us former prisoners can testify to the full years of operation. Some say, "Suffering purifies." I am influenced by the words of Irving Greenberg:

> By 1942 the crowding and the cold and the lack of food in the Warsaw ghetto had reached the point where the Jews were dying at a rate of one and half percent a month. The birth rate had dropped so suddenly that deaths outnumbered births forty to one. At that rate, in six to eight years, all of Jewry would have died. But that was too long for the Nazis to wait.
>
> The next stage was the period of the Final Solution, the concentration camps. By the end of the war the Nazis were determined to finish off the Jews. So every day in the summer of 1944 tens of thousands of Jews were shipped from all over Nazi Europe to Auschwitz where they were gassed and put to death immediately. But in order to make the gas stretch further, the supply used in each chamber was cut in half. This meant that the death time was lengthened from three to seven minutes to fifteen to twenty minutes of gasping and choking. But even that was not the final statement of the

cheapness of human, that is, Jewish life. Hear the testimony of a Polish woman taken from the Nuremberg trial records:

Witness: When the extermination of the Jews in the gas chambers was at its height, orders were issued that children were to be thrown straight into the crematorium without being gassed first.

Smirnov, the Russian prosecutor, asked: How am I to understand this? Did they throw them into the fire alive or did they kill them first?

Witness: They threw them in alive. Their screams could be heard all over the camp. It is difficult to say how many children were destroyed in this way.

Smirnov: Why did they do this?

Witness: It is difficult to say. We do not know whether they wanted to economize on gas, or if it was because there was not enough room in the gas chambers.

5.5 kilogram of the insecticide Zyklon B were used in each chamber load of fifteen hundred people. At that time, that much gas cost $675 or two-fifths of a cent per person. In the summer of 1944, Jewish children were not worth two-fifths of a cent to put them out of their misery before one burnt them.[37]

In all my time at Auschwitz, I never personally heard of children being thrown directly in the ovens. But I did see kids who would be subsequently gassed. We Catholics have a doctrine that to go from this world to the next you have to undergo trial by fire. Will some theologian expound, "Suffering purified those children"? Of what? Will some theologian say that in the face of deliberate mass killing of children Christian Love is intact? Watching our own boys growing up, I think of those kids. I do not believe in suffering. Nothing good is in it at all. No lesson.

It is true that, from a practical point of view, our suffering made for a certain solidarity. Arguments, even occasional fistfights, broke out over normal routines (a place to sleep, a towel, soap, a cup or bread, or between a Pole and Ukrainian). But for the most part, circumstances caused us to try and help each other as much as possible. Work crews assisted a fellow prisoner back from the day's toil. Once Wojtek from Siemianowice, stocky and muscular, came up to me, tears in his eyes. "Zygmunt, I've been called to the *Erkennungsdienst* 'for photographs.'" We were by the back entrance to Block Twenty-four. He cried, "I'll never see the sunrise again," pointing to the bright reddish-yellow glare in the East.

I could not console him; could not even bring myself to say maybe they really did need a new photograph of him. He would see right through it. We all knew they line each guy up and wait for the camp executioner Palitzsch to put a bullet in the nape of his neck.[38] I simply threw my arms around him—I was taller— and whispered in his ear, "Be certain I'll avenge your death."

"*Dziekuje*," was all he answered, "Thank you."

I never saw him again. Did I keep the promise? Never in the way I meant.

"A soldier keeps his word." *Tatuś* is talking to me again, his words shredding my insides like a salad. I can see myself as a child in front of his serious face.

Three Sigmunds. From left to right, Sigmund Sobolewski I, civil engineer; Sigmund III, at 18 months; and Sigmund II, captain in the Polish Army.

Steel in his eye, soft corners around his mouth. They don't come on every human; my boyhood features certainly don't have it. I figure he's got to be the most courageous man in the world. He was a hero—in the Great War, as he calls it. A soldier is the most noble of beings, *Tatuś* is saying; stand true, keep your eye on the target, your target; don't try to go after other people's targets, *Tatuś* tells me. Stand true. Obedience and loyalty and and devotion to God and country, that's what *Tatuś* drums into me. He gets it from his father. I dream of battles: crimson conflicts of bygone days in which I help influence the present; nebulous and bloody new campaigns in which I'll make future history. Bravery wins me the praises of a grateful Polish president.

A few years later it was through the dint of amazing feats in the air. If not for the war, I would likely have become a pilot in the Polish air force; the glider program had already accepted me for initial training. But once in Auschwitz, the other end of a boot impressed on me the horrors a war mentality can breed. With the consciousness of Auschwitz awareness, what were once ambitions are now regarded as delusions. Within a year of our arrival in Fort Assiniboine, I've added a new sign, my hotel's biggest and most significant:

```
┌─────────────────────────────────────┐
│        New Zealand Opted Out        │
│         Montana Refused It          │
│           SAY NO!!                  │
│       TO NUCLEAR ARMS               │
│          in Alberta                 │
└─────────────────────────────────────┘
```

It amuses me when I notice strangers catching their first glimpse of the hotel, nudging their companions, wondering what could be behind a sign like that way up here. And if they are at all inclined to listen, I tell them, no charge. On my urging, an additional referendum has been put to the voters of Fort Assiniboine during the current village elections. I have been campaigning for weeks.

"Yes?" A woman answers the door.

"We're trying to make Fort Assiniboine nuclear-free zone," I say.

"What possible good could that do?" she asks, looking around.

"We'll stand by principle. Besides, I'm very proud of my Canadian citizenship. Why should Americans test over us rather than over themselves? Miscalculation of just twenty kilometres could spell disaster, a whole World War II in a matter of seconds. Alberta government needs to know we're against testing of cruise missiles over our territory."

"Well, it doesn't make all that much sense to me. And who will listen anyway?"

Every door, always the same. How do I drive home ethics over pragmatics? It is very discouraging. But I keep at it. I have become militantly antiwar. "This is my target, *Tatuś*. You can understand that." After Auschwitz, it takes no effort to imagine the terror of a nuclear explosion. *Achtundachtzig* is against fighting. *Achtundachtzig* hates the very idea of killing animals. There are those who can sit cramped all day long in a thatched blind waiting for a bull moose to seek the salty muskeg, alert, passing the lesser ones, calculating their chances for the mature one to cross the threads of their sight. Or those who can wander all over the northern forest, glassing every grassy slope with their binoculars, competing with each other over who can get the buck with the biggest rack and the most points. The thrill of the kill. *Achtundachtzig* has no elk antlers, coyote hides, stuffed eagles or other hunting souvenirs displayed over a door as so many of his neighbours do. One farmer has a barn full of hundreds of antlers, each with its own story. In contrast to my neighbours, I own no gun. *Achtundachtzig* is a pacifist.

And after all that hard work? On election day, 20 October 1986, Fort Assiniboine becomes the 170th jurisdiction in North America to declare itself a nuclear-free zone.

Not many people visit Fort Assiniboine, a hamlet of 179 souls in northern Alberta. Not many passersby, either. In the glossy travel brochures, it is "a land of rugged forests, teeming lakes and untamed rivers where the outdoorsman and fisherman are king, with some of the world's longest hours of sunlight each summer day." (And some of the world's shortest hours of sunlight each midwinter day.) O Canada, the nature preserve. Fort Assiniboine's annual extravaganza, a summer cavalcade of trailers, motor homes and campers, realizes very little for the hotel industry.

Sometimes at night, in this God-forsaken country, I hear the coyotes howling, provoking all the dogs in Fort Assiniboine. Then Paradowski's howls under Bednarek's cold shower come back to haunt me. With Ramona it is exactly the opposite. Compared to the Canadian Rockies, the never-climbed coffee-planted Sierra Maestras are mere foothills. But their beckoning call remains with her. She stops to take in a majestic view: flowers, birds, the hint of the pale green waters of the river, polluted by an upstream pulp mill. "Simo," she says, "you are always in too much of a hurry, you do not see nature."

Our tavern serves as a centre for small-town gossip. Who comes to our tavern? Some couples. A few struggling businessmen. Two of the mechanics from around the corner and down the street. Farmers from nearby sections. Seismic technicians and lumbermen who work in the bush. Aboriginal Peoples. Loners and groups, men and women, who want to talk over a drink, shoot a game of pool, or dance.

Every night at ten o'clock I turn up the volume on the bar TV, and flick to the news. "Hey! Turn the jukebox back on. We don't want to hear that bloody news," the patrons complain. "The service between ten and eleven stinks, and the noise drives you crazy." Since Auschwitz, my mind is alert to every newsflash. In this, the owner gets his own way.

Lately, I seem to get on best with our youngest. Vladimir is also the one I think who has grown to look the most like me. He is much more developed, more athletic, more sports-minded than the other two. Yet I believe it is Vladimir who is emotionally the most like his mother. Once in a while, you can even catch in him a reflection of her face and movements, and he does have her curly hair. He is rough, gets excited, but inside he is quite soft.

Vladimir tries to explain. "Ever been to another bar where the owner turns his back and doesn't care what's happening with his customers? The ashtrays can be spilling over, empties stacked up on the tables, and you'll be watching TV. Like, you play it so loud I can totally hear it all the way upstairs. If I step in for a few minutes, right away they'll gripe, 'Why's your dad here?' 'Vlad, why don't you come down and work for a couple hours and get your dad outta here?' 'Vlad, if you took over the bar, an awful lot of people would start coming.'"

"Yes, you ignore people," Ramona joins in, overhearing.

"You both know I'm not good at small talk. What do we have in common? Besides, who cares if they disagree? News is important. News is world."

With an empty hotel, the bar alone cannot cover the costs. Fortunately,

Sigmund's welding truck.

I still have welding. Here, a farmer needs a combine repaired. There, a piece of a drill from an oil rig needs welding. The field truck travels anywhere—a rolling acetylene tank with lots of hose, an oxygen tank, filler rod and a torch. I approach each job as a new challenge, assessing the stress points, finding just the right way to reconnect the joints. A wire brush removes the dirt and rust, making a polished surface amid the grease and oil of years of service. On heavy metal an arc air torch best removes the old weld. I am the only guy around who has one. Then I grind the edges of the break so the pieces fit, joining with filler metal.

One winter night, I get called out to the bush near Virginia Hills. Snow drifts clot the roads, and they have to tow my truck in with a tractor. A welding truck in the ditch can mean an explosion.

I find the derrick buttered with a slimy oil, the wind cutting through my jacket. No harness or rope secures a climbing man. With one hand, I pull the cables after me. With the other, I fasten to the slippery metal edge above, letting my feet catch up with my arm. Then leaning into the lattice-work structure, I lurch forward again like an inchworm.

I wish Vladimir was here, I say to myself. But he isn't here, I think, only yourself. It's all on you, and you better mind your step.

The wind shakes the rig, which sways noticeably though not as wildly as that time a storm blew up while I painted the top mast of our ship. On the ground, all heads turn upwards, shining feeble lights into darkness. I continue to grope upwards, feeling the rig with my arms and legs, keeping track of the earth by the glimmer from below. Holding with my right leg near the pinnacle, I station myself in the air. I become an elongation of my torch, quickly repairing a broken bracket, then slide down with a flourish. The crew has already turned away—oilmen are always in a hurry—to their separate duties.

These little assignments help to put food on the table.

A normal evening in the tavern, a few guys from the bush are chatting about the spring breakup. At the next table, another guy, a shadow across his face, complains that the vet gave his pigs an injection, and the damn pigs got sick anyway. Through the window I glimpse a red pickup pulling in. John comes roaring up to the bar.

"Just quit Slim's farm," he says throwing off his work parka. "I seen he wasn't never goin' a change. Couldn't get along with the SOB, no way."

I remind him, "You've been mad before and still gone back to——"

"Keep on casual till there ain't no more jobs," he cuts in. "He'd a had no crop if it wasn't fer me."

"He needs you."

"Then why's he such an ass?"

Ten o'clock and the TV volume goes up. Polish cops are beating up on their own citizens. I look for Simon, who is in Poland, hoping not to see him on the TV. The Soviets quashed the Hungarian Revolution with tanks, force against force. But what can their Polish counterparts do against a workers' strike if it spreads beyond the docks? A new Poland is rising from the depths of Polish history, wobbling on baby legs, spirited by an as-yet formless longing. Beyond Gdańsk and its screak of cranes loading minerals, coal, grain, lumber, beet-sugar, and steel for other Baltic ports, a cry goes out: "We will be free again." The lines are drawn: potential Soviet intervention on the one hand, the surging Polish mass on the other; the one contending for its sphere of influence, the other for its home; both seeking destiny. If the Soviets lose, their bloc might swiftly follow in defeat. If the Poles lose, it is unlikely a free and independent Poland will ever exist again.

Wojciech is in tonight. A rangy, pale-topped fellow with a feathery blond face and narrow flat eyes, he always sports a baseball cap, even at night. Buys a beer. Since I moved up here, we have made our own white eagle society of two. Tonight he is glowering at the TV like it could feel his browless scowl.

"The sons a bitches," Wojciech howls, pounding his fist, spilling his beer.

"Those protestors?" I ask not so innocently, while serving John. We speak English. Not that anyone is interested in our conversation, but the customers resent my speaking another language.

"Those protestors?" he stares in disbelief. "Don't be an ass."

"Here you are." Then to Wojciech, "*You* favour *Solidarność?*"

"Hey! You're a Polak, too! Don't you?!" He is drinking his beer. "Those Commies got our country turned into a damned tomb. When workers march, they're attackin' the whole damn workers' party system. Solidarity isn't only workers; hell, this is entire nation."

Vladimir comes in and turns away. "You're definitely not same man you were yesterday," I say.

"You're full of it, I've always been against Commies."

"No, not that," I say. "Only last week you were Mister Conformity."

"Whadaya mean?"

"Well, when subject was Jewish demonstrators, you claimed cops should've beat up on them with clubs." My own words goad me on. "You said they had it coming to them."

"Yeah, Jews control everything. They own the banks, the newspapers. They're Commies, every damn one of them." I am wiping up a spill. A sponge begins to expand inside my stomach. Wojciech makes me realize again how important an Auschwitz awareness is. When I wonder if he finds any inconsistency in his answer, after a bit of characteristic plodding, he explains ingenuously, "It's a fuckin' plot; why—they got everything so they can hide the fact they're communists."

The mind can always find a rationalization for any stance. "If they're communists," I ask, "why did Polish communists conduct in 1968 campaign against Jews? And given that our homeland is practically *Judenrein*, to use ugly German phrase, why fight against group that is all but nonexistent?"

"Look, Zygmunt, don't be a damn fool. Nobody likes those fuckin' Jews. Know your enemy. Stop being a rabble-rouser."

"Rabble-rouser! And Lech Walesa?" I say facetiously.

The guy with the pigs calls impatiently. "Look, there's a new show on. The next drink's on me."

I would have been overjoyed to provide drinks on the house. But we find out about the big event only three days after the fact. Vladimir is nineteen, working in a sawmill. Vladimir still has not forgiven me the embarrassment he suffered "that day" in the lawyer's office. But as far as I know, though the rest of the problems continued, he never 'delivered' again. He and Ramona were cleaning up in the bar after I retired early. "Why did you not tell me?" I am told she screamed.

Soon she is shaking me. "Wake up, Vladimir has a baby."

"Let me sleep. He'll have it in morning, too." But I am awake, and to my distress, it is true. He has been seeing a high-school girl going on a year. "Repeat again what Leesa said," I demand.

Vladimir is looking down at his feet. "She loves me, but she doesn't want to marry me. She says she's going to, like, bring up the child herself."

"That make sense? Girl's in trouble. You offered honourable thing. How can she refuse!?"

"She did, Papa," Vladimir replies, I think a bit impatiently.

"Look at me when I'm talking. Were you sincere?"

"Yes, Papa!" even more impatiently.

"Does she know?"

"O God, yes Papa! Sure she knows!" His young voice borders on shouting. Then backing away with a deep sigh, he moans, "She totally doesn't want to marry me, that's all!" I swim into his sea-green eyes. His frustration recalls my own experiences after the war. I had women, too: a lady teacher who played the violin in Devonport, blacks in Africa; but none for marriage.

We hear about the birth when it turns out Leesa and Vladimir need $500. They had signed to allow an adoption, then changed their minds. They have to pay the lawyer—or, rather, Ramona pays—$500 to annul the adoption agreement.

Ramona visits the hospital. I make other plans. I can hardly believe it—after everything that has happened, a grandchild! As I drive to Barrhead, the sunlight, peaking thinly over the horizon and breaking into tiny halos in the treetops, has not yet burned off the soft morning fog that quilts over the river and countryside. I smile to myself. I have a granddaughter, a surprise to be sure, but a granddaughter nonetheless. Leesa is a sensible girl. Things will work out.

Leesa is living on her own in a modern unit—on welfare. Once in the apartment building hall, which is unlocked, I take a needed few minutes to unwind. It has to be rather straightforward, really. Yet I note how odd it is that, for something so simple, there I am, leaning against the wall, rehearsing my words.

The second floor door opens to my knock. It is Leesa. She is a good-looking girl, blonde. But this morning, a little heavy from giving birth, draped in a loose-fitting rumpled maternity smock, she gives the appearance of a young bag-lady: weary-eyed, somewhat bedraggled, but with smouldering vitality. Maybe she was up all night taking care of the baby. "You! What're *you* doing here?"

I didn't expect to be welcomed with open arms, but her demeanour freezes my carefully thought-out speech in my throat. Vladimir and Leesa have been quarrelling, and I have to word my way in, or more accurately, wedge my way in. If you care about your children, you care enough to hassle them.

Her eyes are flat, her body clearly indicating the door. In front of me: a bare, unprosperous, stale-smelling living room dominated by a big TV blaring the latest instalment of *Hospital* something or other. Not a single picture on the walls. An ashtray overflows with cigarette butts. No one else appears to be home. "I don't really want to see you. Please do me a favour and leave."

My open hands are raised shoulder height, palms forward. "What sense does this make? Leesa, I've spoken to Vladimir. I come in hopes you've got more understanding." With a deep sigh I look her full in the eyes and lowering my hands try and take hers.

She will have none of it. What was weary impatience turns to anger. Her eyes flash.

I continue, "You know I've been through concentration camps? Life is too precious to play games."

"Please, Mr. Sherwood, I have to make my own decisions. Your past makes no difference."

"You're mother. You've got baby to think about. You two should get it together and get married."

Her face loses none of its determination. "And you should mind your own business."

"Vladimir is my business," I volley back, a little feebly, it seems to me. "I'm not, though."

"Maybe you should both go to counsellor."

"And maybe you should go to hell."

"Oh Leesa! You're both completely crazy." I came so absorbed in my own rational agenda, never even contemplated a negative reaction. Bewildered, I turn my head. "I can't understand this."

"You're not as smart as I thought. Look, Mr. Sherwood, I have a child from your son. But I'm the one left with the responsibilities. I have to think." Then perhaps realizing she has exposed, even with that, more than she intended to, her eyes go wet, closing all further discussion. "Just leave me be."

"Leesa——"

"You don't get it, do you, until you're smacked in the face? I'll call the police."

"Okay, okay." The joyous expectation of my earlier thoughts turns. It is her life. The consolation is that, given the circumstances, there was never much chance in the first place. "Before going, let me peek for minute at baby."

"She's sleeping." Her voice cuts again like a knife. This is going too far. Looking down I cannot help but wonder if the soap opera on the TV and the one I am caught up in have anything in common. "Look Leesa, I won't wake her up. It's right of grandfather to see his granddaughter, no?"

"No way. We don't want nothing to do with you or your son." Her brows knit as she gently aims me towards the door. "Get out now, or——"

"Okay, okay." When grabbing up the coat huddled on a chair and flipping it over my shoulder, the cry of the newborn sounds from an adjoining room. Glancing back to catch Leesa's eye, I pause hopefully. The scrape of the latch is her final word.

Vladimir is lucky not to have married her. In my opinion, she ruined his final high school years; she does not have to ruin his whole life. Now whenever he leaves the house, I remind him to wear a condom.

Not until Krystle is five months old do I get to see her face, feel her smooth skin. How is it circumstances make it difficult for me to fathom I am now a grandfather?

Thirteen: Ramona

Fort Assiniboine, Alberta, 1986

few months after Krystle's birth Canada undergoes one of its episodic periods of self-examination. On any given day, a commission is about to be set up, expected to report, or ready to disband. It is our polite Canadian way of pretending to act while doing nothing. But forget murders and rapes, the neat thing about Canada is that the day's commission announcement will usually be one of the headline news items. In this case, Justice Jules Deschênes heads the Commission of Inquiry on War Criminals. The Ukrainian Canadian Congress and Ukrainian National Army urge against prosecution for fear of injustice to possible innocents; the Canadian Jewish Congress and B'nai Brith League for Human Rights favour prosecution in the name of justice for the guilty.

On behalf of the First Polish Transport Association of Ex-prisoners of *K.L. Auschwitz,* I draft a wire supporting the prosecution of war criminals. The signatories to the telegram are: Eugeniusz Niedojadło, No. 213, of Tarnów, Poland, president; Sigmund Sherwood, No. 88, of Fort Assiniboine, Alberta, vice-president. I write, "We should never have, again, Holocaust directed against any group. Prosecution of war criminals would send to world strong message from Canada."

Niedojadło takes me by surprise. "I've got no authority to commit myself on behalf of all the prisoners of the first transport," he says. Right. Jews are involved, so suddenly the former prisoners' organization has "no authority" to speak in favour of prosecuting their own tormentors and murderers.

I fly to Poland with Ramona, glide to a stop before Warsaw's outdated terminal appropriate to any city not larger than one hundred thousand, not to the millions of Warsaw. A tired ground crew waving little red wands wheel mechanical stairs into place. We alight from the fuselage gripping the aluminum railing and troop across the tarmac without the bus customary in European airports. Armed guards are peppered here and there. People in sombre clothes go about the process of passport control. No shops line the terminal except a small restaurant, so all continue directly on their business.

Our first trip takes us to Auschwitz and the *Krematorium IV* complex. I wear my stripers, and, unlike the old days, a second shirt underneath. A newly erected chain-link fence blocks access to the gas chamber–crematorium. I search around for someone to open the padlocked gate. It kills me that Simon spent four weeks in Poland without ever coming here. He turned his back on everything I have lived through. I chalk it up as Simon's way of getting back at me for my discipline—triple. I explain, barely able to point out the details of the distant site, "We were in this very place putting out fire."

Ramona is peering through the fence. She is bundled up, tam stretched over her ears. "Simo, I wish you to tell me, how did you survive in the end? If you knew everything, why did the Nazis not kill you?"

"Right, right! They probably planned to," I reply. "Right before liberation, though, Jewish prisoners' revolt destroyed completely gas chamber and *Krematorium IV*, and burned partially *Krematorium III* complex. That's why we were putting out fire."

She screws up her face in disbelief. "Are you saying a Jewish revolt maybe saved your life?"

I do not know why I never thought of it this way before. "Hmmm, I guess that's true. Yes. Jewish action halted some of killing." My mind fills in the thought: and I have a debt to pay. "You see, that's why we survivors ask: how is it possible Americans refused to do job on crematoria? They found, when it came to Jews, every excuse not to prevent killing."

Ramona lived through the Castro revolution. While she detests war as much as I do, she is also familiar with its intricacies. "Then they knew the crematoria existed?"

"Oh, they knew. After 17 December 1942, it went through camp grapevine that Washington, London and Moscow had simultaneously broadcast that West would hold Nazis accountable for 'carrying into effect Hitler's repeated intention to exterminate the Jewish people.' By 1944, there were those who begged Roosevelt to bomb gas chambers and crematoria. We watched skies for proof outside world cared. We knew world knew. But it seemed they approved. That was devastating. Allies had enough money for words bursting on air waves, nothing for bombs."

"Surely, it is not possible," she says.

She scrunches up her nose the way I have come to know and love. I can see that the reality is difficult for her to handle. I stare through the fence. Something I cannot place. Then I realize. The process of creation has begun again, pushing its way right to the roadside, unmaintained. Ashen, naked limbs of old trees intertwine in tortured embrace, along with huge dark bushes I have no recollection of.

I continue. "According to witnesses, idea was to time uprising with outside action by Polish partisans, killing all SS men. Then, dressed in their SS uniforms, they'd simply walk out, cross river Sola and scud away. But, three days before revolt, guards ordered *Sonderkommando* Kapos to select three

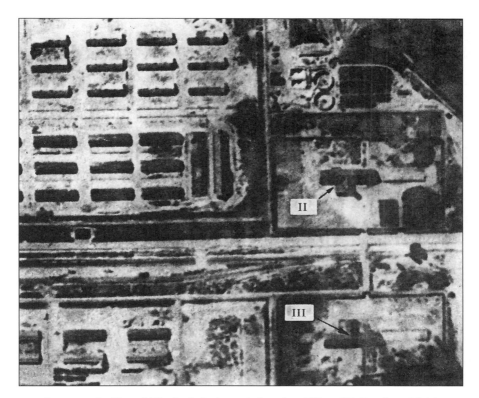

Crematoria II and III. Aerial photo taken by Allies, 25 October 1944.
Courtesy of the State Museum of Auschwitz-Birkenau.

hundred to supposedly clear some bombed buildings in Germany."

Ramona turns to face me. "How does it seem to you? It was another trick, right?"

"Yes, to me it seems so. Only, this time Jewish prisoners sensed deception. Nobody volunteered. So SS ordered Kapos to have, by next day, list of prisoners to make up difference."

"Because they suspected a Jewish revolt?" She stands rivetted to the spot.

"It would seem so," I reply. In the camp, we recognized, even then, that the Nazi crimes were so enormous it would be difficult to believe. The Nazis often laughed about it in front of us. The Jews also knew it. We have, due to their bravery, an inside record of Birkenau's entire extermination process.[39] The diary of Salmen Lewental, found in 1962 buried on crematorium grounds, describes an earlier planned revolt that the Polish Kapo Mietek Morawa (No. 5730) betrayed. I knew him from the "old" crematorium where I repaired doors, and at one time he slept for a few weeks in our *Stube*. He was definitely antisemitic.[40] Under the previous political regime, the Auschwitz Museum rejected a translation of Lewental's diary as wrongly suggesting that an "unfriendly attitude of Polish and Russian prisoners to the Jewish prisoners" caused the revolt's failure. They commissioned another, sanitized translation. In the wake of Solidarity, some Jewish scholar should examine the museum's reinterpretation.

"One witness," I continue, "writes about prisoner and guard who were exchanging information. He claims this Slovak SS man, who was presumably such friend, gave away entire plan. In any case, on 7 October 1944, four trucks of SS rolled up at *Krematorium IV* complex to collect quota of men. Jews either had to submit to selection or begin revolt early under unfavourable conditions."

Ramona's questions start me thinking back over the entire experience. No way a Jew would have expected a Nazi to remain silent about a plan to wipe out his fellow guards. "I think most likely answer is, they had, like everywhere else, their spies in *Sonderkommando*."

"So this is the time they quit killing the trainloads of Jews, no?"

"Not right away. Trainloads do trickle off, though. Just few thousand Jews arrive, gassed along with prisoners incapable of further work. Himmler orders gassing to be stopped on 11 November 1944.[41] Actually, record shows gassing went on until mid-January, though in fewer numbers and only Jews. There were no more Christian victims."

Ramona, probing to understand the bitter fate of what might have unfolded differently, shakes her head. I watch as she cranes her neck, peering out through the fence, then nods, her lids closing slightly over her eyes. She has the picture, shivers, snuggling herself deeply into her overcoat, Wrapping the long scarf up and around her, she reaches for my hand.

When we finally get close, I find the remains of *Krematorium IV* overgrown with weeds and full of garbage. Viewing a major historical site, especially this one, in a state of total disrepair, is devastating. But, more than anything else, it is the unfairness of what I see that draws me to rethink my public advocacy: there is no mention of the *Sonderkommando* revolt on the site. I need a vehicle for my action.

We tour the main camp. When showing Ramona the brothel, conversations buzz my ear. Guys in the fire brigade were always saying things like, "Sobolewski fell for the first girl he ever had." "Don't you ever want to try and see what the others have got?"

"Buzz off," I would reply.

"What should I tell Irka when I see her today?"

"Go to Hell."

"Tell Irka to go to Hell?"

Even Claussen used to razz whenever he saw me, "Hey, *Achtundachtzig!* How's Irka?"

Each Block houses a national exhibit. We find the Jewish exhibit locked and unmanned; I believe, with many, that it begs for serious revision. In our Polish exhibit, one hall shows pictures of adult victims, in the next hall pictures of children. "Look," I point out to Ramona, "here children, who were almost all Jewish, remain unnamed; in first hall, non-Jewish victims had captions identifying them by name."

Ramona gets the idea. "This whole Block commemorates the memory of two Danes, the same space as for one-and-a-half million Jews," she says. Later she points out, six Bulgarians the same. "And look," she says, "not one Jewish star on this Czechoslovakian memorial with crosses all over it."

"Over 150,000 Jews perished from area encompassed by pre-war Czechoslovakia, overwhelming majority of Czechoslovakian deaths." I add the most outrageous of all, "Roman Catholic Austrians, who welcomed, enthusiastically, *Anschluss*, are treated as victims, while Austrian Jews go unmentioned." On the visitors' map, I show Ramona, "Each Block bears legend. However, Block Thirteen, 'Jewish Hospital' where Jewish prisoners were beaten and starved to death, remains unmarked. Why? Similarly, building itself bears no plaque. Map also fails to identify yard of Building C. Then it was gravel pit where hundreds of Jews, Poles and Russian POWs were murdered. Now it's garden of Carmelite convent with fourteen Stations of Cross where, in summer, people come and pray at each station. I think it slights memory of Jews slaughtered here." We visit. "Ramona, sign reads *Żwirownia*,' gravel pit, with no mention of martyred Jews." In Block Eleven, there is a chapel in memory of Father Kolbe. Together we count twenty-three memorial plaques for the some sixteen thousand fellow Catholic Poles executed there, one for Russian PoW's, none for Jews, even though the *Strafkompanie*, or penal battalion, as well as the first *Sonderkommandos*, were located here.

I find also a tendency to submerge the few existing references to the Jews in the fate of other peoples. In the Hungarian exhibit, for example, we actually observe the legend: "The theme of this exhibition is not the fate of the Jewish people. What it wants to narrate is Hungarian history."

"Yet," I tell Ramona, "438,000 Hungarian Jews perished in gas chambers." The camp looks like a place where people of all religions were murdered, presumably in proportion to their representation in the countries involved. This effect results in a major distortion of truth. Instead of national pavilions, the museum should be designed by themes: arrival, everyday existence, SS, Kapos, victims, women, defiance and punishment, business of murder, prosecution of war criminals. It should be explained what caused people to be brought here. And above all, their identity should be given.[42]

During the Keegstra trial, Jack Downey, a get-the-job-done kind of a guy given to a flat leather hat and knotty cane, arranged for two of Keegstra's students to experience the camps. They reported to their classmates at home what they learned. Thank God for communist Poland. For had it been politically possible to arrange, the teenagers would certainly have been sent to the camp that has become synonymous with the word 'Holocaust.' They would then have reported, "Our teacher Keegstra is right on. We didn't find any mention of Jewish slaughter."

If you visit Auschwitz with a Jewish group, you will be shown the Jewish exhibit, you will light your memorial candles, say your *kaddish* prayer, shed your tears. If you visit with any other group, you will not necessarily learn that even one Jew was singled out for murder, let alone the whole people for annihilation."

Remains of Krematorium IV, overgrown and in disrepair.

My survival in Auschwitz sensitizes me to Biafra, My Lai, violence on the streets of 'civilized nations', Pol Pot, later Tiananmen Square and 'ethnic cleansing' in former Yugoslavia, and the upsurge of neo-Nazism all over the world. I discern a continuum that is upsetting even when subsequent tragic events constitute a 'mere' reflection of what happened in Auschwitz. The assembly-line murder of a complete race should be a stark lesson for all the other instances of inhumanity.

I am also sensitized to the actions of the Church. Recently the Vatican initiated steps to make Isabella la Católica a saint. I tell my sons, "I find it interesting, boys, that every country that has had 'Golden Age'—Babylonia, Moorish Spain, Poland, United States—achieved it in atmosphere friendly to Jews. Every time attitude of friendliness soured—Isabella's expulsion of Jews in summer of 1492 being perfect example—Golden Age declined. As for Jews, though, it's my impression they simply regroup and forge ahead, making, wherever there's more favourable political climate, their contributions."

Selections still go on; only with us, we select what we want to care about. I call it "selective conscience." The progressive buildup of frustrations with the Deschênes Commission, with the disrepair of the camp and the lack of

Jewish exhibits, with repeated atrocities and with this Isabella decision—all lead to a decision to develop the Auschwitz Awareness Society.

Making the rounds of Auschwitz with Ramona recalls our fire inspections in Birkenau's *Frauenlager*, always a welcome excuse to talk to the women. Once we went into Block Twenty-five. Crossing the threshold, I was overwhelmed by the sight and smell of a hundred breathing rib cages with nothing in between, semi-naked and female. They were awaiting the open trucks, already relieved of their clothes and food. For what did they need them? In the yard, women were sprawled on the dusty July ground like beasts of the field, nothing at all in their eyes, not even hatred. That they could not even walk the short distance to the gas chambers betrayed how deteriorated these women had become. Some were supporting their heads on one elbow, some were crouching to urinate, some wordlessly pointed to their rat-bitten toes. Arms like bird's legs stretched through the barred windows. We heard, *"Wasser, Wasser"* or *"Brot, Brot,"* as they pleaded for a sip of water or a piece of bread. Daughters struggled to say a few last words to glassy-eyed mothers as *Lagerpolizei* with truncheons continually drove the onlookers away.

At the time I had remembered our religion classes in Nowy Targ, the priest describing to us nine-year-olds how Hell and Purgatory look. But in my worst imagination, I had never envisioned the utter wretchedness of Block Twenty-five. We fled from there immediately.

It has taken me fifty years before I could choke out anything about these pathetic women. Mingled with my thoughts of religion are memories of early childhood in Nowy Targ: My pet sheep dog, Pikuś. The marketplace with its many woollen garments. The Jewish fishmonger on Krakowska Street peddling carp from a galvanized tub. In the nearby Catholic hospital, I took first communion and became an altar boy for Father Łukasik. Often I wish I could recapture the feelings that would wash over me then, before I was baptized by the world. My sister has preserved a photograph of this priest and me. In the picture, on the wall behind the priest, is a portrait of himself. He is depicted with a *tallis* or Jewish prayer shawl, a *menorah*, the seven-branched Jewish candelabra, two wax seals and the number '144,000.' Based on Father Łukasik's interpretation of the book of Revelation, 144,000 was the number of Jewish children—chaste first fruits, guileless, spotless—that must convert to bring about Armageddon.[43] Each child would have his own name and God's name sealed on his forehead, twelve thousand per tribe. In prewar Poland, the solemn aim of many priests was to convert at least one Jew in his lifetime.

For all I know, to convert a Jewish child might still be every Polish priest's desire; that is, if they can find any. Right after the war, the road outside of Nowy Targ became the site where five Jewish Auschwitz survivors were cut down on their way home. Although a huge outcry was followed by a public funeral, a few weeks later another five Jewish survivors were slaughtered on the same bridge. The Polish soldiers of the ultranationalistic N.S.Z. (which still exists here in Poland) took 'credit' for both massacres.

Ramona is exhausted from all the touring. I leave her in the hotel and go out.

"Zygmunt! Zygmunt, after all these years, is it really you? How are you?" I can hear a dog barking in the background.

"Irka, I've been looking all over for you. I've been three times in Poland; I could never find you."

"Who told you?"

"I just found out from somebody. Tell me about yourself." I learn she was married to a Polish officer who has since died, has an adult son, sells newspapers at a magazine kiosk. "Do you remember us standing," I ask, "my arms around you, looking out from the window?"

"Yeah, you were so very young. You didn't know what you were doing."

"I knew what I was doing. I loved you then. I still love you."

"There's a book written by a former Polish prisoner, makes fun of us, laughs that a member of the fire brigade could have been in love with a prostitute, claims you had told me I was supposed to think of you when I had sex with someone else." Irka lets her hand rest on my shoulder, then brushes the spot and darts away, a butterfly in motion. "Oh Sigmund, maybe if we had spoken longer in Belsen, maybe I would've gone with you."

A picture of her at twenty comes into my mind. My eyes wander all over her face and earlobes and shoulders and breasts like searching for buried treasure, and then finding it, I fasten her dress again not doing more even mentally. "There's an operetta tonight," I say. "For old times sake, let's go."

"Yes, oh, yes, I'd love to go out with you."

"Good, I'm here with my wife Ramona."

"Oh? Right. Well, maybe another time, okay?"

"Irka, wait. Don't worry, she knows all about you."

"She does?" A long pause. She is smoking. "Even more reason to make it another time."

"Irka, I've been searching for you for years. It'll be fine, I promise." After we make arrangements, I begin to think: Irka speaks no English, Ramona speaks no Polish. In spite of my assurances, remembering how Iris used to flaunt an English newspaper worries me about how Irka and Ramona will get along after all. And this is not just a past girlfriend I am introducing Ramona to. Can she understand that I was in love with a "prostitute," that camp cannot be judged by the normal standards by which we live today? There were those even in the camp who could not understand it.

Irka arrives at our hotel a little late, plump, poorly dressed, chain smoking. Ramona is her usual spiffy red. Irka later confides that, after I left, she sat for quite some time in shock, heaving dry sobs, pulling on her hair. She seriously weighed whether to keep the appointment. She was afraid to be out with the one who, more than anyone else, represented 'the years of her shame', desperately afraid of being judged by his 'lawfully wedded wife.'

Neither of us need have worried. Ramona smiles, and, somehow, both of them get along beautifully. Practically as soon as Irka arrives, due to the hour, I am forced to excuse myself to hail a taxi. Still, the two who theoretically have no common language find one first. When we take our seats, I am the one who feels funny, out with these two women who both know me. Irka, me and Ramona ... Ramona, me and Irka. The operetta, *Peasant and Knights* by Alexander Fredro, is upbeat, the costuming colourful. It depicts the Polish magnates of the seventeen hundreds. Oh, what could have been.

Seeing Irka is like finding a long-lost family member. She is of sad face, not at all the same proud, outgoing woman she once was; but she still arouses all my warm feelings. In Polish, I confide to her about my marriages. She tells me more about her husband. I do not think she told him what she did in Auschwitz. What the camp does to your life! I wonder what she thinks as she looks at me.

At the end of the evening we meet Irka's son, somewhat hesitant about this strange Canadian visitor from his mother's past. For her part, Irka seems to exhibit what is more than the normal pride in her offspring, maybe her usual self-congratulation, maybe a nervous affectation for her emotion-inducing guests. After our evening, Ramona says remarkably little, and I let it rest.

Ramona is there when I am decorated with the Cross of Auschwitz, a coveted award given to survivors who have in some way preserved the memory

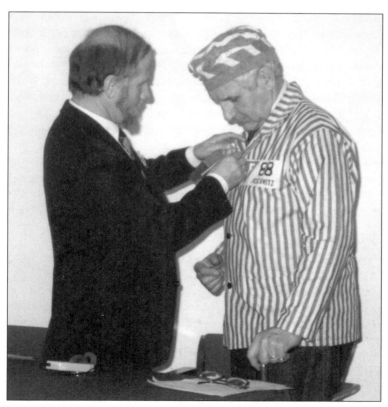

Sigmund receiving the Cross of Auschwitz, Warsaw, 1985.

of Auschwitz. Who would have thought back then that anything like this would happen? The presentation is the reason why we are there at this time. Instituted in 1980 by General Jaruzelski, very few have received it. My citation is for service abroad.

On the way back home to Canada, I show Ramona Sachsenhausen. The U-Bahn from Berlin follows the same track I traversed years earlier when they evacuated the fire brigade from Auschwitz. Signs on the station wall, now suburbia, still read "Sachsenhausen." On the road, we see tourist signs: 'Route of Death March.' The site where tens of thousands perished is a green park. Where the *Krematorium* was, now stands a modest little structure. And like so many others, the building to the right side of the entrance where the fire brigade lived no longer exists; in its place stands a museum. I tell her about the cat. Hard to understand why I did it; it was such a tremendous risk, belonging to a German Kapo and all. I killed it. Slept with it all night. Fluids were coming out. In the morning everyone was wondering what the horrible smell was. Mieczysław Zakrzewski, a fire brigade mechanic in Group One, cooked it.

We spend time in East Berlin, where I have learned there is a tomb, erected during the early Russian occupation, for the unknown Russian soldier. The Russians who liberated Auschwitz, whose prisoners-of-war died there under such brutal treatment, should receive respect. So I arrange to place a wreath on the monument, and, as a survivor from the first transport, I notify the East German press. Since the monument is in the *Tiergarten,* now in the British zone, I have to get permission from the Russians to join the honorary watch that enters the Western zone each morning and evening. I also have to inform the West Berlin police. The British even send a company of soldiers, though the Russian enclave is completely cordoned off and they have to stand several hundred metres away on the street. I plead with the Russian officers to at least let the newsman in—to no avail.

No clouds intervene on our long flight home across whitened Greenland, over the slate-grey Hudson Bay, down over the expansive Saskatchewan prairie. I watch Ramona's darkness silhouetted against the cabin window. Her face is turned, locked to the view of geometric patches, still visible though dusted with snow, where in summer green crops grow along the iridescent rivers slithering across the prairie.

The trip was lost on Ramona. Birkenau is the entire horror of Auschwitz. As far as I am concerned we put in far too little time there. On the train from Poland to Berlin we couldn't get seats for a good part of the way. Of Sachsenhausen, little remained. And when we stopped in Berlin, Ramona was feeling ill. When I scurried around to speak to newspaper reporters the day after we arrived, she had to remain unhappily behind, coughing, alone in the third-rate hotel room. She hated Berlin. It rained. The arrangements were difficult: the Soviets were suspicious of why I wanted to lay a wreath for their fallen soldiers. I was bouncing from one office to another the better part of two days. She became annoyed, and it spoiled the trip for her. "Shall we go out and enjoy night life?" I had said when I came in that evening.

She replied in English. "You're away all the day and think to make it up at the night. No, sir!"

On the plane home she is still grumbling, more quietly now in Spanish. "This was not my idea of a vacation. Auschwitz was cold. Berlin was cold and boring, and the rooming house we stayed in was cold, boring and run-down. I swear, I will never go with you to Poland again."

Later, she pronounces out of the blue, "Irka, she was trapped. Who knows, if I had been there, maybe I would have chosen Block Twenty-four, too." I breathe out.

Soon after our return, I form the Auschwitz Awareness Society—Alberta Venture of Christians and Jews, becoming its vice-president and coordinator. "Auschwitz awareness means new way of looking at world," I tell soon-to-be sponsor Witold Kryzmien, President, Polish Culture Society, Edmonton. "We'll work for better understanding between Christians and Jews. We'll support teaching Holocaust. We'll promote Canadian heritage of racial and religious tolerance."[44]

I motor out of Calgary by the flyover onto Memorial Drive East, then cut onto the Deerfoot North. In no time at all I am in the countryside, gliding through Alberta's flatland, passing bales of hay lounging in stacks as big as a farm house. During the last few weeks I have been asweat with memories, especially when driving, part of the baggage that makes getting from event to event its own emotional ski slope. The harvest hayride in rural Poland suddenly comes back to me:

Surochów, Nowy Targ, Piotrowice, Nisko. In the small communities, everybody including us boys helps bring in the hay. Hay hand-cut with a scythe. Hay piled up four metres above the ground. Higher even than the wooden wagon into which it flies. At the centre top of the pile, running the full length of the cart, a six-metre horizontal pole with chains. Chains attached to both sides of the cart. Keep the pile from breaking apart as the horse-drawn wagon jounces its way over rutted country roads. Could I ever forget this hayride, the sweating horses tugging the shafts? Could I ever forget the Russian PoW's returning from their work details with bodies piled high like hay? Some bleeding. Some still moving. My eyes are punished! Where are the horses? Oh, the *Verdammten Bolschewiken* pull this hayride of the dead. Every day another *Rollwagen* full, every day the "damned Bolsheviks" making like horses.

This is also Auschwitz Awareness.

The steering wheel vibrates in my hand from the northern gusts. Even though I am inside, I button up my coat. A herd of cattle catches my notice. The cows huddle, pushing towards the centre in the Alberta winter wind, visible jets of air spraying from their nostrils. Where is the farmer? More images:

A blue day in November. Russian prisoners naked outside Block Twenty-three. Kapo sprays them with a hose. You filthy, dirty animals; when will you learn to wash? Lowing like cattle, stomping their feet, they press in on each other in the middle for warmth. Steam from their freezing bodies rises around them. Tomorrow? In the *Rollwagen.*

From their first arrival in the camp, the Russian prisoners occupied the bottom of the Auschwitz pecking order, *Untermenschen.* Because Nazi hatred focused on the Russian enemy, the arrival of Russian PoW's even provided a slight respite for the Jews. My internal screen gives me no rest:

Me. Returning from work at SS officer Hans Aumeier's house. On the road, about two hundred Russian prisoners. When did they arrive? The Russians? scarcely a few weeks ago. Abruptly, they break ranks, skitter like cockroaches towards a pile of rotting white beets. Are they crazy? Halt! Halt! the guards call unsuccessfully. Devour the vegetables mildewed from the October rains. If I were not so angry at them for being hungry! Lead in my arms and legs. I am powerless to help them. They are beaten. Do not watch! Avert your eyes! I do watch. Tomorrow? These, too, in the *Rollwagen.*

Another body in a *Rollwagen.* Farmer. Comes into the hotel in Fort Assiniboine. Hungarian. Served during the war with the German army as a male nurse. Today he is heavyset with a stomach, about my age, sixty-six. Has five adopted children, all in trouble. See his eyes. Same eyes I've seen in camp when a person realizes things are hopeless. Recently overheard him talking: Wife died of overdose. Try to picture it: he popped her in a plastic bag, threw her in the trunk of the car and hauled her back to her family in Saskatchewan. There's a *Rollwagen* for you. You shouldn't laugh, but I do when I imagine someone stealing his car while he takes a coffee break, opening the trunk at the chop-shop. Or the RCMP stopping him at a checkpoint. Oh, that? Just my wife.

The whine of a passing truck startles me from my reverie. Out of the side of my eye, I catch written onto its side, 'NSDAP', the sign of the Nazi party soldiers wore on their sleeves. I shudder involuntarily. A second look reveals it's 'NFDAP'. What strikes me is, if I had known in camp that this would happen to me, it would have been a big joke, a tremendous relief. To my left now rise the many tanks of the Bowden refinery. To my right, signs lure me off the highway to take advantage of the wholesale gas prices the refinery offers. Back on the road, the Bowden Penitentiary, watch towers on one leg every so many metres, looms on the left. Merely passing by sends butterflies to my stomach, especially when illuminated at night. In my mind's eye I see Irka and me standing at the window, watching various segments of Auschwitz' fence appearing and disappearing in the moving lights. When I lived in Toronto, my sympathies pulled me to join the John Howard Society devoted to prison reform.

I spot no people at all from the road. A rectangular shadow flits right alongside me in the morning sun. Following my attendance at yesterday's provincial meeting of the Canadian Council of Christians and Jews, I got plenty of sleep. But staring out the windshield at the ribbon of highway is mesmerizing, while thoughts of yesterday's meeting encompass me like skin, absorbing my attention. I was representing the Auschwitz Awareness Society: How to answer a question like that? Could I perhaps have answered her better? She had good intentions. Why do I always get the best responses when it is too late? More flashes, more scenes. Then suddenly, time stands still. A voice rings in my ears: Be careful on the way home, the November roads might be slick. My five-speed Jimmy is poised into the oblivion like a rocket ship ready to launch. I can hear my own breathing, rising and falling like the sea, a sea inside of my brain, too fast. The wind must be whipping up the waters. My body sends messages of pain from all quarters. I crane my neck around. Fortunately, no other cars are involved. The last remains of purple fireweed catch the eye.

The Wetaskiwin Hospital, some one hundred eighty kilometres south of Fort Assiniboine. In the recovery room, the walls are pallid grey, lights dim, the smell of antiseptic, the sound of breathing. Boys are not here yet. Good job, too, I think, for their father is in no shape to give them his blessing.

It is touch-and-go. The patient slides into the corner where wall meets wall. In my delirium, I have become another man watching *Achtundachtzig* wake up in the *H.K.B.*, the prisoners' sick bay, trying to urinate in a bent pot:

Why can't I seem to go? What's wrong? Why are all those other prisoners watching? You are in the meningitis ward, they are saying. Who? what? the meningitis ward? A mystery shrouded in mystery. How How did I get to the sick bay from the *Tischlerei* where I work? What is this thin woollen square over my naked torso? Raking my skin so, want to jump out of it, jump, JUMP out of it. My body, rash all over it, lice-infected, deafness, swelling joints. Can't stand the curdled odour of my own vomit. Can't even blink my eyes for the pain. Please, *Mamusia*, where are you? Cracks in the wall form weird pictographs that disappear and then return, words which *Achtundachtzig* tries to decipher but cannot. A letter goes home. To avoid censoring, it reads: Dear *Mamusia* and *Tatuś*, so sorry to hear Atia's ill. From out of the scrawl, the hand of a fresh-faced second-year SS medical student administers aspirin, boiled water, and injections of alcohol. The dream is weird. In Canada, it notes, they never heard of pure alcohol injections as a treatment. Turning the head is painful. *Achtundachtzig* finds no yellow stars among the patients. Their meningitis treatment is *Genickschuss*, a shot behind the skull. Did once overhear a German Kapo sneer at a Jew: *Ach! ach!* so you say you're sick; well, just lie down on the ground; if you're lucky, by tomorrow morning you'll be dead. What seems like later that day but is not, a form half helps, half pushes *Achtundachtzig* into a special, open-seated reclining chair. Another form battens down my arms, people doing things to my body. Without warning, my spine is punctured to draw cerebrospinal fluid. That me screaming? How is it possible that anaesthesia is a thing of the past? Some become permanently paralysed. A festering abscess in *Achtundachtzig's* leg. Try to walk. Sense of balance not right. How the ground seems to have life of its own! The air here is hot, very hot—no, freezing! From the floor, I recognize the doctor from my home town, my father's physician. Dr. Pizło, remember me?

Sobolewski from Nisko. The object of my pleas is too busy dealing narcotics to help.

Whispering voices come and go, washing over me like from a distant hollow: "Goodnight, Papa." I try to respond, try even to lift my hand. My arms are numb, my head heavy. I shiver. What will become of them if their father does not make it? The boys are not ready to be on their own. I think of *Tatuś*. Did he think me capable, young but resourceful, ready to face the inevitable, when on the night he lay sick Nazis took me, a fledgling from the nest? Tears blur my vision. After a while, seeing and hearing nothing, they depart, murmuring to each other.

Different room, different doctor:

A few months or years have elapsed since *Achtundachtzig* had his spinal. Again, who knows how I arrived at the *H.K.B.?* Someone drags out a body by the feet, I can hear the head bump on each step. Why are you doing that! Am I still breathing? Yes? For how long? *Jezus-Marja*, my shaved head kills! Freezing, even while wrapped in this stupid blanket. What good is it? And what are these dark reddish spots all over my body? Ah, all these fruits and juices at the bottom of my bed. No one wants to give them to me. Please! please! I will die in the midst of plenty; where are you, somebody? Where? I will surely die; oh, Zończyk, so glad you've come. Same Zończyk who used to hang around outside the latrine window for chance at some soup scrapings. Risking his own life, he conjures up some lifesaving smuggled sandwiches and raw onion (vitamin C). It is an old favour returned, no hallucination. Added to the boiled water and aspirin, the medicine for everything, the gift from Zończyk is my only treatment. From the shadows a man is coughing hoarsely. From where exactly? Impossible to tell. A deep sleep. I am licking and flicking through a journal with black stiff covers at the Auschwitz State Museum Archives. I fix on a page, my attention rivetted on the handwritten word *Achtundachtzig*. Prisoner 88 admitted to *H.K.B.* 25 May 1942; afflicted with *Fleckfieber*, typhus; released 6 July 1942. Another journal in the same Auschwitz Archives: 5 July 1942, train of Slovakian Jews arrived; ramp duty: SS Dr. Friedrich Entress. They say, to the sound of Tango Milonga,[45] a macabre joke for a few Nazi ears only, the doctor selected 254 men and 108 women for work; the surplus—old people, invalids, women with small children, numbering 1,636—the same day sent to perish. The doctor? A Polish physician of German origin. Took his degree at the University of Posen. Pretends not to know Polish. Look at him—he tries to out-German the Germans. What luck, barely six weeks after *Achtundachtzig's* release from the *H.K.B.*, they say Entress personally selects some thousand convalescing typhus patients for gassing.[46] The doctor, my doctor.

I hear a scream as a green lab jacket enters my room.

Days and days, twelve days in the hospital, and Ramona never comes. Speaking English again, she tells me after I am released, "All because of the Jews you had an accident and practically killed yourself. Every month you going somewhere else. No wonder you have the accidents."

Fourteen: Sigmund S.

Fort Assiniboine Tavern 1990

The door opens and a couple comes in. Their eyes wander around the tavern. Pink walls, dark brown mouldings, reddish carpet—punk rock colours in the northern arboreal forest; road kill. Until I hear their German, I barely note their arrival. "Ramona," I call through the side door to the trailer, "we need steak." Locals from miles around know Ramona. Travel any place within fifty kilometres, and people will be coming up to say 'hello'. Her cooking holds our operation together. An American steak might be complemented by 'Christians and Moors', a side dish of rice and black beans, or by some other Spanish surprise that keeps people coming back.

I bring their beer. Alexander and Barbara Krebs-Gehlen have come down the Athabasca River in a kayak they brought over from Frankfurt. I guess they saw the hotel sign, *Gasthaus,* I have out on the river. Ramona and I strike up a relationship with them. I move the conversation around to Auschwitz and my work. Many Germans pass through, always on their way downstream to Athabasca, once the gateway to the Klondike; but none show interest in *Achtundachtzig* as do the Krebs-Gehlens. It turns out they know Hans Loewy, director of the Frankfurt Holocaust Documentary Centre.

"And what about your parents?" I ask. I catch them glance at one another, and wonder to myself if I have crossed an unwritten line. They do not have to answer; they could pass it. He takes a breath.

"My father prospered during the war, really prospered. He worked in 'adult education', produced booklets. Was he implicated? He was a member of the party, but I know he did not agree with everything. There was a great business in propaganda and pamphleteering going on. I wonder what my father was doing. But he never told me. Certainly he was no hero. You could not talk and expect to do business. I think about this very much. My friends don't ask such questions. Too hard.

"As for Barbara's father, he was a Russian prisoner doing forced labour in Germany."

"My mother never told him she was pregnant," she interrupts. "He went back after liberation to Russia not knowing I exist. I grew up in a so-called upper-class family. Because I am an illegitimate daughter, nobody told me anything about the family on either side. I grew up with the idea I'm not a person to be loved. I'm fighting. It's true. I'm fighting, I'm fighting, I'm fighting. I asked once my mother about what the family was doing during the war. My grandfather was a businessman. I think he owned the factory where my mother came in contact with my father; something had to have touched him. But she became very aggressive. 'We knew nothing,' she shouted."

"We tried to find Barbara's father through the Red Cross," Alexander tells me. "There was no trace. As a returning prisoner-of-war, Stalin must have murdered him."

"Modern Germany faces important choices," Barbara says. I take the quick change in topics to indicate a closure regarding the parents. If it is painfully incomprehensible for them to face the issue, I can understand that. It is almost as hard for them to figure out what is happening in Germany now. Barbara Krebs-Gehlen goes on. "There are those who speak about the reunification. It is everybody's hope, really. But there are those who speak about it in tones which echo the old Nazi propaganda. And it gets listeners, especially among the youth who are looking for some kind of meaning. All they have is TV; everyone is so busy, no one talks to them."

Later, while I'm wrapping a set of moose antlers as a gift, I hear Barbara ask Ramona why I don't talk about my sons more. "There are problems," Ramona answers.

"It is such a pity his own children don't understand him. Someone told me recently, 'How can human beings draw their sustenance just from family?' Because of my personal biography, because Alexander and I have no children, I think family is a blessing. What do you think about Sigmund's work, Ramona?"

"I wish I lived in Toronto like before. A small town no is for me."

Alexander says later, "Some experiences are so incomparable, we can't take them over generations." Of the two, he is the historian and philosopher.

My friends may be dropping away, but Germans are definitely becoming more interested. Their visit affords me the opportunity to dig deeper into German background. From this and other discussions, I learn that the Holy Roman Empire did not see itself as a multicultural enterprise, as did Poland during its golden age. When the early Middle Ages swirled in the gale of frenzied mob rage loosed by the Crusades, the Jews were buffeted: why go all the way to Palestine when we have worse Devils living right here amongst us? There was mass slaughter. Many Nazi regulations had their antecedents centuries earlier in the Church.[47] Again the role of Christianity gets to me. During the Black Death epidemic, the excesses of the Reformation, and the Thirty Years War, Jews bore the storm along with everyone else, and, then, as a pleasant bonus, found themselves blamed for all the turbulence and strain.

Alexander tells me more about the role of the Church. It is painful to learn that, "on the one hand, the Church encouraged harassment and expulsion of enemies of Christian dogma; on the other hand, some Popes endeavoured to preserve a demeaned Jewish community as an example of what happens to those who lack Divine favour. Thus, after a vicious pulpit-induced rampage against the Jews, a Pope might contend against the blood accusation and other amusements, even intervening on behalf of local Jewish communities. Then, the same Pope might revert to Jewish denunciation, again often resulting in expulsions including invariably the nullification of all debts owed to the Jews." [48]

"What about German Lutheranism," I ask, "didn't the Protestant Reformation bring the Jews relief?"

"Only at first. When the Jews not only refused the old Church but also the new Protestantism, Luther referred to 'the stiff-necked Jews, ironhearted and stubborn as the Devil', assailing them as 'venomous and virulent', 'thieves and brigands' and 'disgusting vermin'. Luther rained on all his perceived opponents in similar language. However, regarding Jews, he also fomented for their forced labour and/or banishment.[49] Centuries later, the term 'disgusting vermin' was appropriated for Nazi propaganda." This opens doors for me.

The grounds and residence of the Governor General of Canada swarm with RCMP. I am amazed by the security. We have to go through two cordons of police. We are in Ottawa to greet the Polish Prime Minister Tadeusz Mazowiecki. Marion Strzelecki, past-president of the Polish Congress, and

Prime Minister Tadeusz Mazowiecki and Sigmund in Ottawa, 1988.
Courtesy of the Ottawa Citizen.

Rabbi Saul Aranov of Ottawa, join me. Our delegation is seeking action in Auschwitz. The Governor General strides side-by-side with his guest, the Polish Prime Minister. They wear black jackets, striped pants. Aides of both trail behind in similar uniform. The pomp and ceremony both captivate and put off. By prearrangement, the Prime Minister's party pauses in front of us. Rabbi Aranov recites a prayer in Hebrew, as is Jewish tradition in the presence of authority, even non-Jewish authority.

"What *is* this?" asks an aide.

"A blessing for the Prime Minister," the rabbi replies.

The aide introduces the dignitaries, and waiting according to protocol for the Prime Minister to first extend his arm, we all shake hands. "For Prime Minister's son," I say in Polish, presenting him with a historical book of Canada.

"How did you know he's an historian?" he asks. I shrug. He hands it to an aide, and adds, "I have delegated the first counsel to hear your concerns after the ceremonies."

When we finally meet the first counsel, he vehemently refuses to allow in the newsman I bring with us. Neither does he listen much. Instead, he subjects us to a long speech, only the ending of which is notable: "The Polish government will establish a special international commission, including Jews, to advise the government on the management of Auschwitz."

Back at home, I stare at the wall. It is early afternoon. Iris has died, the lawyer said. He found my name on the separation agreement. Our marriage, neither angry nor calm, floats silently before me. Through all our differences, didn't she always stand by me, help me over my hurdles? Even after the divorce, she kept my name, never remarried. Did I give her what she deserved? I had no idea how important children would be. I have to think she got a rough deal from me. "O *Jezus-Marja*, I'm so guilty." Yet hardly have I choked out my pain when, in a strange, long-forgotten state of introspection, I find myself marvelling: "All these years since Auschwitz, and death is starting to mean something to me again!"

I am sitting in the empty tavern with my friend, the Jewish historian. His friendship is quite unusual. In the process of losing my fellow Polish friends, I have made too few Jewish replacements. So many Jews view my work with suspicion. They cannot fathom, any more than my sons can, why a Polish Catholic would help Jews. Sometimes their lack of acceptance disheartens me. Most of the time it helps, because, as a result, I know my own motives are neither self-glorification nor pleasure.

Except for my friend Reuven's skull-cap no one could distinguish him. In Calgary, he dresses for business. On the odd time he visits here, he wears jeans. When he comes, we always learn from each other. "Of course you're down. You may have divorced," he says, "but she still shares a part of your life—as Auschwitz does. Although you would not go back to it, you would not want to erase it, either. Yes? She is part of what makes you, you. And yes, your remorse is remarkable. Most of us have not had the experiences to appreciate that."

Later the conversation shifts. "I try not to allow myself to be bitter," I tell him. "Right, bitterness devours. Why let them have the victory?"

Reuven has become my teacher in German–Jewish relations, sometimes testing his lectures on me. He knows I am a history buff, only read historical nonfiction. Naturally, I am interested in Christian-Jewish dialogue and the background of the Holocaust. And ever since the Krebs-Gehlens found their way to the tavern, I have this desire to dig deeper. Once I ask Reuven, "German Jews fled to Poland, bringing with them their Germanic language and their passion for education. Did it have to be that way?"

I watch Reuven stroke his beard. It is what he does when he organizes his thoughts, dividing it in two points, then bringing it back together. "There were periods of respite in Germany. When the Holy Roman Empire broke up into independent principalities, there were different laws in different places. I don't have to tell you about that. The result was that where an occasional 'court Jew' had influence, certain disabilities were eased." He goes on about another descendant of Saul Wahl. "He was born in 1729 in Dessau, the son of a modest Torah scribe. Jewish historians esteem him to be, after the Moses of the Bible, and the noted mediaeval philosopher Moses Maimonides, the 'third Moses', with whom a new Jewish era begins. It was not long until this Moses was revered among the liberal *salon* society folk for his literary and philosophical talent."

We step out from the hotel, turn right past the trailer. Me with a cane, him with his hands behind his back. The sunlight leaps like a Rocky Mountain goat as the clouds alternately mask and unmask the sun's rays. "This is great weather," I say. "I try to get exercise everyday. Mornings I lay on floor exercising abdominal muscles in patch of sunlight, then shadow-box in front of mirror. How strange for me to watch old man with too much flabby skin punching away at air. Yet, I've gotten used to seeing it. Can even smile to know I'm still in better shape than most others my age."

"I would do well to model myself after you," he says, "in many ways. I was telling you about Moses Mendelssohn. The playwright, Ephraim Gotthold Lessing, modelled the protagonist of his *Nathan the Wise* after him. At one point, the Friar in the play exclaims, 'Nathan, Nathan, you are a Christian! By God, you are a Christian! There was never a better Christian!' To which Nathan replies, 'What makes me seem Christian to you, makes you seem Jewish to me.'" When Reuven will first show me act four, scene seven of the German text in the Krebs-Gehlen's Frankfurt library, I'll look for the antisemitism that I automatically suspect. Then I'll realize it is anything but. Some people accuse me of finding antisemitism even where none exists. True, Auschwitz maybe made me suspicious. But the camp did not destroy my head; my reading never stops.

"Watch your step," he says. We have crossed the road where, following the overgrown ruts of a land rover through the bracken and scrub, we pick our way down to the river. Since the accident, it is harder and harder for me to manoeuvre my pulled leg over the soft, uneven tangle. The shuffle of twigs and brush merges with the ever-louder rush of the Athabasca River. "Ah, smell," Reuven says, "pine, muskeg and the river. Do you walk here often? You should, you know. I try to get a month in the woods every year. I do my best thinking in the summer. What were we saying? O yes. Mendelssohn, like his ancestor Wahl, was a product of his times. A great thinker, you know, won a prize Kant competed for. His rationalism joins comfortably with the seeds of Enlightenment that Napoleon sowed on his march eastwards. However, Mendelssohn was also a tragic figure."

"Let me guess, Christianity again?"

"Unfortunately." Reuven raises his voice to overcome the river. "In 1769, a Protestant minister by the name of Lavater publicly goaded Mendelssohn to renounce his religion."

"How did I know," I say. "This is so important to me."

"The consequence was to turn him inward toward the advancement of his people. As a result, Mendelssohn translated the Bible into German. Many rabbis hailed the publication, among them Rabbi Hirschel Levin and his son Rabbi Saul Levin, both also descended from Saul Wahl. Mendelssohn's Bible spread to every little village, helping thousands of *Yeshivoh* students master modern German from his translation. Thus, Jewish youth prepared themselves for the German universities. Yet many Jewish scholars decried his work. They feared that Mendelssohn's translation would only lead to assimilation."

"What doomsayers."

As we have come to the river bank, we pause on a jutting rock. "The weather is changing; I love the shadows on the river. Watch that stick," he says. It swirls in the water, disappears, only to reappear like an arboreal loon several metres away. "By the close of Mendelssohn's career, any passing approval toward the Jews had undergone complete transformation. Rationalists such as Kant ridiculed Mendelssohn's view of Judaism, and German neo-Romanticists conceded to Jews no place at all in modern Germany."[50] We wind our way back to the hotel, again carefully groping with our toes for the ruts hidden in the underbrush, me limping as usual. The sound of the wind replaces that of the water. Reuven continues in a raised voice. "In the Germany of Mendelssohn's time, were fears of assimilation justified? In the early 1800s, the Hep! Hep! riots occurred. German universities excluded 'foreign elements', who 'poisoned' the culture of the *Volk*. You know about this, yes? From your reading. I am convinced everything begins here. Legal and political impediments reached intolerable proportions. Many Jews made conversions of 'conviction', the conviction that it was better to be a professor in Berlin than a Torah scribe in Dessau. Men like Heinrich Heine, the German bard, and Ludwig Börne, the correspondent, underwent conversion as the entry pass to German society. From ten children, Mendelssohn himself left no Jewish descendants."

LOT's Ilyushin turboprop swoops down, a lone white eagle through a grey floor of clouds. The Russian-made claptrap shudders as it descends, causing

Plaque presentation. Izzy Burstyn, Sigmund, Rabbi Shmuel Mann.

passengers to look at one another. Then, rain streaking across the double-paned windows, it lands with two thumps, flattening out onto a slick sleet-covered fairway in the middle of the afternoon. The waiting room is crowded. "Zygmunt, over here."

"Stanisław, right on time. You wait long, man?"

"No, just got here. There's never a problem here." He is right. In the tiny reception area, my friend Stanisław Zakowski has no trouble spotting me. Stan negotiates his taxi through the congestion of the airport boulevard, heading towards central Warsaw. Warsawians with slickers pulled around them huddle under the awnings of street vendors' stands, everywhere sprung up since the arrival of capitalism.

The grey sky matches the grey pavement and massive grey buildings. Warsaw seems like the weariest city in the world. Wherever you go, you are overwhelmed by the stale, stodgy reconstruction of the postwar workers' regime, which must have believed the heavier the cement, the better. In 1939, a full third of its population was Jewish. Today, the remaining synagogue is a museum; and the rabbi, Rabbi Pinhas Joskovicz, as far as I know the only one in Poland at this time, leads a small congregation of mostly foreign transplants. In this presidential campaign period, newspapers are speculating that Jews control the new democratic government of Poland. Four thousand Jews are supposed to control this Catholic nation of nearly forty million.

It is the fiftieth anniversary of the opening of Auschwitz, and our society is also on a mission to commemorate the 1944 Jewish *Sonderkommando* uprising at the *Krematorium IV* complex in Birkenau. In the name of the Auschwitz Awareness Society, Izzy Burstyn, Rabbi Shmuel Mann and I present a plaque to the Minister of Culture, Pani Izabela Cywinska, in Warsaw.

After the Warsaw ceremony, we go to Auschwitz where the plaque will be installed. From my old quarters, I survey the camp. About five hundred metres from the gate, the fire trucks bedded down in garages that also protected several vehicles used for transporting prisoners to the gas chambers. I saw them go every day, spoke to their crew. On this, the fiftieth anniversary of Auschwitz's opening, the fire garages with their characteristic high wooden towers for drying fire hoses still stand out.

I think of Georg Engelschall, the officer who trained us:

Engelschall. More humane than the others. Worst he does? Exhibit us, a sideshow for visiting SS and NSDAP dignitaries. Has us scaling ladders; leaping from the third floor onto a mat, arms and legs swimming in the air; performing other exercises. All to impress some officers from Berlin. At least let Irka watch, why don't you! My first alarm, a fire in one of the delousing saunas near Block Two. Afterwards, Engelschall calls me aside. You, sir, were quite energetic out there; careful not to get too close, smoke can be toxic. He uses the German *polite you*. Usually they use not just *du*, but also you cursed Polish bandit, or you swinehead. This from citizens of a country where, according to a nineteenth-century law, suits are often brought and won for the insult of being called a name. The cross-eyed guard at the *H.W.L.* excavation used to call me, You lazy bum, you. To the Jews he would say, We'll soon finish you off, you Jewish pig, you. So, a Nazi using the *Sie* form of address, very unusual. Spring of 1943, when Zdzisław Tora of Kraków contracts pneumonia, Engelschall makes me group leader. When Engelschall's appointed *Grupleiter* jumps first, he compliments me. For leadership. When I'm caught sneaking out of Irka's window, he intercedes with Hössler on my behalf. Engelschall also has a friendship going with our Kapo, Tamborski. He ever hit or kick anyone? Not as far as I can see. Not even a Jew.

But Engelschall did have a past. For about six months in 1941, he was *Blockführer* in the Bunker. Yet even there, other prisoners recall him as most humane. And according to our comrade Dacko, on at least one occasion, Engelschall took over the Jewish *selekcja* on the Ramp when the SS Doctor failed to arrive. The Nazis eventually got everyone, even the good ones.

"Boys, not all SS were sadists."

On my last trip, taken to attend a reunion of all classes from my Cadet school in Rawicz, I took a side trip to Munich to meet Joseph Engelschall, the brother of our fire brigade leader, Georg. Both Georg's brothers likewise had served in the SS. I also met Georg's daughter, Helga. She volunteered her own advice, "You should forget it. With all that's hap-

Fire house. Three bays for fire trucks still standing outside the main gate. What looks like a chimney is the tower on which the hoses were dried.

pening in the world, forget Auschwitz." Two weeks later she sent a contribution to support the Auschwitz Awareness Society. No letter, just the money.

In the same area is the *Autoschlosserei* where prisoner mechanics did repairs. Towards the end of the war, due to the shortage of petrol, many Auschwitz vehicles were converted to wood gas or wood alcohol. A device similar to a little oven was mounted in front on the driver's side. He stuffed wood in it, causing the machine to jolt along tumultuously, a very crude system given to continual engine blockage. The Polish mechanics were constantly repairing the trucks, not always expeditiously. The Kapo of this repair shop, a German communist, was subsequently shot for helping others to escape.

At the fiftieth anniversary ceremonies, Bishop Julian Groblicki, a senior

bishop from Kraków, lectures about the gravel yard soaked with "Aryan blood."
My mind flitting back to Krankemann pushing Jews to run circles like horses
in this very yard, I protest this obscene misrepresentation to Archbishop
Muszynski, the chairman of the Polish Catholic dialogue with Judaism.

It is the first meeting of the International Auschwitz Council, established
by the new Polish government. *Achtundachtzig* asks for and receives observer
status. Then, on the windswept fields of Birkenau, with the museum director,
government representatives and a priest from the Saint Maximilian Kolbe
Church, we unveil the plaque. A film crew that travelled with us from Canada
records the event.

History must be the record of what happened, and not of what some
political theory says should have happened. Still, what is the big deal with
plaques? Pola Kasprzyk, the mother of the Polish Consul in Vancouver, lives
almost on top of the old Jewish cemetery in Kraków. Later, I meet her and
Dr. Jonathan Webber, rabbi and professor of Judaic studies at the University
of Oxford, Great Britain, appointed as founding member of the International
Auschwitz Council. Pola is like the local chamber of commerce. "Kraków was
the capital of Poland until 1610," our matronly yet stylishly clad, red-haired
guide tells us, as we drive through town. She relates detail to events. "During
the Nazi occupation, Nazi Governor-General Frank appropriated the king's
castle above us on Wawel Hill for himself. You'll be interested to know the
magnificent sixteenth-century tapestries inside spent the war years in Canada."

"Well, we did nice job of it," I mumble in the back seat, as I look up at
the huge dark shadow of ancient ramparts and turrets. "We Poles couldn't
save our Jews, though we could our tapestries. As for my new country, Canada
wouldn't take our Jews, though she would our tapestries."[51]

Pola continues without hearing, "Rubens designed many of them...."
Footing it through the Old Town crowded with people and pigeons, she
explains, "Here, in Sukiennice, the market square dating back to the thirteenth century, the Polish kings were crowned. That lone Gothic tower still
survives; and each day from this redbrick church, a trumpeter sounds 'Hejnal
Krakówski', breaking off midway, when tradition has it a Tatar arrow shot
through his mediaeval predecessor's gullet."

Pola often visits the Jewish cemetery near her apartment, sits in it, pulls
out weeds in a lonely, never-ending battle, even takes visitors there. It is in
total ruin, overgrown and unkempt. "Look at this," she mourns, "no one
remains to care for the gravestones still lying vandalized from the Nazi
occupation."

Markers, some eroded over time, poke out in various directions from the
brush as if in their loneliness reaching one to another. She memorizes the
names of the few Polish inscriptions, then lovingly uncovers a desecrated and
long-abandoned stone, stooping over to pull away the growth that has swallowed it. Its broken crown is missing, but two pillars in sculptured relief still
frame either side of the washed-out inscription. "Come see this one," she
calls. "Look at the design. What can you tell me about it?" A minute later

her voice again rings out, "Ah, here's what I was searching for. It's in Hebrew, but I can tell a great rabbi lies here. Look where his disciples have burned candles."

Dr. Webber goes over. "Shimon Sofer, Rabbi of Kraków, son of our renowned teacher the Hatam Sofer," he says in awe. "Makes you realize how un-Jewish it is that in Auschwitz not even a single Jewish tombstone exists to commemorate the murdered."

We circle the cemetery, the wall of which, she points out, consists of fragments of memorial stones. After the war, mournful Poles gathered the broken and desecrated stones from nearby towns, and fashioned them into the wall. Some names are visible. Others are chopped right off in the middle. "The Nazis used many to pave sidewalks, writing face-up so that is what you walked on. Often there was no way to know their original placement, so we salvaged what we could, building from them this wall." By the exit gate, she shows us a memorial containing dedications to untold millions of Jews destroyed by the Nazis in sundry Polish cities and villages. Even I am dizzy from the enormity of it all.

Pola tells us how as a child she used to help the Jews of the Kraków ghetto. Her cousin Marion Furtak was in the first transport, No. 247, and perished in Auschwitz. She stands at attention as Dr. Webber recites his prayer for the dead, "O God, full of compassion.... May they rest in peace." She crosses herself when he is done. I do, too. Here is a Pole whose heart cries for a people not her own.

Our feet linger as we sightsee through the Kasimierz quarter, the forlorn vestige of Kraków's six-hundred-year-old autonomous Jewish community. When the war began, a full quarter of Kraków's population was Jewish. Passing the buildings on the street, I can still discern the niches in the doorposts where once *mezuzahs* hung. And turning into old yards, I find sections of the old ghetto wall. Behind the small Remo synagogue lies buried the renowned Rabbi Moses Isserles, cousin of Saul Wahl. The oldest existing mediaeval synagogue in Poland, used as a stable by the Nazis, is being converted like so many others into a museum. We bribe a night watchman to enter. Sound echoes off walls dating from 1407. In front of the synagogue we pass a monument to thirty-two 'citizens' who were Polish heroes. "Many were probably Jews," I rankle, "and this monument nowhere mentions that."

Pola, this lover of Jewish history, standing in the heart of the old Jewish quarter, simply shakes her head, "They couldn't have been Jews, or it would say so." With that one statement she fires me up for ten years, demonstrating the significance of even a single memorial. At least our plaque is in place.

This time I am bringing Ramona a painted linen tablecloth. We glide from our place in the Frankfurt tarmac; taxi by the huge air busses, the little trains of baggage cars, the blue planes, tail after tail of blue birds in a gold circle. One seat in front of me, a young mother shakes rattles, coos, sings, rings for the flight attendants to take soiled diapers away, to warm a bottle, to bring a wet rag. Through it all, though, the baby still cries—the whole, interminable trip. I feel sorry for both of them. But sympathy cannot provide a good flight. Competing airlines must have recruited this mother.

After I visit Poland with Rabbi Shmuel Mann of Edmonton, Niedojadło, who had found himself unable to sign our telegram to the Deschênes Commission on the prosecution of war criminals, stops answering my letters altogether. Our relationship meant a lot to me. I cannot fathom the idea that a simple trip with a rabbi could break our long friendship. Two letters do arrive, though. Tadeusz Szymanski, former director of the Auschwitz Museum, asks why Rabbi Mann and I failed to lay a wreath at the cross in the convent garden. Archbishop Muszynski, to whom I complained about Bishop Groblicki's "Aryan blood" comment, also writes. He blesses my efforts to improve relations between Christians and Jews. However, I find nowhere within it any answer to my complaint.

What does give me answers is a deeper study of German culture. Already after the defeat of Napoleon, a distinctly German neo-Romanticism developed in which self is viewed as a product of racial identity. Each people, or *Volk*, possesses from birth its own historic mood that informs its national spirit, or *Volksgeist*. The German *Volk*, superior to all others, is destined to leadership; the Jewish *Volk*, inimical to all others, merits only extermination. Well before Naziism, these beliefs combined in a mounting pile of literature: more than one hundred thousand volumes, encompassing every field. When I heard the extent of this thinking, I had to see for myself: Culture! Education! Faith! Classics! Experimental communities! Science! Eugenics! Political theory! Economics! Politics! Over a hundred thousand volumes![52] I cannot believe how all-pervasive this German *neo-Romanticism* was. A few spoke out against the prevailing atmosphere; but they proved to be lone voices crying in the wilderness.

I tell the boys, "Germans starved, even during WWI, ghettoes they occupied. Had policy of property takeovers, labour drafts and inadequate rations. Following war, Jewish appeals to their record of national service and to accomplishments in science, technology and industry couldn't stem mounting antisemitism. Educated middle classes turned these very contributions into what they saw as Jewish link to negative aspects of modern civilization. What Germany really needed, they said, was *cultural* return. Industrialists, Prussian landed aristocracy, and conservative political parties all joined in attributing Germany's problems to international Jewish conspiracy.[53] Hitler's policies struck, when he finally appeared, chord that reverberated among masses of respectable, knowledgeable folk, those who were elite of universities, German Red Cross, Salvation Army, church choristers, and courts.[54]

"Crash and tinkle of broken windows. On 28 November 1938, *Kristallnacht*, synagogues blazed in hundreds of German towns; Jewish homes and shops were pillaged; Jews themselves vanished, one knew not where. Nazi government fined Jews seven million marks for damage they had provoked."

Barely two weeks later, the following voice rang out:

To: The *Führer* and *Reichskanzler* Adolf Hitler: The three churches of gratitude in Bremen have been inaugurated. They bear your name, *mein Führer*, in gratitude to God for the miraculous redemption of our nation at your hands from the abyss of Jewish-materialistic Bolshevism.

I thank you for having enabled us to express in these new churches what is a deep confession for us who are fully conscious Christian National Socialists. *Heil, mein Führer!* [55]

Do I ever have my work cut out for me. I am always trying to interpret all this to the boys. "You'll hear people say, 'Poles were worse than Nazis.' What they mean is that we often passionately joined in, fingering Jews for Nazis, cheering on SS. You should know, then, that German ideology that led to Nazism was cool and calculated crusade for Europe free of Jews. Compared to Polish heat, it was far more dangerous ... and destructive." The boys want to know if Hitler didn't invent antisemitism. "I wish it were true to say that Nazi Holocaust derived only from one crazy, unbalanced mind. Wish it were true, even, to say it began with Versailles. This night of nights had, many centuries back, its dusk. As Cardinal-Archbishop Clemens August Graf von Galen, who protested against euthanasia but not against treatment of Jews, once said, 'The Jews brought it against themselves for not accepting Christianity.'"

Neither is it over. Von Galen has been beatified, the first step to becoming a saint. And here in Alberta, the whir of buzz-saws. A small sawmill in Caroline, a village in the Rocky Mountain foothills noted for its rainbow trout spawning station. Terry Long, owner-operator, is the founding president of the Christian Defence League established to provide aid to Keegstra. More recently, he has become the Canadian Leader of the Aryan Nations, Church of Jesus Christ Christian. This tall, bearded, athletic man with a ready smile, born around 1948 in California, believes individuals are finally "ready to put a bullet in the enemy's head."[56] Under this man's signature a letter has gone out.[57]

In spite of a postscript asking recipients not to "talk to the media", the invitation gets dispensed and Ron Collister reads it on his CJCA talk show. Subsequently, the organizers confess they knew the media would publicize their message. *Achtundachtzig* responds as well. Normally, most people just make like ostriches; in fact, usually no one reacts at all, so I do. Otherwise, I only tell people about Auschwitz when they ask. Except for this trait of mine to object in person, I would say I lead a life pretty much the same as anyone else.

On a grey day, sky like a smeared blackboard, I arrive early at the Bradley farm in my stripers. The blackboard quickly fills with old experiences. I carry a picket sign:

> # RACIAL HATRED
> ## LEADS TO
> # AUSCHWITZ

A nine-metre cross has been erected, visible for kilometres on the prairie. Has anybody ever wondered what it is about this Christian symbol that it is used for hatred? Has anybody ever heard of anyone burning a Jewish star? The idea almost makes us laugh. So why a cross?

A handful, ten to fifteen other demonstrators also gather outside the gate. To me, real life is this tiny knot of demonstrators. The rest of the world is make-believe. There are other placards:

World has had enough hate

Ignorance + bigotry = RACISM

ALL MEN ARE CREATED EQUAL

God created man—not Blacks or Whites

WE ARE ALL BORN EQUAL—NAKED!

One paraded by Joan Pacquette, a preschool teacher from a nearby town, displays three exquisitely drawn seated babies with the words:

Racism means you're judged
before you can stand up for yourself.

The flip-side reads:

Being White doesn't make you right.

Jack Downey, who arranged to send the two Keegstra students to visit the camps, carries a large Canadian flag and wears his legion blazer and beret. This bear of a man strews flowers onto the Bradley drive as a peace symbol. Something prompts their 'guardsmen' to try and remove them, bending down with grave and dignified military stiffness in their version of full Nazi regalia, picking up the flowers like radioactive waste, their AK 47's slipping from their shoulders and goosing them.

The remaining flowers blow into the mud as cars come careening into the compound. Some wheel in so fast we are forced to leap out of the way. One black-lustre sedan with Nazi insignia halts directly in front of me. An iridescent door swings open, and Saskatchewan gun dealer Carney Milton Nerland alights, squinting and pointing. The simple fact of *Achtundachtzig's* presence enrages. My eye follows his outstretched finger up his arm to find looking back at me a one-eyed raven screeching invective. In the background, a public address system from the swastika-festooned farm blasts out a speech by American White Supremacist leader Jim Wickstrom. Forty-five years later! In Canada!

The guards, some masked and with Dobermans, representing The Brotherhood of Regular People (BHORP), line the gate, which is entirely covered by a white and black sign of greeting:

KKK	BHORP
WHITE POWER!	WELCOME'S
1990	ARYAN–NATIONS

It piques my interest that, off to the side, the welcome has another, smaller sign providing the commentary by which to see through the first:

BEWARE OF DOG

Looking up, I quickly realize this is more than a battle of signs. They carry various types of assault weapons. One self-styled guardsman photographs each of us protestors, writing down our licence plate numbers. I watch the Aryan 'Fest' quickly come to the flash point. Modern-day brown shirts rough up Brad Clark, a freelance reporter, several cameramen and demonstrators.

Achtundachtzig is a lightning rod for their rage. Nerland, a pudgy faced guy with mustache and beer-belly covered by a homespun Nazi uniform, dagger strapped to his side, confronts me swearing.

"Why are you hiding behind dark sunglasses?" I ask. "Why don't you take your glasses off?"

"Come and take them off, you fucking war hero, you survived Auschwitz, you'll survive me."

Like a television camera, I record Nerland and me from off to the side. Since 1967 I do this a lot less than I used to. From where the other protestors have drifted, I see this regalia-bedecked specimen, Canada's self-proclaimed pride, glaring at a sixty-seven-year-old man with a sign—Shame. I am by myself—Double shame. Before my eyes, I see *Blockälteste* Küserow (Kapo No. 17) peering out his window that day I grabbed a piece of bread.[58] It was a similar kind of a day. I am found and beaten. Like that day long ago in Auschwitz, I stand in my stripers facing straight at Nerland, a neutral look on my face. "This is what I survived for?" I reassure myself, "This guy? Big deal! They already cut my heart out in Auschwitz." I say to the world, "This is indeed what I survived for."

"You're one of the ones they didn't work to death," Nerland jeers, frothing himself up. "You parasite. You fucking weren't able to work in the camps good enough to feed the Nazi war machine. What the fuck are you doing over here, you piece of shit! You lying son of a bitch. You tell everyone they got what, twenty million people at Auschwitz? Why don't you tell me they made fucking soap out of your auntie and fucking luggage out of your uncle. They made luggage out of him. I've got it in the fucking trunk of my car. I've got luggage made from your fucking uncle."

I simply turn his ranting and raving off. I am once again a fortified camp, a stone pillar, thick walls against the whole land; this psychic closing is a long-ago acquired skill, a way to get from one day to the next without losing my mind. Since Auschwitz, this survival adaptation had become an impediment to the establishment of close relationships. Today it again helps me. I stand quiet with the sign.

The presence of *Achtundachtzig* works like a truth serum. With one breath he and others like him say, "It never happened." With the next they say, "Let's do it all over."

The suspense is not knowing what this guy is going to do next. Looking at *Achtundachtzig*, Nerland gets progressively angrier. "We're making a gas chamber here today. If you stay around long enough, and you cross this line, we'll put you in it."

I remain in place, silent but eloquent testimony.

Once behind the gate, pumping his shotgun, Nerland screams, "This is called Native birth control." Then turning, "Why don't you come on private property? We'll have to practise some birth control."

Gunshots. A crowd of hooded figures bearing lighted torches appears at dark. They group beside the giant cross. Flames quickly engulf the entire structure, sending sparks spiralling upwards into the crisp darkness. Then, illuminated crimson figures lift their right arms in a Nazi-style salute and scream "White Power!" The leader shouts out "Sieg!" and the followers yell back "Heil!" This is reiterated five times. Then the leader yells "White Power!" and the followers repeat his words in unison. The leader hollers out "Forward march!" and all slowly circle the flaming cross, repeating the calls. Each time they call out their replies, the followers thrust their right arms high in Nazi salutes. "Death to the Jew!" screams the leader. "Death to the Jew!" scream the participants.

They have designed the ceremony to be easily visible from the road. They get extensive press. The presence of *Achtundachtzig* counters their press. The very presence of *Achtundachtzig* testifies.

In Provost, there is some revulsion. A few people march with flowers. But there is a whole lot more non-participation. Agreement? Fear? Indifference? That Saturday the churches are called, but they decline to stand up. Members of the Legislative Assembly are also called; but they, too, stay away. I am told Petro-Canada, the largest employer in the area, warns its employees to stay away or lose their jobs. The RCMP tell us their staff sergeant has gone out of town. He has not. How is it possible they provide nobody on the road! Later, the local United Church minister does speak out.

There is an air of unreality to the episode, but all is not bleak. Here, in Alberta, due to the work of the Auschwitz Awareness Society, we have succeeded in opening some closed doors. For four consecutive years now, annual joint Polish–Jewish memorial activities commemorate Auschwitz liberation day, twice in a Polish church, once in a synagogue, and once in a Lutheran church. Across the provincial border, the small Saskatoon Jewish community sees about 350 turn out for their Holocaust Day observances, more than fifty percent Christian. Even with the cooperation we have established in Edmonton, the Polish community still is absent for Holocaust Day observances. It is possible they are uninvited or unaware of it. Would the Jews invite them? Would they come?

Back in Alberta I face a critical decision. Jim Keegstra has attacked me in a letter to the editor saying only Jews change their names. It makes me think how proud I am to be in that company. It also gets me thinking about my ancestral family. For me, going to "Sherwood" was probably part of a subconscious drive pushing me ever further away from engaging Auschwitz. But, at the time, I failed to recognize it. Which illustrates how seductive escape can be—the little routines by which you convince yourself to believe food and house and material substance is life. And, in contrast to expectations, rather than gain business, I lost compatriots who might have been natural clients.

Funny how even a negative like Keegstra can lead to a positive. Even though my children are Sherwoods, I go and officially change my name back to Sobolewski.

Fifteen: Emilio

Edmonton, Alberta, November 1990

The next meeting of the International Auschwitz Council takes place two months after the Provost incident. I am off with Gary Goldsand, an Edmonton Jewish community worker, and Emilio. Of our sons, Emilio is the shortest and lightest. When the children fought with each other, Emilio was the one to get it. I could never take that. I had enough violence in my life to serve the need of six generations of Sobolewskis. I tried to toughen him up.

Emilio now says, "Papa thinks of strength as a physical thing, for Chrissake, rather than spiritual." I do recognize him as the most sensitive, and probably the most intelligent. He is also the angriest. Emilio says, "Papa, you never explained things. How could we know why we were making that damn embankment at the cottage? It was like that for everything. It was always like that. In Auschwitz, if something was to be done, they just sort of shouted and hit and stuff. You didn't have normal teen growth. You never gave us reasons, just goddamn expectations, all the time expectations."

I am unable to deny it. When my boys wanted explanations, my pain was too fresh. Sensing this, they steered away. Now, when I am eager to engage them, they have already learned not to ask.

Emilio did not actually flunk out of school, but he did leave. At about the time Vladimir took his hike, Emilio had one of those life-changing experiences young people sometimes catch when they try to think too much. His first year at the Southern Alberta Institute of Technology almost completed, a new man came home from a six-day cherry-picking stint to announce, hands in pockets, "You guys have been controlling my life too damn much. I'm taking a one year Sabbatical ... to find myself."

I gaped at him in disbelief.

"It's you, Papa. You're the one that likes the idea of mechanics. The reason I'm practically failing is because I hate it. I mean I *hate* it."

Then I yelled and screamed. "What are you, out of your mind? Have you no shame! You're hardly out of high school and spouting about taking *Sabbatical.*" At that instant I felt I had lost Emilio, that he was a complete stranger looking at me like I was his enemy. For his part, he responded with silence. Recently he told me his quitting school made him realize he could be anything he wanted; do not ask me how, I thought it is just the opposite. A year-and-a-half later, he went into broadcasting at Mount Royal College, which also led him nowhere. His supposed Sabbatical extended through the exact age I was when in Auschwitz. I have noticed that deterioration around the age of seventeen to twenty-one has become a pattern for my boys.

"Emilio is rebelling," Ramona told me.

To me, rebellion is a positive act of reshaping the ground-rules around you. It is an engagement, an attempt to mould the world and your response to it. If Emilio was rebelling against his father, I would have taken it as a type of backhanded compliment. At least it would have meant he was finally taking my life seriously. "What's he rebelling against?" I asked. She, too, used diplomatic silence as her answer. I was never quite certain if her lack of response was a silence of deference to me, ignorance of an answer, denial of the stark truth, or simply a censuring of her inquisitive, stubborn husband.

Emilio's search has steered him down paths expected for a young man whose hormones were shifting from park into overdrive. He has taken up living with a woman. I do not mind that. The two of them belong to a group, like a support group—actually, a kind of a sect. He has to confess every day what he is doing ... God knows what. I do not mind that, either. He is going through his rebellious period now at age twenty-five. Wears his hair past his shoulders, says he was a nerd in high school, swears and drinks for the effect. I do not mind even that. He works only for so long, then goes on unemployment. How can a healthy young man accept welfare? I am afraid he cannot take himself in hand. So I hassle him, tell him he has got to go to college. Mr. Sensitive will probably need another Sabbatical.

I envy people who can look back on their lives without regret. I cannot regret Auschwitz; the forces of the times could not be turned aside. But I do regret my too-hasty decision not to take up an FET grant to study engineering (or maybe even history!). Emilio says, "You're trying to remake us into your own image." I waver in my own mind: Do I pressure them into doing something damaging? What damaging? Can education be damaging? Something so utilitarian, so meaningful, so fundamental to life and values? Can standing on your own two feet be damaging? Can knowing where you come from be damaging?

Since I have not succeeded in getting him back to college, I decided he might as well do something worthwhile, like go to Poland with me. I never told his mother until a few days before. Given Ramona's predictable reaction, I have learned to try to keep an upcoming trip from her as long as possible.

At Simon's suggestion, we now tote over a large painting done in oils, maybe a hundred by hundred thirty centimetres, commemorating the *Sonderkommando* revolt. In a vast empty foreground, shades of grey almost like a pencil drawing (at first I thought it unfinished) portray an inmate's head and shoulders bursting the barbed wire. In the background, murderous reds and blacks depict the *Krematorium IV* complex and its smokestack going up in flames against a narrow band of blue sky. A yellow Star of David floats at the top. The face of the escaping prisoner reveals no joy, only pain and anger. Contemplating the painting, my nostrils fill with the odour of burned explosives, an olfactory illusion from too many years of real experience.

Not yet past the Edmonton airport ticket check, we hear, "Excuse me, sir. You can't take that with you onto the plane."

"No? Then how come they let me take on, last time, plaque?" I answer, clutching the painting tighter. Deep within, my stomach churns.

"O boy, Papa, don't argue," says Emilio.

"Emilio, let me handle this," I whisper. This woman will not persecute me. Turning back to the young Air Canada ground official, unwrinkled hands on her hips, I say, "People always take important items. I've seen draughtsmen with their cases. This is an original painting for Auschwitz Museum."

It is as if she heard nothing at all. "I'm sorry, sir, federal rules prohibit anything that cannot be stowed underneath the seat or in the overhead compartment. We'll store it in the cargo bay for you."

"It's too fragile."

"We'll make sure your painting is handled carefully, sir."

"I'm delivering this painting for Auschwitz Awareness Society, Alberta Venture of Christians and Jews. I'm not allowed to let it out of my sight." I am really afraid to let it out of my care.

Emilio groans and says in an undertone, "Papa, please let them goddamn store it underneath."

"Leave me alone, Emilio!" I undertone back. He shrugs his shoulders. This is how it goes in our family. It increases my resolve. And hers!

"I'm sorry, sir," the unsympathetic cuckoo clock repeats, "you're not going to get on with that picture." The young supervisor turns to the attendant checking tickets at the gate, "This gentleman is not to board the plane unless his package is properly checked." Her even younger partner nods with what I take to be too much pleasure, and the supervisor withdraws, affording no opportunity for appeal.

The line rapidly waves around me. People glare; but others smile, though condescendingly, it seems to me. I stick myself to the painting like glue, maintaining my spot without moving. Luckily, planes have reserved seats. If I wait until the last minute, they will have no choice but to let the picture on. Why am I so foolish? The supervisor, angry now, returns still determined to exercise her shred of authority in the world. "Look, we'll see that your painting gets properly stowed in baggage," she sings.

"There's no longer time to get it in, though," I reply, thinking I have her.

"I'm sorry." That same refrain. She says it too easily to be truly sorry. "Look, either we stow the painting, and you go to Poland, or you do not get onto the plane."

I request the supervisor's supervisor, but the plane is ready to push away from the gate. We board. From the portholes, I cannot watch what is being loaded below. Although the trip is comfortable enough, who can rest? Airport personnel are not renowned for tender care. The whole flight over, I worry about our painting. With reason, it turns out. In Warsaw they cannot find it. I have been complaining already for half an hour when finally they bring it off the plane.

In special ceremonies on 16 November 1990, we present in behalf of the Auschwitz Awareness Society 'Jewish *Sonderkommando* Revolt', painted by Ian Forbes, an Edmonton artist, to the director of the Auschwitz Museum, Jerry Wróblewski. Professor Maurice Goldstein of Belgium, an Auschwitz survivor, speaks. After the ceremony, the officials store the painting away in the museum basement along with everything else that refers to something Jewish.

Torn between the Auschwitz Council meeting and Emilio, I ask him to do Auschwitz on his own.

"Shit. You got me half way around the world for Chrissake, and now you're not going to shag around with me."

"Good! Good! It's just that duty calls. You get feel of Auschwitz with tour guide. Then I'll take you around to special sights and also show you Birkenau."

I attend the International Auschwitz Council, make a place for myself as an observer. Delegates recommend the addition of extra guides. Next meeting they will report that they have fourteen languages represented. I will ask, "Do we provide Hebrew-speaking guide for eighteen thousand visiting Israelis?"

"Mr. Sobolewski, are you an historian?" an angry Władysław Bartoszewski ridicules in German.

"I have no PhD. My credential is my name, *Achtundachtzig*."

"Sobolewski, you're always causing trouble," he shouts in Polish. The final communiqué leaves the issue out. The Polish representatives, who, because of proximity always outnumber the foreign delegates, dominate the International Council. Chairman Bartoszewski worked to save Jews during the Nazi period, spent a year at the Hebrew University in Jerusalem, and is Secretary of the Institute for Polish-Jewish Studies at Oxford. He is a good man who could do a lot. But when criticism of government policy is expressed, as both Polish ambassador to Austria and also head of the International Auschwitz Council, he has been put in an unfortunate conflict of interest. I think his personal sandwich is why he undiplomatically explodes. With straight faces, the government maintains the fiction that the Council functions independently, all the while using it as a fig leaf to cover its own actions.

Good thing I was decorated with the Cross of Auschwitz years ago. They would not do that anymore.

I do show Emilio Birkenau. Our plaque marking the *Sonderkommando* revolt is missing. I look around for where it might have gone. Nothing. We find out that the museum officials removed it, "for safekeeping." But similar inscriptions honouring French Catholics remain standing nearby. So, too, a plaque for murdered Russian PoW's and a plaque for 22,000 murdered Gypsies. I even notice a new plaque: a Jewish woman no less, singled out by name. Many Polish Catholics have their memory honoured, but few Jews. Who is the woman? A German philosopher. She converted to Catholicism, and subsequently became a Carmelite nun. Her efforts did not save her. Of all the martyred millions of pious Jews to mention, they chose Edythe Stein, a convert. While our plaque is safely guarded out of sight in the basement, they have even invented a new symbol for Edythe Stein, a cross superimposed on a six-pointed star. Why is truth so hard to find? The Vatican will probably soon declare her a saint.

"You see, Emilio, Museum visitors easily learn physical details of *what* went on at Ramp: trains, *selektion*, showers, confiscation of clothes and goods, tattoo. But *who*, visitors have no way of finding out from way Museum is currently presented."

"I read that during the summer of 1944, Birkenau once reached, on a mass-production, conveyor-like basis, the killing of a record 18,000 corpses on a single day," Emilio reports.

"At such times, we'd come back from Birkenau with blackened nostrils and particles clinging to our tongues. Usually, though, about five to eight thousand per day was normal. Even though SS officials claimed that they were cremating only those who died, everyone in camp recognized that mass killing was going on."

"How come it's so damned quiet here in contrast to the main camp?"

"Average visitor isn't even directed over here, place where our plaque is supposed to be, place of gas chambers and crematoria, pond, field of ashes. So what most people receive is Polish Christian laundered version of what happened. Why, why should new Poland continue what Communist official policy of silence perpetrated? If we can't show, *particularly at its source*, history with accurate percentage of victims, how can we hope Holocaust tragedy will not be repeated? Yet even if you know enough to want to come, what I call Via Dolorosa of Jews is unpaved, and no buses connect Visitors Centre at Auschwitz-I with Birkenau. Here, bend down and feel, Emilio, cement of gas chamber floor. Mind how smooth. Once it scraped like sidewalk. How many bare feet does it take until cement rough like sidewalk becomes smooth like glass?"

Walking through the area where Kanada was burned down, we find a pile of cutlery still scattered on the ground. Exploration shows it to cover an area about two metres in diameter. We pass the tanks where the Nazis were experimenting with Jewish faeces—every part of the body must be used— in an effort to make methane gas to heat the camp laundry. And here is the International Auschwitz Monument whose dedication I attended in 1967. The cross at its base still makes it difficult for Jews to place their memorial candles here. And how do the authorities know that Jews who were murdered here died for 'world peace and socialism' as it says by the cross?

I'd like to have Emilio's impressions from his own mouth:

Okay, but I get to say what I want. While Papa was talking, I was watching these Polish kids laughing and fooling around on the parade

225

grounds. It made me angry because of Papa's work. "They should be like as if they're going to church," I said, nodding my head in their direction.

"Their teacher should have prepared them better," he said. "It shows you, Emilio, how important Auschwitz awareness is."

"Auschwitz awareness? If they can't succeed here, you damn well can't succeed anywhere. My friends care as much about what happened in Auschwitz as they do about the American Civil War. To them the horrors of the camp are about the same as the horrors of RoboCop."

Anyway, it came out right there on the field that Papa was mulling over a new idea: "Tragedy is, these kids are here in Auschwitz and they won't even see Birkenau. If Auschwitz Awareness Society could arrange some bus service, more of 450,000 annual visitors could visit real death camp."

"I think you're revving your engine in neutral. And it just raises hell in the family. Now you'll be calling people, writing letters all over the place, all about this stupid bus. The same thing here with me. Didn't you tell me you'd take three days for the conference, then we'd have ten days together? Instead, except today, which has been good, you've been spending practically all your time spinning around like a damned top talking to one crummy reporter after another." Warsaw was impossible. As soon as we arrived, it was like he flipped out. Every radio and TV station is supposed to fall over or something because he's Number Eighty-eight. I can't stand the hypocrisy. He has a wonderful way of exposing his public side to the public and never letting them into what he is really.

To my question about reporters, he said, "I have to."

"Shit. You brought me all the way over here to experience Poland with you. And instead of helping me to relive your past, you schedule a damn political whirl. And you come across too superficial, especially with all those gifts of yours. You try to buy the reporters off."

"With few packs of duty-free cigarettes?"

"Yeah, in a poor country, with cigarettes. You goddamn know that."

Later we were at Hanna's. She's a soft-skinned, beautiful woman, the daughter of the girl Papa took to *Mutiny on the Bounty* on his very first date. If not for Auschwitz, I think they might have got married. Then this terrific broad would be my sister or something. So here we were sitting around the living room talking, and Papa got a call from a reporter. He came roaring into the living room, shouting we have to get to the station. Crap, I know my father has gone through a hell I can barely comprehend even after seeing the place for myself. Fair enough. Only, he can't treat people like shit. I finally told him what I thought. "You can't just blitz in and scream: 'We're going to the station.'" I'm sorry, he is socially obtuse. "Papa, we're guests of Hanna. We planned to meet Aunt Barbara. I came here expecting to share your past with you. You're not doing it at all."

He turned to the rest of the room. "Give him time," he said referring to me, "he'll go to college, he'll be all right."

"Papa!"

"Maybe you should read my last article."

"Papa!" Sometimes I get so angry, I can hardly talk. At that instant, I didn't even want to hear about Auschwitz, let alone read his phoney papers.

He smiled again to the others in self-defence. We went separate ways for the rest of the trip. The reason was because of arguments. It was crazy, but funny in a way. We had come with Gary Goldsand of the Edmonton Jewish Community Council. He left him, too. Just stranded him. At the airport, I found Papa already in line.

"You can't just blitz in ahead of all these people," he lectured me, "you've got to wait at end of line." On the long flight back, Papa took an empty seat three rows up.

One thing I can say for myself, at least if I have a fight, with one of my sons for example, I am normal within an hour. In fact, Emilio credits his own tenacity to my example. I took a seat by myself because I had what to think about. What my show-off son calls 'hypocrisy' is really me.

I have learned some new things on this trip. My sister says the next day after our arrest, all my mother's jewellery, except for the rings she wore, was gone. And for the rest of the war, *Mamusia* had to report to the Gestapo weekly. But they survived. However horrible the nighttime arrest, at least the whole family did not suffer like the Jews. Basia keeps the silver items, saved for our neighbours, the lawyer's family. She has them carefully wrapped and tucked away: a ritual piece, something for wine, and maybe a sugar bowl we found and safeguarded from the Germans. To survive during the war, a small metre-square Polish wall tapestry did get sold for flour and lard, as did my mother's own gold rings and even her sheets. But she saved the Habers' silver items. It is logical, but to me it is still shocking, that the Jewish people find it necessary to maintain their own bureau of missing persons. Basia has written twice to the Jewish Agency search bureau looking for the son Shimush (Simon). "That these pieces never got returned bothers me," she says. She wants it advertised.

One thing is certain, my taking Emilio to Poland did not turn out the way I had originally planned. And it is no consolation that Emilio and my sister Basia got along well. Concerning my dedication to Auschwitz awareness, Basia went and told everyone, "He's got a sickness."

So my work, my passion, is plain illness and nothing more. She meant well, my sister. Her intent was that one of our mutual Polish friends would talk some sense into me. But I told them, "Basia thinks my work is some kind of an obsession, that I'm getting sicker and sicker. My son Emilio thinks so, too. But to me, the first twenty-two years, when I was pushed to keep from myself what I knew, *that* was an obsession. Running without any direction, I'd catch myself wondering if I was enjoying myself. Now, after coming to grips with *Achtundachtzig*, I don't question anymore. He pulls me towards higher ground. Yes, we'd be better off materially if I weren't involved with Auschwitz awareness. That's not what counts in life, though. If you've got Auschwitz as part of your life, you know what most people think of as success is pure smoke and mirrors. With each day of my work, I'm happier and healthier."

In me is a person returned from the other side. Returned from a place where a person's dental fillings had more value than his life. A place lacking compassion, lacking truth, lacking any evidence that a beneficent, gracious God exists. These eyes have seen responsible adults tabulate mounds of eyeglasses, toys and shoes. They have witnessed uniformed officers enjoy vegetables enriched on human remains. They have seen civilized people slumber serenely on upholstery stuffed with human hair. And this continues today. Like my son, I have watched children darting through the exhibits of Auschwitz laughing and fooling. Unlike him, I have a message: life is valuable enough to try and change it.

You cannot rob God, but life can rob us of Him. In that Godforsaken place, some people's faith weakened: there were those who believed in God until they were forced to eat of the Nazi poisons. And some people's faith deepened: there were those who lacked God until they found God supporting them through it all, and those who, from their camp experience, learned to fear nothing except God. But for me, Auschwitz inspired neither rejection nor glorious revelation. "Emilio, how can I believe after personally seeing death of Christianity? Only through life task I've chosen to pursue. Could no more give it up than chop off my head."

I bring home for Ramona a painting of an old, wooden Polish church. She does not like it. *That* raises worries, as does her growing opposition to my work. She does not pack for me anymore. And lately Ramona is only communicating through Vladimir. Maybe that is why I see her in him. She is demanding we go to a psychiatrist or a counsellor. Would this counsellor get into *Achtundachtzig* any better than the members of my own family? Would I be simply up against another force? Destined to be torn apart? It bothers me so, that lately I am unsure of my own ability to keep up my work, which is also wracking my nerves more and more.

I catch sight of Husky going under the wheels. No, I cannot sit idly by. "If we Christian Poles, like Christian Danes, had cooperated less, extent of tragedy would've been greatly reduced. Mark well, one crazed leader didn't Holocaust make. It grew everywhere."

The reaction to my words is always intense, especially on the radio talk shows. The security of public anonymity affords people the nerve to express their real opinions: "Why do you blame Christians?" demands one.

"For truth. Somebody has to say it. Europe was centre of Christianity. Perpetrators were either Christian or children of Christians. Several hundred million Christians lived in Nazi Europe. Hard as it is to face, Nazism had many of Christianity's own attitudes in it."

He becomes more agitated. "I get tired of all this media attention on the 'Jewish' Holocaust. How *can* we forget? The Jews are doing themselves a great injustice. God bless the Jewish people, they've got a right to remember. They overlook many victims, though. Proof is you yourself are a Roman Catholic."

The host: "Why are you so angry?"

"I'm not angry. It bothers me the empathy is one-sided. It's almost as if they want us to feel guilty."

"We stood by in silence when our Jewish neighbours were deported to the camps. We stood by in silence when they were trying to hide. We stood by in silence when they were hungry. I think that we Christians really have to come terms one day that we also are guilty. It's Christian world that allows this to continue even after Holocaust."

Another caller tries his version of logic: "Doesn't public programming just call attention to bigotry?"

"Fine, fine. Caller's got point, if only it was true. I've found just the opposite, though. When I visit schools, children rarely even know what Auschwitz is." I think of Emilio. Would he know any better? Even after his visit to Auschwitz, when you get to the real details, the answer is a sad no. "Recently in one high school class of forty-three students, only three had a guess. One confused Auschwitz with Austerlitz, thought it was great Napoleonic battle. Second recalled it was labour camp. Only one knew it had something to do with Holocaust. Their textbooks often have, for what was probably most earth-shattering event of twentieth century, little more than few paragraphs. One beautifully bound, glossy high school history book summarizes entire Holocaust in single paragraph forty-two words long."

"Mark my words, there will be a backlash."

"What, against forty-two words?" I chuckle.

I am on air with Rabbi Mann, who went with me to dedicate the *Sonderkommando* plaque. He motions and answers, "What is the choice? Caller, are you suggesting we don't mention the Holocaust?"

They question teaching the Holocaust. No one ever questions teaching Hiroshima and Nagasaki. No one ever says that belongs to Japanese history only.

A voice calls me "the Devil's conspirator," other endearments. Then she says, "I'll pray for you." At last count, hundreds are praying for me. I appreciate their prayers. Too bad they do not couple their prayers with a little action for Auschwitz awareness.

When the show is over, the phone rings at home. It is Emilio. "Heard you on the radio today. All I can say is you're not succeeding, Papa. Look at you: no friends, nothing; I mean you're like Johnny Appleseed; you fling a seed here, another there. It's pointless."[59]

Ever wonder how people can harbour two mutually contradictory thoughts with utmost conviction? Emilio thinks I am driven by some urge for self-glorification. He also thinks I am foolish to persist in a cause for which there is no public interest or response. To me, it is obvious a futile cause wins no glory.

Among my compatriots, Auschwitz Awareness gets a boost from an unexpected source, none other than Lech Walesa. It is May 1991; we've turned the television volume way up. On a visit to Israel—where the spirit of the six million vibrates—the president of Poland addresses the Knesset: "Among the Poles, there have been some people who did evil. Here in Israel, the land of your culture and the land of your revival, I ask your forgiveness."

The normally boisterous Knesset becomes dead still. Yitzh.ak Shamir rises from his seat. The grizzled man of iron, once a leader in Israel's political terrorist organization Leh.i, now its Prime Minister, grew up in Poland. Shamir's father was murdered in 1942 by Polish childhood friends he had asked for shelter. His mother perished in Treblinka. His speeches never forget. What will the old veteran say? On behalf of Israel, Shamir replies:

> I remember the glory, the colourfulness, the rich Jewish culture, the spirit that beat in the heart; I also remember the degrading poverty and the humiliating antisemitism. We want to hope and believe that your first official visit to Israel is proof of the turning of a new leaf in the relations between our two peoples and states.
>
> We wish Poland economic prosperity, technological, scientific and industrial development, foreign trade and fruitful international ties. As much as it is in our power to do so, we will be happy to cooperate in this endeavour.

"*Sieg Heil!*" Welcome to the streets of Polish Chicago. I am here with Reuven. My co-religionists at the Five Holy Martyrs Church on Pope John Paul II Street have a distinctly European way of saying 'hello.' Nothing surprises me anymore. My priest at home has told me some members of the parish want to do 'something' to blackball me from membership. "Sigmund," they say, "above all people, should realize all the harm Jews have done." So due to my success in finally integrating my inner life, I lost my compatriots, and now my co-religionists.

The church we find ourselves in front of is beige brick. A huge cross tops a stubbed, square belfry appropriately representative of the solid Polish working class who settled the neighbourhood. But to me the square topped church is reminiscent of the entrance to Birkenau so aptly depicted in the painting I recently brought to Auschwitz. Arch-capped steel doors, one-and-a-half-stories high, open onto a broad flight of marble stairs leading to a richly decorated, but modern, nave. Its unusual name honours the memory of Poland's "first fruits of martyrdom," the five brothers: Benedict and John, Isaac, Matthew and Crispin, who shed their blood in defence of evangelical poverty in 1003, less than fifty years after Poland's baptism.[60]

After Walessa's visit to Israel, *Achtundachtzig* stands outside the Chicago church waiting for the arrival of His Eminence Józef Cardinal Glemp.

A day before we are to meet the cardinal, a friend from previous activities visits our hotel. "Sorry for being late. Since my husband died, I often get tied up at the print shop."

"Good to see you any time. Meet my friend Reuven. Reuven, Erna Gans." In deference to Reuven, we speak in English.

"A pleasure." We swap stories in the coffee shop, one of those indoor places decorated as an outdoor garden. Erna is a Jewish survivor. With blonde hair and blue eyes, and a false baptism certificate, truncated from family, she saw it all—from the Polish countryside, not from inside a camp. "Through the entire occupation, I managed to pass as an Aryan. Got no illusions, though; know the feelings of the Polish masses first hand."

"Do Chicago survivors demonstrate much?" I ask.

"Not since the neo-Nazi march in Skokie. Now we do better. Let me show you the Illinois Holocaust curriculum I've helped develop." She is deservedly proud. "Why do you concentrate so much of your time on Auschwitz?" she asks sincerely. "Wouldn't it be better to work on a Polish school curriculum? Then everyone, a whole new generation, would learn; not just those who make a field trip."

"Sure," Reuven replies, "your right. Except what would be taught? Your Illinois program is great, particularly when integrated into the regular social studies curriculum. But, in Poland, Auschwitz is the curriculum. So it is a serious problem that the Auschwitz Museum presents itself as the place where Nazis exploited Poles for slave labour; not as the place where their Jewish neighbours went up the smokestacks. They do not view the annihilation of Polish Jewry as a Polish tragedy."

"Yes, but a new curriculum would teach the young."

"Polish historians," he says, "see Jewish gassing only as an example of what was in store for them.[61] Let's put it this way. If one thinks the primary premise is Polish suffering, then it indeed detracts to say that Nazis killed Polish Jews not as Poles but as Jews. So until there is an *authoritative* broadening of perspective, any curriculum devised and implemented in this ethos would perpetuate the same preconception. The national Auschwitz Museum is the Polish authority, like Yad VaShem for us. This is why we are meeting Cardinal Glemp tomorrow."

"For rest of world, too, Auschwitz is symbol," I add, "so if Auschwitz is presented as a monument to Polish and not Jewish suffering, then that will affect world opinion as well."

More talk shows help illustrate the point:

"Atomic weapons," the voice comes over angrily, defensively, "are as cruel as any crematorium. The two bombs dropped on the Japanese, what about them! Those innocent civilian masses were treated just as bad as anyone in the Holocaust.... I am of German extraction. The day after a Holocaust program aired, I woke to find a huge swastika on my property marked out by someone in the snow."

"The Holocaust has been commercialized," another caller complains. "It's being 'sold' like big business. It's become vulgar entertainment. I recall watching the mini-series *Holocaust*. It was moving in a soap opera sort of way, periodically interrupted by maudlin commercials."

And still another, "Calling the Holocaust 'unique' in history, a pivotal event, is a Judeo-centric point of view. There've been plenty of terrible atrocities in world history."

"This Holocaust stuff," one especially bitter caller protests, "has become an occasion not only for anti-German bigotry, but also for anti-Catholic bigotry and anti-Christian bigotry."

A common undercurrent, which only their tone of voice reveals, contradicts their seemingly balanced attempts at universalization. "Yes," I answer, "I agree; people have caused atrocities of all kinds. I'm Roman Catholic victim. That should speak for itself. But, as victim, I also have eyewitness testimony that, while Nazis selectively killed us Poles, they systematically and totally wiped out Jews. Similarly, Allies killed Germans, Poles and Jewish forced labourers indiscriminately in bombed factories, but specifically refused to destroy gas chambers or rail lines to prevent Nazi mass-killing of Jews.

"Many of you callers seem to find it irritating that event with universal lessons has to have so many Jews involved. We can try to twist away from it. We can ask about bombing in Dresden. We can bring up famine in Ukraine. We forget that, unlike excesses of Hiroshima and Dresden, unlike Nazi killing of us Poles, horrible as all these atrocities of war were, Holocaust was non-functional. Relentless murder of Jews *diverted* Nazis from business of war, tying up men, railroads, energy, technology and weaponry. We can even try and turn, into something anti-Christian, memory of single-minded, planned tragedy directed against total Jewish people. But galling truth still hangs in wind. In end, we can't escape it."

A teenager calls in. "I want to learn more," he says. "Thank you for what you are doing."

Instead of seeing a warning for future parallels, most of the callers seek to belittle the Holocaust as *just* one more atrocity. They harbour subconscious prejudice, sometimes even overt hatred. As my boys so readily note, Auschwitz awareness is an open-ended task. If the blight of antisemitism is to be uprooted from the world, it is something Christians have to do.

Through the media, the people of Alberta, and even Canada, have come to know *Achtundachtzig* better. How did I get tomorrow's appointment with Glemp? *Achtundachtzig* is an idea that reverberates in people's minds: Number 88—first transport! Hard to believe.

Towards the end of 1944, when they call out *"Achtundachtzig!"* even the guards show respect:

Routine visit to a sausage factory. Checking fire extinguishers. Prisoner gives me a *Schinkenwurst* to smuggle back to camp. Hardly have we left the plant, a loud, Halt! halt! Should have known better. Warehouse district piled with plumbing pipes, cement bags, roof tiles, tar and other materials belonging to the department of construction. A shortcut here is enough in itself to arouse suspicion. At least Jurek slipped around the screen of the corner. As if placed in a barrel of cold molasses, I turn around. SS Unterscharführer, ribbons of front-line action, equivalent of U.S. Purple Heart. Doff cap, thrust breast forwards, suck stomach to the spine; it is imperative he does not find the meat belted hard against my belly. Nothing escapes the raven's swoop. My eyes dart first one way, then the other. But where to run? I am a fieldmouse caught in the raven's gaze too far away from its hole. I can hear the little animal squeaking. The young blond Unterscharführer saunters around me murmuring loud enough to hear, Well, well, what are you doing here, *Nummer Achtundachtzig?* The corporal, a *Reichsdeutsche*. Speaks high German with a perfect accent, reflects on my low number. And why is he using the German *polite you;* is he cynical, or does he want something? The corporal, sharp and clean, unlike an ordinary guard, presumably works in an office. I'm dead. For dried peas, *Pfahlhängen.* For a crust of bread, a flogging. For warming soup, a week in the *Stehzelle.* For sausages, what? Economic sabotage, they call it. How long can I hold my breath? He launches into a monologue. It is time for Poles to ally themselves with the Germans against the Bolsheviks; when the Jew Marx spoke about wresting power from the capitalists, he was scheming against us all. He pronounces the words *Jew Marx* with such loathing; either they've been feeding new recruits with Alfred Rosenberg or they've stolen this one from the Nazi university.[62] He's continuing unabated: the evil forces lurk everywhere; they invade our typewriters and our books; then they come in person; if we are not careful, Stalin and his hoards will take over our industries, wipe away the middle class, reduce us to economic slavery. Don't lose eye contact. Hold his eyes and he will not be glancing around at the rest of me. They are pounding down our doors; the consequences will be disastrous; where will there be leisure, adventure, security? Where will there be good family relationships? everything will be stolen from us; you Poles may not share our Teutonic culture, but you can make out political reality; work with us against a Jewish Bolshevism that seeks world domination; what do you say, *Nummer Achtundachtzig? Jezus,* who expected his harangue to turn into an interrogation? *Jawohl, Herr Unterscharführer,* yes, sir, the strangest voice stammers up from my throat while I'm still trying to suck in my stomach. God, he knows.

Abruptly this SS corporal looked at my number and relaxed. "*Hau ab,* beat it, *Nummer Achtundachtzig,*" and, in a mutter, I heard him add, "Everything will be stolen from us." I am certain he knew. Fifty years later, the low number still helps me. It was *Achtundachtzig,* not me, who secured observer status on the International Auschwitz Council. Now *Achtundachtzig* has earned me a meeting with the Primate of Poland, His Eminence Józef Cardinal Glemp, during his goodwill mission promoting better relations between the United States and Poland.

Why am I meeting the Cardinal? In my homeland, Church and government intimately entwine by centuries-old tradition. Even during the era of Soviet domination, the Catholic religion remained deeply embedded in the soil of Polish life. Going to church, or wearing a crucifix, became a nationalistic statement as well as a religious one. On country roads, a shrine beams at you from every crossing. Everyone in Poland avidly follows what Pope John Paul II, still thought of as Karol Wojtyla, does each part of his day. And Polish tradition ordains the Virgin Mary as the queen of Poland.[63]

As for Glemp himself, he has been a close confidante of Lech Walesa, a man whose Catholicism means more to him than his politics. The Primate thus came to America with the blessing of his government. For it is in the interest of my homeland that anyone thinking of the possibility of investing in Eastern Europe, will think Poland.

Some American Jews have been picketing the Cardinal. For members of one faith group to picket the higher echelons of another is hardly a light undertaking. Jews do not picket other cardinals, bishops or priests. This Polish Primate, in his now infamous homily of 26 August 1989, charged that Jews "induced the peasant to drink," "propagated communism," and now spoke "from a position of a nation raised above all others." He also stated that seven Jewish activists who demonstrated at the Auschwitz convent did not destroy the convent nor kill the Carmelite nuns living there "because they were restrained" from doing so.[64] Rabbi Avi Weiss, one of the seven, even served him with a summons for the good Cardinal's defamations. Though completely unprecedented and very provocative, in this, I still have to agree with Rabbi Weiss. A Catholic shrine does not belong on the site where the Nazis had early on killed so many Jews. A Jew, any Jew, has a right to say *kaddish* anywhere in the nearly forty square kilometre space called Auschwitz.

We have already been waiting an hour and a half. "If he's coming, he's really late."

"The Cardinal isn't expected until this afternoon," a rectory priest answers our query. It raises real doubts about his 'appointment' with us.

We meander down the block in the predominately Polish neighbourhood. I am afraid he has stood us up, that we have come all the way to Chicago only to find out he is playing with us. I am thinking about how to make a demonstration from it. The rabbi is urging, "Let's go back to the rectory where we can use the phone to get a clarification."

The rabbi walks towards the rectory, thinking I am following. Instead, I duck behind a house, hiding behind some garbage cans like in my childhood. Rabbi Reuven is calling now. I do not utter a sound; try and make myself small; do not know what I plan to do; simply need to be alone; do not want to be humiliated at the rectory. Properly thought out, we might get some publicity for being stood up. Or maybe it is simply an ingrained habit—the way to survive is to make yourself inconspicuous. Reuven finds me anyway.

Why would a rabbi search back here? I say nothing, like tucking in behind garbage cans is normal. We never discuss it. A newsman arrives. We are standing on the street corner. The Rabbi is mentioning that Auschwitz is one huge Jewish cemetery. A Polish American listening in on the interview interjects, "No, it's a Polish cemetery." With him, I limp back into my destiny.

At 10:45, the Primate's cavalcade rounds the corner. Though the parish priest claimed not to have been expecting a morning arrival, the first sound of the siren brings him flying to open the limousine door. I kneel to kiss the Cardinal's ring, a spontaneous act caught by the media. I notice the Cardinal's hand, then his face; Glemp looks scared, like he wants to take his hand back. Maybe he thinks I am an agent of Rabbi Weiss, there to serve him papers.

The Primate, short in stature, moves with dignity and appears aloof. We see no visible warmth or cordiality about him. He dresses in his formal attire, a red skullcap on his head. The rabbi, at my request for ceremony's sake, wears the *tallis* he prays in, a black skullcap as always on his head. I am in prison stripes with accompanying cap. Against my wishes, the press is physically pushed from the rectory by a parish priest. We are ushered into a cramped, poorly lit room—the Cardinal, his clerk, an interpreter, the rabbi and myself.

I speak in Polish. "As His Excellency is well aware, fate has given me a unique perspective on Auschwitz. We speak to His Excellency out of respect for his influence with the new Polish government: one word from him brings action the next day."

"O no, it might take a month."

"A month we can wait; we're from Canada," says the rabbi in English. I translate. "The American way is to demonstrate and act out; the Canadian way is to meet, discuss and try to find mutuality. We come not for public demonstration, but for what we believe is a shared cause, the cause of truth."

He nods. His clerk takes notes. I pick up the thread again, "The museum officials are trying to transform what was predominately a Jewish tragedy into a Polish tragedy. The Germans face the issue squarely...." The Cardinal is known to have strong German connections. "In Poland, though, when it comes to Jewish suffering, we seem to have amnesia. 'Where are the Jews who used to live here?' 'Oh, they and the Poles were murdered by the Germans.' Quite true, three million of each. In sixty-three days alone during the heroic Warsaw Uprising of 1944, as many Poles lost their lives as Americans in the entire Second World War in both theatres. But thirty million Poles (ninety percent) survived, while nearly all the Jews were killed—men, women and children. The historical reality is there is no Polish family that didn't lose one, and in many cases, more of its members during the Nazi occupation. But, in marking that history, is it also necessary to go and diminish the extent of Jewish horror?"

The Cardinal listens politely.

"Why is no sign placed for the one-and-a-half million Jews who perished at Birkenau?"

Glemp will investigate.

"Why was the Canadian plaque removed while another nearby for Catholics was left standing?"

Glemp will find out.

"The International Auschwitz Council asked for a new guidebook that would underscore the fate of the Jews. The recently released *Auschwitz–Birkenau Informator* is the first Auschwitz booklet published under the new Solidarity government. As the master for copies in other languages, it is no small matter that it once again misrepresents the Jewish tragedy. One example, the most blatant: the female victims of Dr. Clauberg's pseudo-medical experiments in Block Ten are identified as Slavs rather than Jews. Fact is, though, they were Jews in Block Ten——"

"Is that *pravda?*" the Cardinal interrupts, glancing towards his clerk.

I interject, "Yes, that's true. I was there. At the Dering trial in 1964, that the victims were Jewish was never in dispute.[65] What was undisputed in 1964, is in dispute today, not by some neo-Nazi skinheads, but by officials of the Auschwitz Museum."

The Cardinal grows visibly uncomfortable. He preempts the historical question with a fair amount of emotion. "There had to have been others beside Jews."

"In other places, yes. Not in Block Ten, though. Let the Cardinal examine the facts for himself," I declare. "Our legitimate Polish patriotism shouldn't prevent us from telling the truth about others."

The rabbi interjects. "The upcoming meeting of the International Auschwitz Council is scheduled the end of October. As Canadians, we hope your representative, Professor Waldemar Chrostowski, will adopt a helpful stance with respect to these subjects. Not only would this serve the cause of *pravda*," he says, picking up on the Cardinal's own word, "but such an act would also go far toward casting 'new' Poland in a favourable light in the West."

The interview is at its end. If the Primate is anything, he is a diplomat. You do not attain such a high level, even in the Church, without having acquired some extensive skills. Aides assure us as they usher us out, "His Eminence, the Cardinal, will look into your concerns."

Later the press interviews me. "What is the problem at Auschwitz today?"

"In Auschwitz, only odd phrase lets visitors know Jews were involved at all. Nazis first killed Jews in flesh and now Auschwitz Museum kills them in memory. As presented today, Auschwitz repeats what happened then: one standard for Jews, a different standard for Catholics."

"Are you trying to get Cardinal Glemp to make a statement on the convent?"

"No. We're seeking, in future actions, greater sensitivity. On one hand we don't ask as much. And, on other, we ask much more. On one hand, we don't ask Cardinal Glemp to backtrack and publicly admit mistakes. And, on other, we ask Cardinal to take future substantive action."

"Why are you meeting with the Cardinal, then, and not with government officials?"

"We meet political leaders, too. We hope Cardinal Glemp will help correct at least some injustices. Museum officials don't mind, in backfields of Birkenau, some Jewish stars. But they can't stand to see, written into official guidebooks or plaques, word 'Jew' or Jewish names of victims. Is there deliberate policy of antisemitism in Poland? Church could speak to this. Isn't it time for Church to free Jews from its need to make them into demonstration of divine disfavour? Cardinal could help in making that clear."

"You accept the Cardinal then?"

"I believe Cardinal has made some serious errors."

"Then why do you kiss his ring?"

"I try to be faithful Catholic. He still represents my faith and my birth-place. In kissing ring, I pay my respect to Church represented by Cardinal's office." Even pre-war Prime Minister Pilsudski used to kiss the ring.

Believing Christians were both among the victims and among the perpetrators. I waver on the delicate knife edge between faith and doubt. How do we protect ourselves if reason fails us? We have nothing else but faith. Yet, contradictory as it sounds in theory, in practice many Nazis had profound Christian faith. Keegstra proves that being Christian and racist is not contradictory in practice.

My boys, especially Emilio, still cannot catch what motivates me. "Emilio, in Auschwitz two hundred died for one to survive. Jews made up ninety percent. That means 180 Jews died so I could live. As Christian I feel, especially as Catholic, obligation. I have begun to understand, faintly at first, then more and more, whole of my work in terms of resurrection. This is way I can confront, as Christian, tragedy of my life, my passion as it relates to ultimate Passion. And I also believe, after Church's failure in face of Auschwitz, that image of resurrection embodies, as well, only hope for Christianity's renewal. Resurrection absolves guilt that cannot be denied. Resurrection means new order. Resurrection means we can achieve in future what we have negated in past. Resurrection assures us Christianity can mean more than goad to hostility."

No one would call me a great Roman Catholic, but I try to believe in God and respect the Church. While I have difficulty believing Glemp is actually antisemitic, in his insensitivity he sometimes speaks and acts *like* an antisemite. Sadly, I have to agree with Władysław Bartoszewski when he decides it is just Glemp's pre-Vatican II *Weltanschauung* coming out.[66] The Primate never answered the rabbi's subsequent letter, never had his office get back to us on the matters he promised to investigate. Can the media be right? How *is* it possible I knelt to kiss his ring?

"Why should Mama work her butt off while you go traipsing all over the goddamn world?" Emilio, my internal microscope, admonishes on my return.

"Your father's struggling for better world," I say hoarsely. "Hour when you have rest from your enemies isn't time to forget, rather very hour to sacrifice for better world."

"My father is fighting for himself, for Chrissake. Is a cause more important than people?"

I look him up and down. I am thinking, my father sacrificed for his principles in Poland. It affected me, too, and now I admire him for it. But it took me a while. Am I doomed, like Sisyphus, to be perpetually pushing a rock uphill? Will my sons see the point only after I am gone? It is at such times I think to give up my work. Then I am ashamed of even having had the thought.

Emilio catches me off guard. "Papa, where's your sacrifice? Think where? You're entitled to offer yourself. But is it yourself you sacrifice—I know that's what you think—or is it really us that you sacrifice? Go ahead, ask Mama. See what she says."

"Yes, I'm sacrificing, I'm sacrificing you all, everything I yearned for. And I say it doesn't have to be that way; come *with* me, instead. Maybe you and Mama could think of yourselves as partners in accomplishment of needed mission for Auschwitz awareness."

"That really gets me. You just use Mama to run the hotel and do your bidding."

"Emilio, you'll send me to the grave yet. Ever stop to think we've only had for few years our hotel? Before that Mama didn't have outside of home any job."

"The whole thing is gross. You look down on her."

"I knew with your mother what I was doing, and made conscious decision she was woman to be my wife. Certainly she's uneducated; sometimes I catch myself being defensive about it, even. She shows more common sense, though, in one day than most people do their whole life. Yes, we have our problems, and I admit my style isn't housework."

"Come on, marriage means wanting to help each other. You didn't marry Mama for love."

"Ah, and you know what love is?"

"Well you damn well don't; your first wife left you, too. Oh, I don't want to say any bad things."

"Okay, Emilio. People have taught me essentials: personal honesty and, most important, suitability for shared parenthood."

"That's love?"

"Think about it. Whether a person is male or female, to trust your partner as potential parent of your child means you value each other. If you want divorce, you can find many Irises you can have good time with, party with, love. Your own life proves that. For long range, find some Ramona you might want as parent of your child. You don't have to actually have children. Simply to know that you *could* trust given person as your children's parent, whether you will have children or not, means shared values, outlook, goals—everything. You cannot know how much, after Auschwitz, children become confirmation of existence. You boys are my statement of trust in future of humanity."

"I am not your goddamn statement. I am me—damaged from growing up in this household—but me. I think if people keep living together when they don't get along, it's like living in sin."

"You think any marriage is eternal bliss? It's your idea of marriage that's unrealistic, not us. Contrary to your opinion, Emilio, we love each other. I would never divorce, willingly, Ramona."

Sixteen: Ramona

Fort Assiniboine, Alberta, 1991

A past like mine weighs heavily on the present. But the reverse proves true as well. Present problems, perhaps because they are here and now, can for brief periods outweigh the enormity of the past. Our hotel, the principal room being the tavern, resembles many small inns in rural North America today. Everything we have left is invested into it. We bought right before real estate prices collapsed following the Alberta oil crash of the early '80s. Life has come full circle. He who grew up poor and once found the good life is poor again.

The officers from the bank in Barrhead have become regular callers. We can always predict their arrival, so for days, Ramona and I have been scrubbing and fixing up in anticipation. Once we get rolling, we are a real team, and the place shines. When they do appear on the scene, I pretend not to have guessed they were coming. "Well, good day. What a surprise! What'll it be this afternoon?"

They are decent enough, the bank. Always good for a cup of tea, and maybe if you keep it quiet, a drink on the house. "Hello, Sigmund," booms the heavy-set one of the pair continuing my own charade, "the guys who do so much for you are here. Just stopping by to see how the place is." His partner, tall and skinny, light-skinned, is somewhat more reserved. I set a glass in each one's hand. The first downs his in one smooth movement. The other is restrained in his drinking style as well. Lowering and raising his eyes, he sips gently, carefully regarding me from slightly above. Sweeping from side to side, the quiet one's eyes survey the empty tavern sharply, almost as if trying to torture the walls into talking.

I can feel the peeling plaster and panel succumb to the scrutiny, their response plain. "We've seen better days. The oil boom is over. Not too many seismic crews anymore."

Our guests' skilled glances appraise the old acoustic tiles in the ceiling, inspect the upstairs rooms, also empty; the bath and shower down the hall. They view my small office, its books, tapes, and papers in piles on the floor, falling off shelves, everywhere. Stroking their chins, they review the accounts:

hotel and bar receipts, food, two hundred dollars a month from the pool table. I present them the plan of what I hope to do. Showed them a different plan last year. Every year, in fact, it gets redesigned.

The pretty flowered china tea pot comes out. The bank receives the matching cups. We use mugs. "Coffee or tea? Decaf? Milk and sugar? One lump or two?" Ramona serves with poise. She is excellent in this kind of situation. We sit around the table: Me in black shirt sleeves, open collar, T-shirt showing. Ramona, impeccable as always, in a red blouse that makes her dark skin look warm and joyous. And the bank, its stuffy usual in tie and jacket.

"Ramona, your coffee surely tastes good. If you were in Barrhead, I'd be in every day."

"Too bad; we happy to have you."

One of them reaches for a bag of potato chips off the rack. "On house," I declare with a sweep of the arm. The bank does not unstiffen.

The discussion wends its way around the bush, drawing in Ramona as well. "Hear with the spring breakup a few seismic crews will be coming up," she says. Everybody has been talking about it, so hers is more idle conversation than fresh news. She does get to fill in some specifics that relate to the hotel. "The week past we had the music, cost us $300 and we made $312 in the sales. With the oil crews arriving, we expecting some improvement, that is for sure." She does all this in a casual way, never making it seem like she has any purpose to it at all.

I listen to the refrigerator click on, feeling grateful for Ramona's interjections. She is always up on the details of the operation. And, since Auschwitz, casual conversation trickles out awkwardly for me at best. Ramona throws me a queer look when, to prove it, I ask, "So, what's new in Barrhead?"

Both guests begin talking about the senior citizen centre recently done over with bank capital and city help. "It'd be a credit even to Edmonton or Calgary," they are saying. So my question turns out okay after all, and one thing leads to another. "Say, Sigmund, how do you like our mayor?"

"Uh ... somebody like me, survivor of Auschwitz, worries any mayor should ... take in account concerns of minorities."

"I can understand where you're coming from," says the booming voice, reading between the lines while his partner eyes him sideways. A look passes between them. To my relief, the social amenities soon give way to other purposes. The bank moistens its tongue in the delicate cup, leans forward, fires its first salvo. "Payments are a little late, Sigmund."

Before creeping out, the words wind around inside my mouth, "I think ... I think ... got to ... restructure debt."

Brows snap down on the bank's collective forehead. "You realize we can't do that," the boomer leaps in, shaking his shiny head. "A little out of the ordinary, don't you think?" tranquillity jumps aboard, frowning. It is a well-established contest of cat and mouse. But they do not trap me. Actually, we each know the other's game. And each of us realizes the other knows.

"Have any alternatives?" I ask, waiting for an answer. I can see the investigators run the figures around their minds, assessing the situation, searching for any way at all to squeeze money from a stone. Our hotel appraises at $95,000 today. The mortgage is $250,000. They would foreclose in a minute if they had an option. We have some $50,000 in it, all told. We would walk away in a minute if we could. "I am survivor," I say leaping into the lull. "We're in position to make hotel prosper."

Like tired lovers, we are stuck with each other. One of them produces a black-covered, pocket-size notebook. "What do you propose?" he mumbles.

After finishing Concordia University, Simon made some short films, and is now anticipating a special grant from the Foundation for Underwriting New Drama on Pay TV. Simon's old perseverance shows. He presses after the grant persistently, tenaciously, filling out every form, creating his project descriptions, outlines, sample scenes, securing his recommendations. He is telling people, "I learned it from my father. He drilled into us a very strong work ethic. I never realized why until I read about the motto above the Auschwitz gate." Knowing there is much worthy competition does not seem to diminish what I take to be his certainty about his own winning, though he tends not to share his concerns with his papa. Simon tells others, "I learned early not to express too much feeling to Papa. He always used it against me, so why give him the ammunition? And you never knew if Papa might brood, or fly off in a fury. He was volatile, all right; but I can see that it was a result of his concern for our well-being."

So I am forced to infer from hints. For months I envision him waiting for the postal carrier, steadfast in his conviction. "Any day a favourable announcement will come." The supposed prize, as I understand, will be the opportunity to write a feature length film in Mexico under the supervision of one of Canada's most renowned directors. Though I think he needs to rethink his chances, I understand that winning would be an opportunity for growth, advancement and recognition, all in one.

With my advancing age, my dear brother Włodimierz comes often to mind. The list of family cancer victims has lengthened considerably: my grandmother on father's side, my grandfather on mother's side, an uncle on mother's side, and even *Mamusia* herself. I so fear my own violent headaches that I place a new last will and testament in the hands of my lawyer.

Having reached the age of sixty-eight, I am getting fewer and fewer welding jobs. Even when I find work, my back functions for only a few hours. I walk with difficulty. Ramona has a feel for me. She says my new brace—it is very heavy—puts me in a bad mood. Yes, I see myself deteriorating. How could I ever scale an oil rig like I used to?

It's skilled work, excellent pay. If my sons were going to drop their studies—I still can't stand it that Vladimir sits with a grade ten education—I would have loved it if at least one of them would have taken over. I ask

Ramona, "When Vladimir was here last, did you ask him about going back to school?"

"Sigmund, you have talked to him. If Vladimir does not want to study, what can we do?"

"Okay, at least he could've learned welding, or help me with hotel. He's young. Maybe he'd have new ideas and attract new clients."

"You do not leave them alone. To get away, they tell you what you want to hear and then you wonder why they do not do it. That is why they confide in me and not in you."

"Of course, you send them rewards, like when Vladimir ran away to cottage."

"Sigmund, it was a nightmare to know he was at the cottage without the money. Awful, just awful. When he came back he was so thin. But you remember wrong; never sent him anything."

So their mother has much closer attachments to the boys than I have. To her, whatever the boys do is right. My mom was never so protective. She did not come running on the first cry, even when as a small boy I took sick with pneumonia. In Auschwitz, we went for X-rays; I had some residual marks on my lungs, but not enough to send a Pole to the gas. When Simon was first born, I thought maybe Ramona's protectiveness was just the fact that he was the first child; but no, that was her style with all of them. Then I thought maybe there was something wrong with her: after her father died suddenly of a burst vein, she, the youngest child, had gone to pieces. But I have come to realize her style is very good with our children, except for one complaint: when they are off work, she gives them money.

"Ramona, those guys are in their twenties. When your husband was seventeen, he was slave. Imagine! This God-given country of milk and honey, and they can't stand on their own two feet!"

Vladimir tells me: "It was you. You practically drove me to fly the coop. You're always trying to control my life. Like you forced me to read Jeremy Frost and write stories."

"Robert Frost?"

"Whatever. At the dinner table, you quizzed us like a chief judge in court. When things really got hot, each meal had a theme: helping out, good grades, writing skills, grammar. You're fanatical. Papa, you want to be *número uno* or nothing. Okay fine, that's you. I can't put that down. Only...."

"Only what?"

"Only, you can't expect the same from us. I never even wanted to go to college. I wanted to be an actor. But no, you want to go and remake us like you. Naturally I took off."

So much for the mealtime discussions I was so proud of.

In the old days, I would occasionally take my sons with me on a job. When they were with me, my joints were never neater. For a couple of weeks, Vladimir once apprenticed with me on a railroad trestle near Calgary. It was one of those parent-child experiences I will always treasure. Except those few weeks, none of my boys ever learned the trade. I would love to restructure our relationship.

For her part, Ramona tells whoever will commiserate, "Been here too long. Have nothing to do up here in the northern bush. There are some good people—a lot of the old mainly, because a family that is young would no last here. And there is a strength to suck out from the air, so clean, so refreshing; Cuba is too hot. People eat healthy, too, grow their own food, maybe raise a few animals. October, the season of the hunt, they all kill a moose or a deer, then freeze it for eating the whole winter through. For me, it is hard, always on the call; a customer can walk in at any time and order a steak, got no time for myself. When Sigmund is away with the Jews on one of his 'missions,' I have to run everything. Really want to paint, but I no having the chance even to finish the little designs on the cupboards."

Ramona shoulders most of the hotel chores. If not for her, our business would be in much deeper trouble. Emilio says, "My mother, she's a Tower of Strength. While Papa's flying off in the clouds, she's the one holding us together and keeping us out of the poor house."

I have to admit Emilio is right about that. She has the perfect disposition to deal with the public. She will sit down with the women and chitchat. "You went to Barrhead yesterday? What you get?" Maybe having grown up in a small village, she has more affinity with the clients than I do. And details. She is always reminding me: "You order the beer today?" "You collect the bounced cheque?" I think there are more important things to be concerned about than financial matters. I would love to restructure with her, too. If we have marital problems, it is a result of our working together day and night.

Ramona may not have objected to my Auschwitz work at the outset. Now, I have no choice but to go along with a University of Alberta marriage counsellor. Then she tells this Jewish woman, Queena Klein, "Auschwitz is the root of our problems; ever since he started with it, the life is the pits. We are broke. Sigmund says his work is so important for the Jews; then how come they no give more of the help?" She looks around before going on. "Back in Toronto he had a lover, practically abandoned me and the family; is like that again now. No, this is worse than a lover. With her I felt betrayed, but I could manage; from her he would go away once in a while. Auschwitz he is with all the time, that is for sure." Recently, Ramona has issued this ultimatum: "Either me or Auschwitz, take your pick."

Queena just listens. Me, too. I have turned back into the Rock of Gibraltar again. I guess I am like Simon, say as little as possible. This is not easy to endure after thirty years of marriage: "Okay then," she threatens, "I moving out, and you can go and play with the Jews whenever you want." For the time being I ignore it. I know my work tries Ramona's patience, especially over the last five years.

"While she says she would never harm me, that she loves me, no way could I ever make that choice." It terrifies me even to think that eventually I may be forced to.

"Have you thought about a vacation," Queena asks, "to find time for relaxation together? And what about moving all your books and papers from the trailer to the hotel? What is out of sight could be less annoying."

It is in the process of moving my files that I happen on one of Simon's journals. I know he is so set on winning that film grant. Judging from his journal, I am uncertain he could bear the disappointment if it fails to come through. At the time Simon wrote, he was wallowing in self-pity in a cheap Madrid hotel, waiting for a letter from his girlfriend, making, he says, "like Orwell in Paris, broke, eyeing the food on the plates of outdoor diners." Desperate, he had no money to phone her long-distance, and the expected letter failed to arrive. Even though Ramona, the provider, was as close as a collect call, he could not deal with it. He says I have the details all mixed up. Details or not, I am quite concerned about how he will handle it if he does not win this grant he is hoping for.

Now, due to the state of my relationship with Ramona, all typing is done at the hotel very early in the morning when she is asleep. I have been sending letters all over the world, searching for George Ginsbourg, the guy who, against camp regulations, was helping Nowicki, Hulanicki[67] and me with English in Auschwitz. One thing is certain, my typing will not disturb the nonexistent hotel guests. "When do you sleep?" Vladimir wants to know one afternoon. "No matter when I go by, slivers of light always slip through the cracks in between the shade and the window."

"I'm like sleep camel," I reply. I sleep one long night, then work endlessly for several days with hardly a break. Getting on without rest was part of camp routine. That was life then and that is life now. Sometimes in the wee hours of the morning I sit daydreaming, staring out at the black, pining for things to get better. Many years I longed for liberation, longed for marriage, longed for children. Now I long for successful relationships.

There is a sense of well-being within me; but instead of enjoying it, I find my family slipping away from me. It has become harder and harder to discern anything but a welter of individual threads and loose ends, the whole pattern breaking into various dark parts. Should I not be inured already? Objectively, the boys are legitimately resentful: every year we sink deeper in debt. Objectivity, though, is just not what you dream of from your own flesh and blood.

What am I to do? The real issue, I know, is not *where* I work, but the time and money expended. She says I force her to work for the Jews. "You go to Auschwitz, I have double work." When it comes back to that, I worry. How would I ever choose between wife and work? I doubt my own ability to do without either. I wonder what she will do. Maybe, if a miracle happened to allow us to rearrange our lives to afford Ramona more freedom for her own activities, it would help. That is what I am hoping. I think she is hoping somehow *Achtundachtzig* will work its way out of my system. I do not like the chances of either. This banishment of my office is nothing more than a temporary stopgap.

In the midst of my marital problems, the bus project is taking shape. Only in Birkenau are there the ruins of the four crematoria–gas chamber complexes, the open pits where bodies were cremated, the several dozens of wooden barracks housing prisoners in the most primitive conditions, the selection Ramp, and other facilities such as the building-size tubs where body fluids were refined. For a full understanding of the Nazi horrors, *all* visitors should not only see their own national pavilion and the Black Wall of Death, but also the killing fields of Birkenau. Yet, less than ten percent of the visitors get to Birkenau. Neither are they encouraged to do so, the museum as set up under the former communist regime being content to show everyone the non-Jewish presentation in the main camp. The new excuse is that there is no way to transport visitors from one camp to the other.

Ben Rose has written an article in the *Canadian Jewish News* which got the attention of Nathan Leipciger, vice-chairman of the National Holocaust Commission of the Canadian Jewish Congress. I think we have a donor.

Lately, I sit, a servant to my mission, in the pool table room adjoining the tavern. It used to be the restaurant before Vladimir and Ramona bashed down the wall one weekend when I was away. What a time they must have had of it. I was furious. Used to consign out the restaurant, though it caused nothing but arguments. They are thick, those two, always designing how to make me realize that what I do is wrong. Vladimir merely said, "If the walls came down in Germany, they can come down in Fort Assiniboine, too." I have to admit we are more versatile now.

So, first I put up some Quaker Oats in the 'micro-oven.' Then, from the old dining area I keep an eye out for customers while typing, struggling with yet another letter to the Auschwitz authorities. They make me so mad, the way they play down any victimization of Jews, like those Jewish women in Block Ten. But no, they want history to say Polish suffering was at least as oppressive as Jewish suffering. I even located a document sent by an Auschwitz SS doctor to Himmler mentioning the experimentation on the "Jewish women in Block Ten." The historians sit there in Auschwitz while I, Sigmund the welder and barkeep, uncover the document from Fort Assiniboine, Alberta. I paid the Nazi War Crime, U.S. Documentary Service $2 to have it mailed to me.[68]

How does the curator respond? Why—he writes: "The doctor employed the word '*Jude*' to mean 'Slavic.'" Does he expect anybody to swallow crap like that! In glorifying Polish suffering at the expense of Jewish suffering, our Polish government unwittingly provides grist for the neo-Nazis' propaganda mill. There has got to be room for everybody's concerns. I loved my firstborn with all my heart. I thought there was no love withheld, no more to give. Then Emilio and Vladimir came along, and I loved them equally as much. Love and suffering know no limits; there is enough for everybody.

The new museum guidebook never even mentions that 90 percent of those murdered were Jews. It speaks of "unknown victims" in places where we know they were Jewish. A list of victims on page two omits the Jews. Only Polish women are depicted. Page four fails to identify Jews as among the first 728 prisoners. Pages eight and nine actually describe in great detail the whole killing process at Birkenau without even alluding to Jews. The guidebook neglects to state that Dr. Mengele's experiments on twins were on Jews and Gypsies.[69] It glorifies the *Sonderkommando* revolt, and the role of the women, without mentioning that they were all Jews. Pages seventeen to nineteen make no mention that hundreds of Jews were murdered in 1940-42 in the Bunker. But worst of all, it still deliberately misrepresents the Jews who were experimented upon in Block Ten as "Slavs."

A Canadian press report regarding 'Slavic' women in the guidebook got picked up in Poland and caused a furore. My friend Marian Strzelecki, the past-president of the Polish Congress who joined me in greeting the Polish prime minister in Ottawa, tells me, "You're too pro-Jewish." He resigns from the Auschwitz Awareness Society. It is not the first time he has exploded.

"Marian, I didn't create problem; museum stubbornness did. All I did was expose it. Whether it's newsworthy is their decision." My argument does not dissuade Strzelecki, and I lose another friend.

Meanwhile, fourteen newspapers decided to reprint the article, finally forcing our Polish authorities to agree to do something about the booklet. Nothing happens.[70]

The battle drags on. Why does everything have to be a battle? The International Auschwitz Council has authorized signs noting the destruction of European Jewry. The museum has not installed them. In 1990 Dr. Jonathan Webber, my friend from the University of Oxford, prepared an assessment of the Jewish pavilion, which I wholeheartedly support; the museum has yet to carry out any of the suggested revisions. Meanwhile, the Polish Ministry of Culture and Arts arranges meetings of the International Auschwitz Council on Saturdays and other Jewish holy days despite Canadian and British protests.

Museum researchers also claim to be unacquainted with the fact Jews were in the camp from the very first transport. They must know that we know their game. Yet they are informing everyone, "It was a Polish camp; Jews were not taken until 1942." If the museum authorities have their way, there will someday be a Holocaust without Jews at all.

"I was there," I will tell them. Even before Auschwitz was opened, three hundred Jewish forced-labourers from the surrounding area had readied the camp. Some of these were also incarcerated, along with those from the Tarnów prison, as a punishment for infractions such as coming late for work. The rabbi of Tarnów, Israel Joseph Shlichter, ten times great grandson of Rabbi Saul Wahl, his wife Leah and their two children Rebecca and Zeev Dov, remained to be taken later. Eventually, they all perished.[71] Many other

Tarnówer Jews were also with us in the first transport. The officials, who presumably know well enough, refuse to accept my word until I tell them about Father Węgrzynowski (No. 90) and his Jewish choir.

In two areas, activity flourishes: Commemorative citations for Christians continue to proliferate. Contrary to what actually occurred in Block Eleven, Teresa Swiebocka, Auschwitz historian, bargains: "If we change the guide-book, you'll stop bugging us about making Block Eleven a Shrine of Polish Martyrs." Still today, I see Krankemann beating his Jewish horses whenever the word "eleven" is mentioned, even if only in a date. I am supposed to change the history of Auschwitz because she corrects what should have been right in the first place. Postcard salesmen and other commercial enterprises not related to the Auschwitz museum also multiply.

They forget I was in Block Ten during the early days, saw through the cracks in the boarded windows what was going on in the yard between my Block and Block Eleven. I was called back when, in the last few days, the fire brigade had to cordon off Block Ten:

There, naked except for their telltale shirt, a thousand emaciated Jews from IG Farbenwerke.[72] Selected by *Unterscharführer* Oswald Kaduk. Clauberg has closed his sterilization clinic in the Block, the surviving women sent to Birkenau—as these guys are about to be. Are we supposed to catch sight of this? Transport trucks late, so carefully planned sequencing disintegrates. Wonder if I need to remove my group. Jewish guy approaching. Please, I was an officer in the German Army, World War I, highly decorated, two Iron Crosses. Speaks excellent High German. Wave the SS guard over, an Unterscharführer. Seems we have wrong man; he's decorated patriot. Jewish lies, he tells me. After everyone is trucked off, we get a bonus loaf of bread for every two persons. Bread. Eleven in the morning. Happen to glance out on the bakery. Notice three Russians slip into place. One watches the gate, one the entrance to the kitchen, one the road. To anyone else this would be nothing; to the eye trained by four years in Auschwitz, it has teamwork written all over it. Where did they come from? Two others sidle up to the barred window. Brilliant. Broad daylight. Perfect time to arouse no suspicion. You can hardly hear the pane being broken, barely a faint tinkle. At this time of day, could be anything. Not a word is spoken. What next? One scans around abruptly. Quickly joints up a pole from two, two-metre lengths, which he thrusts between the bars. Stabs and retrieves about ten loaves of bread, which passing arms whisk away in the direction of the pool. Those Russians make fools of the Nazis, all right! Leave the window quickly. Do not want to be about if SS come checking up on things. Anyhow, saw nothing.

The pool was built in 1944 for show and, in case of attack, as a reservoir for fire fighting. In all my time, I only knew of it being used twice. Once, *Unterscharführer* Oswald Kaduk ordered the firemen to swim while an SS photographer made a propaganda film. I was not there; I think I was digging Höss's bunker at the time. How I would love to see that movie now. Except that film, not even a group photo exists. Then, in the summer of 1944, a male nurse from the prison hospital, a former Olympic champion from Czechoslovakia, practised somersault dives. I knew him because he gave me massages when I was fighting as a boxer. People were dying all around me, and I was going for a massage.

"Guess what, I'm going to be diving again," he told me while pushing down on my back.

"Here?"

"Yeah, Höss is expecting a high-level Nazi delegation to arrive with representatives of the International Committee of the Red Cross; he's ordered me to perform."

We inmates could never fathom why the Red Cross visited, and yet chose not to issue an exposé of the crimes at Auschwitz-Birkenau.

As far as I am ever able to find out, when it concerns Jews, the Red Cross becomes a stickler for definitions. As their own report later states: "Under National Socialism, Jews had become in truth *outcasts*.... The supervision that the ICRC exercised in favour of *prisoners* and *internees* did not apply to them" (italics added). Red Cross officials are not, of course, consciously antisemitic. No, these Christian gentlemen simply feel a need to be careful about definitions. Aiding Jews contrary to the definitions could jeopardize their role in helping 'legitimate' internees and prisoners-of-war.

At first I was totally mystified. Only gradually has the true picture been confirmed. This is the same ICRC that has approved the Red Crescent and Red Lion symbols, but steadfastly refused to accept the Israeli Red Star of David. It, too, somehow fails to meet the "definition." But the Red Cross has no trouble freely dishing up accusations against Israel. In light of its postwar actions, its decision not to, as they say in their own report, "bang on the table and stir up a scandal" about Nazi murdering of Jews no longer appears so arbitrary.

The neo-Nazis are also always bringing up both the swimming pool and the brothel, as if to say their existence proves there was no murder factory. "Why was there a brothel?" people ask me when I might have mentioned the role it played in my life.

"Who can figure Nazi mind?" I usually answer. "I've got for most things in camp no logical explanation. In Auschwitz, if you tried to understand what was going on, you drove yourself insane. You had to throw away all that old mentality and simply work on the process of survival. Auschwitz' unpredictability, some survivors say 'purposeful unpredictability,' was part of its pain. Maybe reason why Nazis introduced, at Auschwitz, brothels, is because Nazis didn't want pregnant women or births. Sterilization experiments prove that. Maybe they wanted to prevent homosexual activities. Perhaps it was for health of guards. Certainly as a work incentive it was another way to get at prisoners' minds."

"Como está tu desayuno, jefe?" Ramona asks one morning, "How is your breakfast, Chief?" Her hair, cut in short ringlets, emphasizes the morning semicircles underlining her dark eyes.

"Hmmm," I reassure her in the sparse, universal language of those long married. While it is only late morning, my eyes are already heavy. I have been up the whole night working, barely catnapped with clothes on. Now I will plod through the day half-conscious.

I follow her movements, silent in my coma-like state, as she putters about her trailer's little kitchen. In my mind, it is her trailer and her garden, my children, my wife, my table, my welding truck and my hotel. Even so, in the latter, it must be admitted, she does most of the work and the papers are in her name. Some of the rectangles formed by the mouldings on the kitchen cupboard doors have been hand-painted, adorned by delicate matching flowers. This extra touch so characterizes her, but if someone were to ask, I think she would say I overlook details like that. Between filling orders for meals and looking after the tavern, she has had no time to finish her decorated mouldings. Ramona has been taking painting lessons for the last couple years, ten sessions for fifteen dollars. She keeps a little studio in the back of the trailer, would love to paint more. "No time."

One thing she always makes time for is her garden. Unfortunately, the growing season is ridiculously short up here, June to August, but she derives a great deal of pleasure from her efforts. When summer erupts with swarms of black flies and mosquitos, a bouquet of pansies comes alive with an explosion of colour: blue, purple, yellow, mostly yellow, their flowered faces open to the kiss of the sun. Here and again, sticking their heads up like scattered patterns on a bright background, sprout some dwarf sweet peas, and in the back, tea roses and velvety sweet williams, all different colours. Ramona is down on her knees painting with a floral palette, and each plant on her flowerbed canvas is nurtured under her watchful care. On cold nights, which we get several times a summer, it is her hands that cover them with newspaper. When I want to make Ramona smile, I just ask about her flowers.

Before sitting, she turns her head to me, an ever-present wooden spoon in her hand. "Simo?"

"Huh."

"Simo, I have not seen my family for a long time now, miss them terribly, must see them."

I have heard it before, but it gets my attention. As our eyes meet, I detect the slightest hint of a quiver on her thin lips. Ramona is always incredibly controlled, and I look down at once so as not to let her know I saw. She has seven sisters and six brothers, all still in Cuba. She cannot write English, so she has been after me to help her fill out the visa application for four years. How can we, though? My 'life task' absorbs all our funds and then some. Who knows if it will ever be possible? But can I tell her that? After a long pause, I succumb without commitment: "Fine, fine! I know, dear."

"Simo," she pleads, "I wish you to make the papers."

"It'll get done."

We know each other too well. She peers right through my transparent reply, but takes her place at the table without responding. We know our love runs deep—at least I do, maybe too deep. It is buried so far below the surface of our day-to-day existence, it is hard to recognize. Sadly, while she was sympathetic in the first few years, even Ramona does not always appreciate *Achtundachtzig*. As has happened an infinite number of times, she has lost another battle against an army she does not see, fighting for a cause she does not feel. Then I am off on yet another mission to Poland, this time to attend a meeting of the International Auschwitz Council, the third trip in eighteen months. She is so resentful half of me fears the other half is about to be divorced.

It comes even before departing. We are going over the books. "Simo, you spend the money on phone calls, meetings, talk shows, trips. I have needs, too." She is speaking English now. "The hotel is suffering, that is for sure. Your work for the Auschwitz steal you away. You tell me, 'Fine, fine!' but my visa she never get done. Meanwhile, no got the freedom and no got the family. I am so sad, my heart breaking. Why can you no be honest with me for the once? Just say 'no' instead of fool me, raising in me the hopes only to dash them again and again for what? For Auschwitz? Go to your damned Auschwitz! Just cannot take it anymore."

I really want to fulfil her wish. But how can I? Even though Emilio keeps telling me shouting only makes her angrier, my voice rises anyway. "Ramona, Ramona, you can't understand how I feel. How many people ever died for you? How many people did you leave laying on ground you might have helped? You don't know history."

Her resentment like lava from a Central American volcano. "No, Señor Sobolewski, is you who no know the history, thirty years of our history, is you who no understand *my* feelings. You are thousands of miles away in Poland, I am right here." She stares through the window by the table like she is penetrating the entire world, memorizing all its contours. She remains silent for a long interval.

"Oh, I understand all right." Her voice has become subdued, but she is, if anything, angrier than before. Her arms are crossed. I do not think Ramona has ever put her arms around me. She continually withholds. Maybe it is from the Cuban farm where women are treated like slaves. She runs on, talking quickly. "No be able to read but I am not a fool, know the world. Your work over there is like you have another woman. I am the Cuban workhorse, and you got a Polish racer to play the game with." Now she sits in silence on the verge of tears, her back to me.

"You know that's not true!" An overwhelming desire to hug her floods over me. My arm hovers over her shoulder. It urgently wants to reassure her. But she will never know. It does not make contact.

"Then why you making a trip again?"

"Ramona," I say in exasperation, "I can't do anything else."

I can appreciate why even Nazis—who bragged to each other about their 'contribution' to the world—tried to cover up their crimes at the end. When Ramona someday comes before the Maker, and is asked if she has lived up to her principles, she will be able to answer with full confidence, "Yes." I desperately want that, too.

She becomes more brusque, and glares at me. I know what that means. Ramona's way of expressing dissatisfaction is to cross her legs. We will not be in the same bed tonight, as we were not last night, and many nights before that, and probably for some time to come as well. How could everything I yearned for have turned to dust? "Go if you like," she sighs.

And I do.

"Jurek, you know more than anyone else alive," I say to him over the phone, trying for the thousandth time to enlist his support. "You were personal servant to the head Kapo of the camp. You heard the informers, the condemning of people to death. Tell me some of your experiences, and I'll try to publicize them with your name."[73]

"Well, I wouldn't tell you anything because these people have taken over the whole of Auschwitz and the Holocaust."

I feel like slamming the receiver on him, but I do not. If he would only talk, we would have a broad new insight into camp life. "People?" I press him.

Silence. "Well, you should know. You work with——"

"You mean Jews have taken over the Holocaust?"

"Well you said it, not me," he answers in a cagey fashion.

I have come to the conclusion Jurek blocks everything unsavoury from his mind. From listening to him no one could ever find out what the camp was like or what we lived through afterwards. He cannot even admit we robbed villagers on our trek through Germany after liberation. For necessity, you do things that later you would take back if you could. But as he describes it, "If a radio or bicycle was laying there, we'd pick it up." As if generous-minded Germans set aside a cache of bicycles for former prisoners.

If someone would probe him as to the many discussions that have passed between us concerning my work, why—he would say, "We've got no disagreements. He's involved. It's his life. I think what he does is good. It represents what he is."

Again, a longing for a personal restructuring comes to mind. I will confide in my friend, Reuven, "I manage to take his criticism. But when he tells you what he thinks you want to hear, I feel raped."

No sooner do I make it over one hump than another right away looms before me. I have learned that the smooth life is nonexistent. So now that I am sixty-eight, what is my sharpest pain? That towards the end of my life our children cannot yet accept the blessing I have to give.

We have come around full circle from where we started. Fathers and their teenage sons are often at opposite ends of an emotional pole; you expect it. But my boys are already well integrated personalities, well beyond the age of self-revelation: twenty-nine, twenty-seven and twenty-five. Yet ... instead of seeking the blessing their heritage provides, they reject it outright. As if sons could displace their father as I once tried to do with *Achtundachtzig*.

Sometimes I wonder how much of their trouble is simply normal growth; how much is rubbed off from Auschwitz; how much due to my own personality and choices? Would the family have been different if I had never decided to involve myself in my passion? No, involved or not, it would have been the same. In one of those vicious ironies of life, you sacrifice your relationship with the family so you can provide what they need, when what they need really is you. First, business absorbed all my time; and only afterwards, my preoccupation with *Achtundachtzig*.

Whatever I do, I cannot seem to restructure. Their lives are so different from mine. When each went to kindergarten, Ramona cried. When they got to junior high, she cried. When they got to high school, she cried. I was proud they had reached a new stage, but Ramona cried. Ramona knew.

So I ask, why then was I saved? Surely not to pus up old injuries, incite bad dreams, provoke my own people, outrage my fellow Christians and drive painful wedges between me and my family. Beliefs or doubts? Confidence or misgiving? Certainty or ambivalence? The burden is destroying me. And it is all so isolating, sometimes I feel like quitting.

Another night apart.

Ramona drops the coffee in front of me. Some sloshes onto the checkered, plastic table cloth beside the decorative wire chicken basket. Pork sausage slices are sizzling on the stove. "Heard you type at four of the morning; this counsellor is not helping at all; our agreement says you have to do all your typing in the hotel." The usual brunch repartee. It is already past eleven. After closing, Ramona did not get to bed until two o'clock herself; it takes her a while to get back to her usual cheerful demeanour.

"I've got so much to do before my next trip," I yawn, still tired. "The sausage will burn."

She checks the pan. "They will be just right, crisp." She turns back, waving a wooden spoon. Her eyes flash. "So who forces you to fly around the world? You must have a woman over there."

The ghost of my affair still shadows the air between us. I look at Ramona's getup. In the mornings she reminds me of a Picasso painting. I blink, trying to visualize her when first we met, her smooth face, her buoyancy. We have come a long way together, but she has never got over that episode with my real-estate partner. Involuntarily, I yawn again. To my instant regret, the words slip out of my mouth: "I'm taking ... with me, Vladimir."

Everything stops. She stares, crosses her arms, her spoon still waggling meaningfully. "*Callate!* Two thousand dollars extra! Where will the money come from?"

"I cashed life insurance policy." I had hoped to break it to her gently, maybe talk to her about how we might increase our cash flow by saving on premiums. Now it is out in the worst possible way.

"Cannot believe it! *Por qué?*"

"So you won't imagine another woman."

Silence. Then a torrent of English. "What always hurt is you tell everybody I hate the Jews. Is not true. You go away for maybe two or three weeks afterwards, maybe the month that come, the entire hotel is on me. I feel so alone. I am not a brave woman, scared to be here by myself; and after the customers have been drinking, I real scared to go to the trailer at two of the morning. Have we even a next door neighbour to hear me shout? You cannot know how scared I am, you who lived through the camp; by you no one else can be scared.

"And I no just scared for me, am afraid for the hotel. For you, Auschwitz is more important than the business; you no pay the bills as if you no care at all! The hotel is in my name; for you is like hotel no exist. This was supposed to be a joint project. Instead, you go spend practically all your time awake on the work of the camp, go to the bed four or five of the morning, sleep two hours, then you back working. You want to do too much in too short of a time; you are hyper! Is not healthy, you always complaining about the headaches; I am afraid for you. If you would only cut down, yes, I would help you. You say, 'Not to worry for me.' If I did not care, I would not worry; but I care.

"You? You not even go to Queena Klein for yourself; you go 'for Ramona' like is nothing *you* can benefit from. As long as I no say nothing, you believe we got the perfect marriage. You no even want to know what I thinking or feeling. Ever occur to you I am myself, not you? When I say something to the counsellor, you say, 'She never tell me that.' But I tell you, you just not listening. The counsellor tell us to make a trip to Las Vegas to be together. What you do when we get there? Visit a lady who is director of an organization for the Jews, then you go to the newspaper and talk about the camp. Newspapers control you. Went to improve our marriage, to have something for the two of us, and right away you go running out. You not give me a break; no wonder we just go down the hill."

She looks away. What is she looking for, I wonder. Then I catch tears welling up in her eyes. "I am afraid of my own ideas lately; they are not the best. I am not strong enough, not able to go on, not used to fighting all the time, want out, want the peace. And you think my complaint is I no like the Jews, that is what you want to think instead of facing the problems we really got."

This has gone beyond the usual morning chatter. "You like slot machines. I don't," I respond on my own behalf.

Later she reports, hands on hips, she will not sleep in the same bed, nor cook for me, nor do my laundry. Our relationship, I should think, would be much better with love than with punishment. Every marriage I have ever known to fail, my own and those of acquaintances, had previously lost its sexual component. But if sex and laundry is the cost of my work, so be it. The work is more important. A siren wails outside. Noon. Triggered by the siren, my mind thinks escaping prisoner. For a long time, she says nothing. She is staring out the window as she so often does, the one over the kitchen sink, across her garden towards the hotel. I remind myself we had a guest last night. Did he slip out unnoticed, or is he still upstairs? If he has not yet come down, we have to have some breakfast ready.

She must have been thinking about the hotel, too. Perhaps her eye catches its shabbiness. Perhaps she thinks of quieting guys in baseball caps who have had too much to drink. Like my bank visitors, we can each see through each other. We are stuck with each other, too. "Am trapped in a prison," she finally says very quietly in Spanish. "Not as cruel as your prison, but still a prison, that is for sure. We cannot afford to stay, cannot afford to leave. I am a slave to the business. You were four-and-a-half years in Auschwitz; I am practically ten years in the emptiness of this land, and in the darkness of the winter that goes on forever and ever. Think I cannot understand you?" Then she abruptly concludes, "Okay then, do as you like." And, in an exasperated voice edged with what might be almost contempt, she adds, "Your sons think you are *loco*, though. How you think you will help them by running off to Poland wasting everything we have?"

I close my eyes. A man in stripes appears to step out of the darkness, fixes on me. "Did I tell you it would be easy?" I open my eyes. Ramona is looking at me expectantly. The light catches her. How the years have taken their toll. Badges of life have begun to grow across her face. Her eyes have a puffiness to them. She wears a housecoat swept up around her. But she is still one beautiful lady. And even under the folds of the garment, you can tell her figure holds. After all these years, looking at her sends a queer shivery feeling running up my spine. How long has she been waiting for me to answer? No time. The mind works like a flash. A person can review his whole life in a split second.

When I open my eyes, she still stands in the posture she held before. I want to explain to her, "Ravens are everywhere, soaring silently on their flat wings, ready to feed on any social castoff. And so many, who can no longer tell world what they know, who can't even say 'thank you,' need a living voice. This is why I can't choose between you and Jews. You're both part of what makes me, me." I want to say all that, but the words stick in my throat. How could they not? My struggle for an Auschwitz awareness does cause them all problems. Why is it more important than they are?

She takes advantage of the silence. "There, see, I am right." She pauses again, wiping up the puddles on the table. Vladimir calls her a "clean freak." I shift uncomfortably in my chair. Yesterday's clothes feel grimy. "Been thinking," she says, "in spite of it all, everything you do is for the boys— Provost, Chicago, Poland. They are the reason for everything, no?"

I simply gape at her. "Ramona, I do it for my comrades who didn't survive. I cannot free myself from their memory. And I do it for Jews I never knew, for dead, burnt bodies whose voice I am." The thought of those long grey winters at Auschwitz slips in and out of mind, and I am chilled. I see Zończyk, my visitor in the *H.K.B.* when I had typhus. He is waiting with an onion, his hand outstretched as it used to be in life. To Zończyk I owe not only my life, but also whatever shred of Christian brotherhood I feel. "For you," he says, "and for your children." I turn away so she cannot see my eyes.[74]

Her voice is quiet, resigned. "Señor Sobolewski, you say you owe those who died; you cannot even understand yourself; everything you do, you do for the boys; that is why you get so angry with them."

"Do you expect me to go and bow myself down to them?" I demand.

It was one of those fleeting conversations, but it does not slip away.

Seventeen:
Simon, Emilio, Vladimir
Poland, 1992

Katowice is the last major railhead between Warsaw and Auschwitz. You switch trains here. It is a good bet everyone on the platform is going to Auschwitz. Children's laughter greets my ear. About twenty-five youngsters come running and punching, exuberant twelve-year-olds, grade six. Looking to learn the state of young Polish thought, I decide to introduce myself and our mission from Canada.

"Yeah, we're on a school outing, to Auschwitz," they bubble.

The teacher comes caterwauling up. "What's going on here!"

You cannot blame her; how does she know who is talking to her kids? She is a mother hen protecting her brood. "I'm from Canada," I assure her, "a former prisoner, returning, with my son Vladimir."

"Oh, really." She turns to the class. "Children, we are very fortunate. This man is a Polish survivor." Then turning back to me, she says, "They've raised the money for the trip themselves; the school isn't paying for them at all." Capitalism has quickly taken hold in Poland.

Congratulating the beaming youngsters, I ask, "And what'll you find in Auschwitz?"

Dead silence. How is it possible no one's prepared them for a trip like this? Is it merely another outing to the firehouse, or a picnic? They raised the money themselves! Four hundred fifty thousand visitors a year, and this is what all too many come and go with.

"We'll see Father Kolbe's memorial," the teacher interjects for them.

"In winter we lined up outside, nothing but thin pyjamas on," I tell them. "They'd count us, making mistakes on purpose, over and over, sometimes for hours. Right before our eyes, people would collapse and be frozen to death in the snow. They brought here Poles like me, but mostly they brought Jews—"

"Why do you want to tell them negatives?" the alarmed mother hen cuts in.

Why are you taking them to Auschwitz, then? I think to myself. Though no one wants to be rude, you do not want to argue with a teacher in front of her class, either; so I turn to the kids without answering. "Anyone ever seen a Jew?" Twenty-five kids, and not one had. In 1939, I tell them, Poland was thirteen percent Jewish, the largest proportion of any country in the world. Canada is less than one percent Jewish; the United States less than three percent. In a country that was but a few years ago thirteen percent Jewish, not one young student has ever met a Jew. "Why is this?" I ask. "Where'd they all go?" When again no one answers, I tell them about the smokestacks.

"They're only kids," the teacher protests, grimacing.

I simply turn to the kids. "Why do you suppose the Nazis killed the Jews?" I wonder aloud.

I still think this a good question, but in the retelling Emilio disagrees. "In the time man has been on this planet, there's been a lot of killing," he says. "You don't see people trying to make a museum of it."

Anyway, no one responds. Obviously no one has ever discussed this with them. Finally, one clear-eyed lad raises his hand. I nod to him appreciatively. "Because they were rich, and because they were smart," he answers proudly. This time the mother hen says nothing.

I wonder how this guy functions in school if he thinks Auschwitz is what happens to you if you are smart. Slipping on my stripers, I tell them, "I survived because I was a Pole and not a Jew. Jews got treated so bad few could last more than a month or two. And why? Because they were rich? Smart? Because people said they had no right to live. Think about it. Do you imagine this is what God wants?"

In spite of their teacher, all during the train ride, kids keep coming in our car in twos and threes to ask questions. One little girl even gives me her address. You have to believe these small achievements make a difference.

Before we came to Poland, a written summary of our discussions in Chicago was conveyed to Cardinal Glemp. At the previous Council meeting, the Cardinal's representative, Dr. Chrostowski, a priest, had in a final speech effectively jettisoned all positive achievements. This time I abide the whole meeting waiting for the windstorm. In contrast to the previous gathering the year before, Chrostowski remains uncharacteristically subdued. Some small progress occurs when, in the English rendition of the Auschwitz guidebook, the word "Slavic" is eliminated. Small achievements. And there is promise of more "concessions" to come. "Why," I wonder, "does everything have to be a struggle, a concession?"

Father Chrostowski afterwards complains, "Sobolewski, you have undermined my position on the management team of the Auschwitz Museum."

A visit to Birkenau with Vladimir brings back memories:

In our part of the *Konzentrationslager*, the breakdown in discipline is symptomatic of the times. We're saying, The Russian Army has reached the Vistula; just a few weeks, we'll be free; the Nazis have to stop the killing. While marching to Birkenau to inspect fire extinguishers in *Kanada*, running in opposite direction, a group of about twenty prisoners, mostly Jews, protecting their skulls with thin wraith-like arms. Screaming young German foreman chases after, beating those he catches. We step in with a stick, grab the Kapo by the neck, shout at him, Beating is forbidden! Hasn't SS Obersturmbannführer Liebehenschel, camp commandant after Höss, banned certain punishment to protect slave-labour supply? Pattern of maltreatment too ingrained to have an effect? We make a big show of writing his number down. Threaten to report him. How the Birkenau prisoners stare! Even at this date, no Jew can assert *Nie pozwalam* as we do, and not lose his life. God! During our brief conversation, over amongst the birch trees, thousands of Jews are being ushered into the gas chambers.

After the International Auschwitz Council meeting, Vladimir and I tour. I am talking in Polish to a woman in Lublin. She is just the right age. "During the war, where did you live?" I ask in a low tone.

"Outside of town."

"Umm. And what did you do at the time?"

"I was a secretary, in the city."

I mentally calculate her route and suddenly the discussion that began but casually takes on interest. "Then you passed Majdanek every day for years," I say as matter-of-factly as possible.

The reaction is anything but matter-of-fact. With the unexpected change in direction she turns red, screws up her face and affirms with a deep sigh, "I didn't see it, didn't even know it was there."

"No?" I reply, ever so softly.

"I was looking on my side of the road."

"And when you went home at the end of the day?"

Her response is to glance away, probably the way she did then.

"Never mind, what did you do on Sundays?"

Now she answers quickly, "I went to church."

Majdanek was so close to the road one could feel the camp's palpitations in his fingers—yet, it was completely invisible. She turned herself off just like I had to. But I want Vladimir to realize she really has herself convinced she never saw or knew anything about the camp. What can you expect when the whole society fails to own up to the truth?

The dusty road to Nisko from Jarosław winds its way along the river and then onto a turn-off that bumps like a track inside a campsite in North America. Soon there is no road at all, only some deep ruts that the taxi driver, occupied with gab, lets his vehicle follow like it has a mind of its own. "New road is under construction," he has told us. We pass a cemetery where Russians, Gypsies and Jews are buried in mass graves, no names, just numbers. Basia is with us. The driver is a young man; as usual, I have him talking about the Holocaust and Jews in Poland. He uses the phrase, "the Jewish question."

"You know that's a Nazi phrase?" I leap in.

"It is?"

"Yeah. Why isn't there a Protestant question? Why not a Catholic question? Why is it only Jewish life that's in question?" Basia is nodding in agreement. Where does all this come from? I ask myself.

"I'm sorry. I didn't mean it that way," the driver says. "I really didn't."

"In a way, that's even more disturbing to me; why are we Poles still using the phrase?"

Taking care to look back to ascertain my reactions, he chooses his words carefully. "Everybody says the Jews killed Christ. But I believe our just and fair God has chosen the Jewish people. The Polish Pope wants better relations between the Catholics and the Jews."

"The big problem," I remind him, "is that less than half the Polish clergy are for dialogue. If we had supported the Jews the way we did Solidarity, three million Jewish citizens would not have been killed."

Before flying home, I meet in reunion with two members of the fire brigade in the fourth-floor lobby of the Polonia Hotel, the capital's oldest, and one of but a handful of original buildings remaining from before the war. In the dining room artificial skylights soar three stories above, from which hang candle-type chandeliers. Along all sides of the upper level, decorative columns divide a series of French windows, each column graced at its crown by a gilded woolly ram's head. On the middle level, gilded balconies, each with double doors and French panes, overlook the dining area, recalling the glory of former balls.

"You were so young then," Ryszard Dacko reflects with a chuckle.

"What do you mean, 'so young'?" I bend forwards in the overstuffed chair. "How old are you?"

"Seventy-five," replies the still-working maintenance man for *Politika*, a local Polish newspaper.

"Well, I'm sixty-nine." I recline again. "Ryszard, that's only six years difference."

"It doesn't matter. Young/old isn't a question of years, Zygmunt. You were so young, so energetic."

"Yes, so strong-willed, so full of ideas," adds Jan Nowicki beside him on the maroon divan.

"So romantic," says Dacko as two chamber maids chattering to themselves emerge from the old elevator in front of us, pushing their cart on the way to morning duties.

"So naïve," Nowicki adds again.

"That's it, naïve," chuckles Dacko. I see he hesitates to go on.

"You can say it. You can mention Irka," I tell him.

"The whole fire brigade sent her verses in your name. You thought you'd marry her?"

"More than that," says Nowicki, the more intellectual of the two. "You thought life would be so peaceful after the Germans were gone."

"Yeah, just defeat the Nazis and all Poland, all the world, would be transformed for the better." Dacko turns to me. "I also had a girlfriend, a

Jewish woman," he confesses. "I'd tell you her name. Only, she's still alive in California. Why share something that some people will never understand?"

"You saved her life," I remind him.

"Perhaps, yes. I didn't run around mooning, though," Dacko chuckles again.

"Course, maybe that's because you were married," replies Nowicki sagely. Nowicki looks all around, then lights a cigarette. Presently, he turns to me, his mind leaping. "I remember our discussions about escape. The three of us group leaders—I was leader of Group Three—would talk. We knew it had to be all or none." He turns back. "You were——"

I lean over. "I forget completely any such discussions."

"Because," Nowicki replies, "all you could focus on was yourself and Irka."

"You know," Dacko comments, "speaking of Irka, she lived right here in Warsaw; but she never came to any of our survivors' meetings."

"I know," I sighed.

"For us brigade members," Nowicki breaks in, "Irka's absence was as strong as her presence. I think she was embarrassed."

"I think so, yes." My hand goes on my chin. "Saw her years later. She never accepted having been tricked into the brothel. Lived out the remainder of her life feeling dirty. I think ... I let her down."[75]

"You loved her."

"In the end I walked out on her."

"So much for your life of peace, Zygmunt," grieves Dacko.

Nowicki is glancing around at us, sweeps with his arm. "Look at us. We've all been affected forever. Has any of us ever found peace?"

"Good thing she never knew the Auschwitz Museum asked me if I still had any of her letters. They wanted something from one of the women."

"Will the world ever change?" asks Nowicki rhetorically.

"Maybe I'm still young," I muse. "But I think it's got to."

"Keep up the good fight, Zygmunt," Nowicki places his hand on my shoulder. "Don't stop."

"The more the better, even what is already written is not enough," adds Dacko.

"Some people say I do too much."

"Stupid people you don't have to look for," Dacko says. "They grow up like mushrooms."

On the tarmac, our plane inches against the line of planes inching the other direction as we wait in a line bent back on itself for takeoff. When we turn the bend, I catch sight of planes stretched back to the terminal buildings practically obscured by the low-hanging fog that has caused the delay. Finally the engines roar. Once in the air, people with relieved faces begin pulling things out the overhead compartments, and the paraphernalia of travel unfold from their carry-ons. A young Jew in black coat and hat is reading one book and then another in Hebrew or Yiddish—I am too uneducated to know which. Just before we land, out come the straps of his prayer phylacteries. As a Christian, I have to admire his inner strength to observe what his religion calls for, in spite of others around him. How he can concentrate, I do not know. This has been a good learning experience for Vladimir, I think to myself.

Six o'clock, exactly as expected. Vladimir is back up from Calgary. After dinner and a little rest, he comes over to the bar. "Beer?" I offer.

"Sure."

"How's little Krystle?"

"Fine, as far as I know. We're getting together tomorrow."

"Can you bring her around?"

"Well, you know, it isn't up to me. I'll try." Then he says, "You'll be here if I do?"

"You bet."

"Times sure do change." Vladimir checks me out, then goes on. "Papa, I've always admired you."

"Yeah?"

"How many came out from the camps and just concerned themselves with making it? You, you're the opposite. Like you'll drive a hundred kilometres to speak to a class of ten kids. That's serious. When you were taking with Mayor Decore I was very proud. Right on. Papa, the trip has started to make me think. I understand why you do what you do."

"Why?"

"You were there. So many people are saying it never happened; after you're gone, who knows? But Papa?" his voice tightens as he continues, "there are other things in the world, too. Like Krystle." Then he hesitates. "Why do I feel so guilty every time I talk to you, and so aggravated? You're the only person that makes me feel that way."

My own head collapses in my hands. Ramona gave me three sons. The first separated on his own volition and the second is critical. If Vladimir also withdraws, will I not die in grief?

"Papa, I feel like I'm always letting you down. Like, you're a prickly sagebrush whirling in the prairie wind while we're weathering it out in the barn. You return exhilarated but crushed; already making ready to spin off at the next insult; crushed that the rest of us didn't buck the storm with you. Like, you're Mr. Information, Mr. Dates. I can't even remember one-tenth of what you tell me, let alone do what you do."

"You don't have to be martyr. I certainly wasn't. Human being must be *more* than just stone, though. Vladimir, life must have more than eating and sleeping."

He pauses. "Just what I said. Getting a job today is plenty hard, especially a job you enjoy. You try and work, get exercise, eat properly, have friends."

I shake my head. "That's what I thought when I first got liberated. I thought, most important thing is not to be victimized. Then I saw those who have can be defeated, too, like guards."

"So who's a guard? I'm trying to understand you, Papa; I really am."

"Look, Vladimir, other things must be done in the world."

"Like the most important thing is to be free."

"Most important thing is to make right choice." The door opens. With a deep sigh I shift to go to the new customer who has seated himself at a table. "Look, Vladimir, because of Auschwitz, I've learned you can freely decide to be less than free for the sake of some concern for the world."

"You sit. I'll get the customer," Vladimir offers.

No sooner does he get up than the phone rings. Good news, very good news. Emilio and Simon will both be home in a few weeks. Too often now I see them only in the wake that trails after them, the way they help each other out, stand up for each other's choices. I shout to Vladimir, "Perhaps everyone can be home at once? No? Well, at least you are here now."

Achtundachtzig is smoke and mirrors—no, smoke and ashes, without his children.

On schedule, Simon and Emilio are back. That is unusual in itself, especially for Simon. He loathes small towns, particularly Fort Assiniboine. I understand. Everybody in Fort Assiniboine now calls me "the Jew." And every time a fight breaks out in the tavern and I have to eject someone, I then become the "fuckin' Jew." That is the nature of a small community. Every life is bound up in the life of his neighbour—and sometimes the ties that bind can choke. An artist like Simon needs to surround himself in the marketplace of ideas, which only a big city can offer. But we are talking about visiting, not settling. Spiritually, he never came back after I threw him out. It is like he is on one side, the family on the other.

I am dying to ask him about his grant application. Has he heard anything? No, I can see it written all over his face. I imagine him resolutely awaiting the postal carrier every morning. *"Jezus-Marja,* let him get it!" I anticipated a tense visit. Instead, to my delight, we are talking about my current work. I think my friend Reuven's interest is rubbing off on my sons. The discussion turns to Birkenau.

I am telling the boys, "I myself was never on Ramp—wanted to be, though. Good chance to organize foreign currency or wrist-watches."

"I knew it!" Simon cuts in. For me, it was nothing more than an offhand remark. His vehemence comes as a complete surprise. "So all along you knew ... and couldn't wait to take part. I've been seriously afraid of that, seriously afraid of finding out the only ones who lasted so long joined in."

"Yeah, me too," Emilio says, his previously sunny expression turning grey. How distant he seems. "Anyone who survived the whole time has got to have collaborated a lot," he says. "I've read about guards and prisoners, how the guards become cruel before you can even turn around."

Simon has turned his head slightly, and the eyes that look at me eye me sideways. "At first, I'd tell people my papa was lucky, he had a safe job. Then I saw that contraband sketch somebody drew of you. I told myself it wasn't you. But I could see it was. It was the round face that got me. My opinion

Sigmund. In 1960, a German Army officer put several drawings up for sale. They were recognized and purchased by the Auschwitz Museum. Pencil drawing by M. Ruzanicki, c. 1944. Courtesy of the State Museum of Auschwitz-Birkenau.

began to change. I began to ask myself, 'If he wasn't a Kapo, then how'd he survive?' I can't stand it how you pose as a big hero. Why was I so curious? Why'd I even want to know?"

"You were a *Prominente*," Emilio says. "For all we know, your so-called Auschwitz awareness is just to ease a guilty conscience. What are the stories you haven't told us?"

In the beginning I was bashful about it. Now I know it is part of the task. At last, the block in communication unexpectedly outs on the table where I can see it for the first time, and deal with it. Shaken by the intensity of their reaction, but pleased to be engaged on any level, I face them, speaking deliberately, letting my response sink in.

"Certainly we knew. As carpenter's helper I'd been in gas chamber more than once to install doors."

"O God, you really built the place," Simon cuts in. "So it wasn't just the fire brigade who knew?"

"No, not only firemen. Carpenters, mechanics, construction workers. Nazis were proud of what they were doing.[76] Subterfuge of officers got lost in ranks. SS would be telling our guys in Group One, 'Bring me back silk shirt.' 'Find me something I can give my girlfriend.' Unterscharführer Kaduk especially wanted them to get him stuff from ramp duty."[77]

"Where was their famous German discipline?"

"They had no way to keep it secret even if they wanted to. Town was right next door. Townspeople couldn't help seeing so-called invisible trains, trails of smoke that shadowed sky. Many had some connection with forced labour factories. And outside officials, visitors, industrialists, engineers, construction men, repairmen streamed in constantly. We have records of letters from German companies all over *Reich* bidding against each other to build ovens and supply gas. And underground succeeded, through partisan groups, in getting reports to Pope and Allies."

"So word was out?"

"And in. Jews from Birkenau mingled with our people on work details. When Hungarian Jews came, continual bottlenecks occurred. SS couldn't supply enough manpower. Even before, sometimes SS had gone and assigned to ramp duty some *Blockältestes*, or barracks *Stubendiensts*, or male nurses from hospital, usually from Birkenau. Sometimes they used our fire brigade for 'small bit of work', Nazi euphemism for ramp duty. First it was at old freight station or at *H.W.L.*, and then in Birkenau; but it was always Group One. Supposed secret was anything but."

I let that sink in, and then, motivated by their attention, continue. "When Group One was away, our group was supposed to stay in readiness in case of fire. But I was always envious. 'God damn it, when will it be our turn to go on Ramp?' You got used to camp, just wanted to get your share. My friend Jurek even says, 'Camp wasn't that bad.' Of course not—he was privileged prisoner from start."

"You never answered what you were doing. As a group leader, did you face any moral dilemmas?" They must have been harbouring this for years. I think my sons are afraid for me.

"Not really. Only well-trained Poles made up Fire Brigade, so job as *Grupleiter* was easy. If someone didn't pull his weight, I'd give him one of dirtier jobs, like cleaning underside of truck. Mostly, it meant I assigned myself best and most interesting jobs."

Simon restlessly takes another chair. "Then the Fire Brigade didn't have to clean out the gas chambers like the Jewish *Sonderkommando?*"

Finally, a real discussion with my sons! "No, they were on Ramp to help SS make certain cars were empty of baggage, to see no one was hiding underneath the train, that sort of thing. In order to get at hidden valuables, Jews had often been told they would need, to set up in their new location, their money. One of our firemen would sometimes boast, 'Last night I got two Tissot watches and one Schafhausen', or he'd say, 'I found two diamond rings', or 'I got twenty American dollars'. And one guy scavenged big collection of diamonds, which he lost in Sachsenhausen when Russian phosphorous bomb incinerated Block where we lived. He would also report, 'Many women and children today', things like that. They'd go and exchange for food or vodka what they organized. After particularly big transport of Jews, we'd enjoy, for days, leftovers."

A period of silence. Then Emilio, looking at his brother for some approval or, I think, to score a point with him, challenges, "Didn't anyone warn them or something?"

Simon runs his hand through his curly dark hair. "When we were kids, you used Auschwitz as an example for every discussion, but, like the background in a movie, it was never itself the subject. So for me, Auschwitz is just a bunch of disconnected traumatic stories. Give us the basics."

I happen to glance out the trailer's end window. The essence of camp is the impossibility to conduct life by anything remotely resembling free choice. Emilio's is the same question everybody asks me: "Why didn't you do something?" It is the same accusation we repeatedly hurl at ourselves, like that horrible day watching Husky get pulled under the beer truck. Auschwitz is the place where 'doing something' was impossible. First, there was no means. Second, any inner will you might have had, they systematically destroyed. I roll the answer around my head before continuing.

"They trapped you morally. SS continually warned ramp workers that anyone telling deportees about gas chamber would be burned alive. If they caught someone, guards would line up other workers, strap him onto this little cart and push him alive into overheated oven. All his comrades would hear his shrieks. So you contented your conscience with Tissot watches. You want basics, Simon? That's it."

Simon's eyebrows are more arched than usual. "Surely they wouldn't have had to say much; the cries from the gas chamber would have been enough to—"

"It was too far away. You could hear screams if they burned someone alive, but not from inside underground gas chamber. At end, Nazis tried to cover their crimes by dynamite, but they fled in such hurry, gas vents still show; if you'd have gone—"

"Christ, Papa, I'm sorry; if I knew it would hurt you so much, I would've."

"... you'd have seen distance for yourself. *Krematorium IV and V* did have surface gas chambers. They were far, though; and, first, victims entered dressing room. Little signs asked everyone to remember peg number where they hung their clothes. Those Nazis never overlooked even smallest detail."

Emilio moistens his lips. "So what were the SOB's concerned about?"

"Auschwitz took a lot of manpower from war effort. So, rather than stop killing Jews, they tried to kept ratio of prisoners to guards at thirty-five or forty to one. So SS needed to avoid any commotion."

Emilio paces around the table to the window, back again, now turning back to the window, stopping, returning to his chair but not sitting, back again to the window and now to the living room.

"Sit down, Emilio," Simon says in exasperation.

"Lay off." Emilio stops, inclines his head—When will he ever go back to school? I wonder—closes his eyes like trying to visualize the scene and asks softly, "Why the hell didn't everybody revolt?"

"Emilio!" says Simon, "how could there be a revolt?" Then he looks at me. "Who you staring at?"

"Am I? Sorry. It's just that revolt did take place, major one. That's one of events we're struggling to have memorialized. We also want museum to finally make Birkenau's 'Sauna', where those selected for labour were deloused, into long-promised 'exhibit of Jewish suffering'. And they should mark nearby pond, where ashes of hundred thousand Jews got dumped, as mass Jewish grave."

Just then, Ramona comes from the hotel to set out dinner. I am disappointed, but this is not a topic for the table, especially around Ramona. She cares; when we went to Auschwitz, she did not stop crying. It is simply that promoting Auschwitz awareness competes with many family needs. Besides, in contrast to Ramona and the boys, who eat at a normal rate, I do not talk during the meal. To me eating is something to turn your head down and *do*. As the boys say, "At our table, if you snooze, you lose."

The following morning, Simon and Emilio catch me writing letters. After the night before, I have been smiling to myself as though all the problems of the world are solved. As usual, I am right across from the small dance floor by the door, so, if anyone comes in, I can wait on him. "You busy, Papa?"

I push the typewriter away knocking something from the cluttered table. I do not own a word processor. My letters often appear so uneven because I produce everything on an old electric typewriter. The other day a friend stopped by. "Oh, a typewriter. Can I bring my children in to see it?"

"Always have, for you, time," I answer. When they were little, I would have pushed them away. In this, I am the one who has changed: not to let what I myself witnessed ever disappear from my mind; but most important, to teach my children. That a parent changes is hard for children to recognize. When, for instance, I began to resent that they never mentioned Auschwitz, they read it as an accusation rather than as a change in me.

"Tell us about the revolt," says Simon, who is somewhat better read in history than the other two, especially military history. Did I not say he is a lot like me?

"It's fierce."

"Tell it anyway."

"I'll do my best."

Both of them set themselves down at a nearby table, facing me. They must have been thinking about our conversation all night. Maybe my life has some meaning after all. I close my eyes:

Achtundachtzig resting in the firemen's Block, reading letters over and over. All of them from *Mamusia*. Can't get home out of my mind. Home! What's been going on since I've been gone? Basia, one year younger than me, the breadwinner of the family? In a factory that supplies the *Wehrmacht* with milk and cheese. Maybe another package with her cheese will come soon. Suddenly, the siren outside the barracks; then right away, the bell inside. Noise becomes louder and nearer as, slipping on his shirt, *Achtundachtzig* sprints to the gate. A light wind frosts our faces. Irka waves from her corner window. No stopping. Just shout '*Achtundachtzig*' to the guards. SS everywhere, boarding trucks, racing away on motorcycles with machine guns mounted to their sidecars. Black helmets tightened around the guards' chins. An ominous sign! Normally, SS wear ordinary German caps. Only don helmets when they suspect trouble: mass execution of prisoners, shootings in the *Konzentrationslager*, a hanging. Tamborski yells, Big trouble in *Krematorium IV*.[78] Just before departure we hear Engelschall telling a guard, Jewish revolt in Birkenau.

"Going to tell us?" Simon has his elbow on the table, his forehead in the palm of his hand. The fingers of his other hand drum the table. Emilio rocks back in his wooden chair, balanced on two legs.

I shake myself to attention. "I'll try." Always, the memories percolate helter-skelter to the surface: "As we neared Birkenau, clouds of smoke grew thicker and blacker. SS men dashing back and forth, shouting. We could hear continual rifle shots. Without special permit signed by *Lagerkommandant*, no one was to enter gas-chamber area. Huge signs were posted outside of each compound:

ENTRANCE IS STRICTLY FORBIDDEN
TO ALL THOSE WHO HAVE NO BUSINESS HERE,
INCLUDING SS PERSONNEL NOT ASSIGNED
TO THIS COMMAND.

— BY ORDER OF THE LAGERKOMMANDANT

It was so strict not even high-ranking SS were exempt."

"How'd you get in, then?" asks Emilio. He has edged to the tip of his chair.

"Come on, Emilio, he's the fire brigade." Simon answers.

"Lay off, Simon."

I lean forwards. "Actually, even we needed permits."

"But the fire?"

"In spite of fire, crematorium guards held back Group One. Engelschall franticly argued for permission to enter. Without success. Finally raging blaze did dictate its own permission. When our second squad arrived, SS simply waved us through. We found ourselves surrounded by two-metre-high hedges that ordinarily obscured the buildings except for the chimneys and roofs. Here I was busy fire-fighting, smell of explosives in my nose, and all while my head was saying words: 'manicured death.' Hideous as whole extermination process was, I've got to hold, for Nazi neatness and efficiency, some grudging respect."

Emilio sticks out his tongue, making a face. Simon looks dumbfounded. "Oh my God, you admired your captors." His chestnut eyes gleam. His expression is one of both triumph and sadness. It shoots through my mind Simon is waging an argument with his own head, all the while hoping to lose.

I limp around the room with short, rapid steps. Had we not dealt with all that last night? Pretending not to have heard, and, without missing a beat, I continue, hoping he does not notice my agitation. "We entered in between crematorium and pit. In whole of my life, I don't want to see such thing again.

All around SS were roaming, rifles in hand. They were lining Jews up at this lone pine, which then as today, stood beside gas chamber, so stark, stripped of all its branches for its first six metres. At our feet stretched many bleeding corpses. Had to jump over them while working. Bodies everywhere. Engelschall was laying into Zakrzewski, pump operator in Group One, for 'sabotage'. He was pretending engine wouldn't start in order to let crematorium burn. By time he got water going, rafters and slabs were already collapsing."

On the table a paperweight snows on an idyllic scene as I absentmindedly invert the globe. "To right of barbed wire gate near naked pine tree, lay piled about forty still-twitching naked corpses, blood streaking from backs of their heads. SS Oberscharführer Claussen, who sometimes used to get us to clean his boots, this fastidious blond Nazi, was climbing in blood-smeared jack-boots over bodies. Like one-man flock of ravens swarming over some carrion, he was shooting those still alive."

The telling becomes more animated. I am Claussen, springing onto the tavern's homemade stage like it is a heap of corpses. I fire an imaginary carbine into each head.

Simon and Emilio both stare at me, astonished.

Suddenly, I am subdued. Palms forward, I step down remembering how in front of the pile of corpses, rested the murdered prisoners' worldly possessions:

I go over to where the victims each stacked their own clothes. In squares about one foot apart. Neatly folded according to camp regulations: the jacket, the trousers, the underwear—all placed on top of the shoes. *Ordnung muss sein.* It's a German expression: We must have good order. More Jews being herded towards the centre of the yard. With their hands up. Even a few seconds before their execution, these poor souls have got to arrange their clothes, then crawl on the hill of bodies. Lie down, lie down, I hear Claussen say, hands at your sides. Then smoking a cigarette, he shoots them through.[79]

"Other SS men were firing at any moving object, almost killing one of our firemen. 'What are you doing here, you pig?' Only Engelschall's quick intervention saved his life. In about forty-five minutes, when blaze was under control, they ordered us out. What a relief to leave this slaughterhouse alive."[80]

Questions bombard from both sides: "Why hadn't they goddamn revolted long before?" Emilio asks. Like the filmmaker he is, Simon rejoins: "Wouldn't have happened even then if it hadn't been for the German losses, right?" Emilio, looking through me as if some unseen oracle could answer questions of psychology, ponders, "Maybe it's that the SS bastards were a lot less diligent than at first."

To Simon, "Yes." Then turning to Emilio, "And that, too, certainly. Jewish prisoners in *Sonderkommando,* known in prison jargon as *Geheimnisträger,* which means 'bearers of secret', got special treatment to keep them from rebelling."

"What special treatment?" Simon wants to know.

"They could wear civilian clothes, best of men's clothing from transports; eat same food as SS; enjoy library of books, newspapers and magazines. Of

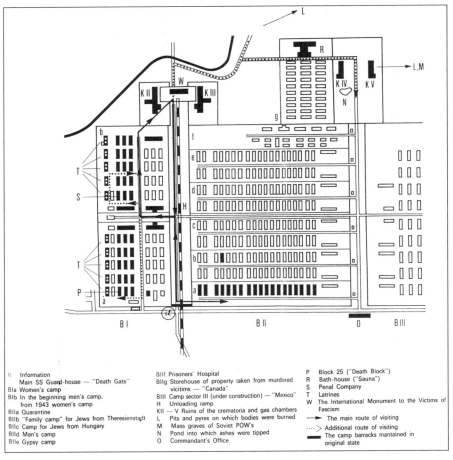

It   Information
          Main SS Guard-house — "Death Gate"
BIa   Women's camp
BIb   In the beginning men's camp,
          from 1943 women's camp
BIIa   Quarantine
BIIb   "Family camp" for Jews from Theresienstadt
BIIc   Camp for Jews from Hungary
BIId   Men's camp
BIIe   Gypsy camp

BIIf   Prisoners' Hospital
BIIg   Storehouse of property taken from murdered
          vicitims — "Canada"
BIII   Camp sector III (under construction) — "Mexico"
H   Unloading ramp
KII — V Ruins of the crematoria and gas chambers
L   Pits and pyres on which bodies were burned
M   Mass graves of Soviet POW's
N   Pond into which ashes were tipped
O   Commandant's Office

P   Block 25 ("Death Block")
R   Bath-house ("Sauna")
S   Penal Company
T   Latrines
W   The International Monument to the Victims of
          Fascism
⟶   The main route of visiting
····>   Additional route of visiting
▬▬▬ The camp barracks mantained in
          original state

Plan of the former concentration camp KL Auschwitz II–Birkenau.

the reading I was jealous as there were no other books in whole of Auschwitz. But, so there could never be witness to testify to whole, Nazis periodically killed each *Sonderkommando* group, usually every three months or so. Why hadn't they revolted before? They lived in so-called luxury with no way of knowing their eventual fate."[81]

"So what caused the revolt when it did happen?" Simon presses. As the more historical, Simon is interested in strategic relationship. To me, this suggests something of me has rubbed off on our eldest.

"Autumn of 1944, Russians reached River Vistula, only four hundred kilometres from Auschwitz."

"You knew?"

"Just as people outside knew what was happening inside, we knew what was going on outside—and swiftly, efficiently, through 'whispering telegraph.'

Conversations were overheard on work duty. *Zugänge*, the neophytes, came in with news. People had ways of getting, past censors, information in their mail. Even some wireless sets were around.

"This is too much."

"We knew defeat of Axis was coming. Our only question was if any of us would survive to see. We had such fear Nazis would do us in, that we grew, as end drew closer, more and more nervous."

"So about the revolt?" Simon presses again.

"Towards end, transports of Polish prisoners were departing for Germany every week. I didn't know then that in August, Nazis had selected from *Sonderkommando* two hundred men. 'For transfer,' they had said. Actually SS murdered them. Then they reassigned, temporarily, all remaining prisoners from *Krematorium III* so only SS—which was very unusual—burned bodies. Their excuse was, 'As these are German civilians who revolted elsewhere, only SS will bury them.' But SS never cleaned up properly. When *Sonderkommando* returned, they recognized, in remains, some of their friends."

"So, unlike other commandos, who didn't know what was in store for them, they knew this was the beginning of their own end, and began to prepare a revolt?" Simon asks.

"Then when SS came for three hundred more, it hastened, prematurely, uprising. Some seventy SS were killed. Jews even threw some German Kapos into oven alive."[82]

I have looked at the German records in the Auschwitz museum: *On 13 September 1944, 847 male prisoners reported for* Sonderkommando *duty*. Two days after the revolt, 9 October, the report reads: *212 prisoners reported for duty*. There was no night shift at all. So, it appears they murdered at least 635 prisoners. Even on the day shift itself, the number killed might have been much higher since shortly after they put down the revolt, they had already assigned new prisoners.[83]

"No revolt leaders made it. SS must've had inside information, because we saw they immediately separated organizers. Then they transferred leaders to Bunker where SS tortured out details they wanted to know: who gave them their weapons, their explosives, everything else. They were then executed."

As it emerged later, Jewish women had smuggled explosives into the crematorium from the Union high-explosives factory located on the camp's periphery. In January, in the last public execution, barely two weeks before liberation, the SS executed four women: Ella Gertner, Regina Saphirstein, Ester Waxblum and their leader, Rosa Robota. They hanged them all publicly "in the name of the law." Surviving participants were Marta Bindiger, Rose Meth, and Malla Weinstein.

I have details from Ester's sister Anna Heilman: Ester and Regina laboured in the powder room, Ella in another area of the same factory. In the Kanada warehouse, Rosa sorted the clothes brought by the *Sonderkommando* from the gas chambers.[84] Anna tells me of her ongoing guilt: Was it her encouragement that led her sister to take up action and thus to die? Yet if

*The Black Wall. Here 16,000, mainly Poles, were executed,
but also some 5,000 Jews and 3,000 Russians.
Courtesy of the State Museum of Auschwitz-Birkenau.*

it had not been for the revolt, would any survive today? For fifty years, the questions have given her no peace. Rose Meth remembers Esther's words: "This depends on us; we can do it. Thousands may die, but some will survive. We must not allow the murder of millions in secrecy. It is our duty to try and make possible a mass escape."

For Polish Catholics hanged only because a comrade of theirs escaped, the museum has dedicated an elaborate plaque with photos of each victim. For these Jewish women, who surviving witnesses tell us used to sing Zionist songs in Birkenau, who were hanged because they actually chose to act, the museum has put up nothing. Nothing. The Bunker's Black Wall, where they executed Polish Catholics, is now a Polish national shrine where burning candles and live flowers are placed continuously. There is no mention of five thousand Jews who were murdered there. And by *Krematorium IV*, where they executed the Jewish prisoners who revolted, there is no shrine, no candle, no flower except what grows wild in the field.[85]

Simon turns to face me while at the same time pulling away somewhat. He speaks very quietly. You can see he has been mulling it over. "Papa, don't you see? Even though you had no choice, you actually helped the Nazis put down the revolt by putting out the fire?"

"Prisoners performed many tasks that could be considered today as assisting SS, but it's a lot more complicated than that. As in every *Konzentrationslager*, prisoners formed organizations. They sent out the odd report about what was going on in camp, and smuggled into camp secret letters. As to real achievement, nothing."

"Come on, you mean all the stuff about Auschwitz underground isn't true?"

"When liberation came, everyone claimed they were in underground. You believe it? Communists glorified underground, especially communist underground. But we saw little to show for it."

"But I always thought——"

"Only *Sonderkommando*, led by Jewish ex-officer Handelsmann, rose against SS. I remember some escapes. After each one, we'd be lined up to witness punishment.[86] But *Sonderkommando* revolt was like open warfare, barricaded prisoners with ammunition. Nothing else like it."

The mood seesaws back and forth. Simon is having difficulty formulating his words. "All my life," his mouth goes dry so the rest emerges as little more than a whisper, "the thought has plagued me: If I'd lived then, I'd probably have done anything to survive, maybe prostitute myself, pimp, maybe even try to be on the Other Side. I know how I used to want women even not being in the camp."

"Yeah, you can't think of anything else," I say.

"So I'm not the only one," says Emilio.

"It seriously frightened me," Simon continues. "But Papa, you were already trapped. What could you lose? You knew and still didn't join underground! You risked more for sex than for freedom."

My shirt collar feels tight. "Simon, you'd want me to have gone and been hero? It's only through grace of God any of us aren't murderers. In place where life was cheap and death swift like eagle, difference often came down to piece of onion, or better-fitting shoes." I lay a hand on his chair back, grappling with the obvious: "I was just normal Polish prisoner, no hero. *Heroes*, practically all dead, were those who chose to rebel. *Collaborators* were those like Kapos who committed atrocities to gain favour with Nazis. Or like physicians like Dr. Władisław Dering, who sterilized, in Block Ten, Jewish women to gain medical stature. To disgrace of museum officials, those doctors have, in their honour, plaque embedded into Block Twenty-one. These, too, mostly found their own end. Those like me, who learned to suffer quietly and blend in, were *victims*. Most survivors come from this group.

"But now, Simon, don't *you* see? It creeps over you slowly; took me many years. In certain way, you're right. What saved my skin is exactly what allows oppression to continue. That's reason why 'Auschwitz awareness' is so important. Person never has to be victim of circumstances only. Not having had it as bad as Jews, I'm doomed to witness for what they suffered."

"The revolt," decides Simon tentatively, "didn't have much of an effect then, did it?"

"For Chrissakes, Simon, body counts aren't the same as impact," Emilio interjects. Simon throws him a look. Emilio shrugs his shoulders and looks away.

"If it hadn't started too soon, revolt would've caused even greater damage.

Even so, revolt cut by one quarter Auschwitz's killing capacity. At that late date, there was no way it could be rebuilt."

I am finished, but they are not. After a rather lengthy pause, Emilio, cracking his knuckles, takes a turn. "Papa, you said this rebellion affected everyone, that there was more hope and all than before. Well how many do you think the *Sonderkommando*'s action saved?"

"Liquidation went on, but at much slower rate. Looking back, I can see that more important was that Auschwitz's entire operation became demoralized."

"Strange word to use about camp," Simon says.

"But it fits."

"Attitudes changed," Emilio understood.

"To us inmates, *Sonderkommando* revolt was sign there could still be will in prisoners to fight. We didn't have to go like lambs to slaughter. Polish prisoners were saying, 'Those docile Jews really showed SS.' 'This time Jews went and made, out of SS, monkeys.' It showed us SS weren't invincible. Even guards became, after revolt, less cocky."

"Maybe due to the approaching Russians; maybe nothing to do with the revolt at all." Simon reasserts himself in the discussion, but he is relaxed now, his body loose with the relief that seems to have washed over him.

"Maybe." I sense Emilio has other questions. But I catch his eye falling onto the open newspaper laying below the typewriter table:

COUP FAILS, GORBACHEV ALIVE

He abruptly switches topic. "Papa, the Jews being killed and all, they were within the compound then?"

"Right! Right! And they couldn't escape. Some few were returned in groups of six or seven from outside. They'd chopped through electrified wire. We could see spot. This was only first of four sets of wire, though. There was this shed, maybe kilometre from gas chamber furnaces. Jews were hiding there. SS-guards had set fire there as well. At one point, Group One went over to put out flames. Rest, I've already told you."

In contrast to Auschwitz, escaping the law in Canada is no trick at all. In response to complaints, the Alberta Human Rights Commission establishes a Board of Inquiry to investigate the Aryan 'Fest' at Provost. The organizers maintain, "It was a *private* party, not in violation of hate laws."

In testimony, it comes out that Bradley, the owner of the farm, constructed the cross from steel pipe. He welded it together, sheathed it in burlap, and drenched it in one hundred gallons of diesel fuel. When completed, the cross for this private party exceeded nine metres in height, visible for kilometres.

Nerland, Saskatchewan leader of the Aryan Nation Church, testifies that the lighted cross symbolizes for him "the light that Jesus Christ brings to the world." It is "a common practice of Scotland," he tells the Board, having cultural, racial and religious significance. Terry Long adds the cross is "a traditional cultural symbol to White Aryan people." The straight arm salute means "openness, friendship, and indicates no secretiveness whatsoever." The chant "Death to the Jew" is a "battle cry of good over evil, and signifies the victory of Christ's people over the children of Satan." Nerland and Long both testify Hitler is a hero, "Elijah the Prophet sent forth by God." Nerland testifies the Holocaust is the "biggest misshapen, misrepresented, sickish joke of the twentieth century." This after his comments about my not having been worked to death, gas chambers, luggage, and birth control. Obviously his mind knows clearly what his mouth both denies and affirms.

Experts testify that the array of symbols: SS, swastika, burning cross, White Power, KKK; display of power, chants and jeers; physical intimidation—all augment the inclination to discriminate which preexists among certain people in our society, promoting hatred of specific groups.[87]

In a report signed and delivered at the City of Edmonton, the Board of Inquiry finds the complaints justified "in whole." Based on the evidence, the Aryan 'Fest' is found to be a "public display" calculated to instill hatred against specific racial and religious groups. The Board further declares:

> This Board had the opportunity of observing and listening to Mr. Long, as assisted by Mr. John Ross Taylor, and Mr. Nerland over several days.... It was patently clear to us these are not simply misguided eccentrics. They are dedicated Nazis....
>
> Neither should it be blithely assumed the few men we saw were working alone. We heard sufficient evidence of the network linking these extremist organizations to convince us there is an international conspiracy to create an Aryan Nation.
>
> ... In light of the evidence disclosed in the Inquiry we trust the advisability of initiating prosecutions will be fully explored in respect of the threats against Brad Clark; the apparent assaults on various media persons; the possession and use of weapons; and the conspiracy to promote racial hatred which appears to be the main reason for the existence of the Respondent Church.[88]

To date, the Province has initiated no prosecution. Terry Long disappeared during the Inquiry.

The RCMP only turns him up a year and some months later. No charges are laid. The optimists call them a lunatic fringe, I call them an ominous fringe.

In a separate case, Nerland is serving four years for manslaughter. He killed Leo LaChance, a Cree trapper, by shooting him in the back with his "Native birth control device" outside the gun store he operates. Why was he brought to trial only on manslaughter? A public investigation has recently suggested Nerland got off easy because he was a police informant. A scandal has developed. People complain, "The damn investigation is harming the entire police-informer system."

And in other cases? After a series of appeals under Canada's hate laws, a new trial was ordered in the Keegstra case, the appeals court finding technical errors in the jury selection process.

"History, in law, is opinion," Justice Arthur Lutz instructs the new jury. "If a teacher wants to espouse and teach the ideas of the Flat Earth Society and require students to regurgitate them in examinations and essays, he is quite free to do so." Then, he added that an individual's right to free speech cannot oppose a group's right to freedom from harassment.

In this, Canadian hate laws differ from those in the United States. Our law is built on the principle that distinctions can be drawn (as U.S. law also does in cases of slander, yelling "fire" in a crowded theatre, fraud, etc.). You are not free to say anything you want. In Canada, we believe the very basis of law is the drawing of distinctions. Our Supreme Court has ruled several times that no individual right is absolute if the exercise of such right threatens the community at large.

Seven years after his first conviction, Keegstra is again convicted of promoting hatred, by a jury he had picked himself. He is again appealing. On Rosh HaShanah 1994, the Alberta Court of Appeal will announce its decision to overturn Keegstra's new sentence on technical grounds: the judge's response to jury questions was faulty. The Province appeals the legal issue to Canada's Supreme Court.[89]

Douglas Christie, Keegstra's lawyer, a man who shows up whenever neo-Nazis are in court anywhere in Canada, has also made the news. Christie was defending a man in British Columbia accused of kicking a policeman in the groin while a prisoner. The lawyer would prove to the court that the charges were unfounded. Let the complaining officer be tied up and try to kick Christie, thus proving the impossibility of the charges. "I wouldn't do that if I were you," said the officer. The lawyer insisted. The officer was bound to a chair in the same way the prisoner had been. He connected with Christie's groin and sent him hopping around the courtroom, whooping in pain. The lawyer lost his case.

For the first time I have begun to appreciate how *Mamusia* must have felt when I fled the European continent without so much as a visit home:

The empty chair—in her face all the while my life hangs in the balance—the chair, which, if her prayers are granted, will be filled again. She's writing military and government, bishop and Pope. Appealing for my release. Gestapo alight from a black Mercedes in front of our house, Why has she written Hitler's sister? Then the war is over. Someone is telling her, Everyone was shot. Then her prayers are answered, I have survived. She's at the window, watching. *Mamusia* glued to the window. Where is he? Why's he taking so long? She reassures herself: He needs time to locate his girlfriend; then they'll both be home. Then she learns Irka has returned. Christmases year in and year out, the chair empty.

Once, a student asks, "My parents are antisemitic, my grandparents are antisemitic. What can I do?" She is the same age I was when I was taken. I give her four words, "It starts with you." Then I think of our own boys. Simon, my firstborn, my might. Emilio, my soul and judge. Vladimir, a buck in the forest. How do I get them to deep down feel the pain of others and still retain my wife and my sons, and, I hope, some day their wives and children, with me? "Think of it like you, too, were inmate of Auschwitz."

Abruptly, apropos of nothing, I remember my most recent trip back, the one with Vladimir. We were in the Calgary airport getting ready to leave. Emilio was there with his girlfriend's kids, his arms crossed as if to say, You're stealing what really belongs to Mama again. We could barely hear each other for the rumble-rattle of carts, the clip-clop of high heels on the tile floor, the scraping of dragged suitcases. Between goodbyes, I was trying to square away at the Canadian Air counter, down past the dinosaur. It was a madhouse. After some futile haggling and delaying, again with an official who kept repeating the same dull litany, I came running back to Vladimir. "They want to charge for my extra suitcase," I told him. "Don't they realize we're on very important mission? Come, Vladimir, we'll fight to get it on."

Part IV
1992–1995

Maybe there are some in the world who have never experienced one of those significant moments that change a lifetime, that become the standard by which all else is measured. There surely are some survivors who have never connected the past with the present except to forget. But twenty-nine years after Sigmund's nocturnal moment in Toronto's humid night, he continues to draw parallels. And the effect? It fills him internally, leaves him devastatingly alone externally.

Then again, maybe it happens to lots of people. Think of the biblical Everyman:

> *Jacob remained alone. A stranger wrestled with him until just before daybreak. When the stranger saw that he could not defeat him, he touched the upper joint of Jacob's thigh so that Jacob's hip joint became dislocated as he wrestled with the stranger.*
>
> *"Release me," said the stranger, "for dawn is breaking."*
>
> *"I will not release you unless you bless me."*
>
> *"What is your name?"*
>
> *"Jacob."*
>
> *"Your name will no longer be called Jacob, but Israel, for you have struggled with God and man, and have prevailed."*
>
> *Jacob then asked, "If you would," he said, "tell me what your name is."*
>
> *"Why do you ask my name?" replied the stranger.* [Gen. 32:25-31a]
>
> —*the Reporter.*

Eighteen: Enter the Reporter

A

Fort Assiniboine, Alberta, June 1992

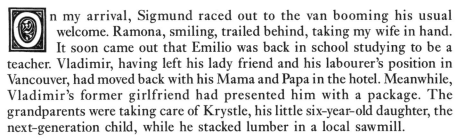n my arrival, Sigmund raced out to the van booming his usual welcome. Ramona, smiling, trailed behind, taking my wife in hand. It soon came out that Emilio was back in school studying to be a teacher. Vladimir, having left his lady friend and his labourer's position in Vancouver, had moved back with his Mama and Papa in the hotel. Meanwhile, Vladimir's former girlfriend had presented him with a package. The grandparents were taking care of Krystle, his little six-year-old daughter, the next-generation child, while he stacked lumber in a local sawmill.

Sigmund observed immediately, "Until Krystle came to live with us, it didn't hit me that I have really granddaughter. To think there was time I'd not thought to see face of *children,* let alone a *grandchild.*" Sigmund and Ramona, both a little drawn from caring for an active child, nevertheless were obviously enjoying having Vladimir and Krystle around. In fact, to Vladimir's talk about moving to Calgary Sigmund reacted, "By yourself? With apartment and child-care expenses? How'll you manage? You'll be back inside of two months. Why don't you just stay in Fort Assiniboine and I'll teach you welding?"

"You're always shooting down my ideas, trying to demoralize me."

"Demoralize you? You don't attend school. You're not serious. You must owe government $5,000 for education you never completed. How could anyone demoralize you? Maybe you should've been in camp so you'd know how hard it was."

Clearly, old patterns do not easily change. One might have thought that, being at home, *Abuelo* would be participating with his granddaughter in ways he never could with his own children. But even this did not change. With the tavern and *Achtundachtzig,* Sigmund could still spare too little time.

"Krystle to start the grade one in September; but she already read," said *Abuela,* almost enviously.

The hotel remained as empty as ever. For a few years already, the only business, such that it was, was in the tavern. And even that, they said, had declined since the province began a localized experiment to allow the sale of beer and wine in ordinary grocery stores. The restaurant, torn out a few years back by Ramona and Vlad when Sigmund was away, was soon to be reinstalled.

Vladimir was assisting when he could. When questioned between serving customers, he sat thoughtfully, speaking over the din of the jukebox, yet softly. "Papa and I are getting along much better than we used to. I love my father. Used to hate him; he can be childlike, totally spiteful and vengeful. But I sort of understand him now. All he wants is that his children be healthy, and above all safe, and above all educated. Still, his ability to forgive the Germans amazes me. I had a nightmare not long ago. Was in a gas chamber. The doors closed on me. I was all out of breath. We often try to protect each other. When a girl is chasing me, without my even saying so, he'll screen my calls, say I'm not around. I've read his stuff, heard his stories. When I was younger, it was hard to get into what he was about. The older I get, though, the more I grasp. When he would put on his stripers it used to embarrass me. Once he changed right in the street. Now I'm used to it. I do think Papa spends way too much time at it; he seems to get a lot out of it, though. I think he's crazy. Guess it's rubbed off on me."

I wandered upstairs. Sigmund's 'office' is a lesson in a man's personality and thought, the overwhelming impression being a cyclone of papers, tapes, and boxes. Gracing the bookshelves were volumes by Ché Guevara, still one of Sigmund's personal heroes. Books on the Nuremberg trials, the

Holocaust, the Final Solution, Auschwitz. Personal testimonies and confessions, diaries. Auschwitz publications. *Pan Tadeusz* by Adam Mickiewicz and other Polish literature. At least fifty volumes in German, untold others in Polish and Spanish. General history and biography. Books on Christianity and on Christian-Jewish relations. *None is Too Many*, a study of Canada's failure to give refuge to the Jewish victims in Europe by Irving Abella and Harold Troper. Many books on Pacelli (Pope Pius XII) and on John XXIII. Many antisemitic works and even more about antisemitism. *The Other Losses*, a treatment of German prisoners of war by Americans and French. A couple of books on the German population's deportation from Poland. One on cruelties committed in the Soviet Union by the Wehrmacht, *Damals in Osten*, with photographs of Jewish women serving German officers. Four books on Dresden.

"I feel very strongly that Dresden was war crime," he had once said.

A slim volume caught my eye, *Commandant of Auschwitz: The Auto-biography of Rudolf Höss*. I pulled it from the shelf, absentmindedly thumbed its pages. Sigmund had inscribed it:

> To Vladimir, my son—to learn how I spent my 'teen' years. We the ex-prisoners of Auschwitz now after 41 years, 'we forgive but we never forget.' I hope that, in your lifetime or maybe your daughter's lifetime, *war* will be condemned by humanity like human sacrifice or like human slavery are condemned by all civilized people.
>
> Papa—Ex No. 88, *K.L. Auschwitz*, Sept/86.

Later, everyone gathered in the trailer's compact living room to make a toast. On the wall above Sigmund hung a richly coloured still-life of bottles and jars on a patterned cloth, one of Ramona's best productions. To the left was the painting she favours, a cabin in the bush entitled "Wild Parsnips," accepted and exhibited at the Fort Assiniboine Art Club. Ramona sat by herself under a picture of Cuban dancers, the flavour of home. Vladimir pulled up a chair. Krystle, in and out, was lolling on the floor near the samovar and porcelain dalmatian. Ringing interrupted the conversation.

"Hello." Sigmund stood in the passageway between the living room and the kitchen. He broke into an expansive grin and a wider voice. "Simon! How are you, Simon?"

Both Vladimir and Ramona perked up. Sigmund was motioning with broad hand sweeps. They had long before been told to expect a call. Even so, one was afraid to assume anything lest it not happen.

"Mama and I? Fine."

Sigmund put a large calloused hand over the mouthpiece, saying more to his visitor than to anyone else, "I can't believe it. He's never asked about my work before." He returned to the telephone. "Well, we've just purchased for Birkenau bus donated by Gerda Frieberg. She's president of Canadian Jewish Congress, Ontario branch. Sixty-two seater. Now tourists can see for themselves Birkenau's killing fields. I'm having it completely overhauled.

They'll be plenty pleased. It's first sizeable donation from outside of Poland, either from government or private. Took two years to negotiate." He appeared excited, then a little apprehensive. "And what's new with you?"

Everyone was leaning forward toward the telephone. "Your girlfriend caught a cold...."

Except for the sound of Sigmund's voice, the room that a minute ago was reverberating with conversation lay strangely still. Even bright little Krystle's bouncing, fair-haired braids were still. The suspense was palpable. "You're getting more sleep lately——"

"You did! Wonderful! I was afraid to ask. Why didn't you say so immediately?"

"Fantastic! Simon got the grant," Vladimir shouted. "We'll be sending his mail to Mexico."

Motherly pride shone in Ramona's eyes. "Isn't that something? Hope Simon will be all right down there. Who will look after him?" she asked no one in particular.

After he hung up, Sigmund told everyone with a happy twinkle in his eye, "Simon's voice was excited, though he tried to pretend it was everyday affair." Later he mused contentedly, "It looks to me like he's become quite some filmmaker. If big directors like his work, he must know something."

"I'm going to Australia," Sigmund's voice came over the phone a few weeks later. Being accustomed to Sigmund's surprises, I just waited to hear what was next. "I've found my friend," he said simply.

A week later a newspaper article from Melbourne arrived. It quoted George Ginsbourg:

> The Nazis used to have regular selections of weak and infirm people whom they were going to take away to the gas chambers. Mr. Sobolewski used to warn me when they were coming around. But it had to be done discreetly. He really stuck his neck out and risked his position. He used to give me bread and soup and a jacket to keep me warm.
>
> In return I used to teach him English. He was very keen to learn. I was grateful to him because a Jew could not last more than six months in those conditions. He saved my life.
>
> I still have his prisoner badge, number eighty-eight. He gave it to me when he was transferred away from Auschwitz as a token of friendship. I have treasured it to this day.
>
> In June 1945, while working in Brussels as a translator for the United States Army, I saw [him] on the street. We stood and looked at each other, and then rushed over and embraced. We exchanged details, but never spoke to each other again.

The pair went their separate ways. Sigmund, however, had never abandoned his search for his friend George Ginsbourg. Recently, he placed a letter and photo in the *Jerusalem Post*. Someone suggested Ginsbourg might have emigrated to Australia. Sigmund followed through with a letter to the

Brussels/1945. Ginsbourg (middle) wanted to go to Palestine; but the British prevented it.

Australian Jewish News. A little detective work and a phone call by a reporter united the two long-lost friends.

"He seems to be very ideologically minded and is making a great *meshugas* with the Auschwitz Museum," Ginsbourg is quoted. "It was unbelievable. This is one of the happiest times of my life."

Auschwitz museum officials did not seem to appreciate Sigmund's questions. They undertook their own campaign to convince sitting members of the International Auschwitz Council that Sigmund should ease up. Thus lobbied, his colleagues told Sigmund he is 'counterproductive.' Sigmund said, "I know they get angry. But how can I shut up? It's only when we make noise that they respond at all. Otherwise, I think Auschwitz would be Polish-Christian memorial only." So he put an add in Polish newspapers: "I Sigmund Sobolewski hereby state that the officials of Auschwitz Museum are not antisemitic and that any references from the Canadian and Polish newspapers that they are antisemitic are completely untrue."

Wróblewski complained, "What kind of statement is that? Why are you repeating two times that we are not antisemitic?"

Number 88, unflagging provocateur, pressed forward, asking aloud: "Sisters have closed convent in building where gas was stored and Jews were killed. Fine. How is it possible they've sublet to Association of War Victims, front for people who talk about 'foreign hands' and 'foreign interests' out to harm Poland? I've heard before these code words. If museum officials are slow to change, couldn't Catholic Church lead way by using its space for proper exhibit instead of housing antisemitic group?"

Sigmund was raising some of his most controversial issues to date: *"It is wrong* that local newspapers describe plans for huge monument for 70,000 Christian victims of Auschwitz while millions of Jewish victims are still denied any monument, not even tourist signs International Auschwitz Council approved back in 1991."[1] *"It is deplorable* that German newspapers complain that funds *Bundestag* donated for Auschwitz museum have been diverted to regional infrastructure programs more than twelve kilometres away."[2] *"It is unspeakable* that local journalists report that former Carmelite convent has become hub of neo-Nazi extremists." Wróblewski, the museum director, stopped speaking to Sigmund.[3]

Sigmund was frantic. It was almost time for the dedication at Nisko, but his magic notebook was missing, the one with all his contacts, phone numbers, addresses, little notes to follow through on this, initiate that. Was I worried? No. It was like the predictable phone call, "I've searched for two days; can't find your last set of questions." I knew from experience that after the panic, the notebook would be found in his suitcase where he had just searched three times.

I was in Poland with Sigmund to become, in the short time allotted, acquainted with significant people and places in Sigmund's life. Then, at the railroad station in Nisko, he would dedicate the plaque, following which Sigmund would cross the Slovakian border to pick up the bus in Zelina and deliver it to Auschwitz while I made my way to Israel. To my chagrin, as soon as we arrived in Poland, Sigmund consumed two full days dragging around to embassies and media offices. Although I was praying otherwise, no one refused *Achtundachtzig* an interview.

The First Secretary at the Canadian Embassy rose to greet us. James Walker, the Canadian official assigned to Jewish affairs in Poland, listened attentively as Sigmund described the mission.

"Did you execute an agreement?"

"This deal's been in process for practically two years. We have signed contract. No way we can pay more. We got our funding from five- and ten-dollar donations."

"Mr. Sobolewski, you actually should be at the consulate for economic affairs," he said helpfully.

"No, Mr. Secretary, we're not talking commerce. They're trying to squeeze, precisely because bus is for Auschwitz, two thousand more out of us. It's *political* manoeuvre. Do you really think two days before we leave Canada they abruptly think to charge extra! In spite of formerly Fascist elements in Slovakia's new government, they need to know in today's world such behaviour will be counterproductive. I'll contact Reuters, AP, UPI. Canada's Jewish community is upset."

The First Secretary mused softly, "I quite doubt company officials are thinking much about that."

And I was silently thinking: I doubt Canada's Jewish Community has any opinion whatever—except, perhaps, why is this fellow presuming to speak for us?

The Canadian consul did call and get us an appointment with Ladislav Stindl, consul in the Czechoslovakian embassy; but our visit produced no results.

In the Polish Cultural Ministry, we sat in upholstered Louis XVI armchairs to a low, round table in the minister's spacious, ornately designed, French-styled office.

"Why do you not approach the Czechoslovakian Embassy?" they inquired.

I answered, "The Czechoslovakian Embassy? We have already been. They greeted us cordially, served tea, gave us contact numbers. Still, they tell us they are Czech. Although division is not yet official, they tell us they no longer carry any influence in Slovakia. No one knows yet who is in charge."

Israeli security halted us at the outside gate. No fancy buildings there. We were surveyed from somewhere inside. A voice through a speaker ordered us to enter the yard. The discussion took place in Hebrew through a heavy glass window in an alcove at the left side of the house. We were never even offered a seat, let alone tea as in the other embassies. The Israeli first consul was even more direct and without apology: "What I am saying is, we simply do not have the workforce to help."

At the American Embassy, after checking our cameras and following the consul through a labyrinth of corridors, they told us, "Czechoslovakia is not the mission of our Polish embassy."

"You could contact in Czechoslovakia your embassy. Americans have now much influence."

"We could?"

Every embassy offered the pretext of help. Every embassy promised to follow through. Sigmund's fervour is contagious. One began to believe, even though reason told one that none would lift a finger.

He did not give up. He went to the radio, television, newspapers. Usually, he was assigned a junior reporter in a room with many desks, stacks of paper and dirty coffee mugs. "Zygmunt Sobolewski, *Achtundachtzig*, coordinator of the Auschwitz Awareness Society of Canada. You've received our fax?"

"Umm, can't remember," his respondent typically hemmed and hawed. "What was it about?"

"Let me find—would you like a cigarette pack?—another copy." After five minutes shuffling, all the while keeping up a pep talk, he would exclaim in surprise, "Ah, here. Can never find anything I need."

"It'll get consideration." The material was tossed somewhere among the other stacks of paper.

Sigmund thought he had triumphed through diligence. I was worn thin merely trying to keep up. "Wait! We have to go back," he shouted.

"Why?" I said, exhausted.

"Left my cane."

"Sigmund, what will you do if the bus company does not relent on these extra charges?"

"Be forced to leave bus and walk away."

"And how will you recoup your five-thousand-dollar down-payment?"

"We'll sue them."

It seemed time for a reality statement. "That will cost you more than the two thousand they are asking. The result will be no bus and no money. *Entre nous*, don't you have any extra money with you?"

"No. And Mr. Leipciger of Canadian Jewish Congress has authorized, you know, no such payment."

"All right," I said throwing my hands into the air.

More telephone numbers, calls, faxes. Being so anxious to get to Auschwitz, who could enjoy it?

At the Polish Ministry of Culture, the hosts were Mutt and Jeff: tall, thin, mustached Mr. Franciszek Cemka, director of museums for Poland; and short, stocky Dr. Bogdan Rymaszewski, who, though executive secretary of the International Auschwitz Council, nevertheless receives his salary from the Polish government. That constitutes part of the problem. They want to maintain the Council is independent of Poland. But one cannot be sitting and claim to be standing.

Sigmund seized the occasion to inquire about Alberta's plaque for the *Sonderkommando* revolt. It has not been displayed since the first day it was dedicated. Both know exactly what he is talking about. "Oh, yes, Panie Sobolewski," Mutt said, "your plaque was very graciously accepted."

"You must be aware, though," Jeff reminded us, "it is a decision of the International Auschwitz Council to install uniform plaques for everything."

"We can understand that. You project a five-year plan, a ten-year plan. It all takes funding, and Poland is short right now. Meanwhile, until new plaques are in place, couldn't you display the one we've given you? That way, the half-million visitors each year will at least have the opportunity to learn what happened. Then when you want to change it, you can."

They exchanged glances; came to a decision. "We will look after it," Mutt promises.

At each stop Sigmund invited our hosts to the plaque dedication that the Auschwitz Awareness Society would hold at Nisko—Nisko, the place of the first cross-boundary concentration camp; Nisko, Sigmund's last Polish home. We had also contacted Rabbi Pinhas Joskovicz of Warsaw. "I wish you had notified me sooner. Unfortunately, Nisko involves a day's journey, and my schedule is full!"

"If you can work it out, we will be delighted to have you," I told him for Sigmund in Hebrew.

Wherever we went, it was clear to me that Sigmund hated my cap. It was easy to guess why. It covered my *kipah* and therefore was out of keeping with his natural inclination to street theatre. He bore no sympathy for my trepidations at being in a place where so many of my brethren perished. He tried to reassure me by laughing, "Nothing's going to happen to you." Then, in the next breath, looking at the newspapers, he would complain, "How is it possible so many here are still so antisemitic!"

At Auschwitz we stayed by prearrangement in a youth hostel established by the German "Action Reconstruction" as a kind of reparations of the soul. Visiting students from all over the world may make use of its facilities. It houses a well-stocked Holocaust library and archive, and boasts a rotating scholar-in-residence. It was actually the nicest place at which we stopped, worlds better than the hotel where the toilet above dripped a water torture on your body sitting below. While there, a Polish student approached timidly. "Would you mind filling out a questionnaire?" she inquired, a bundle in her arm.

"What does it concern?"

"It's for my class, 'What's wrong with the presentation at Auschwitz?'"

From the perspective of our visit, she could not have had a better topic. "That is why we are here."

Together, we considered the Jewish experience in Poland, wondered why none of this history comes out as one views the exhibits. While we were chatting, the curious wandered over. Soon twenty-five students had gathered about. Why the tendency to universalize in a way that minimizes and flattens Jewish suffering—as if Jews, who constituted ninety percent of the victims, were one nationality among many? Why the emphasis on Auschwitz-*Stammlager* rather than on Auschwitz-Birkenau?

Gathered around the table, some leaning, some sitting, we examined the role of communist ideology, of Polish nationality and of Christianity in downplaying the Jewish tragedy. Credit was given where credit was due: Poland did not welcome Hitler as did Austria. Poland never had a Quisling puppet government as in Norway, Slovakia, Vichy France, Rumania, Hungary, and Croatia. It never supplied troops to the *Wehrmacht* or SS as did the Baltics, Ukraine, France, Belgium, Holland, Italy, Spain, Croatia, Slovakia, Hungary, Rumania, and Finland. Nor did it abandon its own cause as did the Vlassov division of Russian soldiers. On the other hand, the Poles did not say, "These Jews are our brothers and sisters" or "We are all Jews," as did, most notably, the Danes. Not far behind were the Bulgarians, Belgians, Norwegians, Finns, and, to a limited extent, Serbs. Nor could it be like unoccupied Sweden, which accepted Jews from Denmark, in contrast to Britain, Canada, the United States and other free countries. Extolling the communist resistance was a way for the postwar People's Republic of Poland to sway the loyalty of its citizens. It was also a way to gloss over the fact that the Nazis, without Polish support, could not have succeeded as they did against their Jewish co-citizens. For even though Nazi occupation forces had encouraged Polish complicity, the slightest reminder of the huge prewar Jewish community raised embarrassing questions for Poland and especially for the Polish Church. We reviewed how democracy obliges a state to allow for expression of manifold and even competing views of truth.

And then we discussed the fragility of history in Polish terms. Katyn is a forest near Smolensk where Polish military officers were butchered during World War II.[4] After Germany attacked the Soviet Union in 1941, violating the nonaggression pact between Hitler and Stalin, the Germans accused the Russians of the Katyn atrocity. The charge led to a break in diplomatic relations between the Polish government-in-exile and the government of Stalin. The Russians, though, blamed the massacre on the Germans; and they maintained the pretence throughout the postwar years of Soviet influence. Today, new evidence has appeared leaving no doubt it was the Soviet secret police who killed the Polish officers. For instance, the soldiers were buried in their winter uniforms, whereas the Germans did not arrive until summer. Public recognition of the truth has become a symbol for Polish nationalism. But it is also clear to everyone that with only a little more time, the truth would have disappeared forever.

Katyn they knew all about. One could see them chewing on the historical implications, running the ideas around their heads. The next day Sigmund showed Höss's bunker and we toured the *Stammlager* together.[5] Sigmund provided a running commentary the likes of which few people in the world can give.

Leaving the bus in Lublin, we were struggling as always with Sigmund's numerous pieces of luggage. We had to transfer to the train station. True to form, he was telling everybody about the "Jewish rabbi."

A stranger approached in the street. "Need a lift?"

"Yeah, it'd be real helpful. We're just going to the train station," Sigmund replied on our behalf.

Of his own accord, the stranger insisted on the scenic route, past the only synagogue remaining from some hundred before the war; past the oldest surviving Jewish cemetery in Poland where, despite, massive Nazi desecration, lie preeminent rabbinic authorities of the sixteenth, seventeenth and eighteenth centuries; past the imposing edifice near the university housing the medical Academy that, before the war, contained the world's largest *Yeshiva*, one of the oldest Talmudic academies in Poland; past the site of the old ghetto to which the Nazis deported some of my family before destroying them and it. "Does the rabbi know that it was there that the Council of the Four Lands met?" He pointed out the place, but the building was destroyed. He would have shown us the Saul Wahl Synagogue; however it, too—gone.

Our 'guide' insisted on taking us to Majdanek where 250,000 Jews were murdered. The death camp lay on a hill right at the outskirts of the city on the main road, in full view of every passerby. The gentleman surprised us by pulling into the parking lot. "Want to stop and go through?"

Sigmund answered, as, dependent on translation, I always lagged behind.

"Can you spare the time?"

"Absolutely."

"You positive?"

"O yes."

We locked the luggage in the car and plodded off together. Preserved undamaged behind the barbed wire and watchtowers we saw: Twenty-four wooden prisoners' blocks, each with its own ghastly exhibit, one completely filled with shoes—high-heeled shoes, low-heeled, men's shoes, boots, children's shoes—another with hats. The telltale "disinfection" chamber where Zyklon B insecticide asphyxiated the Jews from the Warsaw and Lublin ghettoes. The crematorium. And visible from everywhere, the feature memorial of the camp, a 4,429 cubic foot circular mound of ash and bone.

Grateful as I was, I could see we were both getting alarmed. "What is going on?" I whispered, "are we piling up some astronomical bill?"

Sigmund shrugged.

At day's end, however, this anonymous Polish Catholic, too young to remember any Jews himself, would accept no pay, nothing, not even a pack of Sigmund's cigarettes. "I wanted to do this," he said, depositing us safely at the train station. "It's important to me."

Dedication day found no one from our rounds of embassies and news bureaus attending. However, Nisko's square-jawed mayor, Jan Dabek, and his town councillors had posted themselves by the brown and tan cement-block railroad station. The governor of Tarnobrzeg and other district representatives were also present. A unit of the new Polish Army clicked into place. Two local high school classes prattled away. Attracted by curiosity, a sampling of townsfolk gathered behind. Unfortunately, no general announcement had gone out to the local inhabitants, and no public address system had been installed—two oversights. The local Catholic clergy stood front. A local television crew was also there.

When the moment of dedication arrived, Sigmund insisted the rabbi "must speak to Poland" and quickly dissolved into the background. When Sigmund decides, there is no diverting his agenda.

Standing on the very spot where, on October 18, 1939, SS captain Adolph Eichmann told the newly arrived Jews they must provide their own barracks and wells, I started off talking about the golden age Jew and Pole shared together, recalling the bitter story that followed. "For many of you soldiers and students here today, this is the first time you have ever seen a Jew. The absence is even more astounding in a country that, until fifty years ago, was home to the largest, most vibrant Jewish centre in Europe."

From in the crowd, Sigmund translated as the thoughts poured out. "To appreciate why we place this plaque, we can think of Katyn. How many more years of Soviet domination would it have taken until the young people of Poland would never have recovered the truth? On the way here, we passed a cemetery near Pełkinie where, during the war, the Nazis starved to death eight thousand captured Soviet soldiers. The new Polish authorities have removed the plaques commemorating their memory. It is one thing to dismantle the monuments to the Russian Army in every village square—new

Poland has its own army, representing itself in great honour here today. It is quite another to remove the historical markers for those eight thousand specific martyrs." The soldiers nodded slightly in response to the recognition.

"History is fragile. We note this because those same forces that attempted to rewrite the history of Katyn, have universalized the Holocaust for purposes of magnifying their own role. In so doing, however, they have prevented young Poles from knowing what happened to Poland's great Jewish community. Free people have an interest in the truth. There must be *Pravda*.

"Sigmund Sobolewski, No. Eighty-eight, returns today because he was here when that first transport of foreign Jews was unloaded at this very railroad station. A few of you were here with him. Most were not. Sigmund Sobolewski was silent then. Then, six months later, Sigmund was taken from Nisko and imprisoned in Auschwitz where he spent four-and-a-half years. Now he returns to witness for history. Sigmund Sobolewski will not be silent today. Neither will the men and women of this community. There is a new Poland. This plaque represents one small but important effort to reclaim historical truth."

We arrived in street clothes, as did the priest. How would that look on television, Sigmund was evidently asking himself. To me he said, "Priest will be wearing his vestments. You'll have to wear your *tallis*." To the priest he said, "The rabbi will robe; what about you?" The poor priest had to run back to his rectory. After the dedicatory words, the priest, short linen surplice over black cassock overlaid with a green and gold embroidered white silk stole, responded in kind. Then we each concluded with a prayer.

Following the ceremony, we were updated on Nisko's former synagogue. At war's end, the Poles took what the Nazis had made into a warehouse and converted it into a tavern. The city was attempting to expropriate it to preserve it as a holy site. "Yes, but with the proviso that should Jews ever return to Nisko, the city would turn it back to them," Sigmund added in Polish.

We waited at the bus stop. Nisko is a small town, and the group of us were standing on a street corner across from the railroad station conversing about the day's proceedings. Sigmund perched himself on a suitcase, resting his leg. "Ah, finally, here it comes," someone said.

"Basia, quick, the Rabbi's beret," called Sigmund, leaping to his feet as the bus pulled in.

"Where?" she replied, carrying the yellow jacket she had with her the whole day.

"I accidentally left it at the mayor's office."

"Zygmunt, that's two blocks away. How'd you come to have his beret?"

"Lost my own. Hurry. Ask questions later."

We had entered Poland, among the last through the old Warsaw terminal. With only a *kipah* on now, I left, one of the first through the new one: Okęcie 2, polished and austere, totally austere. No pictures, no exhibits. Nothing yet to distinguish it in any way. Officially opened by Cardinal Glemp. No chance yet to even get dirty. Sigmund immediately noticed that Hoch- und Tiefbau, the same company that constructed the Birkenau crematoria in 1942, was building the new international airport in 1992.

I whiled the next week in Israel. By coincidence, Shulamit Aloni, Israel's Minister of Education, had just issued a statement with which nobody agreed. For her, that is nothing new. She critiqued Israel's program of sending students to Auschwitz as promoting mistrust of non-Jews and little else.

Sigmund later said, "Aloni has point. Israelis stick to themselves, use only their own guides, follow strict itinerary. Similarly, on Jewish March of Living, thousands of students from around world sweep into Auschwitz for four hours, march death march, go on to visit Treblinka and other sites, then whisk on to Israel. Contrast this with Germans who send, for week's stay at youth hostel, about fifty students. There they meet with their Polish counterparts to study and to do, in camp, service projects.

"Polish government should be friendlier to such large groups of visitors," he criticized. "But given insular format, is there any wonder Jewish students come back only with horror stories and old prejudices reinforced? Some Jews who support Auschwitz Awareness Society tell me, 'For Poles I wouldn't give a broken penny.' Others say, 'Sigmund, you're wasting your time. Forget it— you'll never change these antisemitic Poles.'" His voice became thoughtful. "Maybe we can't change seventy-year-old antisemitic Pole, or seventy-year-old anguished Jew," he said. "Our hope should be with young people, though."

On the 1994 march, Canadian Jewish students would dedicate a plaque to the four Jewish women whose bravery made possible the *Sonderkommando* revolt. Sigmund would scream, "After they left, museum officials, who participated in ceremonies, promptly removed their plaques." [6]

Sigmund and I met again in Frankfurt for the flight home. Through the help of the Krebs-Gehlens, Sigmund had addressed several meetings of German students while I had been in Israel. Now Sigmund was carrying a reproduction of a painting for Ramona, "The Miracle of the Vistula," commemorating the Polish forces who defeated the Bolsheviks in 1920. The painting featured an Ulan cavalryman and a young woman, the soldier wearing a *rogatywka*, a four-corner, flattop military hat. In the duty-free shop, Sigmund also purchased some body powder with a puff for Ramona. Sigmund was biting his lip. In response to my questions, he told me, "Bus is in place. After six-hour border holdup, it's safely installed in Auschwitz. But we had to pay their extortion fee. Barely bargained them down to $1,600."

"You had the money with you the whole time?"

"Yeah, Barry Slawsky donated it," he said, not realizing the implications of his simple confession, so bothered was he by something more. "You know, Auschwitz's museum officials never even said 'Thank you.' Instead they complained, 'Why isn't it new bus?' 'Why's it so long?' 'Why isn't it undercoated?' And they want to repaint it because it says 'Gift of *Edmonton Jewish News*' on it. It's unbelievable."

On the plane, it emerged that that was not all that was bothering him. "You heard, same as me, head of Polish museums, Cemka," he sighed. "Didn't he promise, until museum carries out its overall plan, he'd put up our plaque? Well, I checked. It's still not up. It's so frustrating. I bought museum guide book in every language; some still have 'Slavic' women being sterilized. If they've got year's supply, fine, let them just put in correction. How many visitors have to go through before truth is taught? What Bartoszewski, head of Auschwitz Council, years ago said was soon to 'be resolved' is still not done."

He worked up slowly. "Spoke to Ramona by phone before leaving," he sighed again. "She was totally cold. Looks like I have to stop my work. This' got to be my last trip to Poland." [7]

"What do you think of Spielberg's being refused?" Sigmund's voice asked through the phone.

"Refused what?"

"Five movies have been produced in Auschwitz. Three Polish, one French, one Czech. All of them about Catholics. Now when Jew wants to film for *Schindler's List,* he gets refused. What do you think?"

"Send me the background. I don't know anything about it."

"Good, good. Can you believe it? They said Auschwitz Council was against it. They use the Council to justify themselves on Jewish issues, like Nazis once used the ghetto councils. At this point, they haven't even had meeting. They said Canadian Jewish Congress was against it, too. Leipziger in Toronto, he doesn't know about it anything. So I called Amblin Entertainment at Universal. They don't know why they're getting hassled. I'll bring it up at next month's international meeting." [8]

Simon wrote to Spielberg; he wanted to secure a position in the production. Sigmund chided, "See, if you'd have gone to Auschwitz, you'd have more to offer him now."

Sigmund said, "When I repeated this to Emilio, he right away jumped to his brother's defence. He thinks Simon's not going was revenge on me. Not that I haven't thought about that myself. But I also feel Simon bears some guilt. Simon is product of my own religious odyssey. After liberation I couldn't pray. Then after experimenting with Unitarian Church, by time Simon was growing up, again I didn't go. Is it any wonder he's not religious; doesn't go to church; criticizes, for its role in history, our Church? Although I, too, criticize, I've found out Church is important, attend on regular basis. When I go, though, I'm always alone; boys don't come. Ramona's right: after Auschwitz, I'm easy about financial problems; there are worse things to worry about, like my children. With them I'm really disappointed. Not one of them is financially independent. And I'm angry at myself. If they'd heard each week priest, it would've given them footing. Simon has made me realize I didn't impress upon boys importance of religion, let them grow like weeds. I'm paying now price. Today, when I go into synagogue and see, celebrating his Bar Mitzvah, some thirteen-year-old, I'm hit with how much my own sons lack.

"Mostly Simon talks to Ramona—mainly about money. Wants us to buy him computer. I work on this battered old typewriter and he wants computer. Don't care if it is his money, he's got to have lesson.

"Emilio doesn't agree on guilt issue. He thinks Simon was afraid he would vomit. 'Auschwitz is a sick place, goddamn perverted', he says. But I told him, 'You went.' 'Sure', Emilio says, 'Didn't like it, though.' 'What do you mean?' 'I felt damn uncomfortable, like you say when you see gays kissing each other and all, especially knowing this is where you were.' To me, this is one telling admission," Sigmund said. "Emilio thinks Auschwitz was 'sick place', so in his mind, it follows that his papa is sick, too."

Then Sigmund leaned forward and without any prompting continued to relate his conversation with Emilio. "Emilio says all his life I mentioned in practically every conversation Auschwitz. 'That's bullshit, and you know it', I told him. So he says maybe I don't say it right out loud; still he's always got feeling that whatever I tell him, Auschwitz goes through my words. He says I'm only in touch with what I want to be. You know what else Emilio said? That I'm criticizing lately Nazis less and going after Church more. He thinks that this is wrong, that I antagonize people.

"I'm seventy years old; was born Catholic; going back to my roots as altar boy in Nowy Targ. People ask me, 'You say Christians were responsible; you're Christian, yet you were persecuted; do you feel responsible for the killing of Jews?' And I answer, 'Yes, I didn't do, in camp, all I could. Maybe because I was afraid; and maybe because I was brainwashed to believe Jews are evil. Before Auschwitz I was not in danger; yet when my priest in Nowy Targ, Father Łukasik, told me Jews killed Christ, I accepted uncritically. Everybody did. So in Auschwitz, I felt, well, maybe these Jews deserve to suffer.' Those who tormented and murdered Jews were baptized Christians, yes or no? And those who stood idly by, before, during and after, in camp and out of camp, in Poland, England or America, were baptized Christians, yes or no? And there were some few who helped, but Church hierarchy failed to respond, yes or no?'"

Vatican II de-Satanized the Church's teaching on Jews. The Holocaust was at least part of the impetus. Then, finally, on December 30, 1993, the Vatican established diplomatic relations with Israel. But, as Sigmund pointed out, the epoch-making breakthrough was clouded. The Pope followed the recognition of Israel by bestowing the Pius Order on Kurt Waldheim, whitewashing his past as a Nazi accused of war crimes by Yugoslavia. Sigmund maintains there are two tendencies within the Church: one toward pursuing a rapprochement with a 'living Judaism', the other, despite *Nostra Aetate* and all its advances, still fixated on the older 'fossil Judaism' theology, promoted by the Vatican's "Opus Dei" group, hoping to make Pius XII a saint.

"I'm still working for next step," he asserted. "I have speaking engagement coming up in Vancouver. They said not to talk about Church. Well, I'm disappointed in my Church. In my mind, Church has failed to complete its own Sacrament of Reconciliation. Despite nineteen hundred years of 'teaching of contempt,' Church has not adequately owned up to its responsibility. Don't we teach that if we confess, we will be forgiven? In Auschwitz there's today visible presence of Catholic priest. Church has forged this link, not me. But it's *negative* presence, mark of Church's own failure. I am working for Church to make promised universal soul-searching statement on Holocaust, if for no other reason than as act of self-purification. And that can only happen if and when it recognizes some responsibility. Reason I criticize Poland is because I care about Poland; it's my native country. And I criticize Church because I care about Church."

Home again, Sigmund quoted Emilio, "'This emphasis on the Church turns people off before they even hear your whole message. It'll really side-track your public advocacy.' This is first time Emilio has volunteered any practical suggestion. This is first time Emilio and I have had together long private talk of any sort. Auschwitz was only small part of it. We talked in 'Earls restaurant,' about some new movie and my marriage with Iris. I think it's maybe first time he saw me as human being.

"And you know what else? Ramona helped me pass out leaflets in Vancouver. And now Vladimir wants '88' tattooed on his arm. And he also wants to change his name back to Sobolewski, like I did."

B

Calgary, Alberta, April 1995

Some observations, are in order. In the preceding chapters, Sigmund's confidant Reuven is the reporter. Together, we met Poland's Ambassador Alojzy Bartošek when the Polish Trade Delegation visited Calgary. Bartošek claimed the problems at Auschwitz are not so serious as to even require solution. Later, we travelled to Chicago to see Cardinal Glemp. *Achtundachtzig* is a key that opens doors; Sobolewski turns it skilfully.

As a narrator, my first principle has been to recount the seemingly disconnected anecdotes that, when placed together, form a retrospective of Sigmund's life. I have chosen to write in the first person, first to more accurately reflect Sigmund's own sharing; and second, to better get inside the head of our subject as affected over the last fifty years by his Auschwitz experience. Family conversations are representative composites of years of interaction, some culled from tapes of Sigmund's own interviews at the time he was discussing the same issues with his family. All the conversations were corroborated with the boys and Ramona. The radio-talk-show conversations were sifted from actual recordings. The words of Nerland are the exact quotes as recorded by the media. Wojciech is a composite, as are Sigmund's other local customers. All other conversations and reported experiences emerge from Sigmund's recollection.

Ramona is correct in saying Sigmund does not see nature. Consequently the descriptions are sometimes the narrator's, most often from visits to the site. Sigmund is alternately loquacious and silent. In response to a question about his life, he will expound at length with rambling anecdotes that uncannily always revert to the topic. At the same time, he is a very private person without interest in tête-à-tête. And although he could pontificate, especially in his younger years as a father, he did not tolerate much verbal interchange, or so the boys unanimously report. Therefore, the very act of isolating specific scenes to represent the family relationship over decades may overdramatize; and the reader is so advised. The organizational structure and the literary vehicles and allusions used to convey a life that wishes to link peoples are also the reporter's. The references to the classics are Sigmund's.

While any biography, even any history, is in some sense subjective, the details of Number 88's life are not altered to make this a better narrative. It was hardly necessary. I once read a piece by Michael Wyschogrod claiming it is forbidden to fictionalize the Holocaust.[9] Why this intentional hyperbole? Art, as a vehicle for catharsis, transmutes and humanizes affliction, or, like religion, glorifies it. Therefore, art is ultimately a gratification even when its subject matter is not. But Auschwitz is history, life and not art. Sobolewski is not gathering dust on a library shelf, boxed in a museum case, or the figment of a novelist's imagination. One can meet him in Fort Assiniboine; or hear him on a talk show; or see his picture on the front page of newspapers all over North America, as happened January 27, 1995. Over the years, in addition to his being decorated with the Cross of Auschwitz, he has been honoured with an invitation to the Knesseth, Israel's Parliament, on its commemoration of the 50th anniversary of the liberation of Auschwitz; awarded an honorary diploma in Community Service from Grant MacEwan College; presented the Celebration Canada Award of Merit by former prime minister Joe Clark; cited in the Board of Inquiry Decision, Alberta Human Rights Commission; and made subject of a chapter in Warren Kinsella's *Web of Hate* (Harper-Collins, 1994) and of a television documentary "Prisoner 88" that premiered in Vancouver, December 6, 1995. His work has been reported in newspapers and journals the world over in English, Polish, German, Dutch, Hebrew and Spanish, and he is a frequent speaker in Germany, Poland, Holland, the U.S. and Canada.

The vagaries of oral history are well known. Sigmund told me twice, for instance, the account of the hospital orderly who pointed upward in answer to his question. Once he related the anecdote in reference to Marian Kornecki (the family friend who informed Sigmund about his father's death), once in reference to Varga Szarkady (the Jew whom he extricated from the debris). It often required many occasions, asking similar questions, to clarify particulars. The mind plays tricks: what seems unmistakable today may be questionable tomorrow. A detail "witnessed" may have been read. A feeling then may actually be a feeling now. What came before may actually have come after.

Sigmund also views the world in blacks and whites. If Ramona complains that he spends too much time and money on Auschwitz, Sigmund interprets that Ramona is anti-Jewish. In all such cases, I have endeavoured as a reporter to incorporate both sides of such questions.

From a psychological point of view, objective reality is irrelevant, for what Sigmund thinks, is what he is. Rather than analyze the general scene, its whys and wherefores, I have chosen to allow the particular, the person then and now, to stand unadorned. Sigmund is his own authority. Nevertheless, I have also taken care to recount the historical details as meticulously as possible and in the multiple voices in which history comes to us. For at end, this is not just a personal story. Owing to the overarching character of the subject matter, Sigmund's life carries societal significance. Sigmund's story documents the human struggle to derive meaning from depravity. At the same time, it attests to the toll such a struggle exacts on human endurance. To afford a sense of perspective, therefore, it must now be asked: regarding major issues, how much of Sigmund's eyewitness account is corroborated by external evidence?

Writing immediately after the war, Erich Kulka reinforces Sigmund's position in his conflict with Auschwitz officials regarding Block Ten, relating that it was "inhabited exclusively by Jewish women." [10] Robert Lifton quotes former prisoner Adelaide Hautval, "Women 'guinea pigs,' all Jewish." [11] Sylvia Friedman, a Block Ten inhabitant, survived and testified about her fellow Jewish prisoners. [12] A Polish Catholic prisoner, Seweryna Szmaglewska, wrote immediately following her own liberation, "In Block 10 medical experiments are performed on the bodies of young Jewish girls. [13] Danut a Czech further supports Sigmund's position in a publication of the Auschwitz museum itself: "Professor Clauberg: research in sterilization. Injection causing closure of the oviducts and thus stopping further fertility of Jewish women." [14] Raul Hilberg cites several documents between Himmler and Clauberg and some survivor testimony all referring to Jewish women. [15] Clauberg, in his own testimony to German newspapers, mentions only Jews. [16] The citations against him in the German trial, rendered moot by his untimely death, also use the word "Jew" in describing his victims.

Elie Cohen, a Dutch doctor, verifies another point regarding the forbidden women in Block Ten: "There were romantic attachments formed between men prisoners outside Block Ten and the women prisoners inside." [17]

Sigmund's recollection of Jews in the first transport, a second issue in contention with Auschwitz officials and many historians, finds backing in another non-Jewish survivor, Józef Garlinski: "There were a number of priests and schoolteachers, and several dozen Jews." [18] Josef Cornillo, an eyewitness, reports: "This was a transport of Jews and Poles from Tarnów and [other places]." [19] The transport included Jews arrested in the spring of 1940 in the *A-B Aktion* ordered by Governor Hans Frank, a staunch Catholic. Cornillo names some of the Jews from Tarnów: two lawyers, Emil Wieder and Isaac Holzer; the director of the Hebrew School, Maximilian Rosenbusch; and the industrialist, Yaakov Schwartz. [20]

That Jews continued to be incarcerated for the first twenty-one months preceding the all-Jewish March 26, 1942 transport is supported by Herman Langbein: "Fritzsch once asked the capo of one of the work commandos—a German criminal—how many Jews he had in his commando. He recounted the number whereupon Fritzsch gave him the following order: 'By Saturday, you will be able to tell me that your commando is judenrein (clean of Jews).'"[21] In this anecdote, Langbein verifies that Jews arrived throughout the first year while substantiating their singularly brutal treatment. Langbein cites another example of this latter point, "One thousand nine hundred eighty Slovakian Jews were delivered to Auschwitz between April 17-23, 1942. On August 15, just four months later, only 7% remained."[22]

On the above issues, museum officials have privately conceded Sigmund's points, though the public exhibit still lacks such acknowledgement. "Why do they fight it so?" Sigmund asks.

Another issue also relates to the Jews. Contrary to other historical summaries of Auschwitz, Sigmund contends that the SS must have had plans for an extermination camp from the beginning. From Karl Fritzsch's speech about the Auschwitz chimney, it would seem that, even before Himmler's first visit, well before Wannsee, back on June 15, 1940, such ideas already existed. Fritzsch came from Dachau, where there was an incinerator in operation. Designs for a similar incinerator were in place, and by September 1940 the first crematorium was operational. However, some prisoners left Dachau alive. Fritzsch's speech implying more sinister designs, repeated again and again, was first enunciated Day One.[23]

There is other corroboration. Years earlier, in *Mein Kampf*, Hitler had lamented that Jews should have been gassed in World War I. Utilizing the west's refusal to accept Jewish refugees as justification, the SS journal *Das Schwarze Korps* editorialized: "These diploma-democrats know the Jewish question very well—one need only look at their immigration regulations.... We shall therefore now take the Jewish Question towards its total solution. The program is clear. It is: total elimination...."[24] Then on January 30, 1939 Hitler prophesied to western democracies who refuse to receive this "valuable race" that a new world war would lead to "the annihilation of the Jewish race in Europe."[25] Julius Streicher, in hundreds of articles in *Der Stürmer*, advocated total extermination of the Jews. On September 21, 1939 Heydrich ordered mass concentration, which he termed "first stages" toward the planned total measures, the secret "final aim."[26] Speaking in 1939, Hitler confirmed, "Fence them in somewhere where they can perish as they deserve." On December 16, 1939, *The London Times* published "A Road to Extermination" announcing that the Germans would deport more than one million Jews into Poland. The title is telling. It is difficult to discern whether the 1940 unimplemented Madagascar resettlement plan was a temporary diversion, a step in the process, or simply a smoke-screen to facilitate extermination. Whatever, Jewish emigration from the *Gouvernement-Générale* was forbidden as of October 25, 1940, which indicates that any internal debate between expulsion and extermination had been settled. "The continued emigration of Jews from Eastern Europe ... would spell a continued spiritual regeneration of world Jewry."[27]

Details for implementing the Final Solution were determined no later than April 1941, the term "Final Solution" first appearing in a letter from Schellenberg May 20, 1941. Höss wrote that in May 1941 he received oral instructions from Himmler to proceed with the gassing of Jews. On May 3, the Polish government in exile sent a formal note to all Allied governments describing the incarceration in concentration camps. Auschwitz, Sachsenhausen, Mauthausen, Belzec and Chelmno were all listed. On July 31, Göring wrote Heydrich requesting "implementation of the planned final solution of the Jewish question," which reference Heydrich understood—no surprise, given his own letter of 1939.[28] Taken with Sigmund's observations, evidence suggests that the January 20, 1942 Wannsee Conference outlining plans to exterminate eleven million Jews merely concretized decisions made long before.[29]

In 1993, Jean-Claude Pressac published the results of research in which he had set out to prove that the gas chambers were designed for disinfection. He made a meticulous and detailed study of plans, orders for material and physical remains, coordinating the three. The one-time Holocaust denier concluded that the chambers were used for killing, and were built only with that intent in mind. For instance, there were shower heads embedded into the heavy cement ceiling without plumbing.[30]

With respect to Father Kolbe, Zenon Frank (No. 156), also a Polish Catholic survivor in the first transport, shares Sigmund's interpretation. "I admired him for what he did, and I don't want to denigrate it; but, you know, I was in that camp for nearly five years, and I saw plenty of people choose death deliberately as a means of escape."[31]

Frank also bolsters Sigmund's point about those who boast about their resistance. "Much has been made about the resistance movement in the camps, which as far as I could see in Auschwitz consisted of a handful of older 'politicals' sitting in a corner nattering."[32] A survivor of Westerbork and Bergen–Belsen reports similarly: "Of course, people wrote books later and probably thought they remembered having great thoughts at the time, which they only actually had afterward."[33] Immediately after the war, Tadeusz Borowski, like Sigmund a Polish survivor of Auschwitz, bemoaned the lack of resistance.[34] Except for the Jewish *Sonderkommando* revolt, the total resistance seems to have consisted of getting a few reports out of Auschwitz.[35] Most testimony on a resistance movement originates from sources glorifying the role of Communists in the camp. Now that the political realities have changed, a reexamination of the accepted 'history' may reveal that there has been more revision than truth.

While corroborating Sigmund's observations, the above reports are dispassionate in presentation, whereas Sigmund tends to be a tornado on the prairie. It is illustrative of Sigmund's character that on checking the first draft, he responded, "No objection to make book even _more_ CONTROVER-

SIAL." (Emphasis is his.) By that he means, do not hesitate to say the truth. The museum officials, on the other hand, attack what is only his style to draw attention from his message.

Many histories repeat that the International Committee of the Red Cross never visited Auschwitz, and museum authorities have not been overly public about correcting the record. Yahil, for instance, reports on the visit of the German Red Cross, but not on the subsequent visit by ICRC.[36] A few, like Martin Gilbert, support Sigmund's contention regarding what has become a sensitive point for the ICRC.[37] And a document filed by the ICRC's own delegate substantiates this visit in late 1944. "A rumour was in fact going round that the camp was equipped with a very modern shower room where groups of detainees were being gassed.... It was impossible to prove anything whatever."[38] Was the ICRC pandering to governments it wanted to work with to justify its own apparatus of 'relief'? Or was it adhering to the rigorous standards of 'proof' required by an international agency?[39]

The BBC publicized the facts behind the Red Cross's "rumour" more than two years earlier, on June 2, 1942. Well before, on November 16, 1941, David Kelly, a British diplomat in Switzerland, had reported that more than half of the Dutch Jews sent to 'labour camps' were now dead. Six days later, Carlos de Macedo, a Brazilian diplomat stationed in Berlin, had independently reported about deportations and subsequent deaths. Then on June 6, 1942, Władysław Sikorski, Prime Minister of the Polish Government-in-Exile, confirmed the BBC report: "The extermination of the Jews is being carried out on an unbelievable scale...." On June 10, specific atrocities were enumerated. On July 17, the Croatian Abbot Giuseppe Marcone announced that two million European Jews had been killed.[40] Decades before public demonstration was in vogue, on July 21, 1942, an outpouring of some 22,000 in Madison Square Gardens condemned the war crimes. The same day, President Roosevelt stated, "The perpetrators of these crimes ... will be punished on the day of reckoning."[41] During August, SS Lieutenant Kurt Gerstein gave an eyewitness account of gassing operations to the Protestant bishop, Otto Dibelius, and to the Papal Nuncio, Monsignor Orsenigo, who rebuffed him.[42] Then, in October, the *Jewish Telegraphic Agency* publicized the Riegner report on the use of prussic acid for the extermination of European Jewry.

That the Allies were aware of what was happening in Auschwitz, however frequently denied, is now proved beyond question. On September 23, 1942 Nazi propaganda minister Joseph Goebbels forewarned sixty German newspaper editors of understandable Jewish hostility. "They know with deadly certainty that as the war progresses they will be packed off to the East and delivered up to a murderous fate." A copy of the speech reached the British Foreign Minister, Anthony Eden, whose initials and notes appear on the document, which surfaced in November 1993 in London's Public Record Office. Eden, described by his personal secretary, Oliver Harvey, as "hopelessly prejudiced against Jews," did nothing. In November 1942, Jan Kozielewski (later Karski) of the Polish underground presented Roosevelt with an eyewitness report of the gassing of Jews in Treblinka and Belzec.[43] On November 14, American Catholic bishops joined an earlier French statement decrying Nazi treatment of the Jews. A Vatican report on the use of gas chambers dated November 25, 1942 is in the U.S. National Archives.[44] On that same day, *The Palestine Post* in mandate Jerusalem printed a full account of Himmler's extermination of Polish Jewry. On December 8, 1942, Jewish representatives met with President Roosevelt. They were advised that diversion from the war effort to save Jews could be detrimental to the Allied cause. The most American Jewry could expect would be an Allied denunciation. This came on December 17, 1942—the same broadcast that Sigmund states spread among the prisoners.[45]

Yet in the summer of 1944 the ICRC delegate could not even bring himself to mention the Jews. The same gentleman reports, "The supplies sent by the Committee seemed to have been distributed. Although there is no proof, we felt the Commandant was telling the truth."[46] His conclusion? Send more parcels.

On the issue of bombing the gas chambers, requests began in the spring of 1944. The idea was rejected by the War Department in June as impractical, even though Washington strategists never consulted the Air Force commanders in Italy who were running daily missions to Auschwitz. Instead, the War Department replied as per a secret policy to avoid any rescue operations. The excuse, as iterated by John J. McCloy, the U.S. Assistant Secretary of War, was: "Such an effort, even if practicable, might provoke even more vindictive action by the Germans."[47]

Sigmund's 1945 eyewitness report that the Americans not only ceded land to the Russians but also 'repatriated' refugees, is a charge until recently denied. As it has now surfaced, the United States agreed, in a top secret clause of the Yalta Agreement, to exchange two million Soviet refugees for approximately 24,000 American servicemen in Soviet-controlled territory. That the United States knew the full consequences of its action is revealed in the name 'Operation Keelhaul', referring to the old torture of tying a sailor, then hauling him under the boat's keel from one side to the other.[48] Close in time and place to Sigmund's own eyewitness report, Nikolai Tolstoy records an American forced transfer of three thousand kicking refugees on May 22, 1945 from Plaven to the Red Army across the Elbe.[49]

Each time Sigmund's points were checked, evidence surfaced authenticating his eyewitness account.

Regarding the relationship between survivors and their children, ours is an extended study of one family. To this date, most nonfiction on post-camp attitudes has been in the form of collected case studies. These provide a comparison that is necessarily missing in a more in-depth, single-family investigation like this one. Thus it is quite pertinent to ask, how much of Sigmund's post-Auschwitz psychology is typical of other survivors? And how much of his sons' response is characteristic of the second generation?

"Concentration camp survivor syndrome" was first described by Niederland in 1961.[50] Among its various attributes, researchers have pointed to hasty marriages contracted to alleviate intense isolation and loneliness, and the supreme importance ascribed to the establishment of a new family.[51] The reliving of past terrors in repetitive nightmares, chronic anxiety and depression, living a socially isolated life, guilt over survival while others have died, are all common. So is a feeling of self-hatred resulting from extreme denigration by their environment.[52] Survivors often possess a surprisingly forgiving attitude toward their oppressors; nevertheless, almost anything will spark a memory.[53] At first, survivors all seem to share a tendency to be alone with their feelings—because they had to repress them during the Holocaust, because trust is impossible, because the past is too painful, or because they have perceived that others cannot, or will not, understand. They frequently compensate by an aggressive determination to succeed at all costs or through a whirlwind of external activity. Often by visiting the place of trauma, a new sense of mastery is gained. To transform guilt feelings into an adaptive mechanism confers meaning to their survival and prevents them from dwelling on the pain and suffering.[54]

Survivor parents often view their children as a source of security and gratification, an undoing of destruction, and a restoration of lost family.[55] As parents, survivors tend toward protectiveness. They frequently expect their children to share their own suspicions of the world, often converting their children into a symbol of what they lack.[56] A survivor's difficulty in dealing with his own aggressive impulses may facilitate aggression in the children, and survivor guilt leads to strong identification with the children.[57] Typical of survivors is concern about fights between their children, a tendency to rate their children as excessively dependent, lacking in maturity and coping skills.[58] The parent alternately nags and humours the child, yet always to mould him or her into an identity useful to the parent.[59]

As Sigmund himself points out, an experience as penetrating as Auschwitz is bound to affect the next generation. A child of survivors may tend toward nightmares and the worry whether he or she, if living then, might have been on the other side. They also may exhibit a propensity to protest social ills. The children of Jewish survivors frequently want to absorb everything they can about the Holocaust, whereas those of non-Jewish survivors seek to avoid it.[60] Children of survivors characteristically become either moderately phobic or rebellious: they make repetitive, fruitless attempts to rebel, or display unusually adverse reactions to even inconsequential setbacks and failures.[61] Often because of guilt in opposing a parent who has already suffered so much, their anger is displaced in fighting others.[62] Children of survivors tend to emphasize the heroic aspects of their parents' past, as opposed to the suffering.[63]

With the call for Auschwitz awareness, Sigmund endeavours to bridge two communities rent asunder by generations of religious strife. Yet Jacob went

*Ramona and Sigmund in front of the Russian soldiers' memorial in Berlin.
Courtesy of Herschel Studio, Berlin.*

forward limping. As always in real life, the weaver's task is incomplete. The threads of Sigmund's religious, ethnic and family tapestry still hang free.

Sigmund recently said, "My life with Ramona is 'jo-jo' with three downs to one up." Nonetheless, he confided, "If I ever get my feet on ground, she gets right away her visa to visit Cuba."

On September 10, 1994, Ramona began a one month trip to Cuba. "Finally, finally," she told me. "I am all excited about it. Been waiting for too long. I am practically on my way."

Sigmund and I sit talking together, he in the black-naugahyde, vibrator chair, me at my desk. Somehow, slowly, painfully, it surfaces. "You know what my problem is? I numbed myself too much. I can't trust. At first, I started with good business and makings of beautiful family, but I had to shut out myself to do it. Then, when my moment came and I finally came to grips with myself, it cost me everything else." He pauses a few seconds to gather his thoughts. "Ordinarily, you don't plan to give up your relationship with your own people … your fellow religionists … your loved ones. You say, 'My case is so logical, people will join on in spite of themselves. Just give them time.' Even as every choice sets path that twists out of sight, your commitments can lead to reverse of what you hoped."

Sigmund continues in a sorrowful voice. "Yet, to sacrifice for something, however painful that sacrifice might be, is to conquer senseless death of Auschwitz. Isn't that ultimate 'Auschwitz awareness'?

"And isn't such awareness Christianity's only chance for resurrection after Holocaust?" he asks.

In my tradition, the stranger with whom the agonized biblical Jacob struggled is often identified with Esau, the non-Jewish brother with whom Jacob must be reconciled.

In the thought of Sigmund's Church, the stranger is occasionally identified with Jesus of Nazareth, through whom Jacob, destined to continue limping, was saved and *renamed*.

When one makes his choices, even death can have meaning. Sigmund has told me, "Due to my experience that day putting out fire in *Krematorium IV*, I harbour deep within close link between me and participants in *Sonderkommando* revolt. My last will states that when my train comes in, I want my ashes carried up from here and put in pond behind *Krematorium* ruins."

Roy D. Tanenbaum
Toronto, Ontario
September 15, 1998

Notes

Part I-1992
One: Enter the Subject

1   H. G. Adler, "Auschwitz," *The Encyclopedia Judaica* (2nd ed., 1973), vol. 3, col. 856.

Push 1945-1966
Two: Jurek

2   William L. Shirer, *End of a Berlin Diary* (New York: Alfred A. Knopf, 1947), p. 56.

3   Prisoners, often Polish, who by reason of their assigned job or length in the Auschwitz Konzentrationslager enjoyed special privileges.

4   Approximately six thousand lose their lives.

Four: Irka

5   Dr. Karl Clauberg's purpose was to find an efficient way to burn the fallopian tubes and induce adhesions to block them, thus reversing his previous research to soften adhesions obstructing the fallopian tubes. The hormonal preparations Progynon and Proluton he had earlier developed to treat infertility, as well as the 'Clauberg test' for measuring the action of progesterone, continued to be employed in the postwar period. Himmler's charge to Clauberg was to develop nonsurgical means of mass sterilization of "undesirables" so they could serve as forced labour without fear of reproducing. Clauberg, as an independent experimenter, paid the camp administration for his female subjects, and the pharmaceutical company Schering–Werke, anxious to benefit from his experiments, supplied the caustic. The "bunny man," Honorary *SS Obergruppenführer* Dr. Karl Clauberg was sentenced in Russia but later released unrepentant on 11 October 1953. He established a gynaecological clinic in Germany under his own name. In the late '50s he was again brought to trial in West Germany. His retrial abruptly ended when he died in prison, 9 August 1957. *See* Philippe Aziz, *Doctors of Death* (Geneva: Ferni Press, 1976), vol. 2, pp. 156–175; Robert Jay Lifton, *The Nazi Doctors* (New York: Basic Books, 1986), pp. 42–43, 269–278. Jurek's friend, Rosa became an X-ray machine operator, survived, was evacuated to Ravensbrück, lived for a time in Warsaw after the war, and (possibly) in Israel.

6   Jupp was later transferred to Birkenau as a senior Block prisoner. In June 1968 in Frankfurt, Jupp Windeck was sentenced to life imprisonment.

7   Close to 27,000 'survivors' perished.

8   In March of 1946, the British hanged SS Hauptsturmführer Franz Hössler.

Five: Ginsbourg

9   Bednarek was eventually tried in the second Frankfurt am Main trials of 1965 and imprisoned. Kala was moved to Anders army base in Italy for investigation. The case against him was dropped because he claimed to an anti-communist.

Six: Iris

10   Heinrich Himmler, Oct. 4, 1943, Nuremberg International Military Trial Document, PS-1919 XXIX, 145–146.

Seven: Ramona

11   The surname probably indicates a Jewish ancestry. Eskanazi is a Hebrew name meaning one who has migrated from a German land. There are many Spanish Catholics with Hebrew names. In 1492, Queen Isabella expelled all Jews from Spain. Jews were permitted to remain only if they became converts.

12   See Tadeusz Borowski, "Auschwitz, Our Home (A Letter)," in *This Way for the Gas, Ladies and Gentlemen* (Dallas, Pa.: Penguin, 1986), pp. 113–114. A latecomer, Borowski was first housed in Birkenau. He arrived in Auschwitz' *Stammlager* only after Sigmund's match, but soon enough to record the prisoners' lingering excitement regarding the fight, "revenging there what the other prisoners had to endure in the field." Borowski renders the story from hearsay, attributing the events to prisoner No. 77. Seventy-seven was Tadeusz Pietrzykowski, transferred to Neuengamme bei Hamburg on March 10, 1943. Since boxing commenced only later, Borowski, in repeating the story from hearsay, obviously confused the doublet. The story of the boxing match is also recorded in Polish in an unpublished manuscript, *Hyenas* by fire brigade member Edward Sokol who notes, "Zygmunt is characterised by a certain softness of moves, and that's why we call him 'Cat', which also reflects upon his rather individualistic character," pp. 482–84. Francis Ford Coppola's film, *Triumph of the Spirit*, released in January 1990, is also about boxing in Auschwitz, though not about Sigmund's fight.

Part II: 1967
Eight: Zygmunt

1   See David Matas, *Justice Delayed, Nazi War Criminals in Canada* (Toronto: Summerhill Press, 1987), pp. 12–13.

2   The first president of the Party was Fritz Thyssen, an original member of "Himmler's Circle," the one hundred top German industrialists who in 1938 financed the SS.

3   "Cardinal Puts Blame on Some Jews for Pogrom," *New York Times*, July 12, 1946, p. 1.

4   See Appendix Three for the text of the Cardinal's speech forbidding physical harm to the Jews but calling for a boycott that would in effect starve them.

5   See also, Danuta Czech, *Kalendarium der Ereignissen Konzentrationslager Auschwitz-Birkenau 1939–1945* (Reibeck bei Hamburg: Rowohlt, c. 1989), p. 834, quoting Lejzor Braun.

6   Jedrek Czurawski, No. 1948, was in camp under an assumed name. He eventually became a recluse, as did Zygmunt Pozniak, another old number who became deranged. Czurawski died in Toronto in 1973.

Nine: *Mamusia* and *Tatuś*

7   Himmler waffled between deporting Jews to Madagascar or concentrating them in Poland. Taking advantage of the situation, Heydrich established a thousand-square-kilometre 'autonomous Jewish reservation' extending southwards from Lublin into the heart of eastern Poland. In this 'Jewish state', Franz Walter Stahlecker chose Nisko into which to 'relocate' Jews from Austria and Czechoslovakia. *See* deportation order of Austrian Jews to Nisko, *Dokumentationsarchiv des österreichischen Widerstandes*, 2536; *see also*, Instructions for Jews leaving Moravia in Zosa Szajkowski, *An Illustrated Sourcebook on the Holocaust* (New York: Ktav, 1979), vol. II, item 335; original on file at World Jewish Congress (New York City).

8   At his 1961 trial in Jerusalem, Adolf Eichmann, head of Department VI of *R.S.H.A.*, claimed responsibility for personally having brought the first group from Čzechy A Morava. "That solution I envisaged as putting firm soil under their feet so that they would have a land of their own," he testified. Thus Nisko became the first concentration camp to which Jews from outside Poland were transported. As such, the Nisko operation provided the model for mass deportation and the prototype for Auschwitz. The Swedish government had exact reports on the Nisko project, but did nothing with them. So for the Nazis, Nisko also supplied the first convincing indication of world indifference. *See* later speech by Frank concerning Madagascar: T. Berenstein, A. Eisenbach, A. Rutkowski, eds., *Eksterminacja... "Extermination of Jews in the Polish Territories during the Period of the Nazi Occupation—Collections of Documents"* (Warsaw, 1957), pp. 51–52; Hans Lindberg, *Svensk flyktingspolitik under internationellt tryck, 1936-1941* (Stockholm, 1964), pp. 271–77; Walter Laquer, *The Terrible Secret: An Investigation into the Suppression of Information About Hitler's "Final Solution"* (London, 1980), pp. 48–50, 87.

9   "You are to build your own barracks, dig your own wells," the Jews were told. "In such a way you can prove yourselves." The Ostrava Jewish community was compelled to supply the materials.

10 Eventually, due to widespread cholera, dysentery and typhoid, which endangered the German troops, the SS' Nisko Project encountered problems with the occupation's civil authorities. In March 1940, many survivors were forced into Russia. In April, a few "flatfoot Indians," as Governor Frank liked to call the Jews, were returned home. Others were driven to death camps in Belzec and Trawniki. *See* Nora Levin, *The Holocaust* (New York: Schocken, 1978), p. 183. Those sent home to Nazi Czechoslovakia were later rearrested and perished either at Theresienstadt or Auschwitz. Frank recommitted himself to Catholicism after the war, confessing at Nuremberg: "The testimony I have heard in this courtroom has shaken me." Found guilty, he was hanged October 16, 1946.

11 For a complete history of Poland, refer to Norman Davies, *God's Playground, A History of Poland* (Oxford: University Press, 1991), 2 vols.

12 For a Jewish history of Poland, refer to Bernard D. Weinryb, *The Jews of Poland* (Philadelphia: JPS, 1973).

13 Nathan Nata Hannover, a contemporary chronicler, recorded in his *Yeveyn Metzulah*: "The pillar of justice ... the [elected leaders] of the Four Lands ... had authority to dispense justice to all Israel in the kingdom of Poland, to safeguard the law, to frame ordinances, and to inflict punishment as they saw fit."

14 A written account is recorded by Rabbi Pinchas Katzenellenbogen, a descendent of Saul Wahl. Preserved in Zevi Hirsch Edelman, *Gedullat Shaul* (London: 1854).

15 Documents dated 1589 attest that Saul was recognized as *servus regis* by Zygmunt III: We, King of Poland, being assured of the singular ardour and notable facility of Saul the Jew, do hereby bestow upon him a position as royal official. That he be assured of our approbation for him, we release him and his property for the remainder of his life from subjection to the authority of any Castellan or local judiciary, or any bench in our realm, of whatsoever type or standing it may be....

16 Saul is the ancestor of some of Europe's leading rabbis, of prominent Hasidic dynasties and of prominent personalities (Jews and non-Jews) in all walks of life. Some noted descendants are Helena Rubinstein, cosmetic queen; theologian Martin Buber; Karl Marx; the Rothschild financiers and philanthropists; Pulitzer Prize winner David Halberstam; Count Johannes, Prince Leopold and Prince Hubertus of the Bavarian court; Albert Edward Harry Mayer Archibald Primrose and Lord Neil Archibald Primrose, the sixth and seventh Earl of Roseberry, respectively. The genealogy of Saul Wahl is set forth in Neil Rosenstein, *The Unbroken Chain* (New York: Shengold, 1976).

17 Chaim Well of Calgary, Alberta still carries what is essentially the same patronymic, slightly anglicized. He is a direct descendant of Saul Wahl through some fifteen generations of rabbis.

18 To secure unity, Polish authorities had designed the Uniate Church in 1595 as a means to bring the Greek Orthodox to Roman authority while still permitting their Byzantine rites and Slavonic liturgy.

19 Nathan Nota Hannover, *Yeveyn Metzulah*, p. 33.

20 Major Kaminski was 'sentenced' in 1943 by the Polish underground army, and two weeks later was executed. Meanwhile, his son joined the SS, only to disappear after the war.

21 Governor Hans Frank had signed the authorization for the *A-B Aktion*, the *Ausserordentliche Befriedungs Aktion*, the extraordinary pacification action. About 10,000 were arrested, 3,000 of whom were immediately murdered. SS General Bruno Streckenbach executed the pre-emptive strike to protect the eastern flank while Germany attacked Holland and Belgium in the west.

22 In 1674, Wojciech Sobolewski, viscount in Drohobycz, voted for Jan III Sobieski, Poland's brilliant general. In short order, nine Sobolewskis sat in the *sejm* during his reign (1674–96). A certain Stefan Sobolewski was, in addition, an officer during Sobieski's gallant rescue of Vienna from the unprecedented Turkish thrust into central Europe.

23 During the reign of the next king, four Sobolewskis sat in the *sejm*. Stanisław Sobolewski served as official of the crown in Grodz. Later, in 1752, he was named Undersecretary of State in the Warsaw principality. All four of his sons held high positions of royal service.

24 During Poniatowski's reign six delegates in the *sejm* were Sobolewskis. If Sobolewskis weren't military officers, then they were religious functionaries like Casimir Sobolewski (died 1791), who was a Jesuit priest.

25 On his way to Russia, Napoleon, with lofty promises of equality, swept through this Prussian portion of dismembered Polish territory. The Polish cavalry joined the 'fight for freedom' loyally following Napoleon around Europe, distinguishing itself

particularly in Spain. Sigmund's granduncle Jan Sobolewski was mortally wounded in a Spanish battle. According to Sigmund's uncle Karol, Jan was reported to have said, "Children, that I must die is nothing; I'm happy there's a victory." Another granduncle was part of a regiment of Polish cavalry sent to Santo Domingo when France was fighting England over control of the Caribbean Sea. Today in Haiti and the Dominican Republic, one can still find several blacks with Polish names. Ignacy Sobolewski became Superintendent of Police in the huge but short-lived free Principality of Warsaw Napoleon recreated. Later he was appointed Minister of Justice, a position he held until 1830.

26 Poland's poet laureate, Adam Mickiewicz, mentions a Sobolewski in his *Dziady*, a drama of personal and national suffering describing the Poles who were, even before the insurrection, condemned and transferred to Siberia.

27 A Sobolewski rose in rank to general in the Polish army. He died nobly towards the end of the First World War. Apparently, the circumstances involved one of those family hurts that get closeted away and are not brought out.

28 Lagerkommandant, SS Hauptsturmführer Karl Fritzsch appeared on the U.S. war criminals list but disappeared in April 1945. Two graves with his name have been found, one bearing a date of death in 1945 and one in 1962.

Part III
Pull 1968–1992
Ten: Achtundachtzig

1 Emil Fackenheim, *The Jewish Return Into History* (New York: Schocken Books, 1978), p. 39. 31:1-30

2 Tiso, who signed the deportation orders for 82,000 Slovakian Jews, was hanged in April 1947. Recently the Catholic hierarchy of Slovakia has pressed the Vatican to declare Tiso a patron saint of Slovakia.

3 Mittelman's figures are echoed by Thomas Keneally, *Schindler's List* (New York: Simon and Schuster, 1993), p. 203.

4 Siegruth was caught hoarding the gold teeth of dead prisoners. For his financial indiscretions, he was sent July 28, 1941 to the Grafeneck "euthanasia centre" in the south of Germany, where carbon monoxide was utilized for killing German invalids and mentally sick. In 1941, no gas chambers functioned yet at Auschwitz. He is said to have committed suicide by hanging himself on the way.

5 The sadistic Roman was arrested early in 1943 for black-market activity. He died six weeks later in prison Block Eleven. Rumours had it that he was killed him with a pick.

6 Mietek Tukaj now resides in Gary, Indiana.

7 Bruno Brodniewicz, Kapo No. 1, was three times imprisoned in the Bunker, for speculation, for relations with German women, and for gold smuggling. Eventually transferred to Eintrachthütte, a small camp about sixty-five kilometres from Auschwitz, he was again appointed Lagerälteste. A few days after Bergen–Belsen was liberated, he was strangled by prisoners who tried him in a kangaroo court.

8 Medical imposter *SS Unterscharführer* Joseph Klehr, accused of ten thousand murders, was tried in 1965 in the third Auschwitz trial in Frankfurt. Judge Hoffmayer sentenced him to life imprisonment for 2,357 cases of murder, no parole for fifty years. Klehr was 61 at the time.

9 The accusation regarding Montini, later Pope Paul VI, has freguently surfaced from various sources; but absolute proof is difficult to sustain through available documents, and the Vatican has consistently disputed all connection.

10 Vincent A. Yzermans, ed. *The Universal Advocate: Public Addresses of His Holiness Pope Pius XII* (St. Cloud, Minn.: offset, 1954), pp. 144–157; *see also* Pierre Blet, Robert Graham, Angelo Martini and Burkhart Schneider, eds. *Actes et Documents du Saint Siège relatifs à la Seconde Guerre Mondiale*, vol. VII, "Le Saint Siège et la Guerre Mondiale, Novembre 1942–Décembre 1943" (Vatican City: Libreria Editrice Vaticana, 1973), pp. 161–167.

11 *See* John F. Morley, *Vatican Diplomacy and the Jews During the Holocaust* (New York: Ktav, 1980). For some of the documents in the Vatican reporting the destruction of European Jewry, *see:* Secrétaire d'État de Sa Sainteté, Pierre Blet, Robert Graham, Angelo Martini and Burkhart Schneider, eds. *Actes et Documents du Saint Siège relatifs à la Seconde Guerre Mondiale*, vol. III, "Le Saint Siège et la Situation Religieuse en Pologne et dans les Pays Baltes, 1939–1945" (Vatican City: Libreria Editrice Vaticana, 1967), pp. 625–628, 631, 633–636, 695–696, 713–717, 738; vol. VII, "Le Saint Siège et la Guerre Mondiale, Novembre 1942–Décembre 1943" (1973), pp. 179–180, 215–216; vol. XIII, "Le Saint Siège et la Victimes de la Guerre, Janvier 1941–Décembre 1942" (1974), pp. 78–79, 466, 534, 669–670, n. 4, 755–757.

12 Sikora survived and lives in Poland.

13 Later Aumeier became *Lagerkommandant* of Vaivara.

14 In his 1933 Advent sermons, Cardinal Faulhaber distinquished between biblical Jews who were the carriers of revelation and the Jews after Jesus who "have received the bill of divorce," and from that time forth are "restless wanderers over the face of the earth." Not everyone picked up on the distinction. When later some foreigners credited him with opposing Nazi antisemitism, he vehemently denied it. *See* Michael von Faulhaber, *Judaism, Christianity and Germany*, trans. by George Smith (New York: 1934), p. 5. Guenter Lewy, *The Catholic Church and Nazi Germany* (New York: McGraw-Hill, 1964), p. 276. Friedrich Heer, *God's First Love* (Worcester: Trinity Press, 1967), p. 324. Daniel Goldhagen brings evidence to show that his attitude was representative of the German Church at large, *Hitler's Willing Executioners* (New York: Knopf, 1996), pp. 109ff.

15 When the Russians attacked Vaivara where SS Hauptsturmführer Hans Aumeier had become commandant, he attempted escape in his pyjamas. Before the Polish court Aumeier declared that he was a "penitential offering for Germany." After being sentenced, he wrote a seven-page letter to the president of Poland begging that his death sentence be commuted, claiming how much he had helped Polish prisoners. In 1947, Aumeier was executed in Kraków along with Grabner, supervisor of the S.D.

Eleven: Simon

16 The major Christian theologians have had a lasting impact on subsequent history. As a means of Christian affirmation, Church father Eusebius stressed God's rejection of the Jewish people. Saint Chrysostom, the 'man of the golden mouth,' accused the Jews of every vice imaginable, arguing that contrary to God's will, Jews obey the Law even though it has been supplanted by Christianity, that Christians should not associate with Jews, that it is a Christian duty to hate Jews, and that Jews are fit for slaughter. Saint

Augustine maintained that the Jews deliberately misconstrue the Bible, that Jews descend not from Abraham but from Cain, and that it is divine will to preserve a remnant of the Jews alive in a degraded state as living witnesses to Christian truth. Justin Martyr proclaimed that as Cain, the Jews must be kept eternally landless. Saint Thomas declared that the Jews, as a result of their sin, are ordained for perpetual slavery and monarchs may therefore treat them as property, provided they are not deprived of every means of survival; the Saint also wanted all Jews to be identified by a badge. Martin Luther called for Jews to be deported and their synagogues burned. There are those who 'explain' that in the context of their day these saints did not mean their rhetoric to be acted upon. However, as Dr. Eugene Fisher of the Secretariat for Ecumenical and Interreligious Relations notes in private correspondence, "The words taken out of context and absolutized by later Christian writers were used to rationalize persecution of the Jews."

For other citations, see Rosemary Ruether, *Faith and Fratricide* (New York: Seabury, 1974). Reuther, frequently writing against Israel and Zionists, is no automatic defender of Jews. For some other Christian authors of this period writing similarly, see James Parkes, *Antisemitism* (Chicago: Quadrangle, 1963), Davies, *Anti-Semitism and the Christian Mind* (New York: Herder and Herder, 1969), A. Roy Eckardt, *Elder and Younger Brothers* (New York: Schocken, 1973), Edward H. Flannery, *The Anguish of the Jews* (New York: Macmillan, 1965).

17 In 1947, when the Holocaust was already on public record for several years, the Yugoslavian court sentenced Cardinal Stepinac to death for his war crimes. The same Pope Pius XII Pacelli, who never even threatened Hitler with excommunication, excommunicated the entire government of Yugoslavia, withdrawing recognition. As a result of the Church's stance against Yugoslavia's action on Stepinac, Marshall Tito commuted the convicted fascist's sentence to seventeen years imprisonment. Nor is this an isolated example. When the National Tribunal of Bratislava sentenced and hanged the Catholic priest Dr. Józef Tiso, leader of the fascist Hlinka party, the entire government of Czechoslovakia was excommunicated. At the same time, Vatican 'compassion' allegedly provided safe conduit for Nazis to escape to havens in South America. In 1994, Pope John Paul II prayed at the tomb of Cardinal Stepinac calling him a "vigilant and true pastor."

18 The World Council of Churches had issued a statement condemning antisemitism in 1948 in Amsterdam that said in part, "The churches in the past have helped to foster an image of the Jews as the sole enemies of Christ, which has contributed to anti-Semitism in the secular world. Anti-Semitism is sin against God and man."

19 The *Nostra Aetate* states: The Jews still remain most dear to God, He does not repent of the gifts He makes nor of the calls He issues. What happened in [Jesus'] passion cannot be blamed upon all the Jews then living, without distinction, nor upon the Jews of today. Although the Church is the new people of God, the Jews should not be presented as repudiated or cursed by God. We cannot in all truthfulness call upon that God who is the father of all if we refuse to act in a brotherly way toward certain men. Since this discussion, several local church bodies have issued statements and the Vatican has recognized Israel. In April of 1998, the Vatican released its much anticipated statement on the Holocaust. It fell on disappointed ears, and they themselves announced that this was but a first step toward formal acknowledgement in the future.

20 For a full study, see Walter M. Abbott, S.J., ed., *The Documents of Vatican II* (New York: Guild Press, 1966).

21 Chramiec contracted typhus and died on August 24, 1942 or was shot.

22 Artur Balke was released in 1943, rearrested in German occupied Greece and brought back to Auschwitz where he was again assigned his old No. 3. He died in 1969 in Hamburg.

23 Sigmund remembers that at the time of the fire in Kanada, SS Judge Konrad Morgen was conducting an investigation of SS officers. SS Untersturmführer Maximilian Grabner was sentenced to twelve years. There was talk. Fire brigade leader *SS Hauptscharführer* Georg Engelschall told the brigade, "It was arson, set to erase the traces of black-market smuggling."
After the war, Grabner, who had been head of the SS in Auschwitz, tried to claim before the Polish court that he had had "no power in the camp." Grabner was executed with Aumeier in Kraków in 1947.

24 Stanley R. Barrett, *Is God a Racist? The Right Wing in Canada* (Toronto: Univ. of Toronto Press, 1987), pp. 172–173, 246 *et al.; see also* Frank Chalk, ed., *The Review of Anti-Semitism in Canada 1983* (Toronto: League for Human Rights of B'nai Brith Canada, 1984), pp. 11–29.

25 Due to the cooperation of the large Dutch Nazi Party, out of 120,000 Dutch Jews, 110,000 perished.

26 Barrett, *Is*, p. 246.

27 Nuremberg International Military Trial Document, PS-3868, XXXIII, 275–276.

28 Yehudah Bauer, citing research by French historian Georges Wellers, himself an Auschwitz survivor, places the total at 1.6 million. Of these 1,350,000 were Jews (85 percent), 30,000 dying of maltreatment and the rest by gassing with Zyklon-B. The remainder were: 83,000 Poles (5 percent), 20,000 Gypsies (1.2 percent), 11,000 Russians (0.6 percent), and 140,000 others considered enemies of the Nazi regime. The inflated figures, according to the Hebrew University Professor Bauer, were a propaganda invention of Polish Communists designed to deny the Jewishness of the Holocaust. Rudolf Höss, *Kommandant im Auschwitz* (Stuttgart: Deutsche Verlags-Anstalt, 1958), pp. 160, 162–163.

29 Ernst Zundel mails anti-Holocaust literature in fourteen languages to 45,000 people in forty-five countries throughout the world. "Race," he is quoted by Stanley R. Barrett, *Is*, p. 158, as claiming, "has been the key to history, and only Hitler had the necessary vision to create a happy, sound society." To businessman Zundel, and others like him, denying the Holocaust can be seen as a useful tool, manipulated for the purpose of attacking Jews.

Twelve: Vladimir

30 See Marilyn McKinley, "Bad Blood in Fort Macleod," in *Alberta Report*, 28 February 1983; Bruce Masterman, "Tavern owner accuses RCMP of harassing native drinkers," *Calgary Herald*, 7 Feb. 1983, quoting the RCMP's response, "There's a lot of exaggeration."

31 Franciszek Piper, "Extermination," *Auschwitz* (Warsaw: Interpress, 1985), p. 115.

32 Piper, "Extermination," pp. 111–127.

33 Danuta Czech, "Konzentrationslager Auschwitz," *Auschwitz* (Warsaw: Interpress, 1985), pp. 29, 32–33; *see also* various reports by Charles R. Allen, Jr. who has written extensively on what he terms "corporativism and the Holocaust."

34 Sikorski perished 25 August 1942 of typhus.

35 Otto Küssel, a German prisoner born in Berlin, escaped with a Pole in 1943, leaving a note fingering *Lagerälteste* Bruno, whom he hated, for gold smuggling. He was rearrested a year later and returned to Auschwitz. He survived, suffering from depression and died in 1965.

36 *SS Oberscharführer* Otto Moll was in charge of this outdoor incineration of bodies. For his service, he received the Iron Cross with Oak Leaves, the distinguished military decoration otherwise bestowed only for bravery in the face of an enemy, and a promotion to camp commander of Gliwice. During the 1944 mass killing of Hungarian Jews, Höss transferred back to Auschwitz because of his gas chamber experience and cruelty. During his trial before the American Military Tribunal, *SS Oberscharführer* Otto Moll was accused of throwing Jewish children into the open fire pits. He was hanged on May 28, 1946.

37 Irving Greenberg, "Clouds of Smoke, Pillar of Fire: Judaism, Christianity, and Modernity after the Holocaust" in E. Fleischner, ed., *Auschwitz: Beginning of a New Era* (New York: Ktav, 1977), pp. 9ff.

38 The inventor of *Genickschuss, SS Hauptscharführer* Gerhard Arno Max Palitzsch boasted of personally executing thousands of Polish prisoners in three years. After his young wife died in the typhus epidemic of 1942, he was caught with a Latvian Jewess. He had apparently betrayed Höss's illicit love affair with a German prisoner, Eleonore Hodys. Palitzsch was arrested and imprisoned in the Bunker where he had previously reigned a semigod. Sentenced to imprisonment by the SS court, some say Palitzsch was shot by the Gestapo (Erich Kulka, *The Death Factory* 1966, p. 236) and some say he was demoted, sent to the front lines, and killed fighting the Russians near Budapest in December 1944.

Thirteen: Ramona

39 Between 1946 and 1960, five manuscripts were unearthed on the gas chamber grounds, buried in waterproof jars by Jews who risked a torturous death to witness to the outside world.

40 Morawa, the Kapo who was foreman in *Krematorium I*, was know to work for the *Politische Abteilung*. He was executed in Mauthausen one week prior to the end of the war.

41 Following Heinrich Himmler's capture by the British Army, he committed suicide.

42 See the last chapter for the results of these complaints.

43 Revelation 7:4–8; 141–5.

44 Other sponsors are Professor Martin Gilbert, London historian; Wojciech Buczynski, President, Polish Cultural Association; Dr. Edward Shaffer, Vancouver professor; Max Sharp, Vice-chairman, Four Seasons Hotels; Dr. Ivo Moravcik, Czechoslovak Arts & Society; Professor Bruce Elman, Dean, Faculty of Law, University of Alberta; Hermann Langbein, Vienna speaker and writer; Dr. Carlos Rizowy, Chicago attorney; Franklin Biolystock, Holocaust Remembrance Centre; Dr. Frank Laurence, Cincinnati historian; Nathan Leipciger, National Holocaust Committee, Canadian Jewish Congress; Barry Slawsky, Publisher, *Edmonton Jewish News*; Father Władek Karciarz, Holy Rosary Polish Catholic Church, Edmonton; Tony Kryzanowski, Edmonton publisher and journalist; Bill and Rhyl Stollery, Project Ploughshares, Edmonton;

Roman Freund, Vällingby, Sweden; Father Gerard Gauthier, Barrhead Catholic Church; M. Strzelecki, Past President Polish Congress, Edmonton; Lawrence Decore, Liberal Party Leader, Edmonton; Mel Hurtig, Hurtig Publishing, Edmonton; Ray Martin, New Democratic Party, Edmonton.

45 Number one on the Polish hit parade, 1936, sung by the "Polish Sinatra," Mieczysław Fogg.

46 Dr. Friedrich Entress was transferred to Flossenbürg in 1943. In 1947 he was condemned to death by an American tribunal and hanged.

Fourteen: Sigmund S.

47 The Fourth Lateran Council (1215) decreed that Jews must wear distinctive clothing to avoid errors in sexual intercourse. The rule was reinforced by Pope Honorius III throughout Christian Europe and remained in force with variations for centuries, often becoming a yellow 'badge of shame.' In 1267 the Synod of Vienna prohibited Christians from attending Jewish ceremonies, and Jews were not permitted to express their views about the tenets of Catholicism. In the same year, the Synod of Breslau created compulsory ghettoes. In 1279 the Synod of Ofen prohibited Jews from buying or renting from Christians. In 1320 the Synod of Mainz defined Judaism as a heresy. The lands that now comprise Germany became the home of the blood accusation, charges of ritual murder and, in 1243, the Host desecration.

48 During the fifteenth century, a full one-fifth of the entire revenue of the major German towns was disproportionately taxed to a small minority of Jews.

49 Both Saxony and the Landgrave Philip of Hesse, in his *Judenordnung*, actually heeded the call.

50 To Kant, Judaism was a relic of a bygone epoch that had grown outmoded—an assertion that Kant endowed to German thought.

51 In one example in 1942, Frederick Blair, Canadian Director of Immigration, refused admission to 6,500 homeless Jewish children over the interpretation of 'family unit.'

52 *See* Appendix Two.

53 The exposition of the intellectual origins of Nazism, here and in Appendix Two, is heavily indebted to George L. Mosse, *The Crisis of German Ideology* (New York: Grosset and Dunlap, 1964). *See also*, the ground-breaking work, Peter Viereck, *Meta-politics, the Roots of the Nazi Mind* (New York: Capricorn, 1965), upon which Mosse is, in turn, dependent.

54 Just how willing the masses were has recently been documented in Daniel Goldhagen, *Hitler's Willing Executioners* (New York: Knopf, 1996).

55 Telegram dated 28 Nov. 1938, addressed to Hitler by the *Landesbischof* Wiedemann.

56 Barrett, *Is*, p. 173.

57 The final report of the Alberta Human Rights Commission, Board of Inquiry re: complaints under s. 2 of the Individual's Rights Protection Act between Harvey Kane, *et. al.*, complainants, and Church of Jesus Christ Christian–Aryan Nations, *et. al.*, respondents, 1992.

58 Max Küserow proved himself cruel and depraved. Appointed Kapo of the penal battalion and later *Lagerälteste* of the *Zigeunerlager* in Birkenau, he surrounded himself with Gypsy girls. He was eventually posted to the army.

Fifteen: Emilio

59 This and the following talk-show scenes are abstracted from Sigmund's appearances on CBC *National Open House,* CBC *Wild Rose Forum* out of Edmonton, CBC *As It Happens,* CBC *Cross Country Checkup* and others.

60 Rev. Joseph F. Mytych, ed. *Pope John Paul II, Pilgrim Among Us* (Chicago: Catholic League for Religious Assistance to Poland, 1980), page referring to Oct. 5, 1979, 8:00 a.m.

61 Himmler called for the extinction of the Jews followed by the disappearance of the Ukrainians, Gorals and Lemcos, and then said, "Whatever is said concerning these splinter peoples applies on a correspondingly larger scale to the Poles." (From a Himmler letter to Hitler May 25, 1940, Nuremberg International Military Trial Document, NO-1880.) On another occasion, he said, "All Poles will disappear from the world.... It is essential that the great German people should consider it as its major task to destroy all Poles." Himmler as quoted in Karol Pospieszalski, *Polska pod Niemieckim Prawem* (Poznan Wydawnictwo Instytutu Zachodniego, 1946), p. 189.

62 Alfred Rosenberg's well-known book was a German best seller, over one million copies sold. Unrepentant to the end, the propagandist was hanged by sentence of the International Military Tribunal in 1946.

63 In 1656, the Black Madonna, Our Lady the Blessed Virgin of Czestochowa, as she is known, a bejewelled icon dating back to at least the year 500, aided King John Casimir and delivered Poland from invading Swedish forces.
She has been parcelling out miracles to us ever since, thereby positioning the Polish Catholic Church in a role something akin to the monarchy of Great Britain.

64 In a later statement, Glemp expressed regret over "misunderstandings" with the Jewish community and appeared to retract the statements he had made two years earlier. Still later, Glemp rejected the idea that the Jewish activists "did not intend to kill the sisters or destroy the convent." He has, in yet another reversal, called antisemitism "evil and contrary to the spirit of the Gospel."

65 Dr. Władisław Dering, Polish prisoner doctor, was released early from Auschwitz as a reward for his collaboration. He then went to work in Clauberg's clinic. After the war, he fled to England and spent several years in Sudan as a physician. In the '60s, Dering initiated a libel suit against Leon Uris, who wrote in *Exodus* that the doctor had performed 17,000 sterilizations without anaesthetic. Technically, Dering won the suit as the figure 17,000 turned out to be inflated, but he lost the case, being awarded one ha'penny, due to the damning evidence presented against him. The case is fictionalized in a subsequent novel by Uris, *QB VII.*

66 Władysław Bartoszęwski, *The Convent at Auschwitz* (New York: George Braziller, 1990), pp. 141–142.

Sixteen: Ramona

67 Józef Hulanicki is now a professor at the University of Melbourne in Australia.

68 Letter from Clauberg to Himmler, June 7, 1943 (NO–212), *Nuremberg Medical Case,* vol. I, pp. 730–732.

69 Dr. Josef Mengele escaped through Rome to South America where he found sanctuary. Mengele was never tried. Controversy surrounds his current status. Some say he is still

alive. Most say he died a natural death. On June 7, 1985 a body was found in a Brazilian cemetery which experts identified as that of Mengele "within a reasonable scientific certainty."

70 Among other magazines, Sigmund's work is picked up and reported in "Response, the Wiesenthal Center World Report," Fall 1991, vol. 12, no. 3, pp. 10-11.

71 As for other descendants of Saul Wahl, hundreds were caught in the maelstrom.

72 Baron Gustav Krupp, munitions industrialist, chairman of the board of IG Farben, was deemed too sick for trial. He died January 16, 1950. The Nuremberg court was asked to try his son, Alfried, who had taken over sole ownership in 1943, and though denied, Alfried was tried before an American military tribunal and sentenced to twelve years' imprisonment and confiscation of all his property. He was released in a general amnesty two years later, the confiscation of his corporate property was annulled, personal property worth $10 million was restored to him, and his company was granted new industries by the Bonn government.

73 Jurek still lives in Ontario. He says he will take all the secrets of Auschwitz' nocturnal politics and murders with him to the grave.

74 Zończyk, having been assigned to the kitchen, survived. He owned a plastic factory in Łódź, and ran a travel agency in New York, where, in 1958, Sigmund visited him with Iris. He subsequently sold the factory, moved to Palo Alto. After Auschwitz, he lost his faith. On 16 April 1993, Zończyk wrote to Sigmund. Sigmund had sent him copies of some of his flyers. It is the old story. Zończyk does not understand why Sigmund "speaks in the name of 'Canadian' Jews," and he is not going to "start an argument" with Sigmund, but "was it the Carmelite nuns who stuffed Jews into the crematorium ovens? ... Do not mail to me anymore your leaflets nor your publications.... Your world stopped in 1945."

Seventeen: Simon, Emilio, Vladimir

75 Irka returned to Poland in 1947 where she found her house destroyed and her immediate relatives gone, lost in the Warsaw uprising. She married a Polish Army colonel, was widowed with one son. Irka died on January 27, 1992, the anniversary of the liberation of Auschwitz. Every six months or so Sigmund receives a letter from her son.

76 *For example*, Heinrich Himmler, Oct. 4, 1943, Nuremberg International Military Trial Document, PS-1919, XXIX, 145–146.

77 In the same trial as Joseph Klehr, *SS Unterscharführer* Oswald Kaduk was sentenced to life. He defended his actions by claiming selective application of the law: The big shots get off, while he, a lowly NCO just doing his duty, is tried. But there were too many witnesses against him.

78 Tamborski, a German citizen of Polish extraction and leader of Fire Brigade One, died in Poland in 1960.

79 Sports fanatic *SS Oberscharführer* Wilhelm Claussen was arrested in 1946 and extradited to Poland. He co-operated with the U.S. military, providing information against Höss, Aumeier, and others. He died mysteriously in a Polish Prison in 1947. Ironically, his brother died as a prisoner in Sachsenhausen.

80 *SS Hauptscharführer* Georg Engelschall, fire brigade commander, was sentenced to two-and-a-half years by a U.S. military tribunal in 1949. He died in 1969 as a result of an industrial accident in Munich. *See also*, Sokol, *Hyenas*, pp. 494-505.

81 Of the thousands employed in the *Sonderkommando* in Auschwitz, only a handful survived the war. Abram and Szlama Dragon, two brothers, escaped from the death march near Pszczyna about twenty-five kilometres from Auschwitz. Both were witnesses during the trial of Rudolf Höss. Alter Feinsilber (in camp under the name of Jankowski) escaped from the evacuation near Rybnik, about thirty kilometres from Auschwitz. Henryk Tauber was another. Then there were Phillip Muller and Miklos Nyiszli, a doctor who worked with Mengele in the mortuary of *Krematorium III*, who both published their stories: *Auschwitz Inferno* and *Auschwitz, a Doctor's Eyewitness Account*, respectively.

82 All this according to Dr. M. K. Nyiszli. The SS version was three Nazis killed, twelve wounded. The real figure is probably somewhere between. Dr. M. K. Nyiszli, *The Auschwitz Inferno* (New York: Fawcett, 1960), pp. 124–125, written in 1946.

83 Nyiszli reports a total of 853 members of the *Sonderkommando* lost their lives. Approximately a hundred fifty escaped; they recaptured all but twelve. Nyiszli reports these, two were recaptured. Only three survived the war and testified.

84 The women in the powder magazine smuggled out the explosive, a spoonful at a time, concealing it in a shred of torn cloth somewhere in their clothing. If it looked like a search were coming, they would untie the rag and let the powder trickle out through a hole previously made. It required months of careful planning and execution to garner but a small amount. Others would then relay the powder to Rosa who would hide it in the *Sonderkommando's* laundry carts. A Russian prisoner named Borodin converted the explosives to bombs employing empty sardine cans as casings. The *Sonderkommando* then cached them for future use. The fingered women were arrested and brutally tortured. They revealed no other names.

85 On the fiftieth anniversary, a memorial plaque was finally erected (October 7, 1995).

86 There were a few escapes, one notable one in 1942 by the *Strafkompanie* digging the irrigation canal, one in January 1944 by members of a previous *Sonderkommando*. And some sporadic killings occurred on the Ramp: A Gypsy woman killed an SS man. Some Jewish women, who came out from Ravensbrück, realized on the Ramp they had been betrayed. One seized the revolver of an SS officer (some say he fondled her naked body). She killed *SS Scharführer* Schillinger and wounded *SS Unterscharführer* Emmerich.

87 The National State Platform of the Church, entered into evidence at the Inquiry, includes the following:
Article [iii] All hybrids called Jews are to be repatriated from the Republic's territory, all their wealth be redistributed to restore our people, and it shall be a capital offense to advocate or promote Jew Talmudic anti-Christ Communism in any manner or any other crimes against nature.
Article [iv] All Talmudism [sic] (Judaism), devil and heathen religions and practices end immediately, and there be an encouragement of the expansion of TRUE POSITIVE CHRISTIANITY.
The Official Religious Platform of the Church includes:

1. We believe the Bible is the true word of God (Yahweh) written for and about a specific people. The bible is the family history of the White Race, the children of Yahweh placed on earth through the seedline [sic] of Adam. Genesis 5:1.
2. Not all races descend from Adam. Adam is the father of the White Race only....
4. We believe that there are literal children of Satan in the world today....

5. We believe that the Canaanite Jew is the natural enemy of our Aryan (White) Race. This is attested by scripture and by all secular history. The Jew is like a destroying virus that attacks our racial body to destroy our Aryan culture and the purity of our Race. Those of our Race who resist these attacks are called 'chosen and faithful'. [sic] John 8:44; I Thessalonians 2:15; Revelations 17:14.

6. We believe that there is a battle being fought this day between the children of darkness (today known as Jews) and the children of light (Yahweh, The Everliving [sic] God), the Aryan Race, the true Israel of the Bible. Revelations 12:10–11.

7. We know that man (Adam) was given the command to have dominion over the earth and subdue it, but that, in great part, our Race has been deceived into rejecting this Divine order....

9. Our Race, within itself, holds divine power....

88 The final report of the Alberta Human Rights Commission, pp. 108-111.

89 In February 1996, the Supreme Court of Canada found against Keegstra. It went back to the lower court for sentencing. The court fined him $3,000, which he paid immediately.

Part IV
1992-1995
Eighteen: Enter the Reporter

1 J. Wróblewski, museum director, stated on March 9, 1994 to International Auschwitz Council that no such plans existed. But see local city council minutes October, 1993 and April, 1994; and local newspaper accounts of the monument from November, 1993 and January and February, 1994.

2 After public exposure, the non-existent deal was 'cancelled'. It now seems to be on again.

3 In 1996, Sigmund was at the centre of a new controversy. Janus Marszalek, Polish developer accused of being leader of the Society for the Victims of War, started construction on a shopping centre within the 1979 United Nations established buffer zone surrounding Auschwitz, less than thirty metres from the main gate. Wróblewski claimed that the International Auschwitz Council had approved construction; Bartoszewski denied it. The federal government halted construction; the developer vowed to continue anyway. A hastily called meeting of the International Auschwitz Council took place April 30. Most foreign Jewish members were conspicuous by their absence, and Sigmund was told he would not be permitted to enter because he is anti-Polish. Those present concluded Wróblewski had done nothing wrong. Sigmund called for a complete review of Wróblewski's stewardship over the museum. In July 1998, the Polish government officially halted development of the shopping centre project.

4 Sigmund's cousin, Adam Fleszar, wrote one letter home to his wife from Kozielsk, then silence. In 1943 the German Red Cross published a partial list of Polish officers executed in the Katyn forest. His name was there along with that of Army Chaplain Baruch Steinberg, a direct issue of Saul Wahl.

5 At the end of the war, SS Sturmbannführer Rudolf Höss was found hiding under the name of Franz Lang in the British occupation zone. He was extradited to Poland, sentenced to death on April 2, 1947 by a Polish court and executed at a site close to the office from which he had governed the camp.

6 A plaque has recently been imbedded on Block Fifteen honouring the Armia Krajowa.

Sigmund complains, "Besides for having little to do with Auschwitz, some units murdered Jews even after war."

7 Władysław Bartoszęwski, *The Convent at Auschwitz* (New York: George Braziller, 1990), p. 158. In March 1995, Bartoszęwski was appointed foreign minister; then when the government changed again, his resignation was accepted. After repeated representations, the booklets have been corrected and a plaque has been installed on Block Ten stating that Dr. Clauberg experimented on Jewish women. Also, the national blocks have been replaced with other exhibits. With the bus, Birkenau has been designated part of the official camp inspection route. The plaque at the International Monument in Birkenau has been replaced, a memorial to the Jewish revolt has been erected at Crematorium IV, and thirty-two markers in the form of Jewish cemetery memorials have been placed along the Ramp and at other locations. In February 1996, museum director Wróblewski was again in the news over plans to commercialize on the 500,000 annual visitors by building a huge shopping mall directly facing Auschwitz, on the spot where thousands of slave labourers were abused and beaten. On the other hand, as of September 1998, Jews murdered at the bunker and gravel pit in the convent garden remain unrecognized, and the Jewish story is still difficult to discern from the museum presentation: The *Sonderkommando* plaque is still not placed. The Jewish exposition in the Sauna building is still "under construction." There are no signs marking the Jews murdered in Block 11 or where Jews were starved to death in Block 13. Crosses proliferate. The SS Commander's building in Birkenau is still a Roman Catholic Church.

8 When the movie appeared in 1994, Sigmund arranged to have 485 rural grade twelve students view it at reduced cost. Two Roman Catholic school boards dropped out at the last minute. Both the historical import of the movie as well as the moral lesson that even a single, imperfect individual can rise to the occasion and act conscientiously, saving hundreds of Jewish lives, were, to the superintendents making the decision, less important than the fact that Schindler was guilty of marital indiscretion.

9 Michael Wyschogrod, "Some Theological Reflections on the Holocaust," in Steinitz and Szonyi, eds., *Living After the Holocaust* (New York: Bloch, 1975), p. 68.

10 Ota Kraus and Erich Kulka, *The Death Factory* (1966 edition), p. 103.

11 Robert Lifton, *The Nazi Doctors* (New York: Basic, 1986), p. 270.

12 Kraus and Kulka, *The Death Factory*, pp. 91f.

13 Seweryna Szmaglewska, *Smoke Over Birkenau* (New York: Henry Holt, 1947), p. 308.

14 Danuta Czech, "Role of the Men's Hospital Camp at KL Auschwitz II," in *From the History of KL Auschwitz* (Kraków: Państwowe Muzeum W Oświęcimie, translated from an earlier Polish version 1976), II, p. 80.

15 Raul Hilberg, *The Destruction of European Jews* (New York: New Viewpoints, 1973), pp. 605–606. *See also* Philippe Aziz, *Doctors of Death* (Geneva: Ferni, 1976), vol. 2, p. 160.

16 Munich's *Süddeutsche Zeitung* after Clauberg was released from Soviet concentration camp 11 October 1955. *See, New York Times*, Oct. 18, 1955.

17 Anton Gill, *The Journey Back From Hell* (London: Grafton, 1988), p. 375.

18 Józef Garlinski, *Fighting Auschwitz* (London: Julian Friedmann, 1975). In other respects, his book is controversial as Garlinski portrays Dr. Dering as a hero of the camp underground.

19 A. Chomet and J. Cornillo, eds., *Tarnów—Sefer Zikkaron* (Tel Aviv: Arzi, 1968), II, pp. 159–160.

20 Chomet and Cornillo, pp. 159-160. *See also* Martin Gilbert, *The Holocaust* (New York: Holt, Rinehart & Winston, 1985) pp. 121–22; *The Macmillan Atlas of the Holocaust* (New York: Da Capo, 1982), p. 46; and Stefan Krakowski, "Tarnow," *Encyclopedia Judaica* (Jerusalem: Keter, 1971), XV, col. 821. The official surviving list of the first transport now preserved in the Auschwitz Museum contains but one ascertainable Jew, a Polish sounding name (Dr. Prof. Zdzisław Simha, No. 452, an assimilated Jewish demographer from Tarnów who perished in 1941). However, ninety-nine unnamed blanks can be counted. To fill in the blanks, Eugeniusz Niedojadło, No. 213 researched and compiled a private supplement of sixty-three names. This is the same Niedojadło who stopped writing to Sigmund after he visited Poland with Rabbi Mann. He attempts to fill in some of these "unknowns." It includes several Jewish sounding names: Baron, Bloch, Abraham Eimer, Klein, Naftali Sack, Emil Simche, and the Rosenbusch corroborated above. No surviving Jews from the first transport remained for Niedojadło to interview for additional names. And since, as in the rest of Poland, Auschwitz Jews constituted a community unto themselves, it is likely that the bulk of the thirty-three remaining unidentified prisoners were also Jewish.

21 Hermann Langbein, *The Nazi Concentration Camps* (Jerusalem: Yad Vashem, 1980), p. 275.

22 Langbein, p. 278.

23 APMO. Materiały obozowego Ruschu Oporu (Materials of the Camp Resistance Movement), t. VII, k. 464.

24 *Das Schwarze Korps,* No. 47, Nov. 24, 1938.

25 N. Baynes, ed., *The Speeches of Adolf Hitler* (London, 1942), vol. I, pp. 737–741.

26 Nuremberg International Military Trial Document, PS-3363.

27 Berenstein, Eisenbach, Rutkowski, eds., *Eksterminacja Zydow na ziemiach polskich w okresie okupacji hitlerowskiej—zbior dokumentow* (Warsaw, 1957), pp. 55–56.

28 Nuremberg International Military Trial Document, PS-710.

29 Nuremberg International Military Trial Documents, NG-2586-G.

30 Jean-Claude Pressac, *The Crematoria of Auschwitz: The Machinery of Mass Murder* (France, National Centre for Scientific Research, 1993).

31 Gill, p. 341.

32 Gill, p. 347.

33 Gill, p. 72.

34 Tadeusz Borowski, *This Way for the Gas, Ladies and Gentleman* (Dallas, Pa.: Penguin, 1986), pp. 112–122.

35 Bruno Baum takes up this very question in a book which otherwise attempts to glorify the resistance movement, *Wiederstand in Auschwitz* (Berlin: Kongress-Verlag), pp. 93–96.

36 Leni Yahil, *The Holocaust* (New York: Oxford Univ. Press, 1987), p. 451. Barnet Litvinoff, *The Burning Bush* (New York: E. P. Dutton, 1988), p. 361, writes: "[Theresienstadt] was the solitary place in the Nazi kingdom of death allowed to receive a visit from the Red Cross." Others write similarly.

37 Martin Gilbert, *Auschwitz & The Allies* (New York: Hold, Rinehart, and Winston, 1981), p. 294. *See also* note 1.

38 ICRC, *The Work of the ICRC* (Geneva: ICRC, 1975), pp. 76–77.

39 Reports of the massacre of individual Jewish communities appeared almost immed-iately in 1939 (*New York Times,* Sep. 13, 1939, p. 11; Sep. 22, p. 1; Oct. 12, p. 56; *et al.*). By January 24, 1940, the *New York Times* editorialized about the absolute authenticity of the reports. On the same day, Congressman Samuel Dickstein read into the House record eleven bulletins recounting numerous atrocities. On January 27, the *Nation* featured eye-witness accounts from a German newspaper (*Nation,* Jan. 27, 1940). The *New Republic* picked up the issue August 7 and September 12. On January 9, 1941 the *New York Times* front paged the State Department's refusal to admit thousands of refugees. As the Nazi attack on Russia proceeded, a handful of Jews escaped, taking messages with them. A thousand herded into a synagogue here, another thousand lined up by a ditch there—the work of the *Wehrmacht's Einsatzgruppen.* A series in *Life* magazine February 23, 1942 provided pictorial corroboration of the reports. The use of poison was described in March, 1942. This was substantiated by the Dutch government in exile, and, on June 8, by an American diplomat. *See also: New Republic,* July 8, 1940, p. 45; Dec. 9, p. 772; cf. *New York Times,* Mar. 8, 1940, p. 6; July 1, p. 4; July 3, p. 1; July 4, p. 5; July 6, p. 4; July 7, p. 1; July 10, p. 6.

40 Gerhard Engel, *Heeresadjutant bei Hitler 1938–1943,* ed. Hildegard von Kotze (Stuttgart: 1974), p. 42.

41 Meir Dworzecki, "The International Red Cross and its Policy Vis-à-vis the Jews in Ghettos and Concentration Camps" in *Rescue Attempts During the Holocaust* (Yad Vashem: Jerusalem, 1977). Two days later, the Federal Council of Churches of Christ in America and the Church Peace Union sent condolences to the Synagogue Council of America. The 12th of August was set aside as a national day of fasting and prayer. Similar protests followed in Boston, Cleveland, Los Angeles and St. Paul.

42 *See* Morley, *Vatican Diplomacy* (New York: Ktav, 1980), p. 114; Saul Friedländer, *Kurt Gerstein—The Ambiguity of Good* (New York: Alfred Knopf, 1969), pp. 128–129, 136. The nuncio's own remarks in July 1942 had mentioned rumours of mass killing of "non-Aryans wearing the distinctive star." Secrétaire d'État de Sa Sainteté, Blet, Graham, Martini and Schneider, eds. *Actes,* vol. VIII, "Le Saint Siège et les Victimes de la Guerre, Janvier 1941–Décembre 1942" (Vatican City: Libraria Editrice Vaticana, 1974), pp. 607–608. Subsequent documents in the Vatican Secretariat of State mention the *cameroni, dove finirebbe sotto l'azione di gas* (chambers where they are finished off with gas), vol. IX, "Le Saint Siège et les Victimes de la Guerre, Janvier–Décembre 1943" (1975), p. 274; *et. al.*

43 Jan Ciechanowski, *Defeat in Victory* (Garden City, N.Y., 1947), p. 182.

44 U.S. National Archives 740.00116 European War 1939/726.

45 For a complete discussion, *see* Alex Grobman, "What Did They Know?" in *American Jewish History,* Mar. 1979, vol. 68, no. 3, pp. 327–352.

46 ICRC, *The Work,* pp. 76–77.

47 David S. Wyman, *America and the Holocaust* (New York: Garland Publ., 1990) vol. 12, p. v.

48 Julius Epstein, *Operation Keelhaul* (Old Greenwich: Devin-Adair Co, 1973); Mark Elliott, *Pawns of Yalta* (Urbana: Univ of Illinois, 1982).

49 Nikolai Tolstoy, *Victims of Yalta* (London: Hodden & Stoughton, 1977), pp. 139–141.

50 W. Niederland, "The Problem of the Survivor," *Journal of the Hillside Hospital,* X

(1961), pp. 222–247. Erica Wanderman, "Children and Families of Holocaust Survivors: A Psychological Overview" in Steinitz and Szonyi, *Living After the Holocaust* (New York: Block, 1976), pp. 115–123.

51 H. Klein, "Families of Survivors in the Kibbutz: Psychological Studies" in H. Krystal and W. Niederland, eds., *Psychic Traumatization* (Boston: Little Brown, 1971), pp. 67–92. W. Koenig, "Chronic or Persisting Identity Diffusion," *American Journal of Psychiatry*, CXX (1964), pp. 1081–1084.

52 Niederland, *"The Problem,"* pp. 222–247. J. Kestenberg, "Psychoanalytic Contributions to the Problem of Children of Survivors from Nazi Persecution," *The Israel Annals of Psychiatry and Related Disciplines*, X, No. 4 (1972), pp. 311–325.

53 Steinitz, *Living*, pp. 35–36.

54 Eva Fogelman, "The Psychology Behind Being a Hidden Child," in Marks, *The Hidden Children* (New York: Fawcett, 1993), pp. 292–307.

55 Klein, "Families," pp. 67–92.

56 B. Trossman, "Adolescent Children of Concentration Camp Survivors," *Canada Psychiatric Association Journal*, XIII (1968), pp. 1221–1223.

57 H. Barocas, and C. Barocas, "Manifestations of Concentration Camp Effects on the Second Generation," *American Journal of Psychiatry*, CXXX, No. 7 (1973), pp. 821ff.

58 J. Sigel, and V. Rakoff, "Concentration Camp Survival: A Pilot Study of Effects on the Second Generation," *Canada's Mental Health*, XIV (1967), pp. 24–26. J. Sigel, *et. al.,* "Some Second-Generational Effects of Survival of the Nazi Persecution," *American Journal of Orthopsychiatry*, XLIII, no. 3 (1973), pp. 320–327.

59 Wanderman, "Children," pp. 121–122.

60 See examples in Steinitz, *Living*, pp. 43–53.

61 Trossman, "Adolescent," pp. 1221–1223. Barocas, "Manifestations," pp. 821ff.

62 Sigal and Rakoff, "Concentration," pp. 24–26.

63 Klein, "Families," pp. 67–92

Appendix One

SS Ranks and their Approximate Equivalent

SS Mann	Private
SS Sturmmann	Lance-corporal
SS Rottenführer	Senior lance-corporal
SS Unterscharführer	Corporal
SS Scharführer	Junior sergeant
SS Oberscharführer	Sergeant
SS Hauptscharführer	Sergeant-major
SS Stabsscharführer	Staff sergeant-major
SS Untersturmführer	Second-lieutenant
SS Obersturmführer	Lieutenant
SS Hauptsturmführer	Captain
SS Sturmbannführer	Major
SS Obersturmbannführer	Lieutenant-colonel
SS Standartenführer	Colonel
SS Oberführer	Brigadier-general
SS Brigadenführer	Major-general
SS Grupenführer	Lieutenant-general
SS Obergrupenführer	General
SS Oberstgrupenführer	Colonel-general
Reichsführer SS und Chef der Deutschen Polizei *(Himmler's personal title as head of the SS)*	(No equivalent)

Appendix Two

The Extent of Pre-Hitler Neo-Romanticism

Germans rejected the French concepts of *liberté, egalité, fraternité* that had been introduced at the business end of Napoleonic muskets. In reaction to French Enlightenment thinking, a distinctly German neo-Romanticism saw each race or *Volk* as determined by its origins. Romantic thinking regarded the Jew as an alien in the land of the Germanic peoples. Theorists claimed the longed-for German *Völkisch* society was like a tree, the hated Jew like a snake at its roots. Long before Versailles, neo-Romantic intellectualization produced more than one hundred thousand tomes—encompassing every field—devoted to Jew-hatred as a healthy palliative for western Christian civilization.

Culture: In the 1800's a weak German confederation appeared. Those who longed instead for German unity looked to culture as a means to enhance German identification, defined in contrast to Semites. Since the nature of the individual soul derives from one's national landscape, the Germans, dwelling in the shadowy mist-shrouded forests, are deep, mysterious and profound; whereas the Jews, being a desert people, are shallow, arid, dry, and spiritually barren. Rootedness denotes fellowship in the *Volk*, which alone renders the human being human. Rootlessness, the Jewish experience, dooms the total person.

Education: The search for social patterns conforming to Germanic longing (i.e., non-Jewish) already led Father Jahn's youth movement, in 1817, to incinerate 'foreign books' corrupting the authentic culture of the *Volk*, of which concept Father Jahn was the inventor. By 1890, all fraternities had declared themselves *Judenrein*. In many of the universities, quota systems were instituted. Jewish faculty were barred. What Jewish students there were, became 'standers' so they would not have to sit in the Jew seats assigned to them.

Faith: Völkisch beliefs were enlarged into a Germanic faith contrasting with the Jewish one. Academics such as Paul de Lagarde (1827–91), and his younger contemporary Julius Langbehn (1851–1907) condemned St. Paul the Jew. It was he who bound pristine Christianity to barren Hebrew legislation, thus suppressing those vital features most authentic to the belief in Jesus Christ. Study of the Christian Bible reveals the Jews to be the arch-fiends of history, from which only a Church purged of Jewish origins by a German Awakening can save.

Classics: Neo-Romantic doctrine added a frame of reference based on an idealized classic Germany that *never* included Jews. Novelist Ernst Wachler identified contemporary Germans with the early Gothic tribes. The ancient swastika linked modernity and antiquity, and enmity between Germans and Jews was portrayed as time-honoured and abiding. Writer Ellegard Ellerbeck proclaimed: "Do you know that you are gods!" To him, Jews prevent the Aryans from assuming their godlike stature and thus have to be eradicated. The art of Fidus pictured nude Aryan youth striding into the sun's rays or ready to fly.

Experimental communities: Just as utopian-minded socialists sought to place socialist islands in a capitalistic sea, so too *Völkisch* thinkers attempted to establish Germanic utopias that excluded Jews. These settlements emphasized return to the land; glorification of an older, nobler peasant economy; racial purity; the ancient Aryan unity between God and the world; body culture; and hatred of foreign labour and traits. Where full agricultural settlements proved impractical, rural boarding schools with similar goals were established. "The Aryan race will prosper only amid the culture of the countryside," Adolph Lanz (1908).

Science: A social Darwinism fostered the idea that human society is an evolving biological organism that can be contaminated by foreign; i.e., Jewish, admixture. The science of anthropology augmented the notion of race with a person's physical structure, and then with worth. The science of philology, based upon the work of Friedrich Max Müller (1823–1900) extended the same through language. One can discern the inner superiority of the Aryan in his very looks and in the tongue which exemplifies his psyche.

Eugenics: There emerged the idea of racial hygiene to purify society. In the words of Ludwig Woltmann, "the Germanic race has been selected to dominate the Earth." There is an absolute duty to breed the fittest, and, correspondingly, to exterminate those unfit. George von Schönerer (1842–1921) excluded conversion as a cure for the Jews, "You cannot resign from your race." To Houston Chamberlain (1855–1927), son-in-law of Wagner, all regressive tendencies stem from the Jew, who as the only other pure race, is locked in mortal combat with the German saviour race. The Jew's very existence, therefore, is a crime against humanity.

Political theory: The dream for an all-German ethos fuelled a political theory opposing civil rights for Jewish 'aliens.' Richard Wagner (1813–83), the composer, wrote: "An innermost aversion against the Jewish nature—not against the religion—is the unconscious feeling of the German people." The philosopher Heinrich von Treitschke (1834–96) justified antisemitic campaigns as a "brutal but natural reaction of German national feeling against a foreign element." He praised the "instinct of the masses which had perceived a grave danger," that of Jewish domination. Publisher Eugen Diederichs' accent on the internal and intuitive was expanded by thinkers like Ernest Bertram and Alfred Bäumler (born 1887) into a praise of force necessary to realize this spirit. Nietzsche (1844–1900) gave voice to the idea of the German *Übermensch*. His concepts of "the Will to Power" and "Transvaluation of Values" were later easily co-opted by the Nazis. Much later, Hitler would term the urge to power "an expression of the heroic will" on behalf of the *Volk*.

Economics: Political theory was appended to an economic theory which militated against Jewish subversion. Eugen Dühring (1833–1921), political economist, in his book *The Jewish Question*, linked Jewish depravity in culture, morals and manners to inherent lustful economic traits possessed by all Jews. Novelist Arthur Dinter and others fused the image of Jewish lust for money with the image of Jewish lust for Aryan women, resulting in the picture of the fat hook-nosed Jewish banker caressing lasciviously a blonde Aryan woman on his knee. Werner Sombart (1863–1941), political and social economist, emphasized the incompatibility of Jewish commercialism with the spirit of the Nordic farmer. He promoted banning Jews from German economic and cultural society. Avant-garde writer Franz Blei claimed the only relationship Jews maintain with the rest of the world is usurious trade.

Politics: The theories extended to practical programs. Already around 1800, identification papers were marked *"Jude."* Bismarck (1815–1898), a liberal turned conservative, embraced anti-Semitism in an appeal to the masses. Adolf Stöcker (1835–1909), a pastor, founded the Christian Social Party, attacking Jews and urging their exclusion from German life. Dr. Otto Böckel, librarian and scholar, was elected to office by raising the spectre of Jewish overlordship. Heinrich Pudor, Bruno Tanzmann, Müller von Hausen, and Theodor Fritsch (1852–1933) all advocated physical force against the Jews. Karl Paasch believed that killing the Jews was the simplest and most practical solution, but shipping them off to New Guinea would also be effective. Hermann Ahlwardt (1846–1914), a teacher and politician whose ideas were repeated by the press and local Roman Catholic clergy, believed that eliminating the Jews was the first giant step toward German dominion of the world, precisely the charge levelled against Jews.[1]

---

1 *See* George L. Mosse, *The Crisis of German Ideology* (New York: Grosset and Dunlap, 1964). For every example, Mosse cites many more. *See also,* the ground-breaking work, Peter Viereck, *Meta-politics, the Roots of the Nazi Mind* (New York: Capricorn, 1965), upon which Mosse is, in turn, dependent.

Appendix Three

Text of Cardinal Hlond's 1936 Speech

So long as Jews remain Jews, a Jewish problem exists and will continue to exist. This question varies in intensity and degree from country to country. It is especially difficult in our country and ought to be the object of serious consideration. I shall touch briefly here on its moral aspects in connection with the situation today.

It is a fact that Jews are waging war against the Catholic church, that they are steeped in free-thinking, and constitute the vanguard of atheism, the Bolshevik movement, and revolutionary activity. It is a fact that Jews have a corruptive influence on morals and that their publishing houses are spreading pornography. It is true that Jews are perpetrating fraud, practicing usury, and dealing in prostitution. It is true that, from a religious and ethical point of view, Jewish youth are having a negative influence on the Catholic youth in our schools. But let us be fair. Not all Jews are this way. There are very many Jews who are believers, honest, just, kind, and philanthropic. There is a healthy, edifying sense of family in very many Jewish homes. We know Jews who are ethically outstanding, noble, and upright.

I warn against that moral stance, imported from abroad, that is basically and ruthlessly anti-Jewish. It is contrary to Catholic ethics. One may love one's own nation more, but one may not hate anyone. Not even Jews. It is good to prefer your own kind when shopping, to avoid Jewish stores and Jewish stalls in the marketplace, but it is forbidden to demolish a Jewish store, damage their merchandise, break windows, or throw things at their homes. One should stay away from the harmful moral influence of Jews, keep away from their anti-Christian culture, and especially boycott the Jewish press and demoralizing Jewish publications. But it is forbidden to assault, beat up, maim, or slander Jews. One should honor and love Jews as human beings and neighbors, even though we do not honor the indescribable tragedy of that nation, which was the guardian of the idea of the Messiah and from which was born the Savior. When divine mercy enlightens a Jew to sincerely accept his and our Messiah, let us greet him into our Christian ranks with joy.

Beware of those who are inciting anti-Jewish violence. They are serving a bad cause. Do you know who is giving the orders? Do you know who is intent on these riots? No good comes from these rash actions. And it is Polish blood that is sometimes being shed at them.[1]

---

1 August Hlond, *Na Straży*, 164-65.

Glossary

cj=camp jargon;
Fr=French;
Ger=German;
Heb=Hebrew;
Hin=Hindi;
Lat=Latin;
Pol=Polish;
Rusn=Russian;
Sp=Spanish;
Yid=Yiddish

A-B Aktion   (Ger) (*Ausserordentliche Befreidungs Aktion*) extraordinary pacification program introduced by the Germans in Poland soon after the conquest in order to forestall partisan reaction.

abstauben   (Ger) dusting off. Aumeier's euphemism for random execution.

abuelo   (Sp) grandpa; f. *abuela*, grandma.

ach!   (Ger) well!

Achtundachtzig   (Ger) 88. Prisoners were referred to only by number.

agents provocateurs   (Fr) a provoking agent used to incite people to some action.

alte   (Ger) old, senior.

Appell   (Ger) roll-call; cj for standing at attention without moving hours on end in freezing snow or rain.

Arbeit macht Frei   (Ger) "Work brings freedom." The cynical slogan emblazoned over the gateway to Auschwitz and many other concentration camps.

Arbeitsunfähig   (Ger) unfit for further work (and thus condemned to the gas chamber).

Aryan   terminology to indicate the master race, which the German *Volk* comprises.

aufgefallen   (Ger) conspicuous, noticeable. Camp language for prisoners who were distinguishable in some way and thereby vulnerable to greater abuse.

austreten!	(Ger) fall out!
ayah	(Hindi) a maid or nurse in India.
barbudos	(Sp) the bearded ones. Slang for Castro's rebels before overthrowing Batista.
belles lettres	(Fr) fine literature.
bis hundertundzwanzig	(Yid) [may you live to be] a hundred and twenty. Common Yiddish expression for wishing someone a long life, based on Moses' life as recorded in the Bible.
bis hundertfünfundzwanzig	(Yid) [may you live to be] a hundred and twenty-five. A play on the above common expression.
blackshirts	*see* SS.
Block	(Ger) Block, barracks. Identical two-storey buildings, ordered in uniformly straight lines. In the main camp, numbered from 1 to 29. Each Block held eight hundred to a thousand prisoners on two floors.
Blockälteste	(Ger) inmate head of a Block, senior prisoner, controlling up to one thousand fellow prisoners through screaming, ferocious beatings and graft.
Blockführer	(Ger) SS leader in charge of a Block.
Blocksperre	(Ger) Block quarantine, curfew, confinement to the Block. In cj, it means the lack of permission to go to the bathroom or to defecate in one's pants even with diarrhoea.
blood accusation	the accusation that Jews use the blood of Christians to bake their matzah for Passover. Derives from the Catholic association of the Eucharist with blood.
Brot	(Ger) bread.
brownshirts	*see* SA.
Bunker	term for the camp prison.
caballero	(Sp) gentleman.
¡Callate!	(colloquial Sp) shut your mouth!
camión	(Sp) truck.
campesina	(Sp) f. peasant.
casquitos	(Sp) Batista's regular Cuban troops.
cicho	(Pol) quiet!
Dali Dali Strasse	(Pol/Ger) Rush-rush Street.
danke schön	(Ger) thank you.
das alte Krematorium	(Ger) the old crematorium.
Deutschland über Alles	(Ger) Germany above all. German na-

tional anthem long before Hitler. In Nazi usage, this phrase connoted "Germany over all," indicating the dual Nazi philosophy of expansion and superiority.

Deutschmarke	(Ger) German currency.
Dreck	(Ger) filth.
Drecksau	(Ger) dirty swine.
Dummheiten	(Ger) stupidities.
durch dem Schornstein	(Ger) through the chimney. A threat repeated many times by the SS.
dziekuje	(Pol) thank you.
erledigt	(Ger) settled!
Elendshaufen	(Ger) pile of misery.
Einsatzgruppen	(Ger) the *Wehrmacht's* special squads that followed behind the advancing German lines murdering Jews.
Engländer sind da	(Ger) the British are there.
Erkennungsdienst	(Ger) Identification Office. A summons usually meant execution by means of a small-calibre gun.
extermination	euphemism for gassing the Jewish people as part of the Nazi policy of genocide. *See* Final Solution.
Final Solution	(source from Ger *Endlösung der Judenfrage*) euphemism for the Nazi policy of genocide against the Jewish people. In June of 1942, Auschwitz became the centre for the carrying out of the Final Solution.
Fleckfieber	(Ger) typhus. In 1942, the epidemic of typhus fever claimed as many as 5,000 lives monthly.
Flüchtlingen	(Ger) civilian refugees.
Frauenlager	(Ger) womens camp.
Führer, der	(Ger) the Leader. Title of Adolph Hitler signifying his role as supreme head of the Third Reich.
Gasthaus	(Ger) inn, hotel.
Geheimnisträger	(Ger) bearers of the secret; cj for members of the *Sonderkommando* and others, mostly Jews, who due to their work were privy to the "secret" of the gas chambers and therefore had to be disposed of.
Genickschuss	(Ger) a shot in the head with a small-calibre rifle, mostly administered at the Black Wall beside Block Eleven.

Gestapo	(Ger = *Geheimne Staatspolizei*) Secret State Police. Hitler's political police force.
Gouvernement–Générale	(Fr) name given, by the Germans, to one of the two districts into which the Nazis divided Poland. It consisted of Warsaw, Lublin, Kraków, Radom and eventually Galicia. Himmler ordered the deportation of the Jews from the other occupied provinces into this district, and implemented the confiscation of their property.
Grupleiter	(Ger) prisoner who served as group leader under the Kapo.
Gymnasium	(Ger) secondary school preparing students for university.
Haga lo que quieres	(Sp) Do as you like.
Hau ab!	(Ger) Beat it!
Heil Hitler!	(Ger) Hail Hitler! German everyday greeting when people gathered. The greeting was accompanied by the "big" Hitler salute with the right arm raised and forward in a fully extended position.
Hep! Hep!	anti-Jewish movement that erupted in Wurzberg in 1819 and spread throughout Germany. The name is said by some to derive from *Hierosolyma Est Perdita*, Jerusalem is destroyed, a slogan of the German knights on crusade. Others say it is derived from the German word "give" shouted before a pogrom: "Give us your money." The English "Hip! Hip! Hooray!" is a variation on this antisemitic chant.
Heraus!	(Ger) Out!
hilfe!	(Ger) help!
H.K.B.	(Ger = *Häftlingskrankenbau*) prisoners' infirmary.
Host desecration	the idea that, if they can get hold of it, Jews will stab the Host until it bleeds.
Horst Wessel Lied	(Ger) the Nazi Party song.
Hurengesindel	(Ger) whore's riffraff.
H.W.L.	(Ger =*Hauptwirtschaftslager*) main SS warehouse.
IG Farbenwerke	German chemical company that established a large plant for the manufacture of synthetic rubber, "Bunawerke," primarily staffed by forced labourers housed in

	Auschwitz-III, Monowice. Due to the cruelty and starvation diet, there was a 300 percent annual turnover in the workforce.
in flagrante delicto	(Lat) in the very act of committing the offence.
Jawohl, Herr Unterscharführer	(Ger) Yes sir, Corporal.
Jezus-Marja	(Pol) Jesus Mary. The Polish Church is decidedly Marian in theological outlook.
Jude	(Ger) Jew.
Judenordnung	(Ger) Jew Ordinance.
Judenrein	(Ger) pure or free of Jews.
kaddish	(Heb) traditional Jewish prayer recited in praise of the Almighty in memory of a deceased loved one.
Kalfaktor	(Ger) personal servant, usually young boys often forced to perform sexual favours.
Kameraden	(Ger) comrades.
Kaninchen	(Ger) literally, bunnies; cj for Clauberg's female patients, and therefore better translated human guinea pigs.
Kanada	section of Auschwitz consisting of about twenty barracks where all the baggage of Jewish victims was sorted out and most of the gold, currency and jewellery was stored.
Kapo	(cj) a prisoner put in charge of a group of inmates; foreman. The term may derive from the Italian *capo* = boss; or from the German *Kameradschaftpolizei* = comradeship police. The SS appointed the Kapos, often from the ranks of German convicts. To win approval from the Nazis, they frequently turned on their fellow prisoners with brutal sadism.
Kaputt	(Ger) broken, smashed in pieces.
kipah	(Heb) skullcap.
klein	(Ger) small.
klutz	(Yid = Ger *Klotz*) blockhead; clumsy.
komisarz	(Pol) Polish police officer.
Kommando	(Ger) crew.
Knesset	(Heb) Israeli parliament.
Königsgraben	(Ger) king's ditch. A huge drainage ditch

	in Birkenau built by prisoners at great loss of life.
Konzentrationslager	(Ger) concentration camp. Besides Auschwitz–Birkenau, the biggest and most notorious, reference is found herein to: Belzec, Bergen–Belsen, Buchenwald, Chelmno, Dachau, Eintrachthütte, Esterwegen, Flossenbürg, Gliwice, Grafeneck, Lichtenburg, Majdanek, Mauthausen, Nisko (Lublin district reservation), Ravensbrück, Sachsenhausen, Sobibór, Theresienstadt, Trawniki, Treblinka and Vaivara.
Krematorium	(Ger) crematorium. There were five at Auschwitz–Birkenau.
Kriegsgefangen	(Ger) prisoner-of-war.
Kristallnacht	(Ger) Crystal Night or the Night of the Broken Glass. A Nazi government-induced pogrom in which terrorists burned or demolished 177 synagogues, destroyed 7,500 Jewish-owned stores. The streets were strewn with broken glass.
Lagerälteste	(Ger) camp senior prisoner.
Lagerführer	(Ger; also *Schutzhaftlagerführer*) chief supervisor in charge of day-to-day camp operation. The marshals and Block leaders were the supervisor's immediate deputies.
Lagerkommandant	(Ger) overall camp commander.
Lagerpolizei	(Ger) prisoner who served as camp policeman.
laissez passer	(Fr) permit for passage, one step lower than a passport.
Lederfabrik	(Ger) leather factory. It housed many departments besides leather-working including a mini-Kanada.
Lehi	(Heb = *Lohamei Herut Israel*) sometimes called the "Stern Group" after Avraham Stern. Conducted underground activities against the British rule of Palestine to win Israeli independence.
Leiter Gruppe II	see *Grupleiter*.
liberum veto	(Lat) proviso by which one deputy in the Polish parliament could reject any proposal by simply exclaiming, "I object."

Justified as the crowning defence of a magnate's liberty, the veto, in effect 1652–1795, was a primary factor in Poland's eradication from the European map.

loco (Sp) crazy.

Los! Los! Ihr
verdammten Hunde (Ger) Go on! go on! you damned dogs.

Luftka (Ger) cigarette holder.

Luftwaffe (Ger) Air Force.

Mamusia (Pol) mama.

Marynarka Wojenna (Pol) "man of war," the name for the Polish navy.

mazurek (Pol) sponge cake dessert filled and topped with rum, plum jam, raisins, walnuts and chocolate buttercream.

Mecenaś (Pol) title used in addressing a lawyer.

mein (Ger) my.

mein Retter ist da (Ger) my saviour is here.

Meister (Ger) master, champion.

Mensch (Ger) man, human being. (Yid/cj) responsible person, upright, honourable.

meshugas (Yid) craziness.

mezuzah (Heb) small container holding a parchment fulfilling the biblical command, "Thou shalt write it upon the doorposts of thy house." This custom reminds the Jew every time he enters his home that the house is supposed to be a place of values and tradition, more than merely a house; and every time he exits his house, that he is to carry the values of godly living with him into the marketplace and wherever he goes.

Mistvieh (vulgar Ger) shithead.

Muselmann (Ger) literally, Moslem (a prejudice); cj for the walking dead; zombie.

Mützen ab (Ger) caps off.

nach vorn! (Ger) step forward!

nein (Ger) no.

Nie pozwalam (Pol) I do not allow. The veto employed by deputies in the old Polish parliament. *See liberum veto.*

NPD (Ger = *Nationalistische Partei Deutschland*) Nationalistic Democratic Party of Germany. Neo-Nazi party formed in West

	Germany in the mid-'60s.
NSDAP	(Ger = *Nationalsozialistische Deutsche Arbeiterpartei*) Nazism. The Hitler-led German political movement patterned after Fascism and advocating physical extermination of the Jews.
Nummer	(Ger) number.
número uno	(Sp) number one.
Ordnung muss sein	(Ger) Rules must be observed.
organize	(cj) smuggle, scrounge, steal (but not from fellow prisoners).
Oxenschwanz	(Ger) ox's penis. Equipped with a steel rod inside used for beating prisoners.
Pan	(Pol; direct address = *Panie*) Mr.; f. *Pani*, Mrs.
Paris ist genommen	(Ger) Paris is taken.
Paris kapituliert	(Ger) Paris has surrendered.
Partja	(Pol) political party.
Państwowe Muzeum w Oświęciemiu	(Pol) Auschwitz–Birkenau Museum opened by Polish authorities in 1967.
Pedziu	(Ger) paedophile.
Peitsche	(Ger) whip.
Pfahlhängen	(Ger) punishment that consisted of fastening someone's wrists from behind and suspending him from a hook in such way that the feet could not touch the floor.
Pipel	(cj) catamite.
Plattdeutsch	(Ger) dialect of North West Germany, near the Dutch border.
Polaco	(Sp) Pole.
Politische Abteilung	see R.S.H.A.
por cierto	(Sp) sure, for sure.
¿por qué?	(Sp) why?
Prominente	(Ger) prisoners who, due to their assigned job or length in the camp, somehow enjoyed special privileges.
pravda	(Rusn/Pol) truth.
Premiumschein	(Ger) camp scrip used to purchase goods and services at the canteen and brothel.
Puffhaus	(cj) brothel. Block Twenty-four–A in Auschwitz. It is not shown to visitors.
Ramp	an earthen, railroad siding in Birkenau where Jews, transported from all over

Europe, were unloaded for the gas chambers. Here the infamous first selection of prisoners took place. *See Selektion.*

Reichsdeutsche   (Ger) German national.

Reichstag   (Ger) today's German parliament.

rex pro tempore   (Lat) interim king.

rogatywka   (Pol) a four corner, flat-topped, stovepipe military hat.

rollen   (Ger) roll.

Rollwagen   (Ger) pullcart.

Rosh HaShanah   (Heb) Jewish new year.

roti   (Hin) an Indian bread.

R.S.H.A.   (Ger = *Reichssicherheitshauptamt*) main security office established under the authority of Heydrich. In Auschwitz, the *R.S.H.A.*, headed by an officer seconded from the Gestapo, stood independent of the commandant regarding prisoners' fate. This office supervised the political department or *Politische Abteilung*; the security police or *SD* in charge of counterespionage; the 'Bunker', a prison within a prison; the trains coming into Auschwitz; registration; reception; inter-rogation; records; and the gas chamber–crematoria.

Rycerz Niepokalanej   (Pol) "Knight of the Virgin Mary." Kolbe's newspaper, still continued by Franciscans.

SA   (Ger = *Sturmabteilung*) Storm Detachment. Known as the brownshirts, the SA were the internal storm troopers.

Saujuden   (Ger) Jewish swine.

Scheissmeister   (vulgar Ger; literally, shit master) prisoner in charge of latrine duty.

Schinkenwurst   (Ger) smoked ham sausage.

Schreiber   (Ger) scribe; prisoner who was second in rank after the *Blockälteste*.

Schutzhaft   (Ger) protective custody. Euphemism for internment in a concentration camp.

Schutzhaftlagereweiterung   (Ger) Two-storey blocks near the main camp built toward the end of the war.

Schutzhäftling Achtundachtzig meldet sich gehorsam	(Ger) protective prisoner No. 88 reports obediently.
Schwein! Da ist der Mist	(Ger) Pig! There is the smell.
Schweinehund	(Ger) dirty dog.
Schweinestall	(Ger) place where the pig fodder was prepared.
SD	(Ger = *Sicherheitsdienst*) see *R.S.H.A.*
sejm	(Pol) parliament.
Selektion	(Ger; Pol = *selekcja*) selection. The infamous euphemism for the process of separating those to be consigned to the gas chambers immediately from those who would be impressed into forced labour before their deaths. Strong men and women were enslaved, while the older and weaker together with children and their mothers were killed. *See* Ramp.
servus regis	(Lat) "royal official."
sí	(Sp) yes.
Sieg Heil!	(Ger) hail to victory!
Ślązak	(Pol; Ger = *Schlesier* or *Oberschlesier*) native of Silesia.
ślepowron	(Pol) blind raven, part of the Sobolewski coat of arms.
Solidarność	(Pol) Solidarity. The movement to free Poland of Soviet domination, led by Lech Walesa in the early '80s.
Sonderkommando	(Ger) special command. Jewish prisoners drafted to serve in the gas chambers. Their job was to untangle the naked corpses, extract the gold teeth, cut off the hair of the women, and stoke the crematoria. Every few months the current group would be executed and replaced with another.
sowieso, Krematorium	(Ger) one way or another, one ends in the crematorium.
SS	(Ger = *Schutzstaffel*) Elite Guard. The military wing of the Nazi party known as the Black Order because of their black shirts and uniforms. The SS had the duty of administering the concentration camps under Himmler. The Nuremberg trials declared any member of the SS to

	be a war criminal.
Stammlager	(Ger) main camp.
Stehzelle	(Ger) a one-metre-square, underground cell with a ten centimetre diameter pipe near the ceiling for breathing.
Strafe	(Ger) punishment.
Strafkompanie	(Ger; abbrev = *S/K*) penal battalion.
Stubendienst	(Ger) senior prisoner in charge of section of a barracks.
Swastika	(In Ger, the *Hackenkreuz*, or crooked cross) ancient 'Germanic' symbol adopted by the Nazi Party as its emblem, thus asserting Nazi identification with its supposed primeval Germanic roots. Actually, the word is Sanskrit and the swastika is an ancient East Indian good luck symbol.
Sudeten Deutsch	(Ger) the German-speaking areas of Czechoslovakia; refers to the mountains south of Germany between Switzerland and Bohemia, thus identifying the peoples of this region with "Greater Germany."
Szwab	(Pol) derogatory term for a German.
tallis	(Heb) prayer shawl.
Tatuś	(Pol) papa.
te quiero	(Sp) I want you; I love you.
Tiergarten	(Ger) zoological garden.
Tischlerei	(Ger) joiners shop.
trabajador	(Sp) worker.
Übermensch	(Ger) superman. In German philosophy, a person destined to lead. Always assumed to be a German.
Untermenschen	(Ger) subhumans. Nazi term for undesirables.
Va'ad Arba'ah Ha'Aratzos	(Heb) Council of the Four Lands. Autonomous council that conducted Jewish affairs in mediaeval Poland, and even collected the taxes on behalf of the government.
varón	(Sp) male; *un varón*, a boy.
Vaterland	(Ger) fatherland.
Veni, Vidi, Vici	(Lat) I came, I saw, I conquered, attributed to Julius Caesar speaking about his conquest of Gaul.

verboten	(Ger) forbidden.
verdamnten Bolschewiken	(Ger) damned Bolsheviks.
Verfluchte Juden	(Ger) cursed Jews.
Vernichtung durch Arbeit	(Ger) extermination through work.
Volk	(Ger) folk. In the German neo-Romanticism of the late eighteenth and nineteenth centuries it was more than simply "folk." It constituted the synthesis of a people with its transcendental quintessence. The assumption that the individual is subject to the ethos of the Folk became the basis for discrimination against non-German peoples.
Volksdeutsche	(Ger) German minority groups long settled in other European countries.
Volksgeist	(Ger) national spirit. Long before Hitler, German thought maintained that each race possesses its own historic genius that ultimately informs the national spirit.
voruzhye!	(Rusn) to arms!
vperyod!	(Rusn) forward!
Wahl	(In this instance, Yid) choice.
Walze	(Ger) cylinder. A chariot from which the Kapo Krankemann would whip the Jews and Poles who pulled it.
Wasser	(Ger) water.
Wehrmacht	(Ger) German armed forces.
Weltanschauung	(Ger) world-view.
wiem o tym	(Pol) I know.
Willkommen Frohe Sängern	(a German song) literally, "welcome, happy singers." The song, which Auschwitz slave-labourers were forced to sing, spoke about women and life, thus constituting a psychological torment.
yeshivos	(Heb; singular *yeshiva*) talmudic academies, literally "places of sitting."
zabyi-go	(Pol) kill him!
zakladnik	(Pol) hostage.
Zettel	(Ger) note.
złoty	(Pol) Polish coin.
Zostaw tego zasranego Żyda niech zdechnie	(Pol) leave this fucking Jew, let him croak.
Zugänge	(Ger) new arrivals.
źwirownia	(Pol) gravel pit. Place on the perimeter of

the camp where Carmelite sisters established a controversial convent. Eighty Jews from the first and second *Sonderkommando* were executed there.

Żyd (Pol) Jew.

Zyklon B trade name for the prussic acid (hydrogen cyanide) used to poison the prisoners in the gas chambers. The firm of DEGESCH (Deutsche Gessellschaft zur Schädlingsbekämpfung) produced Zyklon B; the firm of TESTA (Tesch and Stabenow) distributed it.

PRISONER 88

THE MAN IN STRIPES

by Roy D. Tanenbaum

ISBN 1-895176-74-3 • $19.95

Add shipping: $5.00; international, $9.00.
Canadian orders add 7% GST.
Outside Canada, prices in U.S. dollars.

METHOD OF PAYMENT

Payment or purchase order must accompany order
Please make cheque payable to Raincoast Books.

☐ Visa   ☐ Cheque

☐ Mastercard   ☐ Money Order

Credit Card Number: ———————————————————————————

Expiry Date: ———————————————————————————
(Credit card not valid without expiry date.)

SHIPPING INSTRUCTIONS

Name: ———————————————————————————

Address: ———————————————————————————

———————————————————————————

———————————————————————————

City: ———————————————————————————

Province/State: ———————————————————————————

Postal/Zip Code: ———————————————————————————

Country: ———————————————————————————

PLEASE SEND ORDERS TO:

Raincoast Fulfillment Distribution Services
8680 Cambie Street
Vancouver, B.C., Canada V6P 6M9
Telephone: 1-800-663-5714
Fax Orders to: 1-800-565-3770
Email: custserv@raincoast.com

UNIVERSITY OF CALGARY PRESS